P9-CCX-738

3 9153 00934124 1

DISCARD

JOHN HENRY NEWMAN

JOHN HENRY
NEWMAN

*An Expository and Critical Study
of His Mind, Thought and Art*

BY

CHARLES FREDERICK HARROLD

ARCHON BOOKS
HAMDEN, CONNECTICUT
1966

To B. – F. – J.

Who counseled and encouraged

(*secretum suum sibi*)

Newman, of all men, needs students of active and original and penetrating minds to detect and elaborate the pregnant suggestions of a poetic thinker who had not the habit of scientific statement. Like the slave of Midas, it has been said, he often whispered his secret to the reeds.

— Wilfrid Ward

Une de plus grandes et des plus remarquables preuves de la puissance que les imaginations ont les unes sur les autres, c'est le pouvoir qu'ont certains auteurs de persuader sans aucune raison . . . Leurs paroles, toutes mortes qu'elles sont, ont plus de vigueur que la raison de certaines gens. Elles entrent, elles pénètrent, elles dominent dans l'âme d'une manière si impérieuse, qu'elles se font obéir sans se faire entendre, et qu'on se rend à leurs ordres sans les savoir.

— Malebranche, *Recherche de la Vérité*

A PREFACE

(*Mémoire justificatif*)

Of the making of books on Newman there seems to be no end. It is said that, in 1933, during the centenary of the beginning of the Oxford Movement, no fewer than 10,000 books and articles appeared to celebrate the occasion. We have now arrived at another centennial date, the one-hundredth anniversary of Cardinal Newman's conversion to the Roman Catholic Church, and although we are in the throes of war, more books and articles on the great Cardinal are pouring from the presses. As a contributor to this stream of publication, I feel I owe the reader some explanation for the present study. Two years ago, at the end of the preface to my *Newman Treasury*, I promised "a further volume, on Newman's development as a literary personality, in more propitious times." Not long afterward I realized that "propitious times" in the sense of world peace and individual leisure might remain beyond the horizon for many years to come, and that in fact our own catastrophic times might not be wholly uninterested in, or unbenefited by, a close study of Newman's mind and thought. The materials for my study had been accumulating over a period of some thirteen years. Originally, it was indeed to have been merely a critical consideration of Newman as a literary artist. But two facts led me to enlarge the scope of my work: the publication in 1937 of Fernande Tardivel's excellent, though not altogether adequate, *La personnalité littéraire de Newman*; and the realization that a real understanding of Newman, even as a literary man, required at least an expository study of his religious thought. The reception of *A Newman Treasury*, together with increasing public interest in Newman on the approach of the centenary of 1845, persuaded me that now was as propitious a time as any for bringing my materials to a focus in the present volume.

In many of its pages I have carefully refrained from taking any critical position in fields where I should inevitably be an ama-

teur, namely, those of theology and the history of dogma. I
make no pretense, therefore, of technically judging the validity
of Newman's arguments in the *Essay on the Development of
Christian Doctrine,* or in the *Grammar of Assent.* I am content
merely to explain these works, to account for their genesis, to set
forth pertinent criticisms or comments by qualified critics of Newman, to indicate, where possible, the sources and affinities and
other historical data which might further illuminate his ideas.
That Newman's theory of doctrinal development and his account of religious assent have been attacked on very strong
grounds I am perfectly aware. But as a non-Catholic — I am,
to use a word Newman very much disliked, an Episcopalian —
seeking to *understand* him as a man and as a writer and religious
thinker, I have tried to observe an intelligent neutrality on controversial issues, and have played the critic only where I thought
I knew whereof I spoke — in dealing with his literary method,
with his achievement as poet, novelist, critic, rhetorician. Hence
the greater part of this book is expository and historical rather
than critical. It owes a great debt to authors of special studies
on Newman, to Jean Guitton, Erich Przywara, S. P. Juergens,
J. F. Cronin, Grandmaison, and to the writers of innumerable
articles. It is not, I should add, a biographical study, though
the first two chapters present the chief facts about Newman's life.
The real purpose of Chapters I and II is to throw light on his
mind by answering biographically, doctrinally, and historically
the question so often asked: Why — and also *how* — did Newman come to join the Roman Catholic Church? These chapters
seek also to provide generous information on the religious, social,
and political forces, groups, and ideas which surrounded Newman
prior to 1845.

The other chapters attempt to answer various other questions.
Since many of Newman's individual volumes are out of print,
or otherwise inaccessible, the average reader often wonders:
What is *in* those volumes? — in the *Historical Sketches,* in *Discussions and Arguments,* in *Difficulties of Anglicans?* Is there
anything of value today in the *Lectures on Justification?* — or in
The Present Position of Catholics? How well do Newman's
sermons bear the test of time? Are they as dead as Liddon's or

Maurice's? What is still alive in Newman's two novels, *Loss and Gain* and *Callista?* Considered as poetry, are his *Verses on Various Occasions* as poor as Keble's *Christian Year?* What are the contents of the *Essays Critical and Historical?* I have tried to answer these questions in my over-all attempt to bring out the character and achievement of Newman's mind. In that attempt, I hasten to add, I have not subjected him to any effort at psycho-analysis; I leave that to other and more expert hands. After Chapter II, each chapter is very largely complete and independent in itself. The succeeding chapters will vary in difficulty and interest: many readers will prefer to pass over Chapters III, IV, and VI as being too technical or detailed for their taste; others will find Chapters VII and VIII less appealing than those devoted to Newman as a historian or a man of letters. The book as a whole has been designed for readers of varying levels of interest, and thus permits a considerable degree of selective reading; entire groups of chapters may be ignored or read later without detracting from the intelligibility of the others. In avoiding a partisan approach to Newman, I realize that I am on hazardous ground, open to the charge of indifferentism, or of secret sympathy or antipathy, or of that Newmanian "reserve" which Charles Kingsley thought to be pure guile and duplicity. However, I am willing to be judged by any fair and candid reader, who will see in the present work an attempt at an objective understanding of Newman. To the other kind of reader, let me say of this book what Newman said about his *Grammar of Assent*: "It is what it is, and is not what it isn't — and what it isn't many people will expect that it is."

On the question of Newman's relation to Catholic and non-Catholic readers, I am inclined to agree with the distinguished Lutheran scholar of the Anglican Revival, Dr. Yngve Brilioth, that "it is a presumption if any single communion claims him entirely for its own. In spite of the zeal with which he himself was wont to emphasize the dogmatic differences between groups of Christians, few reach so fully as he that elevated ground where these expressions of the shifting reflections of revelation through different individual and national mediums fade away and disappear." As the activity of Newman's religious endowment led him constantly on, and permitted no real standing still, it came about that, like few men of his century, he enriched the common religious experience of Christendom. Only the indifferent, or the superficially religious, anywhere, can be wholly unconcerned with the issues with which Newman deals, or with his manner of meeting them. Certainly in this time of "the breaking of nations," he is a man, even with all his limitations, whom anyone may read and wisely ponder.

And now I wish to acknowledge my debt to many friends and well-wishers who have helped me in my task. I am especially indebted, for extensive critical aid, to certain of my colleagues at the Ohio State University, Professors Frederick J. Hoffman, William R. Parker, Francis Lee Utley, and John Harold Wilson. To Professor James F. Fullington, chairman of the Department of English at Ohio State, I am grateful for considerations which afforded me some much-needed time at certain stages of my work. I wish to thank the Reverend John Francis Cronin of St. Mary's Seminary, Baltimore, and the Reverend Martin J. Healy of the Seminary of the Immaculate Conception, Huntington, New York, for the benefit of their special knowledge of Newman's epistemology; they kindly and helpfully examined Chapter VI, on the *Grammar of Assent*, and Father Healy made especially valuable suggestions concerning Chapters III and IV. They are in no way responsible, of course, for any of the shortcomings of my exposition. I wish also to express my appreciation for the courtesy of the Reverend Henry Tristram of the Birmingham Oratory in permitting me to quote from some of Newman's unpublished notes. My labors have been materially lightened and safeguarded by the editorial abilities of my typist, Mrs. Myra T. McCrory. I am grateful also to one of my Roman Catholic students, Miss Rosemary Curtin, for cheerfully playing the role of guinea pig in submitting to a test-reading of the manuscript. To certain university libraries — those of Ohio State, Yale, Columbia, and Michigan — and to the New York Public Library, I owe much for a great deal of prompt and skillful aid. Lastly, I wish to acknowledge a deep indebtedness to the late Professor Karl Young and to the administrators of the Sterling Fellowship fund of Yale University for making it possible for me, during a sabbatical year (1938–39), to pursue a close and uninterrupted study of Newman, of which this volume is one of the final results.

CHARLES FREDERICK HARROLD

THE OHIO STATE UNIVERSITY
COLUMBUS, OHIO
February 4, 1945

CONTENTS

xiii

CONTENTS

IV. NEWMAN AND HIS ART

V. NEWMAN AND OUR WORLD

I. NEWMAN AND HIS WORLD

CHAPTER I

THE MAKING OF A LEADER

One day in the autumn of 1845, a certain French priest of the Roman Catholic Church made a momentous descent down the steps of the Seminary of St. Sulpice, in Paris, "never again to remount them," he tells us, "in priestly dress." [1] This priest, some twenty-two years of age, was Ernest Renan, a fastidious, critical, and disenchanted young man who had found it no longer possible to accept dogmatic Christianity, or to submit his mind to the authority of his Church. He was later to gain world-wide renown for books which, for many of his readers, dealt graceful but devastating blows to the orthodox view of the origins of Christianity, the book of *Job*, the life of Jesus. His departure from St. Sulpice, on that 6th of October, was a quiet but epoch-shaping event. Across the English Channel, just two days later, another similarly quiet but pregnant event was occurring, in the village of Littlemore, near Oxford. On the night of October 8, while the rain fell in torrents, John Henry Newman, England's greatest Anglican leader of the day, fell at the feet of the Passionist Father Dominic, whom he implored to receive him into "the one fold of Christ." Like Renan, he had made a long intellectual and spiritual journey. But unlike the great French critic, Newman's quest had taken him from the armchair liberalism of the Oxford "Noetics" of the 1820's, through a grueling study of the early Anglican divines and the Church Fathers of the fourth and fifth centuries, to his present Roman Catholic certitudes, expressed in his uncompleted book, *The Development of Christian Doctrine*. As the cold October rain fell on the little village that night, Newman made his general confession. After it was over, he could not walk. His friends, Richard Stanton

I

and Ambrose St. John, took him by the arms and helped him, stumbling and half fainting, to his bed.

Ernest Renan's defection from the Church of his fathers was an event of importance to all Europe. It was one of many typical culminations of the critical, secular, and naturalistic spirit at work throughout the nineteenth century. Newman's conversion to the Roman Church was no less important an event. The evolution of his thought and belief was but a part of that general European movement known as the Catholic Revival; and his whole career, both as Anglican and Roman Catholic, was devoted, as we shall see, to rendering institutional Christianity acceptable to the critical and historical sense of nineteenth-century man. In achieving this enormous task, to the extent of which he was capable, Newman was happy in his native endowments, though the complexities and mysteries of his nature did not always tell in his favor. It is our purpose to attempt to understand his mind and character, by which he sought to reach the intellect of modern man. We shall not be concerned primarily with the detailed facts of his life, which we shall note only as they illuminate the course of his development. What has been endlessly — and tiresomely — called the "mystery" of Newman we shall soon probe as we turn to those basic character traits which made their first appearance in his early youth.

i.   *"The child is father to the man"*

In the Evangelical middle-class family into which John Henry Newman was born on February 21, 1801, there was much which naturally shaped the boy's character. The Newmans lived in Old Broad Street, London, where John Newman, the father, was a member of a banking firm. Socially, therefore, the boy Newman was surrounded with early nineteenth-century gentility, and he was eventually, at Oxford, to approximate, if not to fulfill, the lineaments of the Victorian gentleman, so memorably described later in his *Idea of a University*. He was the eldest of six children — self-willed, reticent, dreamy, and physically delicate, though never sickly. When Newman was still quite little the family moved to Ham, near Richmond, and though they moved back to Old Broad Street when he was six years old, it was always to the house at Ham that Newman's thoughts went back throughout his life. It is in this period that we find him indulging in the religious daydreams mentioned in the *Apologia*: he "used to wish the Arabian Tales were true . . . his imagination ran on unknown influences, on magical powers, and talismans." [2] He thought life might be a dream, and he an angel, and all this world a deception. What later in his life was to become the Platonic element in his nature is foreshadowed here. A taste for the mysterious, for the supernatural, for the occult, in boys as young as Newman was then, rarely takes such strange and mystic shapes. These early sensations of the unreality of the physical world which Przywara and others have identified as one hallmark of the true Platonist,[3] will soon bring to Newman the conviction that there are but "two and two only absolutely and luminously self-evident beings, myself and my Creator." [4]

He was "very superstitious," and used to cross himself on going into the dark. In one of his school copybooks he drew a solid upright cross and a string of beads. He was never able to discover how these symbols of Rome got into his head, but supposed that he got the ideas from some romance, like Mrs. Radcliffe's or Miss Porter's, or from some religious picture.[5] The hint of superstition — sometimes the reality — was to creep into his writing and his thought to the very end. Yet there was nothing in the mildly Evangelical Newman household to promote either Roman Catholic or superstitious tendencies. On the contrary, at fourteen we find him reading Tom Paine's tracts against the Old Testament, and enjoying the objections which they contained. He also read Hume's *Essays*, including, probably, the essay on miracles, and some French verses denying the immortality of the soul, possibly a poem of Voltaire's. "How dreadful," said the boy to himself, "but how plausible!" [6] Here, at this early age, we see the mind which, years later, could at once accept the legend of the Holy House at Loreto and also sum up the case for religious unbelief so perceptively as to bring bewildered admiration from Thomas Henry Huxley. At any rate, the boy Newman was certainly precocious: Paine and Hume are curious works for a boy to select at an age when *Robinson Crusoe* is more likely to captivate the imagination. In the autumn of

1816, when Newman was fifteen, he had a quiet conversion; he fell under the influences of a definite creed and of "impressions of dogma." He began to read the great Evangelical divines. William Romaine (1714–95), a follower of Whitefield (and not of Wesley), taught him the doctrine of "final perseverance" and convinced him that he was "elected to eternal glory." Perhaps it was Romaine's tender, passionate, eloquently Evangelical *Life, Walk and Triumph of Faith* which thus served to enhance Newman's growing sense of isolation from the material world.[7] Even this early, the dominant side of Newman's intelligence came into play; "the boy," says Jennings, "was a theologian even in his teens."[8]   A deep impression was also made by Thomas Scott of Aston Sanford (1747–1821), "to whom," he says, "(humanly speaking) I almost owe my soul." Two of Scott's doctrines, "Holiness rather than peace," and "Growth the only evidence of life" explain much in Newman: his passionate and militant otherworldliness, and his constant emphasis on the development of doctrine.[9]   Another cardinal theme in Newman's thought, both as Anglican and as Roman Catholic, was "the warfare between the City of God and the powers of darkness," a doctrine which he found memorably treated in William Law's *Serious Call*.   Meanwhile he had made a collection of Scripture texts in proof of the doctrine of the Trinity, and another collection in support of the Athanasian Creed. ' He read Joseph Milner's (1744–97) *History of the Church of Christ*, and became enamored of the long extracts from St. Augustine, St. Ambrose, and other Church Fathers.   This experience was directly prophetic of his subsequent readings for the *Arians of the Fourth Century*, and eventually led to Newman's crucial volume, *The Development of Christian Doctrine* (1845).[10]   At this time also, he read Thomas Newton's (1704–82) *Dissertations on the Prophecies* (1754), and was convinced that the Pope was the Antichrist predicted by Daniel, St. Paul, and St. John.[11]   The effects of this book, he tells us, remained a "stain upon his imagination" until 1843.   And now, though he was not yet sixteen, a deep conviction took possession of him: it would be the will of God that he should lead a single life.   His conversion — so quiet, so intellectual, so almost bookish — was now complete.

Meanwhile, from 1808 to 1816, he had attended a private school at Ealing, where he advanced at a speed no other boy had ever equaled, and where, though he never participated in the games,[12] he was habitually looked up to. In spite of his shyness, he became something of a leader, writing and circulating two papers — *The Spy* and *The Anti-Spy* — and initiating some of the boys into a special Order, of which he was the Grand Master, and with which he had weekly readings of *The Spy*. His intellectual activity seemed endless: he wrote verses, dramas, operas (tunes and all). He devoured *Waverley* and *Guy Mannering*; he kept a diary; he acted in the plays of Terence performed annually at Ealing. In his diary he carefully recorded his readings in Ovid, Homer, Herodotus. "Each year he became more grave, considerate, philosophical, knowledgeable, fastidious, and superior. . . To his mother and sisters he was the Admirable Crichton; to his brothers the slightly insupportable corrector of their ignorance." [13] Indeed the *autocentrisme* of which Abbé Brémond has made so much,[14] begins to show itself this early in the self-willed, aloof, and rather domineering adolescent. Once, when there had been a struggle for mastery between mother and son, she reminded him, "You see, John, you did not get your own way." "No," was his answer, "but I tried hard." [15] On another occasion, somewhat later — in 1820 — he united this egoistic force with unbending conservatism: father and son were discussing the approaching trial of Queen Caroline; Mr. Newman took the "sensible" view, favoring the luckless queen; John sided with the Ministry; whereupon the father, "with a sharp sarcasm," ended with: "Well, John! I suppose I ought to praise you for knowing how to rise in this world. Go on! Persevere! Always stand up for men in power, and in time you will get promotion." [16] This was not altogether a fair reply, and Newman never became known for currying favor; yet there is in this incident a hint of the moral severity and the deference to authority which marked Newman's whole career.

On the whole, it is not difficult to see in the schoolboy at Ealing some of the individualizing elements in Newman's character. In the quick-minded and capable youngster there lurks the mystic's sense of the Unseen. Surrounded by the "unreal" world

of matter, his ego expands under the pious controls of Evangelicalism; his intellect, which admired the "plausible" arguments of
Paine, will not dominate his spiritual intuitions. Shy, and "without a grain of conviviality," [17] uninterested in Ealing's many
games, he nevertheless wins a certain supremacy, by virtue of his
nascent literary talent. Before he is sixteen he has acquired the
theological mentality, and has anticipated his priestly state by
adopting the ideal of celibacy. There is never to be any secret
romance of the conventional type in his life. On the other hand,
there will never be any conscious misogyny; the strength and the
emotional depths of his being will be given to those passionate
friendships with men which were far from uncommon a century
ago, and which were a very significant feature of the Oxford
Movement. In the Ealing schoolboy there is all the potential
force of will, intellect, and heart; all the latent ability to move
and lead; all the potential moralism, aristocratic refinement, delicacy, and personal charm which ultimately, at Oxford, went into
the making of a leader.

ii. *Newman and Oxford* (1817–33)

When Newman was matriculated as a commoner of Trinity
College, Oxford, on December 14, 1816, he was probably unaware that the university was practically the Oxford of the seventeenth century, and a backwater in English intellectual life.
In fact the ethos of Oxford had changed but very little between
the chancellorship of Laud in 1629 and that of the Duke of Wellington in 1834. It was essentially the Oxford of the Restoration Settlement, still bound to the Church of England by the
statutes of Laud. Although nominally a university, it was, in
Newman's early years, really a colony of practically autonomous
colleges, situated in a picturesque Gothic little town, and quite
dissociated from the great world of industrialism, political struggle, and European intellectual ferment. Here in an atmosphere of the Middle Ages, though without the equivalent
intellectual activity, the undergraduate, usually the son of a
clergyman, was placed in the hands of a college tutor, himself an
ordained clergyman. He had, of course, already formally sub-
scribed to the Thirty-nine Articles as a condition of admission to

the university. He was then submitted to a mechanical system of courses in the elements of religion, together with a little mathematics, some philosophy (Plato and Aristotle), and some ancient history (Herodotus, Thucydides, Livy, Tacitus). No modern history was taught for the schools, no modern philosophy, no natural science, and no languages other than Latin and Greek. There were routine examinations whose questions and answers were known beforehand by all who sought degrees. Most tutors in the twenty colleges of Oxford regarded their duties as an unpleasant interlude between their own undergraduate days and their appointment to a lucrative benefice. There was thus a close bond between the colleges and the country parsonages — a fact of capital importance when Newman and his colleagues distributed their tracts in the Oxford Movement. With the exception of poor students known as "servitours," the undergraduates were in reality a congregation of highly fortunate individuals, all members of the Established Church, and all fulfilling a social and traditional obligation to their class.[1]

It is a commonplace to sum up the intellectual situation in pre-Tractarian Oxford by alluding to Gibbon's classic description of Magdalen College as a place of "port and prejudice," under the domination of "priests and monks." [2] However, it is easy to indulge in exaggeration on this subject, and it is well to remember two facts when considering Oxford as a shaping influence on Newman's mind. In spite of the "expensive parties" lamented by Isaac Williams, and the revelry of the college Gaudy, which the young Newman thought of as a "sickening" exhibition of "the sons of Belial," [3] there was, on the other hand, the deeply religious influence of the Non-Jurors, who were stronger in Oxford than in the country generally. Oxford was indeed the "home of lost causes," and still clung to the exiled house of Stuart, watching gloomily the invasion of Whig undergraduates, and still upholding the divine independence of the Church, to the point of regarding Oxford as an *imperium in imperio*. From the Non-Jurors' influence Newman, as we shall see, derived profound spiritual nourishment. The other fact was that although Oxford remained the university of the Tory and church squirearchy, it had begun to shake off the traditions of idleness and licentiousness inherited from the eighteenth century. Some colleges, notably Oriel and Corpus Christi, were awakening to a new intellectual vigor. Many were selecting for their heads men of good character and businesslike capacity for administration. The heads of colleges in their weekly meeting, known as the Hebdomadal Board or Council, were administering the affairs of the university with a new efficiency and zeal. Oriel College itself was ceasing to appoint fellows by reason of rank, or parentage, or social habits, and had begun to elect them solely on the basis of ability. This was one of the results of a spirited attack on the university by the *Edinburgh Review* in the years 1808 to 1810.[4] When Newman arrived at Oxford in June, 1817, and when he was appointed fellow of Oriel in 1822, he found himself in an atmosphere congenial not only to religious habits but also to keen intellectual activity. And he found himself among men of various types, from the wine-drinking wastrels who shocked his Evangelicalism, to the saintly and charming John Keble.

Newman's early career at Oxford may be summed up very briefly. He labored hard and enthusiastically over his studies — sometimes reading between eight and twelve hours a day — and in 1818 was elected scholar of Trinity. Until 1821, law was his destined profession, and he speaks of himself as being "too solicitous about fame." But overwork produced exhaustion, and his failure in the schools in 1820 led him to decide his career in favor of holy orders. If he disappointed himself and his friends by his failure, he atoned for that by gaining the Oriel fellowship in April, 1822, an event which Newman always regarded as a turning-point in his development, since it gave him an assured position, opened up a theological career, and brought him under "various influences, personal and intellectual" which shaped his religious nature.[5] His career at Oriel may be divided, as Ward observes, into three periods. There was, first, the period between 1822 and 1827 when he was under the influence of Whately and the other brilliant Noetics who lured him toward a liberal and intellectual type of Christianity. The second period was marked by his close intimacy with Hurrell Froude — from 1828 to 1832 — which came with the termination of Newman's incipient liberalism, and witnessed his appointment to the vicarage of St. Mary's and his difference with Hawkins, provost of Oriel, over the essentially religious nature of a tutorship. Finally, there were the tumultuous years in the Tractarian Movement (1833–45).[6] We are concerned here primarily with Newman's inner development, and since he had become public tutor at Oriel in 1826, and had begun to sense new and powerful religious stirrings within him, it will be well to glance for a moment at the parties in the Church as represented by various Oxford groups.

The conservative or "Orthodox" party within the Church of England preserved in the main the historic traditions of the High Church divines of the seventeenth century. It claimed to inherit, through a continuous episcopacy which derived its authority unbroken from the Apostles, the true tradition of a catholic, sacramental, priestly church. Its faith rested on the Bible as interpreted by the Councils of the Church, and upon the existence and authority of the Church itself. It was content with the Prayer Book as providing a *via media*, as Newman was to hold, between the "excesses" of Romanism and the "errors" of Protestantism. In Oxford it had an especially strong arm in the Non-Jurors, men whose position dated from the reigns of James I and Charles I, and who had refused to take the oath of allegiance to William III by reason of their belief in the divine right of anointed kings. The temper of the "Orthodox" party was one of passionate and proud belief in a God of unseen splendor, in God's majestic and divinely instituted Church, in authority, in the beauty and power of sacraments and the priesthood.

On the other hand, the Evangelical party of the Church laid little stress on the Church as a visible institution, or on its claim as a branch of the Church Catholic. It was individualistic, vividly conscious of the corruption of human nature, of the efficacy of the atonement, of the "sanctifying influence" of the Holy Spirit, of the individual's need of an unmistakable conversion, emotionally experienced rather than intellectually understood. For the Evangelical, the Bible, literally inspired, was everything; no priest, or ecclesiastical organization, or ritual could avail in saving souls. Baptism and the Lord's Supper were not mysteriously sacramental but merely symbolic and commemorative acts. Theologically, unlike the broad, systematic, and unemotional thought of the "Orthodox" Anglicans, Evangelical teaching was narrow, passionate, unintellectual, without a philosophy of history or religion. If the orthodox could be accused of being "high" and "dry" — involved in high politics, and destitute of fervent faith — the Evangelicals could be, and were, accused of being "enthusiastic" (a word of opprobrium in the eighteenth century), self-righteous, unctuous, and puritanical, if not insincere.

In uncomfortable association with the "Orthodox" and Evangelical parties stood the Liberals or Latitudinarians. Their essential principle was the supremacy of reason. Allied with the Whigs, and armed with intellectual champions from Locke to Butler, they had, in Mr. Faber's amusing words, "helped to maintain that marvelous triumph of manners over matter which was called the Augustan age." [7] They were contemptuous of the "mysteries" of religion; they smiled at the Puritan's conception of a capricious inner flow of grace, and at the Catholic idea of a flow of grace through the sacraments. For the Latitudinarians, religion should be a matter of good sense, respectable morals, a proper orientation of man's nature to God's law as ascertained by human reason. Behind them they had the great tradition of Deism, and around them the great modern movements of science, criticism, and social enlightenment.

Late in life, Newman assigned to these three parties their separate, distinctive principles — to the "Orthodox" the "Catholic" principle, to the Evangelicals the "Protestant" principle, to the Latitudinarians the "sceptical" principle. [8] As an undergraduate, he moved from a mild Evangelicalism, to the Liberal or Latitudinarian position of Whately and the Noetics, to High Anglicanism.

Our glance into the parties of the Church does not, of course, give a wholly adequate or correct picture. Newman, in an appendix to the French edition of the *Apologia*, explained that the Anglican communion was in fact held together by the Toryism and the Conservatism of the Anglican clergy and laity alike; the presence of real and active parties, as such, would have split it into separate sects.[9] Actually the Established Church was nationalistic, rather than Catholic; it had no living theological roots; it feared intellectual inquiry as much as it disdained "enthusiasm"; it welcomed compromise, and hated Rome and Dissent with equal intensity, as threatening it, respectively, from without and from within. Its ecclesiastical Toryism was simply the expression of upper-class Englishmen's unconscious determination to maintain "a monument of ancient wisdom, a momentous arm of political strength, a great national organ, a source of vast popular advantage, and . . . a witness and teacher of religious truth." [10] From the Church as a whole, however, it was possible to gain much; and Newman owed a debt to all three parties. It is enough to note here that Newman was always a "Liberal" in his intellectual audacity and dialectical skill. He was always, we might say, an Evangelical in his "deep and terrifying sense of sin," his Calvinistic emphasis on the contrast between "heaven and hell, divine favor and divine wrath, the justified and the unjustified," in the motive of fear in his sermons, and in the lack of the "sign of joy" which Benedict XIV regarded as indispensable in any real Catholic saint.[11] And of course from the High Anglican party he inherited the notion of the Church as a corporate institution, a reverence for tradition, a belief in authority, in supernatural sacramentalism, in a genuine priesthood. Anglican too is his distrust of emotion, his cool and lucid exposition, his intellectual and artistic refinement.

Between his election to the Oriel fellowship in 1822 and his departure with Hurrell Froude on the Mediterranean journey in 1832, Newman's labors were enormous and his religious and intellectual development rapid and steady. He was ordained deacon in 1824, the year his father died; he accepted the curacy of St. Clement's in May and labored conscientiously with his poor and populous parish, even to the point of being friendly with the "Chapel folk"; he accepted further responsibilities when Whately made him vice-principal of St. Alban Hall in March, 1825; he received priest's orders in May; and a year later, resigning his curacy at St. Clement's, he was appointed one of the public tutors of Oriel. During the year 1827–28, Newman fulfilled the university office of Public Examiner in Classics for the

B.A. degree, and in 1828, when Hawkins was provost of Oriel, he was presented by his college to the Vicarage of St. Mary's, the university church, from the pulpit of which he was to preach some momentous sermons. During 1830, he discharged the duties of proproctor, and in 1831–32 he was the University Select Preacher. Throughout this period of strenuous academic, administrative, and religious labor, Newman was also busy with literary work. Besides his sermon-writing, he wrote an essay on Aristotle for the *London Review*; he contributed to the *Encyclopaedia Metropolitana* essays on Cicero and Apollonius of Tyana, and "composed a considerable portion" of Whately's *Logic*. By 1829, Newman had won a distinguished place in Oxford life. His sermons at St. Mary's had begun to make themselves known. His subtle and mysterious personality, his power of sarcasm, (his "ponderous and icy 'very likelies' "), with which he crushed the unruly undergraduate, his growing intellectual sharpness — largely owing to Whately's "anvil treatment" of him — the increase in his stature as a potential leader, and his severe religious habits — all set him apart and gave the impression that he was marked for some future greatness.

In the meantime, a series of very important events occurred which gave his life a permanent direction: on March 31, 1826, Hurrell Froude was elected to a fellowship at Oriel, and Newman's friendship with him began at that date; a serious illness — possibly a nervous breakdown brought on by overwork — struck Newman down in the winter of 1826–27; his sister Mary died in January, 1828; and early in 1829 Newman and two other tutors had a difference with Provost Hawkins as to the nature of a tutorship. Newman maintained that the work of a tutor was essentially "quasi-pastoral work." The result of the difference was, in the end, that Hawkins ceased to assign pupils to Newman, and Newman was thereby granted time for what was by now his chief preoccupation, the study of the early Church and the Church Fathers. No doubt the illness of 1827–28, together with the loss of his beloved sister (of whom we know almost nothing), accentuated Newman's religious development at this point. It was a stroke of destiny, too, that made Hawkins unwittingly enable Newman to begin that passionately thorough and avid study of the Fathers which was ultimately to alter his whole religious outlook.

At this point we may survey what Tardivel regards as the two great shaping influences on Newman's religious personality: [12] the influence of Oxford itself — its classical studies, its eighteenth-century interests, its brilliant Noetic school of liberalism, its commanding personalities (especially Keble, Froude, 'and Pusey); and the influence of the early Church Fathers.

Whatever of the romantic and mystical there was in Newman — and there was much, as we shall see — his intellectual powers were molded and tempered by Oxford's great classical tradition. To many of us this is so obvious as to need little repetition. It is sufficient here to remember that, having read Ovid at nine and having translated some Homer and Herodotus a year or two later, he plunged delightedly into Oxford's heavy classical reading lists. Throughout his correspondence we learn of his constant preoccupation with Thucydides, Aeschylus, and Sophocles. During his vacations, he read from morning until night in the ancient Greek and Roman authors: in the Long Vacation of 1818, for example, he read and transcribed Larcher's "Notes on Herodotus," and composed a "critique of the plays of Aeschylus, on the principles of Aristotle's 'Poetics.'" He wrote to his mother that, on standing for the scholarship at Trinity, he was required, before the examination, to "do some [Latin or Greek] verses; then Latin translation; then Latin theme; then chorus of Euripides; . . . then some Plato; then some Lucretius; then some Xenophon; then some Livy." [13] And above all, first and foremost, was Aristotle, the Aristotle of the *Logic*, the *Rhetoric*, and the *Poetics*. To be sure, Newman and his fellow-undergraduates had to study Aristotle's *Logic* in Aldrich's emasculated edition, but a severe examination upon the Greek text of Aristotle was compulsory in the final schools. This exacting classical training accounts for a great deal of Newman's rhetorical method, his logical accuracy, his controversial adroitness — here the great model was Cicero — and much of his literary taste. If in his "sense of the supersensible" he was Platonic, in his mode of reasoning he was Aristotelian. He was always ready to submit the powers of reason in service to the demands of faith, but in this restricted domain Aristotelian logic was the great instrument: "in many subject-matters," he was later to say, "to think correctly, is to think like Aristotle." [14]

But, important as were his classical studies, to understand whole ranges of Newman's mind and work it is necessary, as Guitton has well pointed out, to connect him with the English eighteenth century, in which he had his roots.[15] We should never forget that he was born just after the end of that century, in a country which had no moving realization of the European revolution. The eighteenth century, in England, had destroyed nothing; and Trinity and Oriel were merely wrapped in a deeper slumber than the rest of the country. They had no jarring knowledge of *encyclopédisme*, for example, except a general conviction that in France the anti-Christian mind had finally confused itself with the philosophic mind. Yet two classic skeptics of the English eighteenth century never ceased to fascinate Newman, and never, of course, convinced him of the tenability of their position. These were Gibbon and Hume. Gibbon was a favorite for vacation reading: Gibbon and Locke figure in the Long Vacation of 1818, and in 1819 Newman exclaims to his friend Bowden, "Oh, who is worthy to succeed our Gibbon? *Exoriare aliquis!* and may he be a better man!" Dreams of Gibbon filled his nights; his "ears rang with the cadence of his sentences; and he began an analysis of Thucydides in Gibbon's style." Years later he ranked the unbeliever Gibbon as the only English writer who could rightly claim to be an ecclesiastical historian. Newman is never really harsh with Gibbon; the severest condemnation he ever permitted himself was to write of Gibbon's "Five Causes of Christianity": "We do not deny them, but only say they are not sufficient." [16] We shall have occasion later to observe the extent to which Gibbon affected Newman's prose style. (One may also note the surprising degree in which Newman's theories about knowledge and faith echo the atomistic and skeptical doctrines of the other eighteenth-century author who appears so frequently in Newman's pages: David Hume.) We may rank also among Augustan influences the philosopher Locke who, like Hume, figures often in such works as the *Grammar of*

Assent; but Newman was also deeply read in, and influenced by, such neo-Classic writers as Addison (on whose *Spectator* papers he once modeled a small periodical in 1819), Pope, Johnson, Berkeley, Cowper, and Crabbe.[17] However, second only to Locke and Hume as a positive influence, was Bishop Butler, whose *Analogy of Religion* (1736) is ever present in the background or under the foundations of Newman's thinking. He is noteworthy at this point as representing that great tradition, in eighteenth-century English theology, of rational and demonstrative writing, whether it be among Deists like Toland and Collins, or writers on "Christian evidences" like Paley; in all cases, they conducted their discussion with Augustan aplomb, and treated all principles of religion with the good taste of the gentleman. Newman was, of course, to react against their intellectual dryness, but he was ever to retain something of their decorum. In many ways, then, Newman was a man of the eighteenth century. He spent his life, as Dimnet and others have pointed out, in fighting the spirit of Hume, Paley, Tom Paine, and Voltaire, rather than German rationalism or nineteenth-century evolutionism; [18] he remained to the end an eighteenth-century figure, in his general outlook on mundane affairs as well as in the texture of his style. He is Augustan in his definition of a gentleman, in his diction, in his very literary forms — he writes not an "autobiography" but an "apologia," and, like Burke, uses the epistolary form for controversy, as in *The Letter to the Duke of Norfolk*. Nor was he a lonely anachronism; he had excellent Augustan contemporaries who accompanied him in the Victorian era: Macaulay, Hallam, Merivale, and to some extent Cobden and the two Mills.

But even more effective than Oxford's classical and eighteenth-century influences were those of personal association and friendship. For Newman, reality had to make its approach through a person. "Persons influence us," he says, "voices melt us, looks subdue us, deeds inflame us." [19] In the *Apologia* he tells us how he owed certain religious doctrines directly to certain men at Oxford: the doctrine of Tradition to Hawkins, vicar of St. Mary's; that of Apostolical Succession to William James, fellow of Oriel; and that of the Church as "a substantive body or corporation" to Whately. Indeed it was the personal as well as the intellectual appeal of Whately's Noetic group which for a time caused Newman uneasily to "drift in the direction of the Liberalism of the day." The Noetics were the men who set the tone in Oriel in the 1820's — Copleston, Hawkins, Whately, Hampden, Thomas Arnold.[20] Being men of intellectual brilliance rather than of wide learning — they were seriously lacking in historical training, and knew nothing of continental philosophic thought — they shone primarily as thinkers. Liberal in theology and politics, they "sat in their easy chairs," Mark Pattison says, "and thought. . . They called everything in question; they appealed to first principles, and disallowed authority as a judge in intellectual matters."[21] Having little sympathy with the historical tradition of Christian theology, they believed the Church to be burdened with an incubus of formularies and practices which hindered the growth of vital religion; they had shocking things to say about the Thirty-nine Articles, the prayer book, and the marriage and burial services; Whately himself even advocated the disestablishment of the Church; and all of the Noetics believed differences of religious opinion unavoidable, and an infallible authority for deciding religious controversies impossible to find. It was from the brilliant, and often witty, debates of this school that Newman claimed he learned to think clearly and accurately. It was Whately who drew the shy young student out of himself, using him "as an anvil" for forging his own ideas, and drawing him into collaboration on a textbook on *Logic*. Indeed Brilioth believes that it was Whately who "gave Newman's genius the scholastic and antihistorical stamp which was finally to settle his life's destiny."[22] So potent was the Noetics' influence that, for a time, Newman began "to prefer intellectual excellence to moral," and was rudely awakened only by his illness of 1827–28 and by the death of his sister Mary. But Newman bore to the end of his career something of the character of Noetic dialectic, and the Noetic unwillingness, or inability, to be swayed in a moral or religious problem by simple historical considerations.

As Newman drew away from the Noetics early in 1828, he began his momentous friendship with John Keble and Hurrell Froude. Keble had relinquished an Oriel fellowship in 1823 for a humble country curacy, where he helped the poor, preached plain, unpretending, earnest sermons, and wrote the verses which appeared in 1827 as *The Christian Year.* He had been a brilliant university scholar, and was now a plain, unworldly country parson; an old-fashioned English High Churchman and a Tory, venerating his Church and its bishops, equally disliking Rome, Dissent, and Methodism; but with a quick heart, a great contempt for appearances, and an enjoyment of nature. It was Keble's charm and his deliberately undistinguished saintliness, as well as his scholastic reputation, which commended him to Newman. From Keble, Newman derived a greater feeling of the importance of authority, a confirmation of his own, and of Butler's, conception of material phenomena as a "sacramental system," and a new support to Butler's doctrine of probability, namely, the "living power of faith and love" which "gives to probability a force which it has not in itself." [23] This debt to Keble, especially in terms of the *personal* weight it carried, has never been accorded sufficient recognition by Newman's critics and expositors.

Hurrell Froude had been Keble's pupil at Oriel, and was himself elected fellow of Oriel in 1826 and became a tutor in 1827. It was Froude who "brought Keble and Newman to understand each other," about 1828. Froude himself, says Newman, was a man of high genius, overflowing with ideas, with a bold, logical, uncompromising intellect. He openly admired the Church of Rome, and had he not died early — in 1836 — he no doubt would have been among the first of the Oxford converts. His effect on Newman must have been highly exciting, and his influence in the end was enormous. Several years before there was any suspicion of a "Romanizing" tendency in the Oxford Movement, Froude scorned the Reformers, meditated on the perfections of the Blessed Virgin, embraced the principle of penance and mortification, had a deep devotion to the Real Presence, loved to meditate upon the saints, and "had a high and severe idea of the intrinsic excellence of Virginity." Like Keble, he was a Tory; unlike Newman, he had no interest in the Fathers. He loved to shock his friends by gaily and mischievously pushing a religious argument to its limit, usually over into the field

of high Catholic dogma.   Newman admits that from Froude he
got no "precise additions to his theological creed"; again that
was to a large extent a matter of personality.   The relentlessly
logical, irresistibly charming and witty and audacious Froude led
Newman "to look with admiration towards the Church of Rome
. . . and fixed deep in [him] the idea of devotion to the Blessed
Virgin, and led [him] gradually to believe in the Real Presence." [24]

As Newman "moved out of the shadow of liberalism," his
early devotion to the Church Fathers returned.   Here was an
influence upon his life paralleled only by that of Butler, Keble,
and Froude.   In fact, while Froude wished a return to the Middle Ages, Newman himself in the nineteenth century was a contemporary of Origen, Dionysius, and Clement of Alexandria.
As Gorce has ably shown, the early Fathers merely confirmed
what had already lain slumbering in Newman's mind since he
pored over Milner's *Church History* as a boy.[25]   Many years
later he was to state flatly, "The Fathers made me a Catholic." [26]
We shall consider on a later page just what teachings he derived
from their works.   Here it is enough to note that they acceler-
ated the Platonic and mystical in him, that they appealed to him
not only by virtue of their doctrines but because of their charming humanity and their strength of character.   Newman de-
lighted in the letters of Basil and Gregory, in the tremendous
labors of Anthony.   He rejoices that these early giants of the
Church "do not put away their natural endowments, but use them
to the glory of the Giver. . . They are versed in human knowledge; they are busy in human society; they understand the human heart. . . Thus they have the thoughts, feelings, frames
of mind, attractions, sympathies, antipathies of other men . . .
only they have these properties of human nature purified, sanctified, and exalted." [27]   In his poem, "The Greek Fathers," he
admires Clement's "varied page," the sage rulership of Dionysius, Origen's "eagle eye," the "high purpose" of Basil, and the
"royal heart" of Athanasius.   Everywhere in their writings he
finds himself at home, and when he comes eventually to write
The Church of the Fathers, he falls naturally, insensibly, into

the English equivalent of their prose style, and into their tone and manner and method. Mlle. Tardivel no doubt exaggerates when she says that Newman treasured them less for their teachings than for their spiritual history, mingled among their apologetics.[28] Yet there is something to be said in extenuation of such a view. At any rate, so deeply colored is Newman's religious nature by the Fathers, that he has been frequently called "an Alexandrian Greek," "a Greek of Alexandria . . . mystical, ascetic, uncompromising."[29]

During the Long Vacation of 1828 he set about reading the Fathers chronologically, beginning with St. Ignatius and St. Justin. Two years later, with the urging of Hugh James Rôse, he accepted a request to write a history of the great Church Councils for a "Theological Library." He at once set to work on the Council of Nicaea. Convinced that such a work "ought to be derived from the original sources, and not be compiled from the standard authorities," he "was drifted back first to the Ante-Nicene history, and then to the Church of Alexandria."[30] The book which resulted was *The Arians of the Fourth Century* (1833), which we shall examine in connection with *The Development of Christian Doctrine* (1845), to which it provides a sort of preliminary study. By the time *The Arians* was completed, Newman had made his first thorough acquaintance with those early heresies which were to throw modern religious groups into such a disturbing light; he had again dangerously overworked himself; and he had decided to accompany Hurrell Froude and his father on a Mediterranean tour in search of rest and health.

What sort of man was the young Newman when he left England in December, 1832, for a tour of the Mediterranean? He was still rather shy, and gave evidence of having "had a near escape of being a stutterer." He was still sensitive, and apprehensive lest he disappoint the hopes he had raised; yet he had within him a deep fund of "latent undisturbed consciousness of power." In spite of his engrossing friendship with Keble and Froude, he lived in a "real isolation of thought and spiritual solitariness"[31] which was the result of his earlier Calvinistic beliefs; he was developing a strong ascetic tendency — yet, so various was his nature, he chose the wines for his college cellars, and himself drank sparingly.   There was about him that "intense stillness," which Aubrey de Vere noted later; a "humble quiet manner" of entering a room which made one feel, suddenly, that "there was something uncommon in it."[32]   He was one of those people who are never really well, yet seldom really ill — today he would probably be called a "constitutional inadequate," capable of quick recuperation from exhaustion after enormous labors. He suffered from near-sightedness, toothache, indigestion.   His appearance was rather frail, according to most testimony, though Tuckwell speaks of his "ruddy face"; Thomas Mozley alludes to Newman's being "thin, pale, with large lustrous eyes ever piercing through the veil of men and things," a creature "hardly seemed made for this world."[33]   Lockhart saw little that was imposing in his appearance — with his long black coat and white cravat — but Newman gave the impression of entire absorption in an object outside himself; there was a loftiness of mind, a humility, a "virgin purity of heart . . . a wonderfully caressing manner, which had nothing of weakness in it," but which completely subjugated anyone who long remained in his presence.[34] "It would not do to meet him often," said Dr. Arnold a few years later, after spending an evening with him.[35]   Yet this magnetic power was consonant with a curious self-centeredness, an awe-inspiring aloofness, which kept many at a distance; Newman could not readily give himself in love to a fellow man: "I think I am very cold and reserved to people," he wrote in a letter, "but I cannot ever realize to myself that anyone loves me."[36]   At the heart of this aloof man was a baffling paradox, a rare and profoundly nonrational and mystical nature bound up indissolubly with an intellect the acuteness of which easily surpassed ordinary standards.   And within the depths of this nature, Newman carried on a self-mirroring, a merciless self-analysis, which at times approached morbidity.   At the same time, Newman's aesthetic sensibility turned its gaze outward and took in the beauty and the wonder of the world: his letters written during the Mediterranean journey reflect an amazing ability to absorb accurately and to depict vividly impressions of the country around Torquay and Dartington, and of the seascapes of the Mediterranean.

The trip to Italy and Sicily proved to be another of the great turning points in Newman's life. His letters show that he and Froude stayed at Gibraltar, Malta, Corfu, cruised in the Archipelago, and then returned to Naples and Rome. It was not the Roman Church which provided the crisis at this time — it was a "corrupt" system, and he looked on Rome "as a city under a curse"; [37] the crisis was a twofold one — his illness in Sicily, and his sense of a mission to save the English Church from destruction at the hands of the Whig politicians. The Froudes had to leave for home, and Newman was now free to fulfill a cherished project of visiting the interior of Sicily. Such a journey was full of hazards in 1833. But Newman, unaware of the dangers, set out on April 19, with full provisions, a servant, and three mules. At Castro Giovanni, he caught a fever of which he nearly died. He has left us a memorandum, "My Illness in Sicily," which reveals what a deep impression his illness made on him, and to what an intense degree he felt called upon to do some great work before he died. During his fever, which lasted three weeks, he kept saying to himself, "I have not sinned against light"; he morbidly analyzed himself and his past actions — he "had been very self-willed about the tutorship affair" with Hawkins; he reassured himself that "God had some work for him," and that he should recover. The "work" was of course the defense of his Church. In March he had written to Thomas Mozley: "I hate the Whigs (of course, as Rowena says, in a Christian way) more bitterly than ever." [38] The Church seemed in great danger of disestablishment; at least, ten sees of the Irish Church were scheduled for suppression. The Church was not in real danger; the Evangelicals themselves would have stoutly resisted anything remotely resembling spoliation. But Newman, on recovering from his illness, and after severe heartsearching, set off on an orange boat bound for Marseilles, determined to throw himself into a bitter struggle to rescue the English Church from Erastians, Latitudinarians, and politicians. As is well known, while his boat was becalmed off the Straits of Bonifacio he wrote his poem, "Lead, Kindly Light." This poem is not often read in view of what it meant to Newman at the moment. For him the "night was dark," and he was indeed "far from home"; he had hitherto been self-willed ("I loved to *choose* and see my path"), pride ruled his heart; now the Kindly Light will lead him on through struggle amid enemies ("o'er moor and fen, o'er crag and torrent, till the night is gone"). What became a great spiritual hymn was originally a passionate personal confession and a statement of personal faith. Newman arrived in London on July 9: the enemy "would know the difference, now that I am back." [39] The following Sunday, July 14, Keble preached a very quiet and uninflammatory sermon on England's evident desire to forsake her Church; it was entitled "National Apostasy." For Newman, this unpretentious and earnest sermon was the signal for action. He had been through a severe trial; he had thought deeply; he hungered for deeds. The elements of leadership in him had coalesced, and he was ready.

CHAPTER II

EX UMBRIS ET IMAGINIBUS IN VERITATEM

i. A Band of "Oxford Parsons": the Oxford Movement Begins (1833–35)

Newman returned, in the summer of 1833, to a Church beset with dangers from many directions. Waggishly termed "the praying section of the Tory party," the Established Church had been allied with that party for generations, and its bishops had outraged the populace by voting with the Tory lords against the Reform Bill of 1832. But the reforming Whigs, under Lord Grey, were now in power and warned the bishops to "set their house in order." Disestablishment seemed so imminent that Dr. Arnold had recently declared, "The Church, as it now stands, no human power can save." [1] The Whig reformers appeared aided and abetted by the Erastians, who, following Selden and Hobbes, held the view that the final authority in religious belief was neither the Church nor the Bible, but the state. Meanwhile the swell of the French Revolution was at last reaching the coasts of England, bringing in a flood of secularism — a belief that only intelligence, education, and technology were needed to cure all the evils and sorrows of mankind. And everywhere there was, on the one hand, a general ignorance of the principles for which the English Church stood, and on the other, the spiritual deadness of the Church itself.

It has been customary, following Dean Church's classic account in *The Oxford Movement*, to dwell on "the dark time before 1833," when the typical clergyman was much like any one of those in Jane Austen's novels, or in Crabbe's *Parish Register*, or in Dickens' *Pickwick Papers*. The Anglican clergy "had become, for the most part, amiable and respectable gentlemen, who were satisfied to read Morning and Afternoon Service on a Sunday, and to dislike Dissenters." [2] The bishops appear to have been little better. They were politically-minded Tories, ap-

23

pointed by a long line of Tory prime ministers; some of them were not averse to pluralism and nepotism: Bishop Watson of Llandaff held sixteen benefices and never resided in his diocese; Archbishop Manners Sutton of Canterbury distributed sixteen livings and a variety of cathedral appointments among seven members of his family.[3]   There was widespread neglect of form and spirit in church services, in ordination, in examination for holy orders.   Yet this gloomy picture must be corrected by remembering two facts usually omitted from the standard accounts: the general fidelity of the rank and file of the parish clergy, and the natural inadequacy of the Church's mediaeval organization to cope with the rise of industrialism, the rapid growth of towns, the shifting and increasing population, and all the social and moral problems consequent on the introduction of technology into English life.   It was the Ecclesiastical Commission of 1835, and not the Oxford Movement, which removed the abuses of organization, and enabled the Church to meet the social crisis of the time.   Moreover, even in the Church as unreformed, there had been more spiritual life than some of the classic narratives allow: the poet Southey in 1817 considered the Church to be, on the whole, growing in knowledge and zeal; and Wordsworth and Coleridge, in their later years, thought it to be alive with inextinguishable truth.   Furthermore, there were two great religious forces still at work in the Church which made Newman's labors possible: the tradition of the High Anglican school, resting on the principles of the Non-Jurors of the seventeenth century; and the Evangelical revival, which, though it had virtually run its course by 1830, was nevertheless a strong element in Oxford's religious atmosphere.   The Non-Jurors — Ken, Sancroft, Dodwell, Nelson — together with men like Bull and Beveridge, had concentrated their interest, just as Newman was to concentrate his, on the Church of the fourth and fifth centuries, on Catholicity, on the importance of the priestly office, on Apostolical Succession, on the institutional conception of the Church, and on the Prayer Book of Edward VI with its somewhat richer liturgy than the final one.   On the other hand, the Evangelicals had emphasized a need of devotion, a "thirst for holiness," which was to encourage the Movement which Newman brought about.   In fact, "the Tractarians," says Brilioth, "were in great measure recruited from Evangelicals" — from men who had been deeply influenced by Romaine, Thomas Scott, Milner, and Newton.[4] Thus, when Newman returned from the Mediterranean, though the Church was beset with enemies, it was also fortified with hidden resources.

Yet Newman returned more acutely aware of an imperiled Church, and also of a "spirit of the age" which presented a formidable challenge. The 1820's had in many ways been strongly "anti-Church": the repeal of the Test Act in 1828 had admitted non-churchmen into civil and military positions; the Catholic Emancipation Act of 1829 had given broader privileges to Roman Catholics. The old ideal of Hooker, of the identity of the Church with the nation, was banished as an impractical dream. The Reform Bill of 1832 had been a severe blow to the old Tory oligarchy, and thus indirectly to the prestige and power of Oxford and the Church; liberal and mercantile Whigs from both the nobility and the middle class now rose to unprecedented power. The new watchwords were "reform," "economy," "the march of mind," "progress," "reason," "disestablishment." Much of this spirit was an indirect result of the July Revolution in France (1830) — "The French are an awful people," Newman had said in horror; "this Revolution [is] the triumph of irreligion."[5] For Newman, as for Burke, rebellion against constituted authorities was the most tragic of all political solutions; and, like the old Non-Jurors, he regarded it as spiritual dereliction. In a letter to his mother on March 13, 1829, he had said gloomily of this turbulent era:

"We live in a novel era — one in which there is an advance towards universal education. Men have hitherto depended on others, and especially on the clergy, for religious truth; now each man attempts to judge for himself. Now, without meaning of course that Christianity is in itself opposed to free inquiry, still I think it *in fact* at the present time opposed to the particular form which that liberty of thought has now assumed. Christianity is of faith, modesty, lowliness, subordination; but the spirit at work against it is one of latitudinarianism, indifferentism, and schism, a spirit which tends to overthrow doctrine, as if the fruit of bigotry and discipline — as if the instrument of priestcraft. All parties seem to acknowledge that the stream of opinion is setting against the Church. I do believe it will ultimately be separated from the State, and at this prospect I look with apprehension — (1) because all revolutions are awful things, and the effect of this revolution is unknown; (2) because the upper classes will be left almost religionless; (3) because there will not be that security for sound doctrine without change, which is given by Act of Parliament; (4) because the clergy will be thrown on their congregations for voluntary contributions.

"It is no reply to say that the majesty of truth will triumph, for man's nature is corrupt; also, even should it triumph, still this will only be ultimately, and the meanwhile may last for centuries. Yet I do still think there is a promise of preservation to the Church; and in its Sacraments, preceding and attending religious education, there are such means of Heavenly grace, that I do not doubt it will live on in the most irreligious and atheistical times.

"Its enemies at present are: (1) The uneducated or partially educated mass in towns, whose organs are Wooler's, Carlisle's publications, &c. They are almost professedly deistical or worse. (2) The Utilitarians, political economists, useful knowledge people — their organs the 'Westminster Review,' the 'London University,' &c. (3) The Schismatics in and out of the church, whose organs are the 'Eclectic Review,' the 'Christian Guardian,' &c. (4) The Baptists, whose system is consistent Calvinism — for, as far as I can see, Thomas Scott, &c., are inconsistent, and such inconsistent men would in times of commotion split and go over to this side or that. (5) The high circles in London. (6) I might add the political indifferentists, but I do not know enough to speak, like men who join Roman Catholics on one hand and Socinians on the other. Now you must not understand me as speaking harshly of individuals; I am speaking of bodies and principles.

"And now I come to another phenomenon: the talent of the day is against the Church. The Church party (visibly at least, for there may be latent talent, and great times give birth to great men) is poor in mental endowments. It has not activity, shrewdness, dexterity, eloquence, practical power. On what, then, does it depend? On prejudice and bigotry." [6]

Here we see Newman conscious that "the great legacy inherited by Christians in England must be treated as a whole, with the greatest reverence and care, lest what was priceless and irreplaceable might be rudely destroyed in the necessary process of reform." [7] In the 1820's and 1830's he was finding "a philosophical value in the caution of unintellectual conservatism." Something of the spirit of Burke and Coleridge breathes in his dread and scorn for the uneducated atheists like Richard Carlile,[8] the political economists, the Utilitarians, and what Thomas Carlyle was calling the "do-nothing" gentlemen in Mayfair. And above all, he is alarmed at the feeble "mental endowments" of the Church party, and at its complacent trust in "prejudice and bigotry." Uppermost in his mind also is the threat of disestablishment — of "throwing the clergy on their congregations for voluntary contributions," a deadly political move, contemplated by some of the Whigs. He is not unaware, moreover, of the growing influence of the Utilitarian Radicalism of Bentham and James and John Stuart Mill, with its facile maxim, "the greatest happiness for the greatest number." The enemies of the Church, he sees, are no longer "men of wit and pleasure about town," but, as even Whately said, in his *Logic* — did Newman write the passage? — they are "men not only of learning and ingenuity, but of cultivated argumentative powers, not unversed in the principles of logic." [9]

As has been frequently noted, Newman and his fellow Tractarians in 1833 were singularly unconscious — or apparently so — of certain great movements of thought outside the Church, and of those flourishing on the continent. Evidently they knew very little of the spiritual renaissance effected by Wordsworth and Coleridge and Thomas Carlyle; we hear nothing of the brilliant Cambridge school of Thirlwall, Julius Hare, Maurice, and John Sterling. While Newman was writing poetry and gathering up his forces in the Mediterranean, Charles Darwin was away on the *Beagle*, watching the methods of nature in the Southern Atlantic and Pacific islands; Carlyle, on his "Dunscore Patmos" at Craigenputtock, was fashioning out of German literature and thought a new raiment for the substance and spirit of his ancestral faith; over on the continent, transcendental Idealism was in full career in Germany — Hegel and Schleiermacher were lecturing in Berlin, applying to religion and religious documents the new historical method, while in Tübingen, Strauss was developing the Hegelian principles, with results that were to alarm the world in the *Leben Jesu*; in France, Saint Simon had thought out his *Nouveau Christianisme*, and Auguste Comte had begun the *Cours de Philosophie* which showed how the theological and metaphysical ages had been left behind, and how the final positive (scientific) age had come, demanding new approaches to the ideas of God, religion, and society.[10]   It was everywhere a time of stocktaking, of questioning, of doubt.   Though it had certain stimulating qualities, it was, as Carlyle had said, an age rapidly becoming "destitute of faith and terrified at skepticism." [11] This was the epoch — the age of the historical method boldly applied to all fields of experience, the age of full-grown Romanticism, of dazzling and disturbing advances in physical science, of world-creating German idealisms, of world-shattering Biblical criticism, of political revolution and democracy, and of passionate faith in "progress" in economic and social life — this was the epoch in which a little group of Oxford poets, tutors, and preachers hoped to bring about a return to primitive, dogmatic, ascetic Christianity.   Their story — on the face of it, so hopeless — has been told many times.   No story, according to Ollard, in the whole history of the English Church since St. Augustine landed in A.D. 597, is more splendid in audacity, magnanimity, and faith.[12]

Before we consider the first steps they took, under Newman's leadership, it might be well to ask just what was the essence of the movement which they inaugurated.   We cannot hold, with A. P. Stanley, that it was primarily a political effort, nor with Thomas Arnold that it was chiefly an antiquarian movement, nor with Pattison and Jowett that it was merely a sectarian act.[13]   Contrary to general opinion, it had, at bottom, little to do with the Romantic movement.   To be sure, Newman soon recognized, in his essay on "Prospects of the Anglican Church," how much support was indirectly derived from Sir Walter Scott, Coleridge, Southey, and Wordsworth.   And critics and scholars, such as Willoughby and Fairbairn, have not failed to find in French and German Romanticism certain affinities with the Tractarian spirit and effort.[14] It is easy to point to German philosophy and theology, to Schelling, to the mediaeval reaction of Schlegel, Goerres, and Moehler, to the "experience theology" of Schleiermacher and Neander. It is no less easy to point to French Romanticism and ultramontanism — to Chateaubriand, de Maistre, de Bonald, and Lamennais. The Tractarians were indeed akin to the Romantics — if not in fact Romantics themselves — in so far as they shared in the contemporary "sense of the past," in the general reawakening to the spiritual depths of human nature and to its hunger for something more than physical and intellectual satisfaction. But as Fairchild and Brilioth have decisively shown, the Oxford Movement, though prepared for and partially explained by the literary currents before it and around it, even appropriating some of their thoughts, "was not evoked by them, nor can it, unless violence is done to the material, be classified only as part of the Romantic movement." [15]   Just what then, was the aim of that little band of "Oxford parsons" who, as Greville said, had "behaved so abominably" during the Catholic Emancipation days and so utterly routed the Whigs in the Oxford election? [16]

Politically, of course, it was a move to protect the Church from disestablishment, to reassert what Newman had said in *The Arians*, that the Church is "prior in existence to the civil institutions with which it is surrounded," that as a great "ecclesiastical body," it is "a divinely appointed means" for "interfering, or (as irreligious men will say) meddling with the world." [17]   But more subtly and profoundly, it was a call — strange in the days of Bentham, the new railways, and "the ten-pound franchise" — to "repentance, [to] a keen realization of the fearful character of post-baptismal sin." [18]   It was a call to holiness, "holiness rather than peace," rather than the acquisition of the material goods with which the English nineteenth century was about to flood the people.   Newman and his colleagues were determined to realize the primitive "apostolic" conception of Christianity and to apply it uncompromisingly to the "modern" and "enlightened" nineteenth century.   They were determined to ascertain whether Christianity could preserve its spiritual identity in the modern world, or whether it would be transformed by, and absorbed into, the secularized culture of the day.   Withdrawn from the world, living among the books and historical memories of the past, in Oxford, they were not violently alarmed by the insistent and troublesome problems of the great world, problems in religious belief, in scientific discoveries, in social and economic misery. These, they felt — as indeed did Coleridge, Carlyle, and others — would solve themselves when the fundamental moral and spiritual dissonance in man had been resolved. Besides, as James Anthony Froude has said, Newman "took the usually accepted Christian account of man and his destiny to be literally true." [19] The awful sense of the reality of evil and suffering, of the dark mystery of human existence, weighed upon him. Which was the true view of human nature, that of Bentham or that of Isaiah? Did the destiny of man depend on the progress of science and the growth of democracy, or did it lie in the shadow of the mystery of Divine Judgment? It was this call, a challenge for radical otherworldliness, a profoundly searching moralism, that brought the first recruits, as is testified by Pattison, Lord Blachford, and W. G. Ward.[20]

Yet the Movement was also many other things. It was a return to dogma and scientific theology, as against the emotional religiosity of popular Protestantism. It was a return to religion as a devotion and as an art — "religion is not merely a science but a *devotion,*" Newman was to write in 1860.[21] It was a return to definite commitments: "Christianity is faith, faith implies a doctrine, a doctrine propositions, propositions yes or no." [22] It was a reassertion of the corporate nature of the Church, as held by Laud, Bramhall, Stillingfleet. And lastly, it was a turning with eager appetite to the great English divines of the seventeenth century, who had recognized the English Church as a branch of the Church Catholic — Bull, Andrewes, Taylor, Hammond, Thorndike, Beveridge, Ken, Wilson; and also a turning, for Catholicity at its source, to the Church Fathers — St. Ignatius, Origen, Clement, Basil, Gregory, Athanasius. One might add, with Bishop Knox, one other element in the Movement: Tractarianism was attempting to deal with an age-long problem which, in the secular sphere, is treated in such books as Harold J. Laski's *The Problem of Sovereignty*: it was trying to answer the question, "What is the seat of authority in the religious and social life of mankind?" [23]

It has been truly said that "the story of the actual beginning of the Oxford Movement is the story of a crisis in Newman's mind. . . Newman remains throughout the central figure . . . He was the first with no second. . . The rest were all but as ciphers, and he the indicating number." [24] This is true in spite of Newman's insistence that he "never had the staidness or dignity necessary for a leader." [25] He provided the dynamic, progressive force. A more static and respectable effort, on the other hand, was initiated on July 25–29, 1833, at the Deanery, Hadleigh, Suffolk, by Hugh James Rose, a Cambridge man, together with William Palmer, A. P. Perceval, and Hurrell Froude. They proposed founding an Association of Friends of the Church. Out of the meeting, however, came nothing but addresses to the archbishop and the laity, signed by clergymen and heads of families. It was characteristic of Newman (who was absent from the meeting) to frown on such timid and impersonal measures: "No great work was done by a system," he said; "whereas systems rise out of individual exertions." [26] Hurrell Froude demanded that they make a "row in the world"; so on September 9, 1833, the first three tracts, all from Newman's pen, made their appearance. Tract I, a four-page leaflet, deserves a moment's notice. Its clear nervous English, its metallic sound as of a trumpet blast in that quiet world of the English Church, its manly conciseness — all make it typical of the earlier and more influential tracts. Its title is "Thoughts on the Ministerial Commission." Newman addresses his fellow clergymen in a quiet, warning tone: "I am but one of yourselves — a Presbyter; therefore I conceal my name, lest I should take too much on myself by speaking in my own person . . . Speak I must; for the times are evil . . ." Then follow admonitions, exhortations such as must have astonished many a well-fed respectable churchman — "be [to your bishops] what Luke and Timothy were to St. Paul . . ;" welcome if necessary "the spoiling of [your] goods, and martyrdom," proclaim your "apostolic descent," . . . "speak out now before you are forced . . . [The politicians think] they can take away your power . . . Enlighten them in this matter. Exalt our Holy Fathers the Bishops, as representatives of the Apostles and the Angels of the Churches. And magnify your office." [27]   It is hard to imagine comfortable clergymen like George Eliot's Mr. Gilfil, or Mr. Irwine in *Adam Bede*, contemplating with zeal the role of Timothy or St. Luke, or the possibility of spoliation and martyrdom. The tracts therefore brought mixed reactions, of surprise, inspiration, disgust, bewilderment: throughout the parsonages of England there ran the buzz and whisper of discussion. As the tracts multiplied, and as "young clergymen spent days riding around with a pocketful, surprising their neighbors at breakfast, lunch, dinner, and tea," [28] recruits began to pour in; young barristers, like William Gladstone, began to throw in their lot with the Movement. They read eagerly such tracts as "The Catholic Church" (dealing with the Irish Church question), "The Episcopal Church Catholic," "Adherence to the Apostolic Succession," "The Benefits of Fasting." It was, of course, a great age of tract-reading. Now, as Thomas Mozley has humorously pointed out, the usual distributors of tracts to the lower classes — the clergy and other educated people — had the tables turned on them. The tract on fasting marked a fresh stage in the Movement, since the author, Dr. Pusey, by attaching his initials to it, not only gave the movement a name, "Puseyism," but also gave it prestige, since he was professor and canon of Christ Church, and had a vast influence.

With his accession the tracts grew longer, more weighty, and more elaborate. In fact they became rather erudite dissertations. Throughout this earlier Tractarian period, however, Newman himself was buoyant, informal, and confident; his health had been renewed; he felt that he was inaugurating, perhaps, a second Reformation. His manner had at once something of fierceness and of sport; he did not argue at length, but drew men out; he was at times reckless and ironic; his mission was to inflame; and even a measure of excess, he felt, was permissible. "I expect to be called a Papist when my opinions are known," he wrote, "but I shall lead persons on a little way. . . Let me be thought extravagant, and yet be copied." [29]   In the midst of the struggle he labored tirelessly, composing sermons, editing Dionysius Alexandrinus, writing and editing tracts, and carrying on a voluminous correspondence. By 1835 he had written a number of studies of the early Church, such as "Primitive Christianity," and several essays on the early Fathers for the *British Magazine,* which later appeared in his *Historical Sketches,* the most noteworthy group being entitled *The Church of the Fathers.*

In 1834, overcoming "his old scruple against divulging to the world at large what had passed between him and his congregation," which reveals his characteristic reticence and dread of the public gaze, he brought out the first volume of his *Parochial Sermons.* Thomas Mozley testifies to their astonishing popularity: "The volume put all other sermons out of the market, just as *Waverley* and *Guy Mannering* put all other novels." [30] In fact, as Dean Church has said, the Movement was propelled not merely by the tracts, but also by Newman's famous four o'clock sermons at St. Mary's, sermons "plain, direct, unornamented, clothed in English that was only pure and lucid, free from any faults of taste, strong in their flexibility and perfect command . . . in their piercing and large insight into character." [31] These were the sermons which drew crowds of Londoners up to Oxford on Sunday afternoons to see and to hear the man who had so upset the stuffy aplomb of His Majesty's Established Church. Even those who had read the tracts with distaste, or with a suspicion of popery, could hardly resist "the charm of that spiritual apparition, gliding in the dim afternoon light through the aisles of St. Mary's, rising in the pulpit and then, in the most entrancing of voices, breaking the silence with words and thoughts which were a religious music — subtle, sweet, and mournful." [32]

ii. *The Golden Age: Newman and the "Via Media"* (1835–39)

By the end of 1835, Newman and his cohorts were at the height of their confidence in one of the great doctrines which their Movement was designed to prove and disseminate: the *Via Media,* the doctrine that the English Church stood safely free from both the "corruptions" of Romanism and the "errors" of popular Protestantism. The Tractarians were not alarmed that they had grown into a "party," though Newman himself regretted it, as he regretted the mannerisms of some of his disciples — it became a sign of the true apostolic faith, for example, to walk, like Newman, with your head forward and somewhat awry, and, when you reached your place in the pew, to fall on your knees, like Newman, "as if your legs had suddenly been pulled away." There were comic, as well as sublime, aspects of "Newmanism." But the Movement grew. And with its growth there developed, inevitably, opposite tendencies which ultimately brought on a crisis. In fact, 1836 proved to be a year of considerable trial. Hurrell Froude died in February. Isaac William's tract, "On Reserve in Communicating Religious Knowledge," caused scruples in many quarters. To answer insinuations that the Tractarians were promoting popery, they began an ambitious editing of the Fathers of the Church before the division of East and West. But two major events mark the year as a pivotal one in the second period of the Movement: the Hampden controversy, and Newman's lectures on "Romanism and Popular Protestantism."

The Whig premier, Lord Melbourne, appointed to the vacant post of Regius Professor of Divinity a certain Dr. Hampden, Principal of St. Mary Hall. The new appointee had given the Bampton Lectures in 1832, and had thrown doubt on the Creeds and their authority. His appointment roused a storm of indignation, especially among the Tractarians. Here was "Liberalism," openly supported by the government, and forced upon the university. The Tractarians, supported by the Evangelicals, succeeded in enacting a statute depriving Hampden of selecting university preachers. In the midst of the turmoil, Dr. Arnold added fuel to the flames by furiously attacking the Tractarians in an article, "The Oxford Malignants," in the *Edinburgh Review*; and Newman himself published his *Elucidations of Dr. Hampden's Teaching*, which, according to some of his critics, subtly misrepresented Hampden's position and led many to believe his victim a hypocritical heretic.[1] Behind all the tumult stood Dr. Wiseman, an eminent Roman Catholic (afterwards archbishop and cardinal), enjoying its fury, and soon publishing an article in the *Dublin Review*, comparing the supposed Catholicity of the English Church to a convalescing invalid.[2] Out of this bitter struggle, however — one of those virulent factional fights in which the university appeared at its worst — there came the resounding victory for the Tractarians in the judgment on Hampden. But the cost was dear; and the significance for Newman — which is what we are primarily concerned with here — was fateful. In the first place, the controversy brought against the Tractarians the first charges of Romanizing. In the second place, the whole painful affair revealed to Newman for the first time the impotence of his Church to deal with what he regarded as heresy; his dream of a purified Church began to dissolve. In gloomy foreboding, he wrote on a packet of letters:

"March, 1836, is a cardinal point of time. It gathers about it more or less closely the following events: —

1. Froude's death.
2. My mother's death and sister's marriage.
3. My knowing and using the Breviary.[3]
4. First Connection with the *British Critic.*
5. The Tracts becoming Treatises.
6. Start of the Library of the Fathers.
7. Theological Society.
8. My writing against the Church of Rome.
9. Littlemore Chapel." [4]

A new scene gradually opening.

Yet Newman felt secure in his position. And he passed quickly to another and more constructive activity than mere opposition to "Liberalism." He had been in controversial correspondence with a learned French Abbé, M. Jager, about the respective claims of Roman and Anglican Catholicism. He now entered upon the then unheard-of novelty of giving public lectures in Oxford, in the dark and dreary appendage to St. Mary's, Adam de Brome's Chapel. These lectures, on "The Prophetical Office of the Church," [5] a powerful polemic against Rome, unmatched in Newman's writings for biting sharpness, attempted to define the *Via Media* of the English Church, unblemished by the superstitious "additions" of Rome or the caprices of Protestantism. Newman believed that the preservation of a clear corpus of theological truth was the fundamental "Note" of the true Church, and he thought he found it most perfectly manifested in the Anglican Church. Rome had added to this body of divine truth, Protestantism had subtracted from it; only in the English Church, he thought, was there to be found the safe middle way of Catholic orthodoxy — the original Apostolic Church and the faith of the Fathers. Actually, of course, the Anglican Church grievously tolerated Protestant error and neglected her Catholic heritage. Yet she could not forfeit it entirely without losing her identity. She must, on the other hand, maintain her objective body of truth, which was neither Roman nor Protestant; she must return to her original basis, and vindicate her rightful inheritance. This doctrine, briefly summed up for our purposes, is Newman's theory of the *Via Media*.[6] It is essentially a static view of the Church, and should be contrasted with the dynamic view which Newman will develop in his great essay of 1845. It had its other weaknesses: it failed to provide a definite frontier against Protestantism, and, as Newman later said, it was but a "paper theory," and never stood the test of practice. Newman's adhesion to the theory was always somewhat provisional; he trusted the English Church only in so far as she represented the Apostolic Church and the Church of the Fathers. But the lectures attracted crowds of listeners, and had great effect, in various ways, on such brilliant young men as A. P. Stanley and W. G. Ward.[7]

The success of the lectures, however, had been darkened for Newman by the death of Hurrell Froude, and was now to be further darkened by another event — the publication of Froude's *Remains* in 1838. As Ollard says, "anything more indiscreet, from a party point of view, has probably never been done." [8] Briefly, the *Remains*, containing a personal and intimate diary of a devout man, revealed Froude's contempt for the sixteenth-century Reformation, which had been but "a limb badly set," needing to "be broken again to be righted." Froude calls the Hadleigh meeting "the conspiracy"; he reveals that at Rome in 1833 he and Newman had asked a Roman monsignor if the Roman Church would accept them "on any terms to which they could twist their consciences." All this was really written in Froude's characteristic jesting, exaggerative fashion. But the British public was astounded and angered. From that day, Froude's *Remains* have supplied ammunition for every critic of the Oxford Movement. Few people at the time, however, realized that the very publication of the *Remains* showed the Tractarians to be no cunning conspirators or subtle agents of Rome. Yet the episode, like the Hampden affair, again profoundly disturbed Newman's confidence in the ancient Catholicity of his Church.

More and more there was a need for a clear definition of the Anglican position. Newman had condemned the Roman errors respecting Purgatory, Transubstantiation, and the Invocations of the Virgin Mary and the Saints; so with elaborate care he and his friends constructed Catenae of the Fathers, and of the Anglican divines in support of their Catholic views concerning Apostolical Succession, Baptismal Regeneration, Purgatory, the Eucharist. As we have seen, Newman himself, in 1836, had begun to use the Breviary, with its prayers to the Virgin Mary, its Invocation of Saints and Angels; and in Tract LXXV he treated the Breviary as a treasury rather than as a standard of devotion. The Movement itself waxed stronger and stronger; its enemies became bolder and more convinced that its leaders were Romeward bound. To test the leaders, a design was set afoot to erect a memorial to the three reforming bishops who were burnt at Oxford — Cranmer, Ridley, and Latimer. Pusey was inclined to contribute the requested donation for the erection, in order to disarm suspicion of sympathy with Rome, but Newman held aloof. The Martyr's Memorial stands in Oxford today, but it reminds the knowing observer that Newman and many of his fellow-Tractarians were no friends of the Reformation.

In spite of all ominous rumblings, the Movement went on apace. And for Newman, "it was the happiest time of his life." [9] He was master of a great effort, a leader of men. Wonder and awe gathered round him; people feared him, yet were drawn to him. He did not try to proselytize; he respected men's intellectual privacy; but he was accessible, and a stern driver. "He was impatient of mere idle worldliness, of conceit and impertinence, of men who gave themselves airs . . . of pompous and solemn emptiness. . . [He was] courteous, affable, easy . . . a keen trier of character . . . he had his breakfast parties and his evening gatherings." [10] "He seemed always to be better informed on common topics of conversation than anyone else who was present. He was never condescending . . . never didactic or authoritative . . . He never tried to be witty or to say striking things. Ironical he could be, but not ill-natured . . . Prosy he could not be. He was lightness itself." [11] One of his former students, Thomas Mozley, noted that Newman always "looked inquiringly, expectantly, and believingly for the special powers and intentions of his younger friends." [12] He always believed and expected too much rather than too little. If he was not, as some maintain, a good judge of character, [13] he was nevertheless a born leader, stimulating and inspiring his followers with a fiery zeal. He was living in great days: Jowett, Stanley, and Clough hung on the outskirts of the Movement, doubtful but fascinated; even F. J. A. Hort, later so hostile to Anglo-Catholicism, was for a moment carried off his balance; new young men came into the Movement — Oakeley, Faber, Dalgairns; and W. G. Ward of Balliol, who had to be dragged to hear Newman and then was completely overcome. The force of Newman's personality, the charm of his conversation, the power of his preaching — all gave him undisputed eminence and influence. All these, together with the silvery intonation of Newman's voice, whether in a sermon or in an argument, as each separate sentence was spoken rapidly, but with great clearness of expression, made him a magnetic figure. No wonder that "among hundreds of young men, *Credo in Newmannum* was the genuine symbol of faith." [14]

And yet there hung a cloud over all this triumph. Newman always regarded his bishop as his pope. [15] But now, after the Martyr Memorial affair, under the pressure of anti-Tractarian agitation, Bishop Bagot wrote a pastoral letter censuring certain expressions in the tracts. Thus was Newman's foundation in Anglicanism again shaken. Years later, in the *Apologia*, he admitted that at this time he languished in "a state of moral sickness, neither able to acquiesce in Anglicanism, nor able to go to Rome." [16]

iii. *The Crisis, and the "Vision of Peace"* (1839–45)

In spite of vague forebodings, Newman's position in the Anglican Church in the spring of 1839 was at its height. In April he published a sanguine article on the "Prospects of the Anglican Church," in the *British Critic*, summarizing the history of the Tractarian effort thus far, and relating it to other currents of thought in his day, including the Romantic, represented by Scott, Coleridge, Southey, and Wordsworth. It concluded by putting the ominous alternatives: the *Via Media* of Anglicanism or Roman Catholicism. "The spirit of Luther is dead; but Hildebrand and Loyola are alive." [1] Yet even in this hour of confidence, Newman remembered that while the Anglican imputation against Rome was lack of the mark of apostolicity, Rome could counter with denying the Catholic "Note" to the Church of England. He remembered his article, "Home Thoughts Abroad" (1836), a dialogue, in which one of the speakers unsparingly declares: "When a man takes up this *Via Media*, he is a mere doctrinaire . . . The *Via Media* has slept in libraries; it is a substitute of infancy for manhood." [2]

It was in this mood of unsettlement that Newman returned, in the middle of June, to a study of the early heresies, particularly Monophysitism and Eutychianism — heresies which affirmed only the divine nature of the Son, and rejected the decision of the Council of Chalcedon (A.D. 451) that Christ's nature is two, human and divine, indivisible yet distinct, united in one person. In studying the Monophysite controversy, Newman saw his face in a mirror; he was a Monophysite — all his arguments for the *Via Media* were equally applicable to the heretics of antiquity, Eutyches and Arius. His stronghold had been antiquity; and now it seemed that "Rome was where she now is; and the Protestants were the Eutychians. . . The Church then, as now, might be called peremptory and stern, resolute, overbearing, and relentless; and heretics were shifting, changeable, reserved, and deceitful, ever courting civil power, and never agreeing together. . ." By the end of August Newman was seriously alarmed; he had seen a ghost — "the shadow of the fifth century was on the sixteenth." [3]

Then came a new and fateful impetus. A friend, Robert Williams, placed in Newman's hands an article by Wiseman, in the *Dublin Review*, which drew a parallel between the Anglican Church and the Donatists of the fourth century. The Donatists, like the Anglicans, had seceded from Rome and remained, in Gibbon's words, in "memorable schism" in Africa for above three hundred years. The general argument might not have seriously disturbed Newman had not Mr. Williams "pointed out the palmary words of St. Augustine," quoted by Wiseman: *Securus judicat orbis terrarum,* "the whole world judges right" — *i.e.,* the universal sense of the whole Church must be right against one local body.[4] Newman wrote to his friend Rogers: "I have had the first real hit from Romanism which has happened to me . . . Dr. Wiseman's article has given me a stomach-ache."[5] The words of St. Augustine seemed utterly final on the whole question of catholicity which had been plaguing Newman for years. The *Via Media* now looked like a poor thing indeed: "by those great words of the ancient Father . . . the theory of the *Via Media* was absolutely pulverized."[6] But, while for a moment the horrible thought crossed his mind that "the Church of Rome will be found right after all," he regained his composure, and published a considered reply to Wiseman, in an article, "On the Catholicity of the English Church," in the *British Critic* for January, 1840. He was "sore about the great Anglican divines, as if they had taken him in"; yet he believed them to have had the Apostolical succession and the "grace of sacraments"; and he longed for union between the Anglican Church and Rome. His correspondence during the winter of 1839–40 shows a growing unrest: he feels insecure with the authorities of the Church and the university; the Church seems falling into schism between the "Peculiars" (Evangelicals and their adherents) and "Apostolicals." To Mrs. J. Mozley he writes gloomily about an impending "attack on the Bible," about "wretched Socialists," and Thomas Carlyle (who has "settled the wrong way"), and the dreadful Liberals (Dr. Arnold and Milman), and political economists, and "geologists, giving up parts of the Old Testament," and he concludes, what can "withstand the league of evil but the Roman Church?"[7] To add to his discomfort, a young radical faction had begun to cling to him — W. G. Ward, J. D. Dalgairns, F. Oakeley — who had none of their master's prudence, but forced him along the path to Rome with such questions as: "Can the Church of England ever win back its 'Catholic' character?" to which their implied answer was, "No."

And now he contemplated giving up St. Mary's, and spending more of his time at Littlemore, where in that memorable year of 1836 he had built a chapel, and where he could now give himself up to teaching in the parish school, and translating Athanasius. There was as yet no idea of leaving the Anglican Church. But even here in the seclusion of Littlemore, in 1841, three new blows struck him, which, together, threw him into lay communion, put him "on his death-bed, as regards his membership with the Anglican Church," [8] and propelled him definitely in the direction of openly embracing the Church of Rome. The first blow was his discovery, on restudying Athanasius, of the extent to which "the pure Arians were the Protestants, the semi-Arians were the Anglicans, and . . . Rome now was what it was then." [9] The second blow was the reception of Tract XC. The third blow was the affair of the Jerusalem bishopric. Of these three events, it is the publication and condemnation of Tract XC that requires a few moments' attention.

This last and most famous of all the tracts set out to answer the question with which we have already seen Newman confronted: "How can the Church of England win back its 'Catholic' character?" This question, posed by the more radical of Newman's followers — "Ward worried him into writing Tract 90," Archbishop Tait used to say angrily [10] — this knotty question was answered by Newman in an examination of the Thirty-nine Articles in a spirit at once historical and lawyer-like. Many Englishmen admitted that the Creeds and the Prayer Book were capable of a Catholic interpretation, but insisted that the Articles wore an inescapably Protestant aspect. Newman undertook to disprove this. For him the Articles were essentially formulae of a legal character, to be interpreted not according to the theology of their framers but *au pied de la lettre*. Thus he makes a distinction between the Catholic teachings of the first three centuries, the formal dogmas of Rome, and the actual popular beliefs and usages sanctioned by Rome, which he designates as "dominant errors." It was these "errors" which the Articles condemned. Some of the formal dogmas were condemned, too, but not all, and a line had to be drawn between them. The Articles were indeed set up, says Newman, against the political supremacy of the Pope, rather than against the supremacy of the Church of Rome. Further, they could hardly have condemned the great decrees of the Council of Trent, since the Articles were composed several years before the Council was over. They were therefore directed not against Catholic doctrines — teachings on Purgatory, the Invocation of the Saints, the Mass — but against popular abuses of them and the traditional glosses of the schools which the Roman Church protected or tolerated without solemnly sanctioning. Above all, the Articles were expressly intended by the government who devised them to gain over the moderate Romanists, those who would disclaim allegiance to the Pope. Thus the Articles were tolerant of a Catholic or even a Roman interpretation, and Newman thought he had vindicated the Anglican claim to "Catholicity." [11]

He was completely mistaken. And strangely enough, he was totally unprepared for the tremendous outburst of disapproval throughout England. The tract was published on February 27, 1841; on March 8, four tutors (among them Tait, later archbishop of Canterbury) composed a protest against the tracts; a week later, the heads of houses, without waiting for any defence or explanation from Newman, condemned the tract as dishonest. Copies of their condemnation were posted on the buttery hatches and gates of all the schools in Oxford. In every part of the country, in pulpits, at dinner tables, in coffeehouses, in railway carriages, Newman was bitterly discussed as a traitor who had tried to sabotage the time-honored Establishment. One prominent Evangelical of Cheltenham gave his judgment of Newman in a now famous remark: "I should be sorry to trust the author of that Tract with my purse." [12]

Yet something can be said in defense of Newman. Even so hostile a critic as James Anthony Froude wrote later that he "considered Newman's arguments to be legally sound . . . Newman was only claiming a position for himself and his friends which had been purposely left open when the constitution of the Anglican Church was formed." [13] Hutton admits that "there was plenty of room for a sincere interpretation of [the Articles] in Newman's sense." [14] And Sarolea avers that "both logic and history seem on the side of Newman." [15] Newman's great error was to forget, or to ignore, the living interpretation of the Articles which his contemporaries accepted, and to trust to pure logic and the dead past. For the Anglican Church, for good or ill, had become not *less* Protestant but *more* Protestant than in the sixteenth century. He had once written, "the edge of truth is so fine that no plain man can see it" [16] — a saying which gives us the key to much that seems, unfairly, like darkness and guile in him — but the plain British churchman, of course, could not follow him. Indeed, as Sarolea urges, in the affair of Tract XC "it was not Newman who was false and insincere; it was the very position of Anglicanism which was equivocal." [17] Yet the episode gave a very unflattering impression of Newman's mind and for a long time the only conception of him in the mind of the English middle-class was that of a subtle-minded ecclesiastical hair-splitter and special pleader. Unfortunately, nothing less really characteristic of Newman than Tract XC was ever issued by him. In fact, as Ward has truly said, the philosophical basis of Tract LXXXV makes it a far more important document in the history of Anglo-Catholicism than the theological subtleties of Tract XC.[18]

The end of the affair of Tract XC was that Newman agreed, at Bishop Bagot's command, not to suppress the tract, but to discontinue the series. In long letters to the bishop and to Dr. Jelf, now to be found in the second volume of the *Via Media*, he attempted to explain the tract, and to reassert his loyalty to the Church of England, whose single note now is not "Catholicity" but "Holiness." But there remained more blows for Newman to undergo, one of which we have mentioned, namely the affair of the Jerusalem bishopric, which was a political move, in the spring of 1841, to cooperate with Prussia. To Newman's amazement, the Jerusalem bishop was to get his orders from his own Church, yet subscribe to the Augsburg Confession and observe the order of the German Evangelical Church. Again his Church was proving itself neither Catholic nor Apostolic, but simply Protestant. The spirit of Luther was *not* dead. Then followed the two other disappointments — discoveries of how low in the estimate of the Church as a whole the Tractarian principles had fallen.   Isaac Williams, Tractarian poet and good friend of Newman, was defeated in his candidacy for the Chair of Poetry made vacant by Keble's retirement.   This was in January, 1842. In May, 1843, Pusey, who had defended Tract XC in the hour of Newman's trial, delivered in Christ Church a sermon on "The Holy Eucharist a Comfort to the Penitent."   He was careful to quote from the early Fathers, especially Cyril of Alexandria, and also to adhere to the moderate Anglicanism of Alexander Knox (d. 1831), who had actually had some affinities with Methodism. Pusey refrained from explaining the nature of the presence of Christ's body and blood, but bowed before it as an unapproachable mystery.   This was too much for Oxford.   Without a hearing or even the formality of a trial, Pusey was, by the authority of the vice-chancellor, suspended from preaching in the university for two years, for having taught doctrine contrary to the Church of England.

By this time, Newman was settling deeply into seclusion at Littlemore, though the public journals gave him no rest, and prying and peering eyes, even those of heads of houses and doctors of divinity, watched and dived into the hidden recesses of his retreat.   Drawing around him a number of young followers — among them J. A. Froude and Mark Pattison — he worked out a semimonastic organization (the chapel he had built years before, a library, and some "cells"); and planned the series of "Lives of the English Saints," in 1842.   From this strangely indeterminate period in his life, there came also some of the greatest jewels of his eloquence, *Sermons on Subjects of the Day.* But 1843 was the notable Littlemore year: on February 2, he preached for the last time before the university; on September 18, "after a sleepless night," he resigned his living of St. Mary's; on the 25th, he preached his last sermon as an Anglican at Littlemore, the ever-memorable "The Parting of Friends"; on October 3, he resigned his fellowship at Oriel; on October 15, he celebrated his last Eucharist at the altar of St. Mary's.   In the meantime, the religious world was astir over Newman's formal retraction of all the hard things which he had said against the

Church of Rome; this had been published in February in the
Oxford Conservative Journal.[19]

All of the disastrous events of the past three years — Tract
XC, Isaac Williams' defeat, Pusey's condemnation, the Jerusalem bishopric, the personal and public persecution of Newman
at Littlemore (the spying, the suspicion) — all this threw Newman farther along his path. While he conscientiously sought to
restrain his heedless younger followers from going over to Rome,
he himself embarked on a study of the *dynamics* in doctrinal development, as against the old static and shaky *Via Media.* In all
this he was suffering almost inexpressibly, as his letters of these
years testify. He had doubts; he had been mistaken once;
might he not be now, in his Romeward thoughts? "What inward test had I," he later put it, "that I should not change again,
after I had become a Catholic?" [20] What still remained for his
conversion was not a further change of opinion, but a change of
opinion itself into clearness and firmness of intellectual conviction. In this, a study of the evolution of doctrine would serve
perfectly; if he could prove it to be "more certain that *our* (modern) doctrines are wrong, *than* that the *Roman* (modern) doctrines are wrong," [21] and all this with the testimony of history,
then he would know his course. After all, what had the Oxford
Movement been if not an attack on "modern" or "liberal" doctrines? And had not his own Church revealed again and again
its sympathy with them? And did not Rome stand, as always,
for a steadfast refusal to subject to mere human judgment any
of the great dogmas? What, then, had been the history of those
dogmas? What had preserved their continuity? What was
the indestructible element in them, what was their life? And
how and why did they, in their development, make the Roman
Church apparently so different and yet so like the ancient Church
of the Fathers? The more he studied the history of doctrine,
in those years at Littlemore (1842-45), the more

"the force of the great vision of the Catholic Church came upon him,
unchecked and irresistible. That was a thing present, visible, undeniable as a fact of nature; that was a thing at once old and new; it
belonged as truly, as manifestly, to the recent and modern world of

democracy and science, as it did to the Middle Ages and to the Fathers, to the world of Gregory and Innocent, to the world of Athanasius and Augustine. The majesty, the vastness of an imperial polity, outlasting all states and kingdoms, all social changes and political revolutions, answered at once to the promises of the prophecies, and to the antecedent idea of the universal kingdom of God. Before this great idea, embodied in concrete form, and not a paper doctrine [like the *Via Media*], partial scandals and abuses seemed to sink into insignificance. Objections seemed petty and ignoble; the pretence of rival systems impertinent and absurd." [22]

And so Newman labored over *The Development of Christian Doctrine*, a lonely figure, surrounded now, not by his peers as at Oriel ("picked men of a picked college") but by men whom Pattison regarded as decidedly Newman's inferiors, "men like Bowles, Coffin, Dalgairns, St. John, Lockhart, and others." [23] But they loved him, and he never judged by intellectual accomplishments. In the quiet of Littlemore, "he stood," says Ward, "for hours together at his high desk writing, and seemed to grow ever paler and thinner, while the sun appeared to shine through the almost transparent face. As the task neared its end he would stand the whole day, completing and revising it with infinite care." [24]

This is not the place to examine the great work he was spending himself on. It is enough to note that as he progressed with it, convictions deepened, ideas and doctrines expanded in his mind with illuminating power. While, on the one hand, he wrote letters to his sister Jemima and to Mrs. William Froude which show what a mental struggle he was undergoing, nevertheless, on the other hand, the book grew with a life of its own. By October 6, his sister wrote: "J.H.N. . . . adds that now anything may be expected any day." And two days later, he wrote to her: "I must tell you what will pain you greatly, but I will make it short as you would wish me to do. This night Father Dominic, the Passionist, sleeps here [at Littlemore]. He does not know of my intention, but I shall ask him to receive me into what I believe to be the One Fold of the Redeemer. This will not go till all is over." [25]

And so, two days after the archpriest of that "Liberalism,"

which Newman so dreaded and fought, Ernest Renan, had left the precincts of St. Sulpice, John Henry Newman knelt before Father Dominic, while outside the "rain came down in torrents, and the wind howled forth its equinoctial fury . . . and the bell of the little Gothic church at Littlemore sounded more like a knell than a summons." [26] In Newman's mind, however, there was the peace of exhaustion and rest. In fact, he had closed his unfinished book with words which readily fit the occasion of that rainy night: "Such were the thoughts concerning the 'Blessed Vision of Peace,' of one whose long-continued petition had been that the Most Merciful would not despise the work of His own Hands, nor leave him to himself. . ." [27]

iv. *From Anglican Minister to Roman Cardinal* (1845–90)

Newman tells us that after he became a Catholic he had, of course, "no further history of his religious opinions to narrate." He had come "into port after a rough sea." [1] He was now in the Church of his desire. The old Tractarian precautionary piety which, as Hutton says, tinged the whole Movement with an air of anxious adventuresomeness, of hesitating audacity, and careworn courage, now gave way to joyous confidence. Freed of the sober and compromising conventionalism of the Establishment, Newman could now luxuriate in the thought of religion in its totality. He could see it as a synthesis, or harmony, of the activities of man: it included a metaphysical element, in its dogmas (its half-comprehensible interpretation of the problems of existence); it included also an ethical element, in its sanctions and commands; it included, too, an aesthetic element in its graceful and emotion-stirring rites, symbols, and ceremonies; and, properly, it included a political element, in the organization of the Church, as a militant power forever at war with the world. Thus it brought into play every human faculty to transform the religious ideal into the real — cultivation of the intellect, the imagination, the will, the moral sense, and the social sense. To a man such as Newman, the appeal of this all-embracing religion was irresistible. His intellect was enamored of its gigantic edifice of logically articulated dogma. His love of authority welcomed its setting rigorous bounds to the "wild, living intellect of man," and curbing it also with elaborate discipline, ascetic devotions, a spiritual hygiene which was the outcome of nearly two thousand years of experience. On the other hand, he felt at home in the great Catholic mystical tradition, with its elaborate systematic symbolism, its sacraments, its ritual, its miracles, its realistic recognition of the reality of the supersensible world. And, further, he found himself — though he was soon to undergo some disappointments — in a communion where he, as a man of action, might achieve much among other soldiers in the Church Militant.[2]

As for the Church itself, he could also luxuriate in its history and organization and achievement. It was

"in very deed to him a supernatural society, a Divine creation, the spouse of God, the bride of Christ, the Mother of all Saints, the favored yet awful home of the Holy Ghost, peerless in beauty, the channel of every grace, the only bestower of sanctity and immortality, the bosom of repose and sanctuary from the world, the guarantor of blessedness and the peace of heaven." [3]

Years before, in Adam de Brome's Chapel, speaking on the Protestant notion of Antichrist, he had, as it were, prophetically defined the Church he had now entered:

"The essence of the doctrine that there is 'One only Catholic and Apostolic Church' lies in this; — that there is on earth a representative of our absent Lord, or a something divinely interposed between the soul and God, or a visible body with invisible privileges. All its subordinate characteristics flow from this description. Does it impose a creed, or impose rites and ceremonies, or change ordinances, or remit and retain sins, or rebuke and punish, or accept offerings, or send out ministers, or invest its ministers with authority, or accept of reverence or devotion in their persons? — all this is because it is Christ's visible presence. It stands for Christ. Can it convey the power of the Spirit? does grace attend its acts? can it touch, or bathe, or seal, or lay on hands? can it use material things for spiritual purposes? are its temples holy? — all this comes of its being (so far) what Christ was on earth. Is it a ruler, prophet, priest, intercessor, teacher? — it has titles such as these in its measure, as being the representative and instrument of the Almighty Lord who is unseen. Does it claim a palace and a throne, an altar and a doctor's chair, the gold, frankincense and myrrh of the rich and wise, an universal empire and a never-ending succession? — all this is so, because it is what Christ is." [4]

Newman's state of mind in 1845 was, of course, what it still was in 1850 when he delivered the twelve lectures on the *Difficulties of Anglicans*; so we may appropriately express that state of mind in words which he then said, that "what the See of Rome was [in the Byzantine age] such is it now; that what Arius, Nestorius, Eutyches were then such are Luther and Calvin now; what the Eusebians or Monophysites then, such the Anglican hierarchy now; what the Byzantine Court then, such is now the Government of England." [5] Newman had performed what he regarded as an act of the historical method, in *The Development of Christian Doctrine*, and, having established to his own satisfaction that "the principle of development . . . is an argument in favor of the identity of Roman and Primitive Christianity," [6] he now rested in a complete repose of faith.

His sacrifices, in that final act of October 8, had certainly not been negligible. From being a leading figure in the Establishment, he was now to become an obscure Roman priest, generally overshadowed and misunderstood, often deliberately frustrated. Impartial judges will say, with G. H. Harper, that "his motive was intellectual honesty, for he had a conviction amounting to certitude that in the Roman belief alone lay the truth." [7] Behind him, however, lay that beloved world of his youth and his early manhood — the games in Bloomsbury Square, the summer mornings in his father's house at Ham reading the Waverley novels, the snapdragons of Trinity, the Oriel Fellowship, the bells that rang out to proclaim his triumph, the witty and urbane society of the common room, the walks in Christ Church meadow, the violin playing in trios and quartets at music parties, the glory of leadership in the great Tractarian days. From all this Newman turned to a life of obscurity, and often menial intellectual toil. We are not concerned with the external details of his existence — they may be found abundantly elsewhere; so it will suffice to trace here his Roman Catholic career very briefly before we turn to an examination of his works.

As J. Elliot Ross has pointed out, Newman suffered, after his entrance into the Roman Catholic Church, four great failures which would have wrecked a man of less determination.[8]   In 1852, five years after he became a Catholic priest, Newman was made rector-elect of a projected Catholic university in Dublin; but because the Irish priests would not or could not give him the necessary support, he was obliged to resign as rector in 1856, his appointment never having actually been confirmed.   Out of this four-year period of frustration, however, came one of Newman's classic works, *The Idea of a University*.   In the following year, at Cardinal Wiseman's request, Newman undertook a new translation of the Bible.   Again, unsupported by the bishops, Newman had to relinquish his task.   In the meantime, he had founded the Birmingham Oratory, and he now (1858) proposed a branch house of the Oratory at Oxford.   Newman had visions of Oxford as the center of a great Catholic revival of learning, and even went so far, in his trust in his superiors, as to purchase the necessary ground.   But Henry Edward Manning, once a High Anglican and now a potent force in the Roman Church, blocked the plan, and once more Newman had to give up a cherished scheme.   Two years later, still searching for his place in the Roman Catholic world, Newman was made editor of *The Rambler* (1860), a rather liberal Catholic magazine in contrast with the conservative *Dublin Review*.   Within two months this "most dangerous man in England" was compelled to resign. "The years [between] 1859 and 1864 may be called the low-water mark of Newman's life-story," according to the standard Roman Catholic biography of him.[9]   Though his lectures on *The Present Position of Catholics in England* (1851) had been a great popular success, they had involved him in a libel suit with an ex-Dominican friar, Dr. Giovanni Giacinto Achilli, which had resulted in Newman's being fined £100 and costs (£14,000). Even though more than the sum was supplied by loyal Catholic supporters in England and America, the experience had been extremely trying.   He suddenly began to feel old; his books no longer sold so well; he was mistrusted; he ceased to write.   He more and more devoted himself to his school at Birmingham and taught his boys to recite.   "All through my life," he wrote to Henry Wilberforce in July, 1859, "I have been plucked."[10]

But he saw his chance to vindicate his career when Charles Kingsley published in the January, 1864, issue of *Macmillan's Magazine* an attack on his honesty, and indirectly on the intellectual integrity of the Catholic priesthood. Kingsley's charge that truth for its own sake had never been a virtue with the Roman clergy gave Newman the occasion to write an autobiographical narrative, the *Apologia pro vita sua* (1864), which would explain why and how he became a Catholic, and which would lift the general Catholic position to a higher level in the British mind than it had had for centuries. We shall have occasion later to observe his methods and his results. We may note in passing that his *Apologia* placed Newman at once among the great and influential Victorian public figures. It soon became the fashion to quote Father Newman, and to seek his opinions on public questions. Now that he had regained some of his old prestige, he attempted once more to establish a branch of the Oratory at Oxford; but again Manning interposed, and the plan had to be abandoned. Newman's last years were marked by three publications, two of them the products of an immediate occasion, the other the fruit of long and earnest thought. In 1866 he published his *Letter to the Rev. E. B. Pusey on his Recent Eirenicon*, defining and clarifying the Roman Catholic doctrine as to the Blessed Virgin, which Pusey's *Eirenicon* had seemed to misrepresent. In the midst of the turmoil over the Vatican Council, which passed the decree of papal infallibility — which Newman regarded as untimely — he brought to completion his long labors on the problem of belief, of the relations of reason and faith, in *An Essay in Aid of a Grammar of Assent* (1870). Finally, in 1875, he published his *Letter to the Duke of Norfolk*, by way of answering, with his old sinuous eloquence and delicate wit, Gladstone's rather heavy-handed *Vatican Decrees and Their Bearing on Civil Allegiance*, which contained the charge that a Roman Catholic could not be loyal at once to Britain and to an "infallible pope."

The years between 1875 and 1878 increased Newman's sense of isolation; his silence and depression were noticeable to his friends. Ambrose St. John, one of his dearest friends, died about this time, and not even the election to an honorary fellowship in his old college, Trinity, seemed to take away the "winter of his desolation." However, the death of Pope Pius IX in 1878, and the election of Pope Leo XIII, brought a new turn to Newman's fortunes. One of the first acts of the new Pope was to make Newman a cardinal (1879). "This mark of confidence from the Holy See, after the prolonged, aching sense of distrust in high quarters, was so unexpected and so signal, as to be the greatest event as well as the crowning reward of Newman's life. 'The cloud is lifted from me for ever,' were the words in which he spoke of it to his Oratorian brethren." [11]

Newman lived eleven years longer. He preached in Trinity College, Oxford, on Trinity Sunday, 1880, at the Jesuit Church, to an overflowing congregation. He lived quietly at the Birmingham Oratory until the end. In his ninetieth year, on August 11, 1890, he died of a congestion of the lungs. On August 19, he was buried, by his own request, in the same grave with his friend Ambrose St. John, in the burial ground of the Oratorian Fathers. Enclosed by yew and oak and laurel, this little cemetery at Rednal contains a fitting memorial of John Henry Newman: a simple Latin cross which bears his chosen epitaph, an expression of his lifelong quest: *Ex umbris et imaginibus in veritatem.*

II. THREE GREAT LABORS

(1) *THE LIFE IN IDEAS: NEWMAN'S THEORY OF DOCTRINAL DEVELOPMENT — THE EARLY STAGES*

In a note written in the last year of his life, Newman declared: "Very early in life I was troubled with the prospect of an intellectual movement against religion, so special as to have a claim upon the attention of all educated Christians." [1] Much sooner than some of his shrewdest contemporaries, he showed a prescience of the decay of belief, an awareness of the signs of the times pointing to an ever-widening break in the corporate faith of Christendom. The term "agnostic" belongs to the early 'seventies; it was invented by Thomas Henry Huxley at an early meeting of the Metaphysical Society. [2] But far back in the 'thirties and 'forties, Newman had grappled earnestly, in his *Oxford University Sermons*, with the problem, not only of countering the skeptic's arguments with logic but also of providing a more persuasive, concrete, and living appeal to the whole man, by winning over not merely his reason but his heart and imagination. He felt that modern man's enchantment with reason, science, and invention could be broken only by the countermagic of a great Church, "the concrete representative of things invisible." Men needed an authentic organization, with historical credentials, with an acceptable intellectual base, and with a rich and compelling ceremonial life. The beneficent works of Christianity, properly valued, should stand over against the achievements of science as visible and tangible results. If the modern world was to be saved from infidelity, it must be approached with tact, with persuasion, with imagination. "The world overcomes us," he had said, "not merely by appealing to our reason, or by exciting our passions, but by imposing on our imagination." [3]

The central object, therefore, of all of Newman's work was the rational and imaginative justification of existing orthodox Christianity for educated men and for their responsible leaders. This was the aim of *The Development of Christian Doctrine* and of *The Grammar of Assent*; it was also an organic part of Newman's efforts, in his *Idea of a University*, to promote a well-rounded education for the Victorian upper classes. The nature of doctrine and dogma had been a puzzling and fascinating problem with Newman from his early years. How to make dogma — so widely contemned or ignored — once more intellectually acceptable to intelligent men was an even more difficult problem. When, as an Anglican, he turned to the simple message of Christ and the Apostles, he looked in vain for the dogmatic theology which he was expected to preach as a clergyman of the Church of England. How, then, had there risen the complicated intellectual system and the visible ecclesiastical organization in which he was involved? Before he could make all this complex edifice of thought and institution attractive to others, he must first face the historical and theological question of how simple ideas and principles actually grow into complex doctrines. As we have seen, he had abandoned the old "static" view of the *Via Media*, and had committed himself to a *dynamic* interpretation of the very concept of dogma. Perhaps only a mind like Newman's could at once feel completely at home with what he called "the dogmatic principle" and also with the notion of "development." It is necessary, therefore, to observe just what Newman was thinking of dogmatic religion in the years which produced *The Development of Christian Doctrine*.

i. *Newman, Doctrine, and Dogma*

By temperament, Newman had never felt any sympathy with a religion of feeling. What he called "the 'dreamy talk' of modern Protestantism" only stirred his contempt. In a famous lecture "On Preaching the Gospel" he inveighed sternly against the fashionable Evangelicals of the day for merely "stirring up and working up their minds," for "relying on words, vehemence, eloquence," and for pursuing "what is called spiritual-minded-ness." This error, he felt, went back to Luther, who "found Christians in bondage to their works and observances . . . and left them in bondage to their feelings." [1] Newman would never, therefore, have said, with Matthew Arnold, that "religion is morality touched with emotion." [2] From the age of fifteen, he says in the *Apologia*, dogma had been the fundamental principle of his religion — "I know no other religion . . . religion as a mere sentiment is to me a dream and a mockery." [3] And in the *Oxford University Sermons*, he had declared roundly that "what is invidiously called dogmatism . . . is, I may say, necessary to the human mind; we cannot reason, feel, or act, without it; it forms the stamina of thought . . . Sooner than dispense with principles, the mind will take them at the hand of others, will put up with such as are faulty or uncertain." [4] "Religion cannot but be dogmatic," he had written in Tract LXXXV; "it ever has been. All religions have had doctrines; all have professed to carry with them benefits which could be enjoyed only on condition of believing the word of a supernatural informant, that is, of embracing some doctrines or other." [5] Difficulties there would be, of course; every basic religious doctrine affronts reason in her ordinary mood. "Yet what is a mystery in doctrine," says Newman in *The Arians*, "but a difficulty or inconsistency in the intellectual expression of it? And what reason is there for supposing that Revelation addresses itself to the intellect, except so far as intellect is necessary for conveying and fixing its truths *on the heart*?" [6]

Utterances such as these show to what extent Newman was by temperament a dogmatist. They show also to what degree those critics are in error who maintain that Newman had a *hunger* for dogma. On the contrary, he already had the gift for understanding, welcoming, and loving the "dogmatic principle." According to nineteenth-century legend, Newman fled to Roman Catholicism because of his native skepticism and his craving for dogmatic certainties. But this is a survival of that eighteenth-century mode of thinking which held that religion was the spurious product of cunning and power-hungry priests, instead of viewing priesthoods, rituals, dogmas, and ecclesiastical organizations as the product of the religious instinct.   If we are to understand Newman, we must remember, as H. L. Stewart has well said, that "it is not submission to authority that makes the dogmatist; it is rather the temperamental dogmatist who alone can submit to authority.   There was no native skepticism in John Henry Newman.   From childhood he was of the number of those who realize in an exceptional degree the Unseen Power. His was that rare personality marked always and everywhere by 'the practice of the presence of God.' " [7]   He loved to contemplate the "Mysteries in religion."   For him, there was no disappointment in realizing that from the nature of the human mind, no completely systematic Revelation can be comprehended by man.   The great dogmas were Revelation on their illuminated side; the same dogmas and doctrines were Mysteries viewed on the side unilluminated.   Religious truth was, for him, like the dim view of a country seen at dusk, with forms half-visible in the darkness, with broken lines, and isolated masses. Thus, he says, the great dogmas of Revealed Religion, as approached by man, do not make up an intellectually satisfying *system*, "but consist of a number of detached and incomplete truths belonging to a vast system unrevealed, of doctrines and injunctions mysteriously connected together; that is, connected by unknown media, and bearing upon unknown portions of the system." [8]

Yet Newman was always able, at least in his sermons, to make Christian dogmas seem wondrously alive; even in his early parochial sermons, as Dean Church has shown, he combined the most practical methods with the most vivid dogmatic utterances.   His sermons always presupposed a dogmatic religion, and then showed "how what is noblest, most elevated, most poetical, most free and searching in a thinker's way of regarding the wonderful scene of life, falls in naturally, and without strain, with a great dogmatic system." [9]   They proved that a dogmatic system, as such, need not be the cast-iron, arbitrary, artificial, and old-fashioned thing it was often assumed to be.   For Newman, dogmas were by no means things of the past, without sense or substance or interest.   He knew that they were but expedients, as it were, but indispensable for representing what are believed as truths. He showed, by his practice as preacher and writer, that though dogmas may become ugly and untrue in unfriendly and incapable hands, they could become instinct with truth and life in his. Many readers, no doubt, rise from reading Newman on the great dogmas in profound disagreement with their teaching; but few can fail to realize, after their reading, that their whole way of thinking about religion has been quickened and enlarged.

Newman has conveniently summarized for us the dogmas and mysteries which, in a general way, we have just been considering. In one of the tracts written in 1835, in which he contrasted the rationalistic and the Catholic tempers, he wrote:

"It may be right briefly to enumerate the revealed doctrines in order, according to the Catholic, that is, the anti-rationalistic, notion of them. They are these: the Holy Trinity; the Incarnation of the Eternal Son; His atonement and merits; the Church as His medium and instrument through which He is converting and teaching mankind; the Sacraments, and Sacramentals (as Bishop Taylor calls them), as the definite channels through which His merits are applied to individuals; Regeneration, the Communion of Saints, the Resurrection of the body, consequent upon the administration of them; and lastly, our faith and works, as a condition of the availableness and efficacy of these divine appointments. Each of these doctrines is a Mystery; that is, each stands in a certain degree isolated from the rest, unsystematic, connected with the rest by unknown intermediate truths, and bearing upon subjects unknown. Thus the Atonement: — *why* it is necessary, *how* it operates, is a Mystery; that is, the heavenly truth which is revealed, extends on each side of it into an unknown world. . ." [10]

Having summarized the great Catholic doctrines, Newman proceeds to draw some practical inferences as to how to meet them, inferences which show again, in contrast to the triumphing Latitudinarianism of the day, his own steadfast orthodoxy, his stanchly Catholic temperament. Thus, he says, one should be very "reverent in dealing with Revealed Truth"; one should avoid all rash theorizing and systematizing; one should be solicitous to hold the Truth safely and *entirely*, and to guard it zealously. But further, in even more conservative words, he says: "We should religiously adhere to the *form of the words* and the ordinances under which it [the Truth] comes to us, through which it is revealed to us, and apart from which the Revelation does not exist, there being nothing else given us by which to ascertain or enter into it." [11]

This intense conservatism may, at first sight, seem very unpromising of any dynamic conception of doctrine; and, as a matter of fact, in 1835, when Newman wrote these words, he was resting contentedly on the static view of the Church and its doctrines. But he was soon to undergo, as we have seen, a drastic change in his convictions. For several years he had been studying the nature of doctrine itself — a speculative truth or working principle — and of dogma — that doctrine laid down with authority, clothed in formal wording, and drawn into the integral confession of the Church. In the early 1840's he was concerned with the *life* in ideas and doctrines, and with the patterns which they repeated in the Church of the early Fathers. This study was but the culmination of a long development in Newman's own intellectual history.

ii. *The Early Growth of Newman's Idea of Development*

We have already noted that from the great Evangelical divine, Thomas Scott of Aston Sanford, Newman had drawn, even while still in his teens, two mottoes: "Holiness before peace," and "Growth is the only evidence of life." Just as Scott seems to have helped Newman preserve himself from subjectivism in religion,[1] so he also supplied the young Newman with an objective criterion for development. It happened that Scott's criterion of "growth" was supposed to apply only to the individual; but it was not hard for Newman to see how equally applicable it was to ideas and institutions.[2] It was Joseph Milner's *History of the Church of Christ*, however, which had a most signal effect upon Newman's later thinking about the early Church and the doctrinal changes with which it struggled. There is a certain irony in this, for Milner's whole work is designed to show that the Lutheran doctrine of justification by faith alone had been the sign and seal of true Christianity from the first, and that it had been the open or concealed source of strength to the Fathers of the Church and to the saints in all the ages. To prove this, Milner presented long extracts from the Fathers — Irenaeus, Tertullian, Pantaenus, Origen, Clement, Ambrose, Augustine — with passages of which Newman says he was "nothing short of enamored." One wonders what he thought of Scott's severe condemnation of Origen's "presumptuous spirit," and of Tertullian's "unhappy mixture of philosophical self-righteousness and superstition." [3] But, as Brilioth observes, Milner's leading ideas — the "evangelical excellencies" of these Fathers when inspired with truth — passed through Newman's mind without leaving a trace behind.[4] "I read them," says Newman, "as being the religion of the primitive Christians" — and the word "primitive" is the key to Newman's statement.[5] For he was always to seek Christianity in what he regarded as its original purity and simplicity. Milner's work, then, played a part, which has almost never been recognized in shaping Newman's theory of development. Its part was small, to be sure, but it came at a time when Newman was extremely impressionable.

One other Evangelical writer seems also to have contributed to his doctrinal theories: Jones of Nayland. Here the contribution was the notion of "veiled language." Newman was eventually to make much of the doctrines of "reserve" and "economy" in communicating religious knowledge, doctrines which in time plunged him into the great controversy with Kingsley. In Jones' sermons, Newman found eloquent accounts and justifications for God's "economy," *i.e.* God's communicating with man "by signs, shadows, and figures of visible things." He also found Jones giving precisely the same reasons which Origen and Clement had given for the Church's use of "veiled language" — the language which tells only that which the hearer can assimilate, and which uses images or figures in varying degrees of literalness according to the hearer's capacity.[6] All of these Evangelicals, we may conclude, had predisposed Newman to take up his spiritual abode in the ante-Nicene period, and in the great Church of Alexandria. When, preparatory to writing *The Arians,* he came to read the Fathers, he had already heard the music of Origen's and Clement's teaching; he had already known something about Alexandrian mysticism and allegorizing and *oeconomia.*

The seeds of the developmental hypothesis lay not, however,

merely in books; they lay also in Newman's mind.   In a notable
letter to his mother, of March 13, 1829, he gives evidence of
having thought long and intensely upon the phenomenon of the
transmission of wisdom from one generation to the next.   "Listen to my theory," he says, and then proceeds to justify what, in
matters of religion, is called "prejudice," yet what is, he thinks,
really an inherited wisdom, of which many of us are nearly if
not entirely unaware.

"As each individual has certain instincts of right and wrong antecedently to reasoning, on which he acts — and rightly so — which
perverse reasoning may supplant, which then can hardly be regained,
but, if regained, will be regained from a different source — from reasoning, not from nature — so, I think, has the world of men col-
lectively.   God gave them truths in His miraculous revelations, and
other truths in the unsophisticated infancy of nations, scarcely less
necessary and divine.   These are transmitted as 'the wisdom of our
ancestors,' through men — many of whom cannot enter into them,
or receive them themselves — still on, on, from age to age, not the
less truths because many of the generations through which they are
transmitted are unable to prove them, but hold them, either from
pious and honest feeling (it may be), or from bigotry or from prejudice.   That they are truths it is most difficult to prove, for great men
alone can prove great ideas or grasp them. Such a mind was Hooker's,
such Butler's; and, as moral evil triumphs over good on a small field
of action, so in the argument of an hour or the compass of a volume
would men like Brougham, or, again, Wesley, show to far greater
advantage than Hooker or Butler. Moral truth is gained by patient
study, by calm reflection, silently as the dew falls — unless miracu-
lously given — and when gained it is transmitted by faith and by
'prejudice.' " [7]

By the time Newman had written this letter, he was deep in the
Fathers, in preparation for *The Arians*.   But even in his parochial
sermons he let drop, now and then, a suggestion that he was
pondering the developmental side of religious doctrines.   He
was, as it were, listening anxiously to catch from tradition any
hint of direction or purpose.   Once, with his characteristic mastery of imagery, he compared the visible Church to a memorial,
which Christ had left behind, and "let drop from Him as the

mantle of Elijah, the pledge and token of His never-failing grace from age to age." [8]   If it is true that the Church is the mantle of Christ's glory, left behind on earth, would it not follow that he who takes up but a fold of it is obliged to seek for more?   Here is the seed of the progressive or dynamic conception of the Church.   Yet in these early Tractarian years, Newman is still more concerned with doctrine and dogma themselves than with their development.   He is seeking a justification for dogmatic formulations.   And though the notion of doctrinal development lies slumbering in the depths of his thoughts, he is consciously striving to make the beauty and necessity of dogma self-evident to other men.

In writing *The Arians* he proved for himself, at least, that Christian doctrines must preserve their original purity and unity or perish. The early Church, he found, had set up its creeds and dogmas as protections for the original deposit of faith.

iii.   *"The Arians": Dogmas as Defenses*

As we have seen, Newman had been frequently disturbed by the thought that the elaborate theology of the nineteenth century which he was teaching from the pulpit of St. Mary's, and which was expressed in the liturgy in which he took part, seemed to have only a remote relation to the simple message of the Beatitudes preached by Christ to the multitude.   In one of the central chapters of *The Arians of the Fourth Century*, "The Principle of the Formation and Imposition of Creeds," he faces this fact. He seems to hold that the simple teachings of the early Church, prior to dogmatic definitions, represented an ideal state of things; but that, "much as we may wish it, we cannot restrain the rovings of the intellect," and sooner or later, nothing "is left to the Church but to speak out, in order to exclude error." [1]   What Ward has called "protective additions" were necessary.   In fact, as Ward puts it, the beginnings of dogmatic definitions are somewhat like the genesis of laws: the rule of peace by exhortation, oral tradition, and example may work very well in a small community, but it is impossible when that community attains a certain size and complexity.   Thus the primitive Christian society gradually demanded a more defined creed.   Subtle minds began

to speculate: how could the Scriptures bid men to worship both
God and His Son without bidding men to worship two deities?
A system of doctrine at once became unavoidable, "being framed,
let it be observed," adds Newman, "not with a view of explaining, but of arranging . . . of providing, not a consistent, but a
connected statement.   There the inquisitiveness of the pious
mind rests, viz., when it has pursued the subject into the mystery
which is its limit."   Yet this is not all.   Intellectual expression
of theological truth not only excludes heresy, but it also "assists
the acts of religious worship and obedience," fixing and stimulating the spirit, and tranquillizing the mind.[2]   But it was with
dogmas as defenses that Newman was primarily concerned.
And he noted that the Gnostics and, later on, the Arians, introduced speculations which damaged the essential character of the
Christian message.   It is a commonplace to repeat the words of
that very unorthodox Victorian, Thomas Carlyle, in connection
with the Arian controversy; great as was Carlyle's contempt for
Christian orthodoxy, he nevertheless admitted to J. A. Froude
that if the Gnostics, Arians, and other heretics had won, Christianity "would have dwindled away into a legend."[3]   Newman
keenly realized this, and, while admitting that dogmatic formulae lacked the beauty and symmetry of the whole of which
they were but aspects, he maintained that they nevertheless provided the necessary bulwarks against the vigorous and prideful
intellect of the individual.   Thus as Newman investigated the
true nature of Arianism, Sabellianism, and Semi-Arianism, he
became more and more convinced that historically the elaborate
dogmatic system so prominent in Catholic theology had arisen
of necessity from earlier and simpler Christianity, not as rival-
ing or as changing it, but as protecting it against essential corruption.

Furthermore, as the apostolic period receded into the distant
past, the "sacred impressions" of Christianity — "the Word was
God," "the Holy Ghost which proceedeth from the Father"[4] —
these lost their original vividness, and dogmatic creeds became
necessary.   Newman admits that at first "the Church was unwilling to have recourse to the novel, though necessary, measure
of imposing an authoritative creed,"[5] and he is certain that the

original "impression" of Catholic truth was something far more living and moving than the propositions in the creeds which were eventually imposed. He takes the doctrine of the Trinity as an example,[6] and analyzes the process whereby the simple language of Clement, Basil, and Origen is replaced by the dogmatic propositions of the Athanasian Creed. These propositions, he knows, are necessarily imperfect. Yet — and here is where Newman differs from men like Coleridge and Carlyle — Newman regards them not as mere "symbols of a philosophy . . . the mere accidental types of principles," [7] but as expressions of objective facts, and as the truth so far as human limitations permit man to know divine truth.

Another line of argument which appears in *The Arians,* and for which he owes much to the early Fathers, is that Christianity is a further and truer development of those truths of religion which had been from the first revealed to mankind. That is why, in the *Apologia,* Newman specifies his debt to "the philosophy, *not* the theology," of the great Church of Alexandria, of Origen, Dionysius, and Clement. "Portions of their teaching . . . came like music to his inward ear": the mystical or sacramental principle, the idea of "economies" and "dispensations," according to which he understood that "Nature was a parable: Scripture was an allegory: pagan literature, philosophy, and mythology, properly understood, were but a preparation for the Gospel." [8] A directly divine dispensation had been granted to the Jews, but an indirect, partial, "economical" dispensation of divine truth had also been granted to the rest of the world in the degree in which it was capable of receiving it. Newman thus points out, in *The Arians,* that as God only partly and sometimes bafflingly, grants insights to certain men, and leads them into truth even by ways of error, so St. Paul, like Clement after him, in preaching to the Greeks, "while strenuously opposing all that is idolatrous, immoral and profane in their creed, yet professes to be leading them on to perfection and to be recovering and purifying, rather than reversing the essential principles of their belief." [9] Here is the seed of one of the great principles so skillfully argued and illustrated in the *Essay on Development,* that as the mind and practice of the Church expanded, it utilized, transformed, and absorbed the heathen doctrines and forms of those it converted.

By the time Newman had completed *The Arians*, in June of 1832, he had saturated his mind with Alexandrian thought. While engaged in narrating the rise and suppression of ante-Nicene heresies, he had absorbed the essence of Alexandrian Platonism — its mystical and sacramental view of the external world as "but the manifestation to our senses of realities greater than itself." Already steeped in the theology of Butler, he welcomed Alexandrian doctrines as to "the various Economies or Dispensations of the Eternal." [10] In Butler he had long ago read that "Christianity is a scheme as much above our comprehension as that of nature . . . one dispensation [of truth is] preparatory to another . . . and so on through an indefinite number of ages"; [11] he had also absorbed the idea "of an analogy between the separate works of God leading to the conclusion that the system which is of less importance [the earthly] is economically or sacramentally [one might say, by token or symbol] connected with the more momentous system [the Divine]." [12] Intermittently connecting these analogical worlds were the "dispensations" and "effusions" of divine grace, of which Newman had also read in Milner.[13] This doctrine, found anew amid the Alexandrians, strengthened Newman's conviction that miracles happen in one age and fail to occur in another for lack of the necessary divine "effusion," and also that the religious life of man as a whole is in constant change (of growth or decay), and must necessarily be guided by some great authoritative institution which should guard the *depositum* of faith while at the same time permitting it to expand with the expanding mind of man. On the other hand, Alexandrian mysticism confirmed Newman's belief that while "room is made for the anticipation of further and deeper disclosures of truths still under the veil of the letter . . . the visible world still remains without its divine interpretation." Even Holy Church, with all her sacraments and appointments, will remain, he says, to the end of the world, only a symbol of "those heavenly facts which fill eternity." In the *Apologia*, Newman concludes his discussion of his debt to the Alexandrians by saying, as well he might: "It is evident how much there was in all this in correspondence with the thoughts which had attracted me when I was young" — when the influence of Milner and Butler had made its impress on his mind.[14]

We may conclude our consideration of *The Arians* by observing, with Jean Guitton, that it is undoubtedly, though a dull book to most readers, an excellent introduction to Newman's thought as it was shaping itself in his apprentice years. In it we find prefigurings of his theology and of his methods of exposition, and at moments a hint of the doctrine of development. It shows Newman characteristically isolated in his labors, untouched by the new German philosophy of religion — he had only scorn for Schleiermacher's "religion of the feelings" [15] — untouched likewise by Roman theology and Scholasticism, or by the great immanentist and organismic doctrines of the Romantics. Yet there were compensations: he was never ensnared by nineteenth-century intellectualism, sentimentalism, and despair. His masters had been neither Latin nor German, but Anglican and Greek: Oxford and Alexandria had been his spiritual home. Bull, Taylor, Law, Butler, Clement, Basil, Theodoret, Chrysostom, these had been his teachers; and they had all been, so Newman thought in 1832, sons of the same Church, the Church of the Apostles. As we have seen, however, by 1839 his patristic studies had led him to view his Church in far less flattering colors. Anglicans had become, to his horror, the Semi-Arians of the nineteenth century.[16]

As Newman developed his later University sermons, Antiquity seemed to him less and less valid as a test of dogma, and Catholicity became more and more significant. If the Church of the present was to be regarded as in some way identical with the original Church, some theory of *development* must be brought forward to account for the enormous difference between the former and the latter. One of the most prophetic of Newman's utterances on this subject occurs in the fifteenth Oxford university sermon.

iv. *Late Anticipations: The Last Oxford University Sermon*

Between the years 1833 and 1836 Newman wrote for the *British Magazine* a series of papers later collected under the title,

"Primitive Christianity," and published in Volume I of the *Historical Sketches*. In these papers, he canvassed the opinions of St. Ambrose, of Vincent of Lerins, of Apollinaris, and of Jovinian as to the notes of a true Church. The Church of Athanasius and St. Ambrose, he maintained, rested not on human law and government but on "popular enthusiasm, on dogma, on hierarchical power, and on a supernatural Divine Presence." [1] This was strong language for early Tractarian readers, but Newman was determined to prove that modern Protestantism, not modern Catholicism, was a corruption of the early Apostolic faith. Above all, he wanted to find the true Catholic note in the early Church; and he thought he found it in Vincent of Lerins' famous canon, *Quod semper, quod ubique, quod ab omnibus*, that which is believed always, everywhere, and by all. [2] His conclusion was that primitive Christianity, judged by the Fathers and the Apostolical canons, was "distinguished by its high sacerdotal, ceremonial, mystical character," and had ever a universal and unitive nature. One might argue, of course, that the Church of St. Ambrose was not the "primitive Church"; but Newman is concerned with showing that, with the dearth of documents of the first and second century, we may be able to view that primitive Church through the eyes of the Fathers, taken not as authorities but only as witnesses. Whatever may be the validity of Newman's argument, the important results of his researches, in his own mind, was to show him that of the two modern representatives of Christianity, the Catholic and the Protestant, it was the former which seemed to have a more vital continuity with the Church of the first centuries. This was a bold conclusion in the early 1830's, and it committed Newman, no doubt unconsciously, to an investigation of the process by which the simple Church of the Apostles became in time the vast organism of the nineteenth century.

Another paper, published in the spring of 1836, entitled "Home Thoughts Abroad," [3] and taking the form of a dialogue between a Romanist and an anti-Romanist, stated the argument in behalf of Rome with such perspicuity and force that Newman's friends cried out, "How imprudent, how insidious." [4] Newman's desire to bring the Roman argument out with all its force, in order to meet it the more effectively, led him to put into the mouth of the Romanist some words which might very well have been set down in the *Essay on Development*: the so-called "corruptions" and "additions" made by Catholicism to the early faith are, he says, "those necessary developments of the elements of Gospel truth, which could not be introduced throughout the Church except gradually." [5]   Here, in an article which tries to show how the Anglican Church enjoys the benefits of Catholic faith without submitting to popery and "corruptions," Newman has touched on an argument which in time would expand and take complete possession of his mind.   As we have seen in an earlier chapter, he did not have long to wait.   His study of the Monophysites in the summer of 1839, the publication of Wiseman's article, and the fateful quotation from St. Augustine — *Securus judicat orbis terrarum* — all seemed, for the moment, to pulverize the theory of the *Via Media*, which his recent essays and tracts had so laboriously constructed.

The Catholicity of the Church of England no longer looked so certain; hence Newman's article in the *British Critic* of January, 1840, on the "Catholicity of the Anglican Church."   Here again far back in Newman's mind is the thought that simple, primitive articles of faith develop into intricate doctrines and dogmas. Once more stating the Romanist position so well as to frighten his more cautious readers, he allows that the Roman theory "seems to be that the whole faith was present in the minds of the Apostles, nay, of all saints at all times, but in great measure as a matter of mere temper, feeling, and unconscious opinion, that is, implicitly, not in the way of exact statements and in intellectual form. . . . The Roman Catholics would maintain that the Apostles were implicit Tridentines; that the Church held in the first age what she holds now; only that heresy, by raising questions, has led to her throwing her faith into dogmatic shape, and served to precipitate truths which before were held in solution." [6] Newman's whole essay is, of course, designed to defend the *Via Media*, and even though Wiseman's quotation from St. Augustine has jarred him severely, he wónders if, after all, the saint's words need be taken "as a theological verity equally sacred as an article in the Creed." [7]   In spite of St. Augustine and Wiseman, "the English Church is [still] the Catholic Church in England."

If it has not the note of Catholicity, it has at least the note of *life*;
and reunion with the Roman Church — which Newman has now
come ardently to desire — is impossible "till she ceases to be
what she practically is." [8]   Yet, if we look carefully into this
essay, we shall see that Newman has, perhaps unconsciously, absorbed the Roman doctrine of development.   After summarizing the doctrine fully and, in a degree, sympathetically, he comes
out flatly with the words: "We think there is a great deal of
force in this view." [9]   And though the context of his words shows
him still clinging to Anglicanism, it is clear that Newman's mind
has found intellectual nourishment especially suited for it.

Three years pass, and then on the afternoon of February 2,
1843, Newman preaches his great University sermon on "The
Theory of Developments in Religious Doctrine."   Here at last
Newman is applying openly the maxim which he learned from
Scott, that the true test of life is growth.   He applies it in what
was then an extremely novel way, to the dogmatic development
of the "impressions" derived from revelation.   Doctrines, he
says, have a way of *using* the minds of men, of growing, and of
perfecting themselves by the very act of rejecting heretical off-
shoots.   Thus a few words, "uttered, as if casually, by the fishermen of Galilee," expand and develop; they have a life of their
own, "which shows itself in progress; a truth which has the token
of consistency; a reality which is fruitful in resources; a depth
which extends into mystery." [10]   Reason has not only submitted;
it now ministers to faith — illustrating its documents, elevating
illiterate peasants into philosophers and divines, and eliciting
meanings from their words which their immediate hearers little
suspected.   "Its half sentences, its overflowings of language, admit of development." [11] Centuries pass before the formal expression of the truths of these simple pioneers of religious knowledge
is required to guide and steady the millions of believers.   "Thus,
not till the thirteenth century was there any direct and distinct
avowal, on the part of the Church, of the numerical Unity of the
Divine Nature, which the language of some of the principal
Greek fathers, *primâ facie*, though not really, denies." [12]   The
religious mind gradually "reasons out a series of dogmatic state-

ments, one from another . . . not from those statements taken in themselves, as logical propositions, but as being itself enlightened and (as if) inhabited by that sacred impression which is prior to them, which acts as a regulating principle, ever present, upon the reasoning, and without which no one has any warrant to reason at all. Such sentences as . . . 'the Word was made flesh' . . . are not a mere letter which we may handle by the rules of art at our own will, but august tokens of most simple, ineffable, adorable facts, embraced, enshrined according to its measure in the believing mind." [13] Revelation has provided in the Bible the main outlines and some of the chief details of the dogmatic system. But one dogma creates another — Scripture has but begun a series of developments which it does not finish. The fully developed dogmas, however, mark out, as it were, so far as it is possible, the real range, depth, and character of the original "sacred impressions" — today we should perhaps call them "intuitions" — prior to the dogmas themselves. And these dogmas or propositions "imply each other," and form a whole, to be accepted as a unity, and not piecemeal (which is the badge of heresy).

Newman is never weary of reminding his readers that dogmas by no means convey a true or adequate idea of divine realities. Like children, men are best taught "by an accommodation, on the part of their teachers, to their immature faculties . . . What is short of truth in the letter may be to them the most perfect truth, that is, the nearest approach to truth, compatible with their condition." [14] The very nature and limitations of language impose an accommodation or "economy" on the method of teaching religious truths; so also do the "moral diversities between parties" and individuals — "they seem ever to be dodging each other, and need a common measure or economy to mediate between them." Thus fables, myths, legends, accounts of miracles and heroic deeds, all of which are the "spontaneous produce of religious feeling under imperfect knowledge . . . may be considered facts or narratives, untrue, but like the truth, intended to bring out the action of some principle, point of character, and the like." Newman instances the tradition of St. Ignatius as the child whom Christ took in His arms as perhaps unfounded but nevertheless as intended to "realize to us his special relation to Christ and His Apostles."   If the alleged facts did not occur — and here Newman's language goes to audacious lengths — "they ought to have occurred (if I may so speak); they are such as might have occurred, and would have occurred, under circumstances . . ." He shuns the question of casuistry; and he further declares that "some [religious stories] are immoral [or fraudulent], common sense tells us; but it is enough for my purpose, if some are necessary." [15]   As for dogmatic propositions, they also are of an economical character, partly revealing and partly concealing the truth.   Being of such a character, they naturally multiply, as men meditate upon dogma.   But the multiplicity of propositions implies no multiplicity of dogmas themselves; propositions are added to propositions in the definition of dogma, not because the Divine reality described is complex, but because, in order to fix our thoughts upon it, we must describe the impressions it makes upon us from a great many different points of view.   Yet no matter how much dogmatic propositions multiply, they fall far short of the realities which they affirm. And this, says Newman, should not grieve the mind; for just as our senses cannot be proved to suggest any real idea of matter, and we yet proceed in our affairs without uneasiness, so our intellectual formulations of divine truths fall short of satisfactoriness, and yet we need not "vex ourselves to find whether our deductions are philosophical or no, provided they are religious." [16]

Newman tells us, in the *Apologia,* that when he preached his last University sermon, he had come to feel that "the principle of development not only accounted for certain facts, but was in itself a remarkable philosophical phenomenon, giving a character to the whole course of Christian thought . . . [And] it served as a sort of test which the Anglican [teaching] could not exhibit . . . The principle of development in the truths of Revelation [was] an argument in favor of the identity of Roman and Primitive Christianity." [17]

CHAPTER IV

(2) *THE LIFE IN IDEAS: NEWMAN'S "DEVELOPMENT OF CHRISTIAN DOCTRINE"* (1845)

i. *The Origin and Nature of the "Essay on Development"*

Newman's work on doctrinal development had both a personal and a theological genesis. It is common among hostile or semi-hostile writers to stress the personal and practical origin of the essay. It is true, as Cross maintains, that the work is not primarily "a treatise of pure abstract theology," and that it was indeed written, to some extent, to "justify a profoundly significant practical step" — entrance into the Roman Church. One may even agree that "it might be called the *Apologia* of 1845." [1] There is no doubt that Newman conceived the theory of development, as it finally appeared, for the purpose of explaining how he could intelligently reject one of his chief theological principles — the appeal to the doctrines of "Primitive Antiquity." For ten years he had been proclaiming the incompatibility of primitive and Roman Christianity. Now suddenly he ceased to believe in this incompatibility. And so the *Essay* was composed (beginning at the end of 1844) to set some limit to what he later called "vague misgivings," [2] and to show himself and others that he had now revised his notion as to what Antiquity might be expected to conceal and to disclose. If, after writing his book, his convictions in favor of the Roman Church were not weaker, then he should know his course.

But there was more than the motive of personal justification. Cross has ably shown — and it should have been evident to any observer of the footnotes of Newman's writings — that behind the work there stands the Bull-Petavius controversy of the seventeenth century. [3] Since Newman wrote before the days of Migne's *Patrologia,* and, after the custom of the time, relied on secondhand authorities in his studies of some of the Fathers, we find him frequently quoting them from such secondary authorities as Bull and Petavius. Bishop George Bull (1634–1710) published in 1685 his *Defensio Fidei Nicaenae*, which tries to show that the doctrine of the Trinity was held by the ante-Nicene Fathers of the Church. This weighty and Catholic-spirited work, together with the *Dogmata Theologica* (1644–50) of Dionysius Petavius (1583–1653) were, as Cross says, "continuously at Newman's hand as his two chief sources from the time that he began to work on *The Arians* until he finished *The Development of Christian Doctrine*." [4]   Petavius had applied the concept of development to the doctrine of the Trinity as held by the early Fathers, but had obviously written with his eye on the "modern" doctrinal form. He held that though the substance (*substantia*) of all Catholic doctrine was bequeathed to the Primitive Church, the form which it later took was determined by subsequent definitions. Bull's work was written in reply to Petavius, in an effort to show that the *whole* of truth was to be found in the Church at the outset. This, of course, was one of the teachings in Bull's writings which made him, in Newman's eyes, a pillar of the *Via Media*, of the static view of the Church. But the moment Newman's reliance on the note of Antiquity as marking the true Church had ceased, then, as Cross wittily puts it, "Bull had to be sacrificed on the altar to Petavius." [5]   That Newman was directly influenced by Petavius' teaching has not yet been demonstrated, but there is every reason to believe that the Bull-Petavius controversy contributed in no small degree at least to the early beginnings of Newman's theory about development. "As long as Antiquity was to be accepted," says Cross, "Bull was an invaluable stand-by. Now that Antiquity was [to be] rejected, why not attempt to do so by the method adopted by Bull's adversary? Moreover, Bull's adversary belonged to 'the straightest sect' of the Communion to which Newman was contemplating giving his adherence. What better authority than a Jesuit could he have had for his task?" [6]

The fact that Newman found a clearly developmental theory of dogma in Petavius reminds us that he was in no sense the originator of it. As Juergens has pointed out, "the idea of the evolution of dogma existed more or less clearly throughout the history of theology" and Marin-Sola has pointed out traces of the idea in St. Irenaeus, Origen, St. Basil, St. Jerome, and St. Gregory Nazianzen.[7] Like Darwin, Newman was not the inventor of a hypothesis, but a bold and illuminating applier of the general nineteenth-century idea of "growth" and "development" to a particular field. The idea of organic continuity and growth is of comparatively modern origin; ancient thought was relatively static. The concept of humanity as a developing organism, for example, had been glimpsed by Condorcet, by Kant, by Burke; and was clearly formulated by Comte in his "Positive Polity." The French Revolution had given the concept a powerful impetus; and even the Catholic reaction to the Revolution produced some works which are informed by the same general idea — Bonald's *Connaissances Morales* and Lamennais' *Essai sur l'Indifférence*. At the same time, Hegel's metaphysical speculations viewed humanity as a developing organism, and the same theme, of course, underlies his *Philosophy of History*. Herbert Spencer in sociology and metaphysics, and Charles Darwin in the study of biology carried the organismic view of the world to what seemed unanswerable conclusions. For centuries the European frame of reference had been the *Summa Theologica* of St. Thomas Aquinas; now it seemed to be adumbrated in books informed with the new "historical spirit." And some of Newman's admirers hastened to bracket him with Hegel and Spencer.[8]

At this point it is well to inquire into the nature of "development" as Newman uses the term. A great deal of misapprehension about this term appears in Newman literature. It ought to be clear to any reader of Newman that his doctrine of development was in no sense an anticipation of Darwinism; from such a supposition Newman would have shrunk with horror. Darwinism postulates the possibility of deterioration, as the corollary of progress, and teaches that all species were contained in some original germ, and that environment alone was sufficient to account for variations. Yet critics like Hutton, Barry, Tardivel, Flood, May, Ross, and Fawkes, have uncritically associated Newman's concept with that of Darwinian evolution. Barry's statement is typical: "We cannot but see on every page of the *Development* Darwin's advancing shadow." [9] Nearly every Newman critic fondly emphasizes the number of years — some fifteen — by which Newman's *Essay* antedates *The Origin of Species* (1859).

When we turn from the Darwinian interpretation of Newman's term, we find critics at variance in other directions. Some believe, with Sarolea and Geoffrey Faber, that the term merely means "the unfolding of possibilities and consequences contained in the premises . . . Although Newman repeatedly uses the analogy of organic development, his conception reminds us rather of a *logical process* than that of an organic growth," the implicit becoming explicit. Sarolea concludes that "to assert that Newman has been the Darwin of theology would therefore be as historically true as to assert that Darwin is contained in Heraclitus and Lucretius." [10] Newman's "development," after all, is merely *explication*. This concept of dogmatic development had had the support of certain authorities since the time of Suarez, the great Spanish scholastic (1548–1617). Yet writers like Barry and Elbert and Jean Guitton have interpreted Newman's doctrine in terms of biology; "this 'eclectic, conservative, assimilating, healing, moulding process' is not mere explication, but *epigenesis*." [11] Elbert, probably following the lead of the Spanish Dominican, Marin-Sola, sees Newman's process as "homogenous evolution." [12] And Guitton, carefully summing up and dismissing Sabatier's view that Newman adapted biological evolution to theology, and Tyrrell's view that Newman merely applied skillful dialectic to Roman theology, and Storr's conclusion that the *Essay* uses an incoherent *mélange* of logical and biological criteria — Jean Guitton sweeps these notions aside and classes Newman among those Romanist theologians who regard the progress of dogma as a genuine development: "the progress of dogmatic formulae is not, for [Newman], mere 'explication'; it is a *life*; time does not simply unfold it, time truly develops it." [13] Ideas have a life of their own; a great dogmatic proposition does not, therefore, advance according to the scholastic notion of "preformation," all its future products, down to the very last, lying secretly in the original germ, awaiting only a kind of mechanical unpacking; on the contrary, every stage of its growth becomes a causative impulse to a new stage, the new elements being assimilated under law in a synthesis not hitherto realized. Development is a process of incorporation, in which a vital principle is at work, conserving the old and developing the new through a continuous organic growth. This, as we have said, is epigenesis, and it involves a certain amount of transformation, though never, of course, a metamorphosis.

Unfortunately Newman's various definitions of "development" leave, in some minds, the impression of ambiguity. Writing in 1871 a footnote to his essay on "The Prospects of the Anglican Church," correcting his old Anglican self rather severely, he makes the following guarded statement: "The hypothesis about the *depositum fidei* in which I gradually acquiesced was that of doctrinal development, or the evolution of doctrines out of certain original and *fixed dogmatic truths*, which were held inviolate from first to last, and the more firmly established and illustrated by the very process of *enlargement*." He repudiates the idea of "*metamorphosis* and recasting of doctrines into *new* shapes." [14] Newman here seems to be stressing the immutable character of dogma, the impossibility of anything really new being added. But four years later, writing of the Vatican Council, he thinks of development as being "the new form, explanation, transformation, or carrying out of what in substance was held from the first, what the Apostles said." [15] In these words we have, perplexingly, at once the idea of "explication" (in *explanation*), of "epigenesis" (in *new form*, and *transformation*), and also of primitive purity (in *what the Apostles said*). This last notion, an implied horror of innovation, is expressed a few pages later, where he says with finality, "No simply new truth has been given to us since St. John's death." [16] As one examines Newman's various pronouncements on the subject, it becomes clear, however, that his use of the term "development" includes, on the whole, *all* of the interpretations thus far considered. It is, as Father Perrone agreed with him, an increasing logical comprehension of the original *depositum*, [17] but it is more than a process in the believer's mind. It is also the peculiar *life* in ideas — that living wisdom which is the outcome of deep thought in the Church on the field of knowledge under the guidance of "the Spirit of Wisdom." There is thus, for Newman, a mystical, at least a mysterious, power of growth in religious ideas which permits them to produce what *seem* to be "additions" but which are but the natural outflowering of the seed in such ideas. As Guitton observes, Newman came later to prefer the term "enlargement," which preserves the idea of original purity along with subsequent growths.[18] Much of our perplexity over Newman's meaning arises no doubt from the fact that, as Bertram Newman has noted, the *Essay* tries not only to account for the development of doctrine but also for the expansion of an institution informed by a "living idea." These two sides of the subject run parallel in Newman's mind, and the *Essay* is accordingly dominated by the conception of organic growth, but only by such as is compatible with the belief that dogmatic truth is incapable *ex hypothesi* of material increase or innovation.[19]

Yet it is not easy to fix Newman's mind in any neat category. If he saw further than his contemporary Macaulay, who held, in his essay on Von Ranke, that "in divinity there cannot be a progress analogous to" that in the sciences, he also had moments of extraordinary audacity and insight. One would never guess, for example, judging from the insular and non-scientific spirit of the Oxford which shaped his mind, that he would make the remark recorded by Blennerhassett. One day in 1857, says Blennerhassett, Newman sat on Killiney Hill, in Ireland, with his friend Dr. Sullivan, president of the Queen's College in Cork, enjoying a singularly beautiful sunset. "Suddenly Newman turned to Sullivan and said: 'I wonder whether the tests I have applied to theological development would hold water if they were applied in the physiological order.' This was two years before the appearance of Darwin's book." [20] Several years later, Newman discussed *The Origin of Species* with Blennerhassett, but never evidenced any alarm over its possible effects on Christianity. In this, Newman was strikingly unlike most mid-Victorian clergymen, who, like Bishop Wilberforce, took an indignant, frightened, and belligerent attitude toward the new biological theories. Even though he would no doubt have sternly rejected any "Darwinian" interpretation of dogmatic developments in Revealed Religion, his faith in supernature was so firm that he had no fear of genuine scientific inquiry into nature.

ii. *Newman's Final Argument: Development vs. Corruption*

We are now prepared to look into the contents of the *Essay on Christian Doctrine*, sometimes regarded as "undoubtedly Newman's greatest, though not his most attractive work." In spite of its being, as Bertram Newman says, "a model of subtle argumentation, lucid eloquence and orderly arrangement," [1] it is, to some extent, a formal treatise, informed by great learning, and devoted throughout many pages to the technical examination of particular doctrines. It is not, on the whole, easy reading. However, there is a frequent and powerful imaginative appeal, a bold sweep, and a subtle intellectual music which, at least for the moment, take the mind prisoner. One should always remember, in reading the *Essay*, that the author is not engaged primarily in formal argument in behalf of the Roman Catholic Church, but is urging that, if the hypothesis he advances be valid so far, a powerful presumption is provided that it may be trusted to go the rest of the way. Newman was a master rhetorician. And in the *Essay* all the resources of his literary art are employed in bringing the reader's mind into harmony with his own, in enhancing the full weight of his hypothesis by focusing all his lines of argument and suggestion upon his desired conclusion, and in deftly marshaling to that end an overwhelming array of facts and considerations. Newman's method, on the whole, as Przywara notes, is apologetic rather than dogmatic, more historical, empirical, and analytical than systematic.[2] Like most of his books, it was called forth by an occasion, and like most of them, it seeks an immediate response by using a direct and practical appeal to the mind and the imagination.

We shall examine the *Essay* in the edition of 1878, in which, as we learn from the Plummer letters first published by Frank Leslie Cross, Newman "half-re-wrote, or rather whole-rearranged" the work.[3] This edition presents the *Essay* in the final form in which Newman wished the public to judge it.

The book falls into two Parts — Part I dealing with doctrinal developments viewed in themselves, Part II setting up tests to differentiate between developments and corruptions. Newman begins his argument, in the Introduction, by asserting the objective and historical character of Christianity: "Christianity has been long enough in the world to justify us in dealing with it as a fact in the world's history.   Its genius and character, its doctrines, precepts, and objects cannot be treated as matters of private opinion or deduction, unless we may reasonably so regard the Spartan institutions or the religion of Mahomet." [4]   If one concedes that this historical Christianity presents apparent inconsistencies and alterations, one may attempt to apply the Vincentian canon (*quod semper, quod ubique, quod ab omnibus*); but the test of Antiquity and of Vincent must be abandoned because of the lack of unanimity in the early Fathers on certain important doctrines — Purgatory, Original Sin, the *Disciplina Arcani*.   We are therefore compelled, says Newman, to take the view, already illustrated by continental writers like de Maistre and Moehler,

"that the increase and expansion of the Christian Creed and Ritual, and the variations which have attended the process in the case of individual writers and Churches, are the necessary attendants on any philosophy or polity which takes possession of the intellect and heart, and has had any wide or extended dominion; that, from the nature of the human mind, time is necessary for the full comprehension and perfection of great ideas; and that the highest and most wonderful truths, though communicated to the world once for all by inspired teachers, could not be comprehended all at once by the recipients, but, as being received and transmitted by minds not inspired and through media which were human, have required only the longer time and deeper thought for their full elucidation.   This may be called the *Theory of Development of Doctrine*." [5]

Newman's whole effort in the succeeding argument is, he says, "an hypothesis to account for a difficulty," an effort to meet the rising tide of infidelity which "already has its views and conjectures."

The first formal section of the *Essay* opens with an admirable account of the process by which "living ideas" (such as "the divine right of kings," "utilitarianism," "the rights of man") are subjected to action and reaction, to a general "agitation of thought and action of mind upon mind."   This account leads to one of the memorable passages of the book, a remarkable fusion of argument, metaphor, and illustration:

"Whatever be the risk of corruption from the world around, such a risk must be encountered if a great idea is duly to be understood, and much more if it is to be fully exhibited. It is elicited and expanded by trial, and battles into perfection and supremacy. Nor does it escape the collision of opinion even in its earlier years, nor does it remain truer to itself, and with a better claim to be considered one and the same, though externally protected from vicissitude and change. It is indeed sometimes said that the stream is clearest near the spring. Whatever use may fairly be made of this image, it does not apply to the history of a philosophy or belief, which on the contrary is more equable, and purer, and stronger, when its bed has become deep, and broad, and full. It necessarily rises out of an existing state of things, and for a time savours of the soil. Its vital element needs disengaging from what is foreign and temporary, and is employed in efforts after freedom which become more vigorous and hopeful as its years increase. Its beginnings are no measure of its capabilities, nor of its scope. At first no one knows what it is, or what it is worth. It remains perhaps for a time quiescent; it tries, as it were, its limbs, and proves the ground under it, and feels its way. From time to time it makes essays which fail, and are in consequence abandoned. It seems in suspense which way to go; it wavers, and at length strikes out in one definite direction. In time it enters upon a strange territory; points of controversy alter their bearing; parties rise and fall around it; dangers and hopes appear in new relations; and old principles reappear under new forms. It changes with them in order to remain the same. In a higher world it is otherwise, but here below to live is to change, and to be perfect is to have changed often." [6]

But developments are of various kinds: mathematical, physical, material, political, logical, historical, ethical, metaphysical. There is not space to follow Newman in his many skillful illustrations of these types of developments, but we can observe his conclusion, "as to Christianity, supposing the truths of which it consists to admit of development."

"That development will be one or other of the last five kinds. Taking the Incarnation as its central doctrine, the Episcopate, as taught by St. Ignatius, will be an instance of political development, the *Theo-*

tokos of logical, the determination of the date of our Lord's birth of historical, the Holy Eucharist of moral, and the Athanasian Creed of metaphysical." [7]

Since it cannot be maintained that the Scriptures "comprise a delineation of all possible forms which a divine message will assume when submitted to a multitude of minds," Newman declares that developments are indeed to be expected. The prophetic, doctrinal, and political developments contained in the historical parts of Scripture anticipate the development of Christianity both as a polity and as a doctrine. And since Christianity came into the world as an idea rather than as an institution, a developing infallible authority is also to be expected, to impart, in matters of morals and faith, decision to what is vague, and confidence to what is empirical, to ratify successive steps and changes. "In an age in which reason, as it is called, is the standard of truth and right, it is abundantly evident to any one . . . that, if things are left to themselves, every individual will have his own view of them, and take his own course." [8] Thus, Christianity which is both social and dogmatic, and intended for all ages, must have an infallible expounder to guarantee unity of form and of doctrine. Newman now surveys the existing developments of doctrine and concludes that they are indeed the probable fulfillment of the expectations. In a very skillful passage he points out the numerous doctrinal "additions" which have become a part of the *organic whole* of Catholic teaching:

"These must be the very developments which they profess to be. Moreover, the very scale on which they have been made, their high antiquity yet present promise, their gradual formation yet precision, their harmonious order, dispose the imagination most forcibly towards the belief that a teaching so consistent with itself, so well balanced, so young and so old, not obsolete after so many centuries, but vigorous and progressive still, is the very development contemplated in the Divine Scheme. These doctrines are members of one family, and suggestive, or correlative, or confirmatory, or illustrative of each other. One furnishes evidence to another, and all to each of them; if this is proved, that becomes probable; if this and that are both probable, but for different reasons, each adds to the other its own probability. The Incarnation is the antecedent of the doctrine of mediation, and the archetype both of the Sacramental principle and of the merits of Saints. From the doctrine of Mediation follow the Atonement, the Mass, the merits of Martyrs and Saints, their invocation and *cultus*. From the Sacramental principle come the Sacraments properly so called; the unity of the Church, and the Holy See as its type and centre; the authority of Councils; the sanctity of rites; the veneration of holy places, shrines, images, vessels, furniture, and vestments. Of the Sacraments, Baptism is developed into Confirmation on the one hand; into Penance, Purgatory, and Indulgences on the other; and the Eucharist into the Real Presence, adoration of the Host, Resurrection of the body, and the virtue of relics. Again, the doctrine of the Sacraments leads to the doctrine of Justification; Justification to that of Original Sin; Original Sin to the merit of Celibacy. Nor do these separate developments stand independent of each other, but by cross relations they are connected, and grow together while they grow from one. The Mass and Real Presence are parts of one; the veneration of Saints and their relics are parts of one; their intercessory power and the Purgatorial State, and again the Mass and that State are correlative; Celibacy is the characteristic mark of Monachism and of the Priesthood. You must accept the whole or reject the whole; attenuation does but enfeeble, and amputation mutilate." [9]

This mark of indivisibility, integrity, and oneness convinces Newman that the Roman Church of his time is the successor of the Mediaeval Church, which in turn was the legitimate heir of the Nicene and of the Church of the first century. He is sure that if St. Athanasius or St. Ambrose came suddenly to life they would see in the Roman communion, rather than in the members of any other, the essential Church of their own day.

Newman next considers the most appropriate method of proving that the modern doctrinal system is indeed a genuine development from earlier and simpler forms. The method is that which he learned from Bishop Butler: "Probable proofs, by being added, not only increase the evidence but multiply it." [10] Lord Bacon could afford to recommend induction for the physical sciences, says Newman, "but it is otherwise with ethics," with matters of faith; he is content to fall back on deduction. He must also employ traditions, authorities, antecedent auguries, analogies, parallel cases. God may bless "antecedent probability" and deduction in religious inquiries, he says, "who blesses experience and induction in the art of medicine." [11]   Turning to "instances in illustration" of development, considered from the point of view of antecedent probability, Newman examines The Canon of the New Testament, the doctrines of Original Sin and of Infant Baptism, Communion in One Kind, the Homoüsion, the Incarnation, the Blessed Virgin, the doctrine of Saints, and of Papal Supremacy.   Typical of these examples is Infant Baptism, on which subject Newman characteristically throws the weight both of argument and of patristic authority, and concludes:

"It was on retrospect and after the truths of the Creed had sunk into the Christian mind, that the authority of such men as St. Cyprian, St. Chrysostom, and St. Augustine brought round the *orbis terrarum* to the conclusion, which the infallible Church confirmed, that observance of the rite was the rule, and the non-observance the exception." [12]

Possibly Newman's most eloquent writing in this part of the *Essay* (Chapter IV) is that devoted to "The Papal Supremacy," but space does not permit more than a noting that he is aware, even with all his eloquence and show of reason, that "all this is a theory."   But it is, he adds, "a theory to account for facts as they lie in the history." [13]

No doubt it is the next chapter, the fifth, which gives the *Essay* its most original and modern character.   Here, by seeking to give his argument something of scientific precision, he exhibits an elaborate technical apparatus, and lays down criteria (some of them from biology) which will enable us to distinguish a doctrinal development from a doctrinal corruption.   The seven tests or "notes" of a true development in any field, says Newman, are (1) *preservation of type,* as the type of the child is preserved, though altered and strengthened, in the man; (2) *continuity of principles,* in the sense that some languages "have a capacity for compound words, which . . . is denied to others"; (3) *power of assimilation,* as exemplified in a plant which will assimilate more or less foreign material in any *habitat* in which it will grow; (4) *logical sequence of ideas,* as in the history of Lutheranism, which began with "private judgment" and eventually led to "the philosophy of Kant and the open infidelity of Strauss"; (5) *anticipation of its future,* as illustrated in the Russians who, as mere pirates on the Black Sea, were unconsciously anticipating their later aims toward Constantinople; (6) *conservative action upon its past,* as observed by Blackstone, that "when society is once formed, government results of course, as necessary to preserve and to keep that society in order"; and finally, (7) *chronic vigor,* as the chronic continuance of the American Union shows that the republican principle is still alive, whereas the gradual appearance of imperial institutions in republican Rome showed that the republican principle was dying out.

The rest of the *Essay* consists simply of the massive and eloquent application of these seven tests to the Church, to its doctrines, practices, reputation, status, fortunes, and misfortunes. As Guitton points out, and as is evident from even a glance at the page numbering, the seven tests had, for Newman, an unequal importance.[14] Only the first is treated with great thoroughness: doctrinal *preservation of type* in the Church of the first, fourth, and fifth and sixth centuries is given 113 pages; whereas the second and third tests receive only from 23 to 26 pages. With the fourth note, there are signs, if not of weariness, then of haste and of rapidly developing decision. The seventh test is quickly dealt with in nine pages. We feel, as we read these last pages, that Newman has for some time considered his demonstration to be conclusive; there is little more to say.

It is impossible, of course, to examine here in detail all of Newman's arguments and illustrations in his treatment of the seven tests — with their scores of brilliant or passionate or subtly persuasive passages. In Chapter VI alone, where he is arguing the "Note of *identity of type,*" he gives an unforgettable picture of what Christianity looked like to such sensible and respectable men as Tacitus, Suetonius, and Pliny. He dwells on the "superstitious," "secret," "proselytizing," "gloomy," "magical" features which made Christianity repellent and alarming to all "right-thinking" Roman citizens and their magistrates. He shows how the early Christians, with their mysteries, their secret organizations, their apparent "sorcery," were considered as undermining the established government and the established religion. He shows how they, in a strangely obstinate, virulent, and contagious spirit seemed to be "the enemies of mankind." He tells

how a traveler encounters a group of these "light haters," later
called monks, and is shocked at their effect on people of "good
family and fortune." "Is not this herd," asks the traveler,
"worse than Circean poison? then bodies were changed, now
minds." [15]   As Newman enumerates other characteristics of these
early Christians, he seems to see the outlines of a type which
appeared to continue in its identity down to his own day.   And
using his gift for analogy with an unsurpassed cumulative power,
he sums up his review of Christianity in the first three centuries,
so as to imply that the very imputations leveled at nineteenth-
century Roman Catholicism were the badge of her divine identity:

"If there is a form of Christianity now in the world which is accused
of gross superstition, of borrowing its rites and customs from the
heathen, and of ascribing to forms and ceremonies an occult virtue; —
a religion which is considered to burden and enslave the mind by its
requisitions, to address itself to the weak-minded and ignorant, to be
supported by sophistry and imposture, and to contradict reason and
exalt mere irrational faith; — a religion which impresses on the serious mind very distressing views of the guilt and consequences of sin,
sets upon the minute acts of the day, one by one, their definite value
for praise or blame, and thus casts a grave shadow over the future;—
a religion which holds up to admiration the surrender of wealth, and
disables serious persons from enjoying it if they would; — a religion,
the doctrines of which, be they good or bad, are to the generality of
men unknown; which is considered to bear on its very surface signs
of folly and falsehood so distinct that a glance suffices to judge of it,
and careful examination is preposterous; which is felt to be so simply
bad that it may be calumniated at hazard and at pleasure, it being
nothing but absurdity to stand upon the accurate distribution of its
guilt among its particular acts, or painfully to determine how far this
or that story is literally true, what must be allowed in candour, or what
is improbable, what cuts two ways, or what is not proved, or what may
be plausibly defended; — a religion such that men look at a convert
to it with a feeling which no other sect raises except Judaism, Socialism,
or Mormonism, with curiosity, suspicion, fear, disgust, as the case may
be, as if something strange had befallen him, as if he had had an initiation into a mystery, and had come into communion with dreadful influences, as if he were now one of a confederacy which claimed him,
attested him, stripped him of his personality, reduced him to a mere

organ or instrument of a whole; — a religion which men hate as proselytizing, anti-social, revolutionary, as dividing families, separating chief friends, corrupting the maxims of government, making a mock at law, dissolving the empire, the enemy of human nature, and 'a conspirator against its rights and privileges'; — a religion which they consider the champion and instrument of darkness, and a pollution calling down upon the land the anger of heaven; — a religion which they associate with intrigue and conspiracy, which they speak about in whispers, which they detect by anticipation in whatever goes wrong, and to which they impute whatever is unaccountable; — a religion the very name of which they cast out as evil, and use simply as a bad epithet, and which from the impulse of self-preservation they would persecute if they could; — if there be such a religion now in the world, it is not unlike Christianity as that same world viewed it when first it came forth from its Divine Author." [16]

If the Church of the first three centuries was marked by these distinguishing and persistent features, it was no less marked in the fourth, fifth, and sixth centuries by other features equally characteristic and enduring. Newman runs through the story of the early divisions of the Church, the rise of the Arians, the Semi-Arians, the Nestorians, the Monophysites, and shows how these divisions arose from thinkers who rebelled against mystery in theology and who hoped to simplify the truth handed down; how, after the empire accepted Christianity, the great heresiarchs, like Arius, almost uniformly sought, and often obtained, help from the state, which naturally objected to the dogmatic independence and tenacity of the Church; and how it became almost the badge of heresy to lean on the civil power — here Newman glances reproachfully at the Anglican Church — instead of adhering to the doctrinal tradition of the Fathers. Everywhere, he says, the Church was one, the sects were many, independent, and discordant. The Church was a kingdom — and a kingdom admits the possibility of rebels. Moreover, besides being Catholic, "co-extensive with the Roman Empire," it was exclusive also, and incessantly "denounced the idolatries and sins of paganism." Even in these early centuries, its intolerance toward what it considered error, its ceaseless war on other bodies called Christian, its claim to be alone called "Catholic"—this brought upon it the vilifying names of "seducer," "harlot," "apostate," "Antichrist," "devil." [17]   But whereas in the fourth century the Church lay in the midst of a multitude of sects, "in the fifth and sixth we see the same Church lying in the West under the oppression of a huge, farspreading, and schismatical communion." [18]   Heresy is no longer a domestic enemy, but occupies its own ground.   Although the Council of Chalcedon settled the Nestorian and Monophysite heresies, these heresies continued to flourish and spread.   The Nestorian heresy, "when cast out of the Roman Empire, addressed itself . . . to a new and rich field of exertion [in Persia], got possession of an Established Church — [here, again, Newman glances at the Church of England] — cooperated with the civil government, adopted secular fashions, and, by whatever means, pushed itself out into an Empire." [19] And thus Newman is led to his final cumulative, analogical conclusion:

"If, then, there is now a form of Christianity such that it extends throughout the world, though with varying measures of prominence or prosperity in separate places; that it lies under the power of sovereigns and magistrates, in different ways alien to its faith; that flourishing nations and great empires, professing or tolerating the Christian name, lie over against it as antagonists; that schools of philosophy and learning are supporting theories or following out conclusions hostile to it, and establishing an exegetical system subversive of its Scriptures; that it has lost whole Churches by schism, and is now opposed by powerful communions once part of itself; that it has been altogether or almost driven from some countries; that in others its line of teachers is overlaid, its flocks oppressed, its churches occupied, its property held by what may be called a duplicate succession; that in others its members are degenerate and corrupt, and surpassed in conscientiousness and in virtue, as in gifts of intellect, by the very heretics whom it condemns; that heresies are rife and bishops negligent within its own pale; and that amid its disorders and fears there is but one Voice for whose decisions its people wait with trust, one Name and one See to which they look with hope, and that name Peter, and that see Rome; — such a religion is not unlike the Christianity of the fifth and sixth centuries." [20]

This brings us to the end of the great climax of the *Essay*.   For in none of the other test-passages is Newman so magnificent in his scope, so dramatic in his re-creation of that segment of history which Gibbon and the Fathers had made so alluring to him.

In dealing with the second test of a true development, *continuity of principle*, Newman uses for illustration the adhesion of the early and the later Church to the mystical rather than the literal interpretation of Scripture; her resolute assertion of the supremacy of faith over reason; her consistency in theology and dogma. The third test or note, *assimilative power*, is exemplified both in dogmatic truth and sacramental grace. Thus the Montanists, the Donatists, the Novatians, though heretics, all supplied "the raw material . . . which the Church, by means of the continuity and firmness of her [dogmatic] principles, could convert to her own uses." [21] St. Gregory of Nyssa well illustrates, on the other hand, Newman thinks, the assimilative power of sacramental grace. The Church followed his "economy," his practice of adopting, imitating, or sanctioning the existing rites and customs of a populace which had been converted to Christianity.

"The use of temples, and these dedicated to particular saints, and ornamented on occasions with branches of trees; incense, lamps, and candles; votive offerings on recovery from illness; holy water; asylums; holydays and seasons, use of calendars, processions, blessings on the fields; sacerdotal vestments, the tonsure, the ring in marriage, turning to the East, images at a later date, perhaps the ecclesiastical chant, and the Kyrie Eleison, are all of pagan origin, and sanctified by their adoption into the Church." [22]

The fourth note, *logical sequence*, "one doctrine leading to another," is illustrated in pardons, penances, satisfactions, purgatory, meritorious works, and the monastic rule. Briefly, for example, "if in consequence of death, or in the exercise of the Church's discretion, the '*plena poenitentia*" is not accomplished in its ecclesiastical shape, how and when will the residue be exacted?" Clement answers that if the 'purifying discipline does not take place in this life, it must after death; hence the doctrine of Purgatory. The fifth note or test, *anticipation of its future*, Newman illustrates with resurrection and relics, the virgin life, the cultus of saints and angels, and the office of the Blessed Virgin. The first example is perhaps the most skillfully presented. The old Paganism, both educated and vulgar, had held corpses and sepulchres in aversion. Christianity, however, preached the doctrine that matter, a creature of God and in itself "very good," had become corrupt, needed redemption, and had received it in the bodies and relics of the saints. Thus Newman, having summed up the awe-inspiring doctrine that God "had taken a portion of that corrupt mass upon Himself, in order to the sanctification of the whole," proceeds as follows:

"As a first consequence of these awful doctrines comes that of the resurrection of the bodies of His Saints, and of their future glorification with Him; next, that of the sanctity of their relics; further, that of the merit of Virginity; and, lastly, that of the prerogatives of Mary, Mother of God. All these doctrines are more or less developed in the Ante-nicene period, though in very various degrees, from the nature of the case." [23]

Of the several illustrations which Newman uses for his sixth test, *preservative additions,* one of the best is the foundation of the Society of Jesus, which did indeed, as clearly an "addition," tend to preserve the Church as the Church then was; another is the use of the cross as a symbol of holy war. As for the seventh test, the reader, whether Catholic or non-Catholic, may be inclined to agree with R. H. Hutton: no illustration is needed of the Church's *chronic continuance*.[24] Newman, however, dwells in admiration on the way in which the Church survived peril after peril — the bitter persecutions under the pagan empire; then the empire's sudden conversion, and the hazards of liberty in Christian worship, the cult of the saints, the development of Monachism; then the irruptions of the barbarians from the north (and later the Saracens from the south), the long controversy over the Incarnation; then the Dark Ages, and afterwards the great struggles incident to the rise of the ecclesiastical monarchy and the theology of the schools; and lastly the great changes consequent upon the controversies of the sixteenth century. "Could such a theology as Arianism," asks Newman, "have lasted through the scholastic contest?" Could it have survived "the Barbarians of the Empire, or the feudal system?" [25]

He looks back over the Church's tumultuous history, and is convinced that her "wonderful revivals" after all sorts of disaster are "further evidences of the absence of corruption in the system of doctrine and worship which she has developed." There are times, indeed, when she lapses into almost a state of *deliquium:*

"She pauses in her course, and almost suspends her functions; she rises again, and she is herself once more; all things are in their place and ready for action. Doctrine is where it was, and usage, and precedence, and principle, and policy; there may be changes, but they are consolidations or adaptations; all is unequivocal and determinate, with an identity which there is no disputing. Indeed it is one of the most popular charges against the Catholic Church at this very time, that she is 'incorrigible;' — change she cannot, if we listen to St. Athanasius or St. Leo; change she never will, if we believe the controversialist or alarmist of the present day." [26]

With these words, Newman's *Essay* abruptly breaks off. Demonstration had ceased to be necessary. It is as if he had suddenly dropped his pen as he stood at his desk, pale and thin, convinced that he had attained the fullest conviction, and that he must no longer delay his submission to Rome. He wrote one more paragraph, gravely beautiful in the Biblical rhythm of its longer sentences, passionately intense in its shorter imperative exhortations, exquisite in the pathos it throws over the exhausted writer. The paragraph is addressed to the reader; it is a postscript and a prayer:

"Such were the thoughts concerning the 'Blessed Vision of Peace,' of one whose long-continued petition had been that the Most Merciful would not despise the work of His own Hands, nor leave him to himself; — while yet his eyes were dim, and his breast laden, and he could but employ Reason in the things of Faith. And now, dear Reader, time is short, eternity is long. Put not from you what you have here found; regard it not as mere matter of present controversy; set not out resolved to refute it, and looking about for the best way of doing so; seduce not yourself with the imagination that it comes of disappointment, or disgust, or restlessness, or wounded feeling, or undue sensibility, or other weakness. Wrap not yourself round in the associations of years past, nor determine that to be truth which you wish to be so, nor make an idol of cherished anticipations.   Time is short, eternity is long.

NUNC DIMITTIS SERVUM TUUM DOMINE,
SECUNDUM VERBUM TUUM IN PACE
QUIA VIDERUNT OCULI MEI SALUTARE TUUM."

CHAPTER V

INTELLECTUAL EXCELLENCE: THE IDEA OF A LIBERAL EDUCATION

Newman's attempt to define a liberal education has become highly pertinent in recent years, especially since the economic crisis of the 1930's and the exigencies of war have led us to re-evaluate our experiences, our educational ideals, and our institutions. In the current debate over "What is a liberal education?" * Newman doubtless stands with such advocates of a non-utilitarian education as Robert Maynard Hutchins, Mark Van Doren, and Jacques Maritain, but not wholly for the same reasons. His ideal is not founded, like Hutchins' and Van Doren's, on a return to the trivium and quadrivium. Nor is it informed by the spirit of Scholasticism. Though he deplores the tendency to confuse training with education, and the tendency toward excessive or too early specialization and professionalism, he has no intention of "educating for freedom," or of specifying the "hundred great classics" which should supply a liberal-arts-college curriculum. His liberal education is not intended primarily to make "enlightened citizens for Democracy" or for any other polity, though if he is pressed he will admit, as we shall see, that "good citizenship" will be one of the invaluable by-products of such an education.

Newman's theory is at once more individualistic and more narrowly intellectual than that of most present-day champions of the non-utilitarian education. He would never say, for example, as does A. G. Henderson, president of Antioch College, that education is to prepare "the best brains for sound democratic leader-

* Recent representative works on the subject are Robert M. Hutchins, *Education for Freedom*, Louisiana State University Press, 1943, and *Higher Learning in America*, Yale University Press, 1936; Mark Van Doren, *Liberal Education*, N.Y.: Henry Holt and Co., 1943; Algo D. Henderson, *Vitalizing Liberal Education*, N.Y.: Harper and Bros., 1943; Jacques Maritain, *Education at the Crossroads*, Yale University Press, 1943.

91

ship, to produce liberal individuals ready to facilitate needed change and thus advance culture." Newman was anything but democratic, and as a mid-Victorian gentleman, aware that the mid-century social pattern in England was rapidly stabilizing itself, he probably did not contemplate, or desire, any important social change. His educated man would be truly a "liberal individual," but closer to the pattern of a Roman gentleman in the days of Cicero than to that of a twentieth-century social and economic leader. As for "advancing culture," Newman probably thought that English culture was in no need of advancing; England's gentlemen and their world seemed capable of withstanding the heaviest onslaughts of reformers. The stratified, opulent, stable world of the decade which saw the publication of *The Idea of a University* knew very clearly what a liberal education was, and for whom it was intended — the gentleman, the financially independent and well-bred man of leisure. This man, British in his individualism and conservatism, could afford that "intellectual excellence" which is the crown of Newman's concept of liberal education. In the 1850's Newman's gentleman had little premonition of the demands of science and technology as we now know them.

Thus Newman's thinking in education is both an ally and an opponent of the liberal educators of today. He is with them in opposing the degradation of real education to the level of specialized training; he is with them in emphasizing the discipline of the mind as of central importance in the liberal program. He is with Mark Van Doren in particular in implicitly affirming that there is no such thing as "education for democracy" but only good education and bad education, which make good and bad men. But he parts company both from those who would return to mediaeval or Scholastic patterns and from those who would "socialize" education until all individuality has left it. — The best way to ascertain Newman's position on these problems is, after all, to turn to his own words. The implications of his statements are so clear, in the wonderfully lucid analytical style of *The Idea of a University*, that the reader is left in very little doubt as to the relevance, in numerous ways, of Newman's ideas to those which challenge us today.

i. *Newman's Irish Campaign*

Of all Newman's writings, the *Idea of a University* has the widest appeal. Catholic and non-Catholic readers can agree on nearly all that Newman says in that work, about which it is customary to repeat, often uncritically, Walter Pater's judgment that it is "the perfect handling of a theory."[1] Too seldom, however, do admirers of the book know or remember all of the circumstances under which it was written. Those circumstances, together with certain traits in Newman's character, when studied carefully, reveal the true nature of his conception of an ideal university, of an ideal education, and of their ideal product, the "gentleman."

The Oxford which Newman left in 1845 was conservative and ecclesiastical. After his secession from the English Church, theology went out with dramatic suddenness, and science came in as the ruling principle of Oxford thinking. A "flood of reform" followed, as Mark Pattison tells us, and did not cease until it had produced two government commissions which drastically remodeled the curriculum, withdrawing "education by the parsons" and offering a new education by specialists.[2] The new spirit was secular and naturalistic. The atmosphere at Oxford, once so charged with religious potencies, was now the rationalistic atmosphere of biologists, geologists, empirical thinkers like John Stuart Mill. We need only remember such names as Matthew Arnold, Mark Pattison, Arthur Hugh Clough, and James Anthony Froude, to recall to what extent the Tractarian period had given way to an era at Oxford in which the secular spirit had begun to undermine effectual belief in orthodox Christianity. Education was being severed from religion; agitation for the withdrawal of religious tests continued vigorously; and the Church was thrown into an uncomfortably defensive and obscurantist position. Thus when Newman was invited in 1851 to give a series of lectures in Dublin against "mixed education" — Catholics and non-Catholics submitting to the same curriculum — Irish Catholics had already become acutely alarmed over secularist education, seeing it only as a part of a vast anti-Christian campaign. Newman never succeeded in allaying their fears.

He himself was certain that the only way to meet modern intellectual infidelity was on its own grounds — through a courageous
program of higher education.

Higher education for Catholics in Ireland in the middle of the
nineteenth century was deplorably inadequate. Irish clergymen
were educated at seminaries, such as Maynooth. The laity attended such Catholic colleges as Oscott, Ushaw, St. Edmund's,
Downside, Stonyhurst, Ampleforth, where they received a liberal
education no more advanced than that of the great public schools
of England, such as Rugby or Eton. No Catholic college had
the right to grant degrees recognized by the state. Recently,
under Peel's influence, the Queen's Colleges were supposed to
offer a non-sectarian education, which was, in fact, Protestant.
This was even less satisfactory for Catholics than Trinity College,
Dublin, which enjoyed in Ireland the prestige of Oxford in England, and which, though thoroughly Protestant, did not, like
the Queen's Colleges, divorce religion from education. The
intellectual inferiority of Irish Catholics was a reproach and a
danger. And by 1850 many Catholics were convinced of the necessity of a Catholic University in Ireland. In that year, the National Synod of Thurles decided upon the advisability of founding such a university; Pius IX had already given his approval to
the idea. The decision, however, was reached by a majority of
only one. The Synod was split between what Newman called
"the political and devotional party" and the champions of intellectual interests. Archbishop Cullen (who invited Newman to
give the lectures) represented the first group, which dreaded the
whole modern scientific and liberal movement; Dr. Russell and
Dr. Moriarty represented the other party, which shared Newman's conviction that the liberal and secular movement should
be counteracted, not by mere repression or evasion, but by a
university training at once religious and scientific. The Queen's
Colleges excluded theology. Newman hoped for a university
in which theology and science should flourish freely side by side.
He had recently declared his larger hope in his lectures in Birmingham on *The Present Position of Catholics in England*: "I
want a laity, not arrogant, not rash in speech, not disputatious,
but men who know their religion, who enter into it, who know

just where they stand, who know what they hold, and what they do not, who know their creed so well, that they can give an account of it, who know so much of history that they can defend it. I want an intelligent, well-instructed laity." [3]

Unfortunately, Newman found too many Irish bishops quite unconcerned with producing a "well-instructed laity." In addition to this initial handicap, there were such problems as lack of adequate funds, the poverty of the Irish people, the ever-present effects of the great famine of 1846, the lack of a clear understanding of just what a university should be, the political differences which appeared in Dr. Cullen's stubborn opposition to the appointment of Young Irelanders to the university faculty, the lack of unity among the Irish bishops in desiring a university at all, and, finally, Newman's own lack of executive ability and his ignorance of the administrative problems which harass a university, however ideal. In Discourse IX, Newman very disarmingly and honestly admits: "Neither by my habits of life, nor by vigour of age, am I fitted for the task of authority, or of rule, or of initiation." [4] One may well ask, Why did he attempt to go through with the enterprise? "A more worldly-wise man than Newman," writes J. Elliot Ross, "once he had realized the situation, would have found some excuse gracefully to withdraw . . . ; a very pugnacious man might have brought the Bishops to terms. But Newman was too shy, too sensitive, too proud, and too submissive to apostolic authority to fight." [5] If too few of the Irish hierarchy had Newman's implicit trust in Pius IX's wisdom, Newman himself, for whom Bishop Bagot had been his pope, could strengthen himself for the unlikely task by saying "St. Peter has spoken; it is he who has enjoined that which seems to us so unpromising." [6]

Further difficulties arose from Newman's failure to grasp certain elements in the Irish situation. He failed to realize how little the Irish were interested in the English idea of a "gentleman" as the product of university training. He failed also to foresee how shocked the Irish would be at his doctrine that "a gentleman may be 'gentle,' and have no religion." [7] The Irish could not share his belief that, given a vitalized religion, intellectual excellence may be pursued as its own end. He failed,

further, to appreciate to what degree the Irish would be opposed
to a Catholic university which should be "a university for England as well as for Ireland." [8]   Finally, in spite of his assertion
that he was most inclined to "the Louvain plan" of a university,
he nevertheless wished, to some extent, to "import Oxford into
Ireland" — "the Oxford of his own time, 1816–1845." [9]   Newman was aware of the boldness of his venture: "It is a most
daring attempt," he wrote to Mrs. William Froude, "but first
it is a religious one. . . Curious it will be if Oxford is imported
into Ireland, not in its members only, but in its principles, methods, ways, and arguments.   The battle there will be what it was
in Oxford twenty years ago [against liberalism] . . . While I
found my tools breaking under me in Oxford . . . I shall be
renewing the struggle in Dublin." [10]   There is considerable
pathos in this, in view of what the sequel was, but there is also a
strange blindness to realities.   One recent Irish critic and editor
of Newman has thus summed up Newman's error: "He read his
new appointment to mean that the Church and the Irish people
were to line up behind him, and be at his disposal in renewing,
many years after its definitive collapse, a set of local controversies, Anglican in provenance, and academic or quasi-religious or
both, with which neither the institution to which he was called,
nor the Irish people for whom it was being established, had any
connection or concern." [11]

It is not implausible to attribute to these circumstances some of
the tone, the method, and the style of *The Idea of a University.*
Newman's discourses have a tentative, probing, sometimes uncertain quality, as if he were not sure that his Irish audience is following him.   He defines, and redefines; he approaches his subject
from many angles; he illustrates copiously, and quotes from his
favorite authorities.   Considering the gap between Newman and
some of his hearers, and considering how Newman failed to
bridge that gap, at least in his own time, *The Idea of a University*
is not altogether "the perfect handling of a theory."   Indeed,
the discourses are a very strange product of that whole "Irish
University affair."   One other circumstance helps to explain
them: they were written and delivered during the agonizing
time of the Achilli trial.   Newman was, as it were, doubly in-

sulated from his hearers: he was freshly arrived on the Irish scene, and he had vivid memories of a libel suit.   It was natural that Irish realities should fail to reach him fully, and that in conceiving a new university he should turn inward and see the image of Oxford on his heart.   His treatment of the ideal university is therefore highly intellectual, and more autobiographical than is generally realized.

Newman has given the story of the Irish university, and of his relations with the bishops, in a little volume privately printed in 1872, and not included in his collected works, *My Campaign in Ireland*.   In it, together with Ward's account, we learn how Newman's formal appointment as rector was delayed from November, 1851, until June, 1854; how the Irish bishops, sensitive to outside influences, and jealous and afraid of Newman, prevented Wiseman from having Newman made a bishop; and how, in reality, the bishops wanted not a university as a practical project but as a political and ecclesiastical weapon against "mixed education," and had therefore used him and his name as a valuable asset.   The whole narrative makes sorry reading, with here and there a passage of memorable humor or wit as Newman recognizes that even in the midst of failure and frustration there are always droll experiences.   Before he severed relations with the project, however (in 1857), he founded *The University Gazette*, editing it himself for a year, and publishing in it those discourses later entitled the *Rise and Progress of Universities*.   He also founded a medical school and a school of science, established a professorship of Celtic literature, and made numerous appointments to the university faculty.   Thus there was much more accomplished than one would have expected possible in view of the difficulties which had beset Newman from the very start. The greatest accomplishment, of course, was the series of nine discourses which make up the first half of the volume now known as *The Idea of a University*.[12]

ii.   *Newman and the Idea of a University*

When Newman delivered his lectures in May and June of 1852, he was addressing not only his immediate audience but all England as well on the conservative view of what a university and a liberal education should be. He was remembering the issue of Tractarian days, when the reformers had determined to nationalize, secularize, and modernize Oxford. At that time the Tractarians were equally determined to keep Oxford strictly an Anglican academy in which theology would remain "the queen of the sciences." They had looked with disdain and disapproval on the encroachments of physical science, and regarded the British Association and the Royal Society as the source not only of new knowledge which might, with great caution and prudence, be accepted by the Church-controlled universities, but also of shortsighted utilitarianism and of narrow specialized training. So faithful is *The Idea of a University* to the mentality of the Oxford Movement of thirty years before, that one writer declares it to be "as integral a part of the Tractarian Movement as was Newman's *Arians of the Fourth Century* or the *Oxford Sermons*, because it sums up the Catholic view which Newman and his friends held in common concerning the idea of Oxford." [1] This accounts for certain elements in his conception of universities which strike many present-day readers as strange or antiquated. Newman insists, for example, that a university is "a place of *teaching* universal knowledge . . . rather than [of] the advancement" of such knowledge. [2] He is content to leave research to such societies as the British Association, the Royal Society, the Antiquarian Society. He has no premonition of what the world's universities were to become, centers not only of the humanities but also of vast scientific learning and investigation contributing to human knowledge and welfare. He is no doubt right in saying that "to discover and to teach are distinct functions," rarely found united in the same person; [3] but he has no knowledge of how an instructor's research may enrich and vitalize his role as a teacher. True to the spirit of pre-scientific Oxford, he asserts that "the great discoveries in chemistry and electricity were not made in Universities," and that "Porson had no classes." True to the spirit of the age of Newton and Butler, when scientific experiment was still an activity of isolated individuals, he is sure that "the natural home for experimentation and speculation is retirement." [4] For him, universities are institutions for conserving and propagating the inherited knowledge and wisdom of

the race; in them men are to become "deeply read in the philosophy of ancient truth, and serenely prescient of the future from
[their] comprehension of the past." To the charge that such
institutions would be old-fashioned, Newman would answer, as he
did in writing in 1838 of "Medieval Oxford," "it is their very
place to be oldfashioned." [5] In all this we readily see wherein
many a page of *The Idea of a University* bears the mark of its
own day. The book was published almost simultaneously with
the publication of the Royal Commission's Report recommending
drastic measures in the direction of liberalizing and secularizing
Oxford and Cambridge. Newman's purpose, therefore, was not
merely to define university education for his Irish audience but
also to sum up the conservative view of liberal education at a time
when political liberalism seemed, from Newman's point of view,
to threaten with destruction all that philosophy of humanism
which Oxford, in the long course of its development, had so successfully evolved.[6]

On the other hand, Newman's discourses contain passages of
permanent value on the nature of an ideal university in any time
or place. He sees it, for example, as a make-weight against
popular, journalistic pseudo-knowledge. Like Carlyle, he is
acutely conscious of the new power of periodical literature, from
which the "intellectual man, as the world now conceives of him,
is one who is full of 'views' . . . from the Personal Advent to
the Cholera or Mesmerism . . . [from] German philosophy,
the French Empire, Wellington, Peel, and Ireland" to "agriculture, emigration, and the colonies." Newman abhors the new
reading public which demands of its favorite journalist "his
lucid views, leading ideas, and nut-shell truths for the breakfast
table." [7] To counteract the tremendous influence of this pseudo-
education, Newman wants the people "taught a wisdom, safe
from the excesses and vagaries of individuals, embodied in institutions which have stood the trial and received the sanction of
ages." [8] Universities of this sort would be "seats of universal
learning, each with its *genius loci:*

"An assemblage of learned men, zealous for their own sciences, and
rivals of each other, are brought, by familiar intercourse and for the

sake of intellectual peace, to adjust together the claims and relations of their respective subjects of investigation. They learn to respect, to consult, to aid each other. Thus is created a pure and clear atmosphere of thought, which the student also breathes, though in his own case he only pursues a few sciences out of the multitude . . . He apprehends the great outlines of knowledge, the principles on which it rests, the scale of its parts, its lights and its shades . . . Hence a habit of mind is formed which lasts through life of which the attributes are, freedom, equitableness, calmness, moderation, and wisdom." [9]

Such a seat of learning "will give birth to a living teaching, which in course of time will take the shape of a self-perpetuating tradition, or a *genius loci* . . . which haunts the home where it has been born, and which imbues and forms, more or less, and one by one, every individual who is successively brought under its shadow." [10]

Indeed this tradition, in an ideal university, would be so strong as to enable the university to exist, says Newman, even if there were no one to teach the young men. A "multitude of young men, keen, open-hearted, sympathetic, and observant" could so mingle that "the conversation of all [would] be a series of lectures to each"; all would "gain for themselves new ideas and views, fresh matter of thought, and distinct principles for judging and acting, day by day." Such an experience would be, for the student, "seeing the world on a small field with little trouble," [11] and the process would result in the whole assemblage being molded together and gaining one tone and one character. Newman thus makes a radical distinction between the *formal instruction* of a university and the *informal intercourse* of students among themselves and with their instructors. He is emphatic that a university ought to be "an Alma Mater, knowing her children one by one, not a foundry, or a mint, or a treadmill." [12] In his discourses on the *Rise and Progress of Universities*, he is equally explicit: "An academical system without the personal influence of teachers upon pupils, is an arctic winter; it will create an icebound, petrified, cast-iron University, and nothing else." [13] Abhorrent to Newman's mind was the thought of "system without personality," of institutional size and routine. For him, a university was a human, and a humanizing, institution or it was nothing.

Since the dominant theme in Newman's nine discourses is the *unity* of education, and since Newman was always opposed to a purely secular education, it was only natural for him to vindicate the place of theology in a university. Three discourses out of the nine are devoted to this subject — "Theology as a Branch of Knowledge," "Bearing of Theology on Other Knowledge," and "Bearing of Other Knowledge on Theology." Newman holds that if a university is to impart *universal* knowledge, it cannot properly leave out theology, since, for him, religious doctrine, "whether from Reason or Revelation . . . is knowledge, in as full a sense as Newton's doctrine is knowledge." [14] Moreover, theology "gives a unity and coherence to all other knowledge in the light of ultimate ends." In order to have "possession of truth at all, we must have the whole truth; and no one science, no two sciences, no one family of sciences, nay, not even all secular science, is the whole truth . . . Revealed truth enters to a very great extent into the province of science, philosophy, and literature, and . . . to put it on one side, in compliment to secular science, is simply, under colour of a compliment, to do science a great damage." [15] Yet Newman does not mean to imply that his university would be a "glorified theological school." He was indeed surprisingly realistic, compared with some of his Irish associates. He knew that his students expected to live in the world as it was. "Why do we educate," Newman therefore asks, "except to prepare for the world?" He reminds his audience that a university "is not a Convent, it is not a Seminary; . . . we cannot possibly keep [the young] from plunging into the world . . . ; and it is not the way to learn to swim in troubled waters, never to have gone into them." [16]

On the organizational side of the projected Catholic university, Newman showed an astonishing degree of creative thinking. He anticipated many of the features which, either in theory or in practice, figure prominently in modern university organization. He believed, for instance, in vesting authority and responsible leadership in the rector, in somewhat the same fashion as they are vested in an American college president. He sought to prevent such a predominance of colleges over the university as had developed at Oxford. In two other respects he was in advance of his time: he tried to blend the professorial and the tutorial systems, so that the same person would act in both capacities to the same students; and he laid careful plans for the establishment of "a school of useful arts" — what we today would call "colleges" of engineering, agriculture, mining, and the like. With the same care which he gave to safeguarding the prerogatives of the rector, he sought security and freedom for the teaching staff. The professors of each faculty, for example, were to elect annually out of their own body their dean and secretary. None of these plans appear in the nine discourses, but they were as genuine a portion of his program as that set forth in the famous lectures.

The same may be said of his standpoint in regard to academic freedom. It is not discussed in the lectures on theology and its bearing on other knowledge; yet in 1855, after the university was actually open, Newman insisted eloquently and courageously, in a lecture on "Christianity and Scientific Investigation," that "the investigator should be free, independent, unshackled in his movements . . . allowed and enabled, without impediment, to fix his mind intently, nay, exclusively, on his special subject." [17] Newman is assuming, of course, "good faith, honest intentions, a loyal Catholic spirit, and a deep sense of responsibility." [18] He is convinced, furthermore, that a true Catholic is sure that "nothing can make him doubt, that, if anything seems to be proved by astronomer, or geologist, or chronologist, or antiquarian, or ethnologist, in contradiction to the dogmas of faith, that point will eventually turn out, first, *not* to be proved, or, secondly, not *contradictory*, or, thirdly, not contradictory to anything *really revealed*, but to something which has been confused with revelation." [19]   So long as scientific investigation does not forget the "moral weakness and the intellectual confusion" of most men, so long as it works in a "grave and business-like character, answering to the mediaeval schools of philosophical disputation," then free inquiry may be conducted with safety. Newman reminds us that for centuries Aristotle was considered by the Church as a "more serious foe, beyond all mistake, than Bacon has been since," yet in the great "age of Universities" St. Thomas made him "a hewer of wood and drawer of water to the Church." [20] In like manner, says Newman, all scientific truth can, when properly tested and set forth, be assimilated into the Church.

iii. *Newman and the Idea of a Liberal Education*

One of the best ways to approach Newman's theory of a liberal education is to ask what, in his view, such an education is *not*. He tells us, for one thing, that it is not a "loading of the memory of the student with a mass of undigested knowledge." It is not "an unmeaning profusion of subjects . . . implying a smattering in a dozen branches of study"; neither is it merely "an acquaintance with the learned names of things and persons," nor "attendance on eloquent lectures," nor the witnessing of "the experiments of a platform." Modern universities, especially in America, are plagued with the popular demand for "easy" and superficial instruction; the educational institutions of Newman's day had no less a problem: "All things now are to be learned at once," says Newman mournfully, "not one well, but many badly. Learning is to be without exertion, without attention, without toil; without grounding, without advance, without finishing," with "nothing individual in it." [1] And just as a superficial acquaintance with science and literature do not constitute an education, in the same way recreations and accomplishments fall short of Newman's ideal: "All I say is, call things by their right names . . . You may as well call drawing and fencing education, as a general knowledge of botany or conchology. Stuffing birds or playing stringed instruments is an elegant pastime . . . but it is not education; it does not form or cultivate the intellect. Education is a high word; it is the preparation for knowledge, and the imparting of knowledge in proportion to that preparation." [2] Nor is cultivation of the intellect achieved by what is popularly known as "seeing the world, entering into active life, going into society, travelling . . . coming into contact with the principles and modes of thought of various parties, interests, and races. . ." [3]

Again, education is not merely instruction. Newman thinks of the word "instruction" as more properly belonging to "manual exercises," to training "in the fine and useful arts, in trades, and in ways of business; for these are methods, which have little or no [strictly educative] effect upon the mind itself," but "are contained in rules committed to memory, to tradition, or to use, and bear upon an end external to themselves." [4] Instruction, lectures, examinations, experiments, prizes — all these, says Newman, may lead to knowledge, but "the end of a Liberal education is not mere knowledge, or knowledge considered in its *matter*." [5] In fact, "it is not mere application, however exemplary, which introduces the mind to truth, nor the reading of many books, nor the getting up many subjects; . . . a man may have done it all, yet be lingering in the vestibule of knowledge." [6]

It goes without saying, then, that Newman will deny to utilitarian or professional instruction any of the values of a liberal education. Calling in Aristotle and Cicero as authorities, he differentiates between "*liberal* knowledge" and "*servile* knowledge." He does not deny that "commerce and the professions afford scope for the highest and most diversified powers of mind. . . . [Yet] what is merely professional, though highly intellectual, nay, though liberal in comparison of trade and manual labor, is not simply called liberal, and mercantile occupations are not liberal at all." Why all this distinction, he asks, anticipating objections. He answers by declaring, with Aristotle, that "that alone is liberal knowledge, which stands on its own pretensions, which is independent of sequel, expects no complement, refuses to be *informed* (as it is called) by any end . . ." [7] In so answering, Newman is replying to the objections not only of some of his immediate hearers but also to writers on education from John Locke down through Lord Jeffrey and Sydney Smith to Lord Macaulay and the members of the Royal Commission of 1850. Locke, in his *Some Thoughts Concerning Education*, had attacked the conventional classical education which "neglected all the while the writing a good hand, and casting accounts, which are of great advantage in all conditions of life, and to most trades most indispensably necessary." [8] It was from Locke's point of view that Sydney Smith, Lord Jeffrey, and Professor Playfair, from 1808 to 1810, published a series of book reviews in the *Edinburgh Review* attacking Oxford and Cambridge for clinging to an outmoded and inadequate curriculum, and for obstructing the progress of science and commerce.   These attacks were answered by Edward Coplestone, Professor of Poetry at Oxford, in an earnest and dignified pamphlet, which, together with its review by his Oriel colleague, John Davison, in the *Quarterly*, constituted a stanch defense of the educational value of literature and logic as contrasted with science.   According to Professor Knickerbocker, Newman "had before him, as he composed his lectures, the outlines of defense of the Oxford scheme which Copleston and Davison had written in reply to the first *Edinburgh* criticisms." [9]   One might add that evidently Newman also had before him Macaulay's brilliant but uncritical essay on "Bacon" (1837), in which the "ancient philosophy" of Plato, Aristotle, and Seneca is held up to ridicule, as unfruitful, in comparison with the Baconian "philosophy of Utility."   Newman cites Macaulay's essay, and admits that "The Philosophy of Utility . . . has at least done its work; . . . it aimed low, but it has fulfilled its aim." [10]   Yet to all the arguments favoring a "useful" education, whether adduced by Locke, or Jeffrey, or Macaulay, Newman has but one answer: a liberal education does not aim to make men better, morally or economically; "it is as real a mistake to burden it with virtue or religion as with the mechanical arts"; its one aim is general cultivation of the mind; and its method is the pursuit of knowledge as an end in itself. And this leads him to the final rejection of a false aim — that education should have a moral purpose.   On the contrary, education is "no guarantee for sanctity"; it "makes not the Christian, not the Catholic, but the gentleman."   It is well to have the cultivated intellect, the delicate taste, the candid, equitable, dispassionate mind of a gentleman; but these qualities "do but seem to be what they are not; they look like virtue at a distance."   It would in fact be as easy to "quarry the granite rock with razors, or moor the vessel with a thread of silk," as to "hope with such keen and delicate instruments as human knowledge and human reason to contend against those giants, the passion and the pride of man." [11]

Thus does Newman dismiss the various false conceptions of education, as he sees them, flourishing in the middle of the nineteenth century. His own conception may be most readily understood by noting the several definitions of liberal knowledge and education which appear as a series of climaxes through Discourses V–VIII, and by observing what Newman considers to be the final product of such an education, namely, the "gentleman."

We have already seen that, for Newman, a liberal education pursues knowledge as an end in itself, and that it ultimately produces a "habit of mind . . . which lasts through life, of which the attributes are, freedom, equitableness, calmness, moderation, and wisdom." [12] This habit of mind is elsewhere in *The Idea of a University* elaborated upon in terms of "enlargement of mind" and "philosophical knowledge." The former expression designates, not the mere communication of knowledge — instruction — but "the mind's energetic and simultaneous action upon and towards and among those new ideas, which are rushing in upon it. It is the action of a formative power, reducing to order and meaning the matter of our acquirements." A truly cultivated intellect is one which takes a connected view of old and new, past and present, far and near. It has knowledge not only of things but also of *relations*. The well-read man, the annalist, the naturalist, the man of information and statistics — these "have not," says Newman, "what specially deserves the name of culture of mind"; they do not "fulfill the type of Liberal Education." They do not possess that "true enlargement of mind which is the power of viewing many things at once as one whole," a power which Newman sometimes calls "illuminative reason," since it never views any part of a subject matter without recollecting that it is but a part. Thus Newman concludes in a famous passage:

"To have even a portion of this illuminative reason and true philosophy is the highest state to which nature can aspire, in the way of intellect; it puts the mind above the influences of chance and necessity, above anxiety, suspense, unsettlement, and superstition, which is the lot of the many . . . The intellect, which has been disciplined to the perfection of its powers, which knows, and thinks while it knows, which has learned to leaven the dense mass of facts and events with the elastic force of reason, such an intellect cannot be partial, cannot be exclusive, cannot be impetuous, cannot be at a loss, cannot but be patient, collected, and majestically calm, because it discerns the end in every beginning, the origin in every end, the law in every interruption, the limit in each delay . . . The perfection of the Intellect, which is the result of Education . . . is the clear, calm, accurate vision and comprehension of all things, as far as the finite mind can embrace them . . ."

From this point in his discussion, Newman proceeds to show how near to divine wisdom this illuminative reason may attain, and to imply, incidentally, why he has no fears of a thorough training of the mind apart from religious considerations, so long as those considerations are elsewhere borne in mind. This illuminative reason is, therefore, "almost prophetic from its knowledge of history; it is almost heart-searching from its knowledge of human nature; it has almost supernatural charity from its freedom from littleness and prejudice; it has almost the repose of faith, because nothing can startle it; it has almost the beauty and harmony of heavenly contemplation, so intimate is it with the eternal order of things and the music of the spheres." [13]

And the knowledge with which this illuminative reason operates is not "useful" but "philosophical" knowledge — "something intellectual, something which grasps what it perceives through the senses, something which takes a view of things; which sees more than the senses convey; which reasons upon what it sees, and while it sees; which invests it with an idea." What makes "philosophical knowledge" superior to "useful knowledge" is that the former tends to rise toward general ideas, to a synoptic view of all things. "Not to know the relative disposition of things is the state of slaves or children; to have mapped out the Universe is the boast, or at least the ambition, of Philosophy." [14] It is with this knowledge that a liberal education has to do: "Liberal Education, viewed in itself," says Newman, "is simply the cultivation of the intellect, as such, and its object is nothing more or less than intellectual excellence." Just as there is a physical beauty or excellence, an excellence of moral character known as virtue, and a beauty of personality, so there is a perfection of intellect. In true Aristotelian fashion, Newman here, as elsewhere in *The Idea of a University*, dwells on the classifiability of human powers, and avers that the cultivation of the mind may properly be carried on in complete distinction from the cultivation of virtue: "To open the mind, to correct it, to refine it, to enable it to know, and to digest, master, rule, and use its knowledge, to give it power over its own faculties, application, flexibility, method, critical exactness, sagacity, resource, address, eloquent expression, is an object as intelligible . . . as the cultivation of virtue, while, at the same time, it is absolutely distinct from it." It was this "philosophy of severance," as one recent critic has called it, that made Newman's conception of university education a stumbling block to many of his Irish listeners.[15] But Newman, unperturbed, admitting intellectual excellence to be "but a temporal object," nevertheless follows his humanistic theory to its logical conclusion: "We attain to heaven by using this world well, though it is to pass away; we perfect our nature, not by undoing it, but by adding to it what is more than nature, and directing it towards aims higher than its own." [16]

If Newman is pressed to prove the "utility" of a liberal education, he replies that "though the useful is not always good, the good is always useful. Good is not only good, but reproductive of good . . . Good is prolific." If therefore our intellect is so excellent a portion of us, it must be not only beautiful, perfect, noble in itself, but also useful — "not in any low, mechanical, mercantile sense, but as diffusing good, or as a blessing, or a gift, or power." If, more precisely, Newman is obliged to define education in terms of practical ends, he is willing to say that it is the "training of good members of society. Its art is the art of social life, and its end is fitness for the world." And just as it does not confine itself to professional training, it has no aspiration to produce heroes or men of genius. Universities are not the birthplaces of poets, founders of schools, conquerors of nations. "A University training is the great ordinary means to a great but ordinary end." The social utility of Newman's "liberal education" may be stated in terms first of society itself, and then of the individual. It will be noted that Newman accords

three times as much space to the latter as to the former; he is
more concerned with the individual than he is with those less concrete entities, social patterns and social forces.   University training, therefore, so far as it has a social purpose, "aims at raising
the intellectual tone of society,[17] at cultivating the public mind,
at purifying the national taste, at supplying true principles to
popular enthusiasm and fixed aims to popular aspiration, at giving enlargement and sobriety to the ideas of the age, at facilitat-
ing the exercise of political power, and refining the intercourse of
private life."   No sentence of Newman's contains a greater quantity of compact or latent meaning; when analysed phrase by
phrase, Newman's concept of the social value of a liberal education is tremendous.   Yet Newman himself, a master of analysis
and elaboration, never followed out the implications of his sentence.   He preferred to confine his attention to the individual
man for whom university education was originally intended.

That education was to give a man:

"a clear conscious view of his own opinions and judgments, a truth
in developing them, an eloquence in expressing them, and a force in
urging them.   It teaches him to see things as they are, to go right
to the point, to disentangle a skein of thought, to detect what is sophis-
tical, and to discard what is irrelevant.   It prepares him to fill any
post with credit, and to master any subject with facility.   It shows
him how to accommodate himself to others, how to throw himself into
their state of mind, how to bring before them his own, how to influence
them, how to come to an understanding with them, how to bear with
them.   He is at home in any society, he has common ground with
every class; he knows when to speak and when to be silent; he is
able to converse, he is able to listen; he can ask a question pertinently,
and gain a lesson seasonably, when he has nothing to impart himself;
he is ever ready, yet never in the way; he is a pleasant companion, and
a comrade you can depend upon; he knows when to be serious and
when to trifle, and he has a sure tact which enables him to trifle with
gracefulness and to be serious with effect.   He has the repose of mind
which lives in itself, while it lives in the world, and which has resources
for its happiness at home when it cannot go abroad. He has a gift
which serves him in public, and supports him in retirement, without
which good fortune is but vulgar, and with which failure and disappointment have a charm. . ."[18]

Almost as if carrying his consideration of the possible "utility" of a liberal education over into the domain of religion, Newman attempts in Discourse VIII to show how the truly educated mind may be "at once a defense yet a disturbance to the Church." As a defense, it may "rescue [man] from that fearful subjection to sense which is his ordinary state." Being "level with our nature," it may "employ nature against itself," and rescue "the victims of passion and self-will." It can hardly supply religious motives, or be the proper antecedent of anything above the level of nature; but Newman grants that it "does a work, at least *materially* good (as theologians speak). . . It expels the excitements of sense by the introduction of those of the intellect." [19]   It may also, in spite of the dangers of secularism, go far toward solving many urban ills: "When in the advancement of society men congregate in towns, and multiply in contracted spaces, and law gives them security, and art [*i.e.* invention] gives them comforts, and good government robs them of courage and manliness, and monotony of life throws them back upon themselves, who does not see that diversion or protection from evil they have none, that vice is the mere reaction to unhealthy toil, and sensual excess the holyday of resourceless ignorance?" (One might add, parenthetically, that in this remarkable sentence, nowhere elaborated upon in Newman's writings, there is the essence of whole volumes of Ruskin; and that far from being unaware of Victorian social ills, as he is often charged by his critics, he was actually conscious of them, but found no occasion, and had no desire, to offer some easy nineteenth-century panacea.)   Intellectual culture, then, may aid religion in doing a work — saving the victims of social upheaval — which could not be done, he held, by "cheap literature, libraries of useful knowledge . . . lectureships, museums," zoos, and public parks.   It may develop in social *leaders* the very qualities of "the type of Christianity . . . veracity, probity, equity, fairness, gentleness, benevolence, and amiableness." [20]

Yet there is in this very similarity to Christian virtue, a grave danger in intellectual culture. Such culture, in a civilized age, may develop a "Religion of Reason," in which conscience will give way to "a moral sense," duty will become "a sort of taste," and sin not an offense against God but merely against human nature. According to this "philosopher's or gentleman's religion," vice is not a thing to weep about, but to laugh at. Ridicule becomes the test of truth. Newman, of course, has in mind certain great eighteenth-century exponents and models of this "Religion of Philosophy." Gibbon had painted with pleasure the "godless intellectualism" of an ancient "modern," the Roman emperor Julian; Lord Shaftesbury had drawn out the idea in theoretical form in his *Characteristics of Men, Manners, Opinions, Views*; and Lord Chesterfield had exemplified it. Edmund Burke had given it classic utterance in his famous cry: "The age of chivalry is gone. . . . It is gone, that sensibility of principle, that chastity of honor, which felt a stain like a wound; which inspired courage, while it mitigated ferocity; which ennobled whatever it touched, and under which *vice lost half its evil by losing all its grossness.*" [21] In such an age, the glories of its outward life cannot entirely hide the evil and suffering to which it dooms its victims. It " 'skins and films the ulcerous place,' which it cannot probe or heal,

> 'Whiles rank corruption, mining all within,
> Infects unseen.' " [22]

Its intellectual culture creates the gentleman, while the Church is trying to create saints. Today it creates the "modern" J. Alfred Prufrock, of Mr. Eliot's poem — disillusioned, introspective, proud, secretly despairing and fearful. Newman writes one of his most penetrating passages, as he puts his finger deftly on the weakness of any merely intellectual "modern," whether he be of Periclean Athens, Augustan Rome, Renaissance Florence, eighteenth-century Paris, or nineteenth-century London:

"Their conscience has become a mere self-respect. Instead of doing one thing and then another, as each is called for, in faith and obedience, careless of what may be called the *keeping* of deed with deed, and leaving Him who gives the command to blend the portions of their conduct into a whole, their one object, however unconscious to themselves, is to paint a smooth and perfect surface, and to be able to say to themselves that they have done their duty. When they do wrong, they feel, not contrition, of which God is the object, but remorse, and a sense of degradation. They call themselves fools, not sinners; they are angry and impatient, not humble. They shut themselves up in themselves; it is misery to them to think or to speak of their own feelings; it is misery to suppose that others see them, and their shyness and sensitiveness often become morbid.   As to confession, which is so natural to the Catholic, to them it is impossible; unless indeed, in cases where they have been guilty, an apology is due to their own character, is expected of them, and will be satisfactory to look back upon.   They are victims of an intense self-contemplation." [23]

Lord Shaftesbury began his teaching, says Newman, where he should have ended it — "if his flowers [consistency, 'beauty of sentiment, grace of actions, a right taste in life and manners'] do but last to the end of his revel, he has nothing more to seek." His "philosophical morality" sought mere external embellishment.   It had no conception of such a profound moral virtue as humility; it was content with modesty, whose province is outward deportment.   The driving force of pride is, under such a teaching, turned to account: it becomes *self-respect* — "delicacy and gentleness are its attire, and good sense and sense of honour direct its motions."   This self-respect is no longer a restless agent, but is channeled into industriousness, frugality, honesty, and obedience.   It becomes a safeguard of chastity, the guarantee of veracity.   It "is the very household god of society," inspiring uprightness in everyone, from the servant girl to the head of the family. It develops a horror of exposure, notoriety, ridicule; it shrinks from what are called "scenes"; it is merciless toward the mock-heroic, toward pretense, egotism, adulation.   It teaches men not to eradicate an appetite, or to discipline the emotions, but merely to suppress their feelings, control their tempers, and mitigate the severity and tone of their judgments.   Its sensibilities are shocked by the tragic and the bombastic; hence it brands as "simply out of taste" the unchristian practice of dueling.   In all these respects, the "Religion of Philosophy," the intellectual counterfeit of true religion, appeals only "to what is in nature, and it falls under the dominion of the old Adam."   But its product, taken on its own merits, has a genuine and permanent value.   For that product is the "gentleman."   And the gentleman as a type may be found equally well exemplified in a saint and in an apostate: "Basil and Julian were fellow-students at the schools of Athens; and one became the Saint and Doctor of the Church, the other her scoffing and relentless foe." [24]

iv. *Newman and the Idea of a Gentleman*

Most readers of *The Idea of a University* fail to realize that Newman's famous definition of a gentleman is preceded by a most searching analysis of the eighteenth-century ideal as set up and exalted by Lord Shaftesbury. We have just seen how thoroughly he explores its limitations. Yet in the next, and final, section of Discourse VIII, he presents that ideal as the *beau ideal* of the world, and as the final product of intellectual cultivation at a university, "apart from religious principle," at once assisting and distorting the development of religious character. Newman's definition is, in view of the nature of his auditors, a feat in audacity. He accepts the worldly ideal (remembering the Oxford approximations to it) and sets it up as a value, in the secular sphere, parallel to soul-development in the religious sphere. From his vantage point in the Roman Church, and on the basis of his own unshakable faith in the reality of the Unseen, he has little to fear from a program of education for "gentlemanliness." Hence he boldly and eloquently defines the gentleman in words which, though they are known everywhere, must not be omitted here:

"Hence it is that it is almost a definition of a gentleman to say he is one who never inflicts pain. This description is both refined and, as far as it goes, accurate. He is mainly occupied in merely removing the obstacles which hinder the free and unembarrassed action of those about him; and he concurs with their movements rather than takes the initiative himself. His benefits may be considered as parallel to what are called comforts or conveniences in arrangements of a personal nature: like an easy chair or a good fire, which do their part in dispelling cold and fatigue, though nature provides both means of rest and animal heat without them. The true gentleman in like manner carefully avoids whatever may cause a jar or a jolt in the minds of those with whom he is cast; — all clashing of opinion, or collision of feeling, all restraint, or suspicion, or gloom, or resentment; his great concern being to make every one at their ease and at home. He has his eyes on all his company; he is tender towards the bashful, gentle towards the distant, and merciful towards the absurd; he can recollect to whom he is speaking; he guards against unseasonable allusions, or topics which may irritate; he is seldom prominent in conversation, and never wearisome.   He makes light of favours while he does them, and seems to be receiving when he is conferring.   He never speaks of himself except when compelled, never defends himself by a mere re-tort, he has no ears for slander or gossip, is scrupulous in imputing motives to those who interfere with him, and interprets everything for the best.   He is never mean or little in his disputes, never takes unfair advantage, never mistakes personalities or sharp sayings for arguments, or insinuates evil which he dare not say out.   From a long-sighted prudence, he observes the maxim of the ancient sage, that we should ever conduct ourselves towards our enemy as if he were one day to be our friend.   He has too much good sense to be affronted at insults, he is too well employed to remember injuries, and too indolent to bear malice.   He is patient, forbearing, and resigned, on philosophical principles; he submits to pain, because it is inevitable, to bereavement, because it is irreparable, and to death because it is his destiny.   If he engages in controversy of any kind, his disciplined intellect preserves him from the blundering discourtesy of better, perhaps, but less edu-cated minds; who, like blunt weapons, tear and hack instead of cutting clean, who mistake the point in argument, waste their strength on trifles, misconceive their adversary, and leave the question more in-volved than they find it.   He may be right or wrong in his opinion, but he is too clear-headed to be unjust; he is as simple as he is forcible, and as brief as he is decisive.   Nowhere shall we find greater candour, consideration, indulgence: he throws himself into the minds of his op-ponents, he accounts for their mistakes.   He knows the weakness of human reason as well as its strength, its province and its limits.   If he be an unbeliever, he will be too profound and large-minded to ridicule religion or to act against it; he is too wise to be a dogmatist or fanatic in his infidelity.   He respects piety and devotion; he even supports institutions as venerable, beautiful, or useful, to which he does not assent; he honors the ministers of religion, and it contents him to decline its mysteries without assailing or denouncing them.   He is a friend of religious toleration, and that, not only because his philosophy has taught him to look on all forms of faith with an impartial eye, but also from the gentleness and effeminacy of feeling, which is the attend-ant on civilization.

"Not that he may not hold a religion too, in his own way, even when he is not a Christian.   In that case his religion is one of imagination and sentiment; it is the embodiment of those ideas of the sublime, majestic, and beautiful, without which there can be no large philosophy. Sometimes he acknowledges the being of God, sometimes he invests an unknown principle or quality with the attributes of perfection. And this deduction of his reason, or creation of his fancy, he makes the occasion of such excellent thoughts, and the starting-point of so varied and systematic a teaching, that he even seems like a disciple of Christianity itself. From the very accuracy and steadiness of his logical powers, he is able to see what sentiments are consistent in those who hold any religious doctrine at all, and he appears to others to feel and to hold a whole circle of theological truths, which exist in his mind no otherwise than as a number of deductions." [1]

If this ideal seemed dangerously secular to his audience of 1852, if it seemed so to his later readers, and if it appears equally so to certain readers now, Newman's thought must be seen once more in the context of Oxford in the 1830's. During 1833, on his return from the Mediterranean, he had written his *Church of the Fathers,* a series of sketches for the *British Magazine.* If we turn to the third sketch, "Basil and Gregory," we shall find Newman observing with approval that Basil "would make the monk the true gentleman." He notes that Basil demands of the monk:

"knowledge how to converse; to interrogate without over-earnestness; to answer without desire of display; not to interrupt a profitable speaker, nor to desire ambitiously to put in a word of one's own; to be measured in speaking and hearing; not to be ashamed of receiving, or to be grudging in giving, information . . . The middle tone of voice is best, neither so low as to be inaudible, nor ill-bred from its high pitch. One . . . should be amiable in social intercourse; not aiming to be pleasant by smartness, but cultivating gentleness in kind admonitions. Harshness is ever to be put aside, even in censuring." [2]

We are reminded again, as we read these lines, that Newman's mind and thought were shaped not only by the humanism of Oxford but also, as Tardivel and Gorce have so well emphasized, by the Christian humanism of the early Fathers. Paradoxical as it may seem, the gentleman of Lord Shaftesbury and the gentleman of St. Basil have, to a large extent, the same virtues. And this identity of character, "apart from religious principles," supported Newman in his appeal, over the heads of his Irish audience, as it were, to Catholics throughout the British Isles, for a university education equaling if not surpassing that which Oxford offered, an education which would equip the religious man to live successfully, with dignity and intelligence, in the modern world. He clearly felt that he was presenting an ideal which was valid both in the world and in the Church, one which, if followed, would lift Catholics to the intellectual level of cultivated non-Catholics.

Since we have briefly noted the intellectual context of Newman's idea of a gentleman, a word may be said about its *social* context. Newman's definition was, after all, but a part of a long Victorian effort to clarify a social type. We find this effort in Ruskin's remarkable chapter "On Vulgarity" in *Modern Painters*, where the gentleman's nature is defined in contrast with the vulgarian's "deadness of heart" and "deathful selfishness"; in Tennyson's prolonged preoccupation with the character-traits of his friend Hallam, and of King Arthur; in Thackeray's satires against snobbery and in his Colonel Newcome, whose simple guilelessness makes him "founder in a world of mean, clever people"; in Dickens' repeated failures to portray what he admired but never understood; even in Trollope, though we must go to his *Autobiography* for his most telling and penetrating statement. By the end of the century, says H. V. Routh, "it was apparently difficult to avoid the subject, whether in conversation or in writing a book." [3]   In former ages men had had a perfectly clear conception of the gentleman as a type — neither Chaucer, nor Castiglione, nor Shakespeare, nor Peacham, nor Lord Chesterfield had any doubts. But by the middle of the nineteenth century the industrial revolution had so altered or obliterated the boundary lines between the upper and middle classes that definitions were in urgent demand. The newly powerful middle class aspired to the manners of the well-born, and refused to be enslaved by their commercial prosperity. They determined to keep alive that eighteenth-century tradition which Newman knew so well; that aristocracy of morals and manners, that cult of self-possession and self-respect, which Shaftesbury had represented; at least that "surface Christianity" which was Scott's definition of good breeding. [4]   They added, of course, the strengthening ingredients of middle-class piety, frugality, self-control, patriotism, and puritan devotion to work. By the early 1850's, this effort had resulted in the discreet moralization of the "gentleman," even if, and sometimes because, he had taken up his career in business. The Victorian gentleman might be a merchant, but he sought endlessly to immunize himself from modern, overcrowded, mechanized civilization; he set up his "gentlemanly" ideals as a counterpoise to the industrial revolution which had brought him into being. He cultivated his ideal also as a moral defense against "the stern avatar of democracy." And his final aim was to live the life of a man of good ancestry, good manners, good fortune, and leisurely accomplishments.

Newman's definition is, of course, largely one of intellect and manners. But its social assumptions are unmistakable. If Newman did not follow Aristotle's *Politics* so far as to model his "liberal education" according to the "slave-state system" of ancient Greece, he did have in mind the English social equivalent of the Greek aristocracy. Newman's discourses, as Corcoran has pointed out, reflect the mind of the "landed gentry of England, with its outposts in the English Civil Service, Established Church, Army, and Public Schools," a caste which had a real and legal monopoly of political control over all English life until its decline in the years between 1845 and 1867.[5] In the middle decades of the century, when the English *bourgeoisie* read *Modern Painters* in order to know what pictures to admire and to buy, when they built baronial country houses in which to live like the proudest peers of the realm, when leisure and aristocratic delicacy were becoming an attraction, then it was that Newman's splendid paragraph appeared. In its supple phrasing and liquid rhythm, in its exquisite balances and contrasts, and in its perfect statement of what Newman conceived to be the highest type of intellectual and social excellence, so far as education may produce it, his definition set up a standard both new and old, and always beyond the reach of men. It inspired his contemporaries; it challenges the present day. On its formal side, it belongs, as Dean Stanley said of something else Newman had written, not to provincial theory, but "to the literature of all time."[6]

CHAPTER VI

"THE LOGICAL COGENCY OF FAITH": HOW WE BELIEVE

Shortly before Newman completed the writing of *The Grammar of Assent* (1870), he wrote to a friend: "I suppose [this book] will be my last . . . I have written in all (good and bad) 5 constructive books. My Prophetical Office [the *Via Media*] (which has come to pieces) — Essay on Justification — Development of Doctrine — University Lectures (Dublin) and this." [1] In two respects this brief summary of his work fails to do Newman justice. In the first place, only five years later, in 1875, he was to publish one other substantial book, the *Letter to the Duke of Norfolk*. In the second place, Newman's summary omits a work which his admirers rank high in the literature of apologetics, the *Oxford University Sermons* (1843). This reminds us that Newman's preoccupation with the problem of belief goes back to some of his earliest sermons — that on "The Usurpations of Reason" was preached in 1831. [2] A glance at the word "Faith" in Rickaby's *Index* ("a guide to Newman's thought") will show how continuous and homogeneous was his thinking on the subject of *how we believe*. Passages in the *Grammar*, which we shall later consider, have their foreshadowings, their prefigurings, sometimes their exact anticipation in the *Parochial Sermons*, in the essay on *Development*, in the *University Sermons*. One theme, among others, runs through all these earlier works: faith is committed to "probabilities," and "a good and a bad man will think very different things probable." [3]

By the 1860's Newman was profoundly disturbed by the inertia of the Church in the face of widespread skepticism. He noted that in the current school treatises, if the question arose, "How can a man unschooled in theology and apologetics have sufficient reason for belief in Christianity?" the answer generally was that such a man had reasons sufficient to satisfy his own limited intellect. Little attention seemed to be given to the possibility of holding the right beliefs for the wrong reasons, with the further possibility of repudiating the beliefs at the first pricking of fallacious reasoning. Newman was even more disturbed on finding that educated Catholics received the credentials and the doctrines of the Church mechanically and passively, without weighing their cogency. Too many believers accepted religious doctrines on the word of a Church whose authority the proofs themselves were supposed to establish. To examine this vicious circle seemed to the uncritically devout an admission of a doubt against the faith. Wilfrid Ward records that his father, W. G. Ward, and Newman had found even so able a man as Cardinal Wiseman laboring in a surprising confusion of thought on this subject. In a conversation among the three men in 1859, this confusion became vividly apparent when Newman, with characteristic bluntness, staggered the cardinal by asking, "Then pray, your Eminence, what is the difference between Faith and Prejudice?" [4]

Much as Newman welcomed the "faith that outstrips argument," much as he favored a religion even "more superstitious, more bigoted, more gloomy" than "the religion of the day," he nevertheless realized the titanic challenge of the secular intellect to the Church of his time.[5] He therefore took it upon himself to treat what, in the *Apologia,* he had called "the logical cogency of faith." [6]

i. *Newman on Knowledge and Faith: 1833–68*

What has been called Newman's "Alexandrian mysticism" is clearly apparent in a passage of *The Arians* which foreshadows the great work of 1870. In outlining the teachings of the Church of Alexandria — of Clement and Origen, in particular — Newman writes, in an approving spirit, of the Alexandrian doctrine that the external world "beguiles the imagination of most men with a harmless but unfounded belief in matter as distinct from the senses." From this doctrine, which reminds one of the teachings of Berkeley or Kant, Newman passes on to the Alexandrian idea that the popular argument from final causes is but an "Economia" suited to the multitude, as teaching the existence of God, who "after all dwells intelligibly, prior to argument, in their heart and conscience." [1] In passages such as these one finds the gist of at least one-half of the *Grammar of Assent*.

Similarly Newman's final position regarding the nature and content of faith is anticipated in the *Lectures on Justification* (1838). As Brilioth has noted, in these lectures "Newman maintains a doctrine of *fides formata* in conscious opposition to Luther, but also under the impression of the theory of religious knowledge, which later was to take definite shape, first in the University Sermons, and then in the 'Grammar of Assent.' " [2] Faith is, according to Newman in 1838, "an original means of knowledge, not resolvable into sense, or the faculty of reason, confirmed indeed by experience, as they are, but founded on a supernaturally implanted instinct, an instinct developed by religious obedience." [3] Here we observe an early expression of Newman's teaching of "a right state of heart" or of conscience — in this case an "obedient" state — as preparing us for a kind of knowledge that transcends the knowledge delivered by formal reasoning. We are reminded again that, for Newman, "Man is *not* a reasoning animal; he is a seeing, feeling, contemplating, acting animal," a creature endowed with will and moral judgment.[4] It is in Newman's brilliant letters to *The Times* (1841) — the Tamworth Reading Room articles — that his relative contempt for logic makes its earliest and most brilliant appearance; here it is that some of his finest passages on the primacy of conscience appear. Indeed he was so satisfied with his line of thought that he quoted in the *Grammar* a passage five pages long from the Tamworth letters to point up the distinction between belief as a principle of action as contrasted with knowledge, logic, or argument, which have never converted with a syllogism — "many a man will live and die upon a dogma: no man will be a martyr for a conclusion." [5]

In certain of the *Oxford University Sermons* (1843), which Newman himself regarded as "of the nature of an exploring expedition," there is further study of the nature of faith and knowledge which foreshadows the *Grammar of Assent*. These sermons seek to show the grounds on which the logically untrained believer justifiably holds his belief, namely, through "implicit" or unconscious reasoning. Even when this reasoning is set forth in logical fullness as "explicit reasoning," it is never adequate to account for all that was believed.[6] The unlettered believer thus holds his faith not on explicitly demonstrable grounds — though Newman believes such grounds to be accessible — but by virtue of a "right state of heart."[7] The action of his moral nature has a far deeper *rational* import than is commonly realized. Conscience gives him a glimpse of reality behind the physical world so piercing and convincing that Newman places it on a level with his knowledge of himself, and much higher than his knowledge of the external world as derived through the senses. That this higher knowledge cannot be stated in logical terms is, to Newman, perfectly understandable; indeed he denies that logic is equal to the complete expression of any mental process, since so much of our reasoning is done subconsciously, mingling memories, associations, and emotions with its ratiocinative elements.[8] However, it is all this complex of subconscious activities which propels the mind toward assent. And any account of how we believe must deal with the "whole man," not merely with his conscious reasoning faculty. Newman directs his University sermons at two schools: at the "evidential school" of Lardner, Paley, and Whately, who overvalued "expertness in logical argument," to the exclusion of the nonrational element in belief; and at the Evangelicals, who overvalued the nonrational, the emotional, in religion, to the exclusion of "carnal reason."[9] This explains Newman's preoccupation with "reason *and* faith," his desire to show the "*logical* cogency of faith." Since the University sermons are but exploratory in nature, and incomplete because of the affair of Tract XC, and since their tentative lines of thought are completed in the *Grammar of Assent*, we may pass on to three later attempts to deal with some of the problems treated in 1868–70.[10]

In one of the Dublin lectures, "A Form of Infidelity of the Day," Newman anticipated some of the late-Victorian agnostic objections to considering religious knowledge as any longer "scientific." According to the secular mind, Newman discovered, "religious persuasions are not knowledge, they are not scientific. . . . Christianity has been the bane of true knowledge, for it has turned the intellect away from what it can know, and occupied it in what it cannot." [11]   Such an attitude called for a vigorous and well-thought-out reply.   The *Grammar of Assent* was the ultimate formal answer.   It attempted to show that the modern mind is not violating itself in certain acts of assent which transcend logic, but is following certain laws or patterns which bring certitude in all fields, not merely that of religion.   Modern infidelity must be met with intellectual weapons as sharp as its own, so that religious knowledge can be seen to be as "objective" and "rational" and "ordered" as is secular knowledge.   A few years later, in 1857, we find Newman again wrestling with the problem of a logic or grammar of belief.   He is in the midst of plans for a new translation of the Bible; he designs an elaborate *Prolegomena,* which will counteract the influence of agnostic propaganda.   All that is left of the manuscript — it is believed he destroyed the unfinished text in 1877 — are some notes.   Among them we may observe the following: [12]

"It is as difficult to acquiesce in that we are made for nothing, or that there is no end [purpose] of our being, as to believe the dogmas of a revelation.

"This again is a reason for not being put out at difficulties in revelation when it is made — for while (as I have shown) revelation must be strange, scepticism is as strange or stranger.

"Then there is a God: i.e. utter scepticism is false . . ."

Finally we may note a memorandum which Newman made in 1860, in response to the urgings of W. G. Ward that he compose a sequel to the Oxford sermons on faith and reason.   Unlike many of his Catholic associates, he could not lump together all agnostics and unbelievers as being insincere, or as intellectually blinded by moral corruption.   He knew that many agnostics were thoroughly honest.   He also knew their arguments, sometimes better than they knew them themselves.   Indeed the memorandum, entitled "The Fluctuations of Human Opinion," reveals how thoroughly he understood the skeptic's position.   As Ross has said, "a confirmed unbeliever could not have put his case better than Newman does": [13]

"(1) We cannot get beyond a judgment such that it denies itself soon and melts away into another — nothing fixed and stable.

"(2) Hence what does Catholicism do but arbitrarily fix what is not fixed, and perpetuate by an unnatural and strained force what else would be transitory?   It assumes and wills that this or that should be true which is not true to the mind except for a time or more than something else.

"(3) We cannot get beyond a certain degree of probability about anything, but Catholicism enforces a certainty greater than Mathematics,

"(4) and making it a sin to doubt, artificially prolongs an opinion. It is but an opinion that the Church is infallible, but we commit a man to it and make it a sin to doubt it.   If he argued himself into it, why may he not argue himself out of it?   If it is a conclusion from premisses at first why not always?

"(5) How can there be a revelation; for the certainty of it must depend on uncertain premisses?   Such seems to be the state of human nature.   In this state of things what does Catholicism do but unnaturally prolong a particular state of opinion and pretend to a certainty which is impossible?"

Such is Newman's summary of a very plausible view of the inherent uncertainty of religious opinions.   He so well understood this view — and other agnostic arguments — that Huxley was in time to make his celebrated remark that from certain of Newman's works he could, if he were called upon, "compile a Primer of 'Infidelity.' " [14]   Doubtless no one was better equipped than Newman, by mental endowments, to make a cogent reply to some of the most persuasive arguments of mid-Victorian agnosticism.

ii.   *The Writing of the "Grammar of Assent"*

Ten years before the publication of the *Grammar of Assent*, Newman had contemplated writing a book which would disclose the basis on which minds unacquainted with either philosophy or theology could and did rest their religious belief.   Thus in January of 1860, in a letter to Dr. Meynell, Professor of Philosophy at Oscott, and an admirer of the *Oxford University Sermons*, Newman revealed that he had seriously considered, partly at the urging of "a dear old Protestant friend," the writing of a work which would expand the subject treated in some of the Oxford sermons. "If I wrote a new work," said Newman, "it would be on 'the popular, practical, and personal evidence of Christianity' — *i.e.* as contrasted to the scientific, and its object would be to show that a given individual, high or low, has as much right (has as real rational grounds) to be certain, as a learned theologian who knows the scientific evidence." [1] He would show not *why* men believed but *how* they believed, and this on practical, personal grounds. He would avoid the terminology of the schools — he was always repelled by technical, learned, impersonal language; he would also shun the abstract, and rest his argument on the concrete experience of the individual.

In August, 1866, while Newman and Ambrose St. John were "up at Glion over the Lake of Geneva, a thought came into [his] head as the clue, the 'Open Sesame,' of the whole subject, and [he] at once wrote it down, and . . . pursued it about the Lake of Lucerne." [2] He was to make more attempts at the formulation of his theories than he could enumerate. Many of his ideas no doubt proceeded from some of the notes he had jotted down twenty years before, notes still preserved in the Birmingham Oratory.[3] Apparently he had begun with an examination of the nature and grounds of certitude. This, he felt, was a false start. "It struck me," he wrote in his journal, after the *Grammar* was off the press: " 'You are wrong in beginning with certitude — certitude is only a kind of assent — you should begin with contrasting assent and inference.' On that hint I spoke, finding it a key to my own ideas." [4] And that hint, incidentally, is a clue to the reason for the very unprepossessing initial chapter of the *Grammar of Assent,* opening up, as it does, with a textbook-like series of definitions and distinctions, concerning propositions, inferences, apprehensions, assents.

The actual writing of the book cost Newman many pains. Interruptions were frequent: the negotiations concerning the proposed Oxford Oratory broke in upon his labors in 1867. But the writing was resumed in the summer of that year, and by the summer of 1868 the first draft was nearly finished. When he showed his manuscript to some friends familiar with the theology

of the schools, he was discouraged to find how little they realized the urgency of the difficulties which he was trying to meet,
and how quickly they pounced upon his vocabulary and phrasing
as being at variance with standard Catholic modes of expression.
He had a "haunting fear," as Ward tells us, "of the men who
knew much and understood little," who would think they shat-
tered his teachings when they brought up an array of "orthodox"
expressions.[5] "Every word I publish," he said nervously, "will
be malevolently scrutinized, and every expression which can possibly be perverted sent straight to Rome . . . I shall be fighting
under the lash."[6] Moreover, he was keenly conscious of his
ignorance of the vast literature of metaphysics. With Dr. Meynell, who read the proof sheets, Newman corresponded at length,
sometimes concerning Newman's highly individual use of words,
such as "instinct," often concerning Newman's want of familiarity with philosophical language. "It sometimes amazes me,"
he confessed, "that I have ventured to write on a subject which
is even accidentally connected with" metaphysics.[7] Indeed he
had some very bad half-hours, when it seemed only proper and
reasonable to give over the work altogether. But he toiled on,
writing and rewriting, as was his method, until he had said precisely what he had intended to say. According to some reports,
he wrote some of the chapters ten times, and the last chapter
"perhaps twenty times."[8] There were moments when he was
"quite frightened lest the labor of thought might inflict on
[him] some terrible retribution at [his] age."[9] One thing that
aided him in his labors was the peace and quiet of his seclusion.
Jennings, who lived in Birmingham during Newman's Oratorian
period, has told, in his little book, *Cardinal Newman,* of the "tiny
country house of the Oratorians, a few miles distant, at Rednal
. . . a pretty little spot, well away from the smoke and din of
Birmingham . . . [where] Dr. Newman [would] sometimes
spend days in absolute seclusion . . . It was here that the most
closely reasoned of his works, the *Grammar of Assent,* was composed."[10]

The book was ready in February of 1870; a specimen bound
copy was sent to Newman on February 21 — his sixty-ninth birthday. The dedication was to his friend, Serjeant Bellasis "in

memory of a long, equable, and sunny friendship" — a dedication
which, according to stories more or less apocryphal, nearly passed
in the final proof as "in memory of a long squabble and funny
friendship." [11]   Newman's book met with prompt criticism.
Leslie Stephen and Fitz-James Stephen both attacked it in
Fraser's Magazine.   By the end of the year, Father Harper, the
Jesuit, had published an elaborate attack on it from the scholastic
standpoint; [12] Newman's method, of course, had indeed run
counter to scholastic precedent, in dwelling almost exclusively on
conscience as the argument for the existence of God.   Other
critics quarreled with Newman for appearing to discount the
argument for theism from the evidence of "design" in nature.
It is worth noting that long before the evolutionary theory had
altered its tenability, Newman had had profound suspicions of
Paley's famous argument from "design" in his *Evidences of
Christianity* (1794) and his *Natural Theology* (1802).   On
this point Newman seems to have been intellectually in advance
of Huxley, who remained satisfied with the argument from "design" until the appearance of *The Origin of Species* in 1859.[13]
"I believe in design," Newman replied to his critics, "because I
believe in God; not in a God because I see design." [14]   In spite
of all adverse criticism, the *Grammar of Assent* had a wide cir-
culation and made Newman deeply happy.   He knew that he
had merely sketched in his theory — his book was but an *Essay
in Aid*.   With self-consolation, he wrote to a friend: "It is what
it is, and it is not what it isn't — and what it isn't most people will
expect that it is."   To another friend, he said quite simply: "I
have got a great burden off my mind." [15]

iii.   *Aims and Methods*

One will look in vain for a copy of the *Grammar of Assent*
among the books of logic on library shelves.   This is because
Newman's work is primarily descriptive; it is a treatise on the
psychology of assent or acceptance of a belief.   Furthermore, it
is predominantly empirical, not theoretical.   It makes no attempt to show men how they ought to think, but rather how they
do think, in the field of religious belief.   Most of the *Grammar*
is devoted to an elaborate study of the mental operations under-

lying the processes of inference, apprehension, assent, and certitude; a great deal of it is devoted to pointing out and illustrating (often with great force and poetic beauty) the differences between formal and informal inference, and "real" and "notional" apprehension or assent. The work itself is directed at a chosen body of readers: those who accept Newman's postulates — the existence of God, the immortality of the soul, the freedom of the will, the existence of sin and virtue, the possibility of a revelation and of a mediator between God and man. "Even after these postulates are accepted," as the Abbé Dimnet has noted, "Newman does not think that faith will necessarily follow." [1] A "right state of heart" must be present. It is futile to try arguing men into believing.[2] Hence the *Grammar of Assent* makes no attempt to win converts to Christianity; it only attempts to enlighten believers as to the proper intellectual grounds for holding the beliefs they already hold. "I am not proposing," Newman warns us, "to set forth the arguments which issue in the belief of [Christian] doctrines, but to investigate what it is to believe in them, what the mind does, what it contemplates, when it makes an act of faith." [3] He is simply defining, ordering, and classifying certain mental processes which lead up to the act of faith.

Thus the title of the book should give less trouble than it has to certain critics. Hutton, for instance, denies that the book is a grammar in any sense whatever.[4] But Hutton, like many other critics of Newman, seems never to have noticed a very revealing expression, dropped casually into the Preface of the third edition of the *Oxford University Sermons*, an expression which illuminates at once Newman's whole approach to the problem of reasoning. Newman writes that reasoning, when retrospectively analyzing itself, is "called *logic*, which is a sort of *rhetoric*." [5] This means that, for Newman, logic is hardly an instrument for gaining new truth, but rather a verbalizing of truth gained by other methods; it means also that logic may properly be used for *persuasion*. Hence it is that many Newman readers, ignorant of his conception of logic — which was that of Whately — are shocked by what seems an unscrupulous employment of reasoning to support or attain to conclusions which flout the first principles of logic. If, however, logic be conceived as merely a method of analysis ánd persuasion, it takes on something of the nature of rhetoric. And Newman's book might well bear the title, *An Essay in Aid of a Rhetoric of Belief: or How to Hold One's Belief Most Cogently and to Express It Most Persuasively.*

If, then, Newman's aim is mainly psychological, justificatory, and persuasive, what is his method? In general it may be said to be what the aim demanded: not a metaphysical, demonstrative, theological procedure, but a highly personal, empirical, inductive method. It is in fact, as were most of Newman's efforts, remarkably autobiographical. Newman writes for the average educated man, in an easy, familiar, personal style, professedly only tentative rather than final in his thinking (as the full title of his book indicates). Though inductive in his method — generalizing from a host of concrete experiences — he nevertheless aims at wholes, at broad, general effects. He "always leaves the impression," as Juergens well observes, "that he is investigating a living subject; there is a complete absence of scientific formalism, of adequate definitions and divisions, of clear-cut distinctions and a strictly logical order." [6] There were drawbacks and hazards, of course, in this method; but Newman was convinced that "words are incomplete exponents of ideas," and that "it were as easy to create what is real as to define it." [7] Hence he is willing to suggest rather than to define: "Instead of using one word for a strictly determined idea, he prefers to check up his terms, to limit their meaning, or rather to suggest his idea, by the use of several words, each only an approximation of that meaning, but all of them converging in such a manner as to lead the reader into the full notion of the writer. In other terms his method is descriptive." [8] Here we see again the Ciceronian manner observed in *The Idea of a University* — surveying the subject from various lights, advancing and retiring from it, illustrating, confirming, comparing, "till at last the hearer feels ashamed of doubting a position which seems built on a foundation so strictly argumentative." [9]

Structurally, Newman's book is as individual as his general method. At first glance it appears curiously arbitrary. One critic has remarked that Newman's method throughout "suggests less logical sequence than musical arrangement, where a single theme is presented again and again, with manifold variations and ever-shifting harmonies." [10]   Newman loved the music of Beethoven; in some ways the patterns of the *Grammar of Assent* may remind one of the complexities of a Beethoven quartet; in both cases the full import of the work is discernible only after the work as a whole has been experienced, and after the mind has had time to view it in all its parts and as a unity.   Strictly speaking, however, the *Grammar* falls into two Parts, the first Part dealing with assent and apprehension, with especial reference to "real assent"; the second Part contrasting assent and inference, in order to set out in relief the faculty of "implicit reasoning" (long ago dealt with in the *Oxford University Sermons*), now defined and treated as "the illative sense."   These two principles, real assent and the illative sense, are applied, as we shall see, at the ends of Parts I and II to matters of faith or religion.   The Abbé Dimnet, however, suggests that Newman's two-part plan is in reality a three-part plan: first, a discussion of all possible intellectual attitudes toward a given proposition (Chapters I–IV); second, and most original, a treatise on "the art of thought" (evidently Chapters VI–IX); and third, a consideration of the proofs which satisfy Newman in regard to Natural and Revealed Religion (Chapters V and X).[11]   However one may wish to view the structure of Newman's book, many readers will always regard it as not altogether successful.   It bears the marks of Newman's isolation from so much of contemporary thought; it conforms to none of the recognized categories, but is a fabric interwoven (with a skill which delights but sometimes puzzles) of many strands of thought — logical, psychological, historical, and literary.⟩ Moreover, Newman departs from his usual custom of informing the reader at once of what he is to expect; instead he opens his work with two rather formal chapters on the "modes of holding propositions."   It is not until the beginning of the more important half of his book (the opening of Part II) that Newman states definitely the real nature of his inquiry, namely, the analysis of the psychology of belief.[12]   Yet, in spite of all that may be said against Newman's method, it will always have its admirers. They will note a kind of artistry — almost a sly, mischievous artistry — in a book which begins with the dry classification of propositions and ends eloquently with a passage from the Fourth Gospel, "I am the Good Shepherd, and I know Mine, and Mine know me . . ."

Another feature of Newman's method is his individual, sometimes arbitrary, use of language. It is not only arbitrary and personal, but also sometimes quite loose, and very frequently "old-fashioned." And underlying his informal use of words, there is his genuine despair of language. "He has no confidence in a single word's power to convey his idea in full . . . He [knows] that words have different connotations with every person"; hence he purposely multiplies synonyms and practically equivalent expressions. Juergens has compiled from the Oxford sermons alone a list of some sixty-five expressions, varying in length from one word to an ample phrase, which Newman employs to describe the moral state which ordinarily precedes and coexists with faith.[13] With such a skeptical view of language, Newman naturally breaks with the schools and gives to such words as "opinion," "presumption," and "speculation" a meaning all his own. For him, to "investigate" is right and proper; to "inquire" is not;[14] the *Grammar of Assent* is an investigation, not an inquiry, for "inquiry presupposes non-assent," or doubt. Newman also handles his language loosely: for example, as Juergens has shown, "certitude," or the mental state of being certain, is used in two quite different senses throughout the *Grammar*; and "probability" — one of the key words in the book — is nowhere given a clean-cut definition, but, like "certitude," is employed in two senses.[15] D'Arcy has observed, in addition, the extent to which Newman's vocabulary bears the denotations of the seventeenth and eighteenth centuries. Thus for Newman "speculation" means not a conjecture or a venture on chances, but the contemplation of mental operations and their results as opposed to experience; the word "probable" is constantly used in contrast with "demonstrable"; "sense" is frequently used where we today should say "intellect."[16] In stating the moral basis of religious belief, Newman regularly uses the words "notional" and "assent" in precisely the fashion in which his old favorite Evangelical,

Thomas Scott, employed them in his *Essays on the Most Important Subjects of Religion* (1793).[17]   In 1881, Lord Blachford noted that in discussing religious belief, in an informal conversation, Newman "recurred to the familiar topic that *instinct*, which is unanalyzable argument, is often truer than what is logically cogent" — showing a use of "instinct" which is found throughout the *Grammar* and which perplexed Newman's good friend and counselor, Dr. Meynell, the Catholic philosopher.[18]   All this means, quite simply, that Newman's terminology must be understood in its historical relations.   The present-day reader of the *Grammar of Assent* will do well to remember that the author who in 1885 as well as in 1859 relied on Dr. Johnson's dictionary for his definitions of "reason" and "body," respectively,[19] was employing a terminology in 1868–69 which comprised not only current English words and expressions, appropriated for his own special purposes, but also the traditional vocabulary of Anglican divines and Oxford scholars.   Newman's language is essentially the language of Locke, Butler, Whately and the Noetics.

The diction of the *Grammar*, one may say in conclusion, is striking evidence of Newman's limited objective.   In a decade reverberant of argument over the impact of Darwinism on religion, Newman continued to answer the older and now less formidable agnosticism, which tended to substitute the God of natural philosophy for the God of conscience.   In his very choice and use of words, he continues the battle with Paley and the Evidential School of Apologists in England; he aims in 1870 at meeting the arguments of the Oxford common room in the 1830's.[20]

If Newman's *Grammar of Assent* is to be understood properly only in its historical relations, in respect to certain of his ideas and much of his terminology, it is necessary to traverse what for many readers is a rather tiresome domain, the field of sources and affinities.   Let us examine, however, as briefly and as profitably as possible, Newman's chief debts to the past.

iv.   *Sources and Affinities*

The deepest source of Newman's theory of assent was, one hardly need say, his own temperament — the nature of his own mind, and the data supplied by his personal experience in morals and religion.　By nature he was "Platonic"; he took a spiritual or mystical view of the world, in which the natural and the supernatural are but related planes in one divine system.　We know that he was confirmed in this view by his readings in the Fathers, especially Clement and Origen, whose broad "philosophy" — in the sense, almost, of "philosophy of history" — came, as we have noted, like music to his inward ear.　They emphasized in him that "real" hold on the supernatural which is so characteristic of him, and which is the source of the "mystery of Newman."　As he had written in the *Essay on Development*, the Fathers were not "opposed to inquiries into the intellectual basis of Christianity," but held "that men were not obliged to wait for logical proof before believing; the majority were to believe first on presumptions and let intellectual proof come as their reward." [1]　Even some of his terminology, as Przywara has shown, comes from Clement.　"Clement of Alexandria's trio," says Juergens, "πίστις — (γνῶσις — ἀγάπη) — ὅρασις, which St. Augustine borrowed and rendered '*credere* — (*intelligere* — *diligere*) — *videre*,' should, then, be the source of Newman's 'Love — Faith — Wisdom or Enlargement.' " [2]

On the other hand, along with this highly mystical element in Newman's nature, there went a strongly empirical one.　Here the great confirmer and influence was the English philosopher, John Locke.　Though Newman could never agree with Locke's statement that assent admits of degrees, or that assent should be directly proportioned to inference, nevertheless, as John Francis Cronin has shown, he found in Locke much that was immediately assimilable: e.g. that "man knows first, and then only is able to prove syllogistically"; that the syllogism is "not the only nor the best way of reasoning"; that men often see the connection between proofs without recourse to logic; that "God has not been so sparing to men as to make them barely two-legged creatures, and left it to Aristotle to make them rational." [3]　Indeed, like Newman, Locke admits that probabilities may so group themselves as to lead to certainty.　As for the value of logic, Newman's whole concept of its nature and value may be found in Locke's assertion: "Syllogism, at best, is but the art of fencing with the little knowledge we have, without making any addition to it." [4]   Moreover, Locke's nominalism appears here and there in the tissue of Newman's argument, giving rise to the charges of Lebreton, Grandmaison, Baudin, Fairbairn, and D'Arcy.[5] Locke dismissed abstract ideas as merely names, mental fictions useful in ordinary speech, but expressing no real relation and having no independent reality of their own.   There can be no doubt that Newman was more concerned with the real, the concrete, than with mere notions or concepts: "In this world of sense we have to do with things far more than with notions." [6]

In the conduct of argument Newman was, of course, deeply influenced by Whately and by Aristotle.   The latter was by far the greater source of Newman's epistemology.   Yet it is not to Aristotle's *Logic* that we must turn for Newman's originals, but to the *Nicomachean Ethics*, particularly the sixth book.   In Aristotle's teachings he found that reason and logic are not coextensive, that there is a personal element in thought which transcends logic.   The use of logic never brings us to first principles; this is the function of intelligence (νοῦς), which intuitively grasps these truths.   Nor, at the other end of the chain, can logic attain concrete facts; this is the function of prudence (φρόνησις).   In another passage, as Cronin points out, Aristotle speaks of the νοῦς in a way which is virtually a definition of Newman's "illative sense": "Ultimates as well as primary definitions are grasped by the Intelligence (νοῦς) and not reached by reasoning: in demonstrations Intelligence apprehends the immutable and primary definition; in practical inference it apprehends the ultimate and contingent fact, and the minor premise." [7]   Like Newman, Aristotle regards the personal and intuitive element in thought as so important that the "unproved assertions of experienced and elderly people, or of prudent men, are as much deserving of attention as those which they support by proof, for experience has given them an eye for things, and they see correctly." [8]   From Aristotle also came the confirmation that it is not the notional (abstract thought), but the real that leads to action; Aristotle notes that prudence (*phronesis*) deals with action and with the particular facts which are connected with them.[9]   Finally from Aristotle, the "oracle of nature and of truth," came the doctrine that "a special preparation of mind is required for each separate department of inquiry." [10]

Another source of Newman's thought in the *Grammar of Assent* was Bishop Butler's *Analogy* and the *Rolls Sermons*. From Butler, Newman derived three main teachings: (i) that, in religion, conscience is the chief source of most men's real motives of credibility; (ii) that there is an analogy or parallel between nature and supernature, the former only "economically" or "sacramentally" connected with the latter, and therefore leading one to believe in "the unreality of material phenomena"; and (iii) that "Probability is the guide of life." Cronin has drawn attention to a common misunderstanding in regard to the third of these doctrines. Newman tells us in the *Apologia* that his own view of "probabilities converging to certainty" is distinct from the teaching of either Butler or Keble. Keble did not hope for certainty through any act of reasoning, but was satisfied with an assent based on love.[11] Butler's teaching was that only God knew truth with certitude; to man, however, only "probability is the guide of life." [12] From an examination of Butler's doctrine in general there emerges the fact that for Butler "probability" is simply a *practical* guide for action, and not, as for Newman, a speculative principle by which one may attain to certainty in complex moral matters. Butler's statement was thus more of a stimulus to Newman for further thinking than an expression which Newman merely elaborated upon. Thus the Butlerian doctrine of probability as the guide of action becomes, for Newman, the guide of reasoning in matters of religion where a real, concrete assent is desired.

The influence of Keble followed the same lines as Butler's, except that Keble as a living person whom Newman loved gave greater substance and vitality to the doctrines involved. Keble reinforced the idea of analogy between the natural and the supernatural worlds; and he improved on Butler's theory of "probability" by adding the doctrine of "love," which became in time "the right state of mind and heart." Juergens has admirably summed up the respective influences of Butler and Keble on Newman as follows:

"Butler broadened his intellect, Keble warmed his heart and imagination; Butler's teaching was notional, Keble's real; Butler worked on Newman's conduct through intellectual principles, Keble through images and acts; Butler was a book, a method, Keble, a living person; Butler was what a philosopher's treatise is to a disciple, Keble, what a mother's ways and words are to a loving son; Keble was Butler's philosophy 'realized' and personified." [13]

Passing from influences to affinities, one is struck at once, in the literature on Newman, by the frequency with which the names of Coleridge, Kant, and Pascal appear in connection with the *Grammar of Assent* and the *University Sermons*. Contrary to the opinions of many, Newman owes no debt whatever to Coleridge, whom he did not read until 1835, when his own theory of knowledge and faith was fully outlined.[14] In fact when Newman in 1839 credited Coleridge with helping prepare for the Oxford Movement, he declared unequivocably that the great Romantic "indulged in a liberty of speculation which no Christian can tolerate, and advocated conclusions which are often heathen rather than Christian." [15] So little mark did Coleridge seem to leave on Newman's mind that in old age he stated in a letter that he had "never read a line of Coleridge" — an instance of Newman's memory being at fault.[16] Between the two men, however, there is a curious affinity which, when examined, further illuminates Newman's thought. Both men are concerned with the distinction between what Coleridge calls the Understanding (*Verstand*) and the Reason (*Vernunft*), between what Newman called, respectively, logic and the illative sense. Both men believed that man arrives at religious truth differently from the way he arrives at the truth in formal science. In the latter field, conclusions are drawn solely by the logical faculty, the *Verstand*, which deals with evidences and demonstration. In attaining to supernatural truths, however, a particular disposition or quality of mind is indispensable: the *Vernunft*, or the illative sense, which accepts rather than defines,[17] which gathers up into one act of knowing a mass of implicit reasons, memories, associations, desires. In all this, according to both Newman and Coleridge, personality and the will have their part in the knowledge and acceptance of truth. All is concrete and real; true knowledge is

never merely abstract.   Finally, both thinkers give a large place
to conscience in their respective theories of knowledge.   The following might very well have been written by Newman: "That
I am conscious of something within me," says Coleridge, "per-
emptorily commanding me to do to others as I would they should
do to me; — in other words a categorical (that is, primary and
unconditional) imperative; . . . is a fact of which I am no less
conscious . . . than I am of an appearance presented by my outward senses." [18]   This paralleling of the data of conscience with
the data of the senses, the suggestion that the epistemological
value of the former is as great as that of the latter, is a remarkable instance of two great minds, wholly uninfluenced by each
other, arriving at virtually the same conclusion by different
routes.[19]

That Newman's thought is at times peculiarly Kantian has
been remarked by many critics.   Here the possibility of an influence would seem to be very great.   Yet, although Newman
actually read Kant shortly before sketching his plans for the
Grammar, there is little in his book which reminds one directly
of Kantian thought.[20]   Indeed there is more to remind us of
Berkeley (though Newman in 1863 warned a correspondent,
"You may call me a Berkelian, which I am not").   Thirty years
earlier, we find him writing in a Berkelian spirit, in words like
the following (1834):

"while a man holds the moral governance of God as *existing in and
through his conscience,* it matters not whether he believes his senses
or not.   For, at least, he will hold the external world as a *divine* intimation . . . To what extent Berkeley denied the existence of the
external world I am not aware; nor do I mean to go so far myself
(far from it) as to deny the existence of matter, though I should deny
that *what we saw* was more than accidents of it, and say that space
perhaps is but a condition of the objects of sense, not a reality." [21]

The passage, as a whole, is very close to Berkeley, though for
Newman the existence of an object is not, as for Berkeley, its
"being perceived" — *esse* is *percipi.*   We shall see later that
Newman attributes to "instinct" the fact that man and brute are
aware, in their senses, of something distinct from and beyond the

mere phenomena they perceive. In Cronin's paraphrase, "man can do, what the brute cannot, rationalize to a notion of a *cosmos*, a system of order, law, and unity, of which the various perceptions of his senses are but effects and phenomena." This attitude, Cronin observes, would be called by modern scholastics "perceptionism." [22] To this extent, at least, Newman's thought approximates that of Berkeley.

Evidence that Newman was reading Kant and meditating on the problems of sensation, consciousness, and faith is supplied by entries in his diary, first published by Przywara. In February and November, 1859, he set down some notes on the basis of our knowledge of the external world:

"I have a sensation of colours and forms — this is one thing. I have a persuasion that these colours and forms convey to me the presence, etc. of external objects — this is a second thing. I have said that the sensation is not the object of faith but of consciousness — but the second is an object of faith — its truth [the presence of external objects *in themselves*] is not bound up in that act of consciousness by which I know I am [but is the result of an act of *faith*] . . . I grant or I assume, that the soul would not think without some external stimulus; that if it were cut off from all external communication from the external world, it would pass this life in a sort of torpor." [23]

Here we find Newman dwelling on what Kant calls the *noumenal* world (things in themselves) and the *phenomenal* world (things as they appear to our senses); the former he takes on faith, the latter (the world of "colours and forms") he knows through his consciousness, by which he knows that he himself exists. In another entry, dated February 4, 1860, Newman is directly and subtly arguing with Kant:

"Kant, whose philosophy I have been reading in Chalybaus, would say as to consciousness: 'Yes, it bears witness to internal facts of the mind, but it is impossible to connect them, whatever they are, with anything external to it.' Well then, I say: — You can indeed reduce me to a state of absolute scepticism about everything external to consciousness — but this is a reductio ad absurdum of all knowledge external to us whatever, of senses as well (I should add much more than) supersensuous knowledge — but if you do not go to this extreme length which makes it hopeless to reason or investigate at all you must allow something — and all I ask you to allow is this — that it is true that I am — or that my consciousness that I am represents the fact external to my consciousness (viz.) of my existence.   Now see what is involved in this one assumption, viz. My consciousness that I am is not immediate, but indirect — Sentio ergo sum.   In this is involved therefore the presence of a faculty by which from what I have experience of I acquire the certainty of that which I have not experience, viz. my existence, my existence being a fact external to consciousness. — But if one external unexperienced fact may be known by reasoning upon experience, perhaps another may.   Therefore the idea is not absurd that as from 'sentio' I infer the existence of myself, so from 'conscientiam habeo' I infer the existence of God, and again from the phenomena of sense I have the existence of matter." [24]

To what extent Newman does justice to Kant in this passage or draws valid inferences, it is not our present business to determine — we should need, for one thing, more than this isolated entry in the diary, and also a knowledge of just which of Kant's works Newman was reading.   It is enough here to observe that in writing the *Grammar of Assent* Newman had already traversed at least a substantial portion of Kantian thought, and that he decided, in the end, to return to his original starting point, to that moralism which informs all his thinking, to that witness of the conscience which for him is as eloquent as the witness of the senses.   And we are reminded also that throughout his thought it is personality which alone is real — the great Self and Newman's self.   Here, as Jean Guitton penetratingly observes, he is like Berkeley: "he sees in the world only persons; whatever has not that character is shadow, symbol, or notion." [25]

The affinity between Newman and Pascal, noted by nearly all writers on Newman, is discernible at several points.   That faith cannot be produced by acts of ratiocination is at the root of Pascal's famous aphorism, "The heart has its reasons which the reason cannot know."   Both Newman and Pascal knew that to believe we must wish and will to believe; further we must engage in "acts of religion," mortifications, observances: "This," says Pascal, "will make you believe by the very laws of your nature and will stupefy [*abêtira*] your reason." [26]   Pascal's choice of *abêtira* has all the daring realism associated with Newman; both men knew what simplicity is required of true believers. They also knew that religion requires something *heroic* in man: faith must be a "wager," says Pascal; faith has its *ventures*, says Newman.[27]   Even Newman's doctrine of "probability" has a parallel in the great French mystic, as Stewart has shown in *The Holiness of Pascal*: man is shown as he is, and then as he ought to be; the reader is perplexed; then Pascal shows him a "particular people," the existence of the Bible, the fact of man's "fall." "The free thinker mutters the word 'illusion,' " — but Pascal reminds him that in view of man's predicament, the "probabilities" make the venture of faith worth taking.[28]   This is roughly Newman's method.   On the whole, though no influence can be determined, there is an extremely interesting similarity between Newman's method and thought and those of Pascal.   Actual mentions of Pascal are frequent in Newman's works: he once recommended the *Pensées* to a lady who was troubled in spirit;[29] and in the *Grammar* he gives long quotations from that work in comparing Pascal with Montaigne.[30]

Newman had affinities, finally, with at least two other groups of thinkers: the Pragmatists, and the Scholastic philosophers (the continuators of the thought of St. Thomas Aquinas).   That he could remind one, at times, of two such divergent schools of philosophy is evidence once more of the complexities and paradoxes of his teachings.   His closeness to the Pragmatists is much greater, on the whole, than is his closeness to the Scholastics. Wilfrid Ward tells us in his *Last Lectures* that the eminent Pragmatist, F. C. S. Schiller, declared in a letter to him that "Newman was one of the forerunners and anticipators of pragmatism."[31] Newman's pragmatism and that of Schiller, William James, or John Dewey are alike, however, only in a negative way; that is, both protest against identifying actual human reason with "the description of it in logical textbooks"; both insist on a personal equation in the attainment of truth; and both remind us of the implications in philosophy of the idea that "Life is for action." Schiller's objection to formal logic is very similar to Newman's: in abstracting the meaning of words as used by the concrete individual, says Schiller, we render logic practically useless; we drain words of their meaning. Actually we cannot abstract from the psychological processes of thought; in logic, judgment is central, and, according to Dewey, "judgment is not logical at all, but personal and psychological." [32] Besides this protest against intellectualism, pragmatism, on its negative side, protests also against the impersonal approach to truth, which issues in skepticism about the "real world" of our daily lives, in the "idealism" of Kant and his followers. On the other hand, when we look at certain facts with our whole being, "it seems," says William James, "as if our passional and volitional nature lay at the root of all our convictions." [33] Newman, of course, agrees with this line of thought, but he parts company with the Pragmatists when he declares that this personal and concrete way of thinking may lead to error if the "right moral disposition" is absent. Finally, if, as Newman emphasizes, "Life is for action," then knowledge is "not something separate and self-sufficing," but experimental, practical, purposive, involved in the process by which life is sustained. Knowledge and belief are rules for action; thinking is one step in the production of active habits. However, Newman is more willing than the Pragmatists to consider the functions of merely "notional" thinking. Nor would he accept the popular watchword of pragmatism, that "truth is what works." We have no right to disparage dogmatically any truths of which we cannot see the pragmatic value; they may, according to Newman, have a bearing on our welfare which our limited faculties cannot apprehend. The Pragmatist's disparagement of metaphysics and theology finds no echo in Newman.

One of the objects of J. F. Cronin's *Cardinal Newman: His Theory of Knowledge* is "to show that the teaching of Newman can, in all major points, be harmonized with the philosophy of Aristotle, St. Thomas, and the neo-scholastics." [34] How far the author has succeeded in his attempt it is not our purpose to determine; we may, however, summarize his discussion for the light it may throw on Newman's aims and methods. In so far as Newman was Aristotelian in epistemology, he was scholastic. But there are scholastic affinities also in his conviction that *truth is attainable*: skepticism seemed to Newman unreasonable. He could not sympathize with Descartes' famous initial step of universal doubt; he thought of truth as verifiable by objective evidence, tested by its consistency with itself. Like the scholastics, also, he upheld the validity of the ordinary sources of knowledge. He valued the reflection of the mind on the data of *consciousness*, which, though not an initial faculty of knowing, enables men, on thinking and reasoning, to "know that they know." [35] He valued also the *senses*, as being the chief means for acquiring knowledge of the material world; they have their limitations, and do not convey knowledge other than of the "phenomenal" or "accidental," yet they may be tested, corrected, verified, and trusted as far as they go. Newman had the scholastic's unwillingness to think of the senses with the transcendentalist's disparagement. Above all, he valued *reason* as a source of knowledge. Not limited to time or place, reason supplies the deficiencies of sense, though it does not perceive many things directly. As Cronin summarizes:

"It is a faculty of proceeding from things that are perceived to things which are not, it asserts one thing because of another thing. It is an act of the mind by which, knowing one thing, it advances to know another. The reason receives the data of sense and advances to notions, to universal ideas which have no formal existence in the external world. In doing this it compares phenomena, perceives how they are alike and unlike at once, groups and discriminates, forms classes and divisions, thus from the particular and singular data of sense forming ideas valid for all classes and groups." [36]

A final source of knowledge, for Newman, is the validity of human *testimony*. He is willing to rely on the broad generalizations of history, to believe in the value and reliability of manuscripts and other documents.

This is not the place to discuss what Cronin calls Newman's "potential contribution to scholasticism," but we may note in passing that this contribution consisted in his analysis of assent, the "counterpart of the supernatural act of faith"; his theory of implicit reason and of converging probabilities; his realistic handling of human thinking, apart from textbooks; and, perhaps most important, his emphasis on personality, the "whole man," in the reasoning process.[37] In all this, Newman may reasonably

be said to stand out as a potential *ally* of scholasticism, so definite
are his affinities with it at certain points.

v. *"The Grammar of Assent"* (1870): *"Cor ad Cor Loquitur"*

No analysis of Newman's treatment of assent can be made easy.
To simplify his statements is to run the hazards of distortion and
misrepresentation.   Nor can the subtly spun arguments be para-
phrased or enlivened without, to some extent, falsifying Newman's purpose.   It is impossible to condense or dramatize the
Grammar for the lazy-minded reader, or for anyone who has no
taste for intellectual exercise.   In short, no wholly satisfactory
summary of Newman's book is possible.   "Of all the works of
Newman," writes Dr. Benard, "not excepting the *Essay on Development*, the *Grammar of Assent* is the most difficult to summarize.   We might almost as easily reduce to its 'essentials' a
landscape by Corot.   Every detail, every tiny illustrative point
we eliminate, turns out, to our surprise, to have been indispensable to the general effect." [1]   Hence, the reader who wishes
profitably to follow the present comparatively brief exposition
must be prepared for a considerable loss in the proportion, richness, subtlety, and completeness of the original argument.   It
will be to his advantage, however, to accept Newman's terms accurately, and to follow closely the course of his reasoning to the
end.   We shall cling to as much of Newman's illustrative matter as space permits, and, at the risk of doing him some injustice,
we shall judiciously select and simplify in following the various
lines of his thought.

a. *Newman's Three Guiding Principles*

Before we turn to the contents of the *Grammar of Assent*, we
should observe the three key-principles which open the secret of
his system to us, and which have been admirably summarized in
Cronin's study of Newman's epistemology.   The *first*, as we
know, is that "Life is for action . . . Life is not long enough
for a religion of inferences . . . To act you must assume, and
that assumption is faith." [1]   If all men followed the logic of
Whately, or the demand of Locke and the Victorian scientists for
rigorous demonstration, little would be left for most men but

skepticism. "Certitude is for the intellectual *élite*." [2] Further-more, logical consistency or coherence is after all but a static test of truth; life gives a dynamic test; and action as well as thought takes part in the pursuit of truth.

Newman's *second* principle is that "the whole mind reasons," not merely the formal intellect; thought is personal as well as universal. In contrast to Aristotelian logic — an unvarying in-strument of thought — Newman sets up what McRae calls "the living reality of immediate life." [3] In the *Apologia* he had al-ready declared that "it is the concrete being that reasons; pass a number of years, and I find my mind in a new place; how? the whole man moves; paper logic is but the record of it." [4] New-man's theory of knowledge will take into account such facts as prejudices, extraneous influences, and above all the will. Since, as Newman says in a letter to Wilberforce, "syllogisms and states of mind are incommensurables, it is obvious what room there is for interference of the will" in the attainment of knowledge; "none are so deaf as those who won't hear." [5] A good will, the right moral disposition, are necessary to preserve men from skep-ticism, to enable them to attain certitudes never attainable by the speculative reason. In this, as we have seen, Newman shows a remarkable affinity with Kant, who in *The Critique of Pure Rea-son* makes precisely the same observation.[6]

The *third* key-principle in the *Grammar of Assent* is that rea-soning should be treated as it is actually found in life, not as men are told it should be. Newman regarded abstract reasoning as "always dangerous," since it had little contact with life. Certain of his critics, fearing nominalism, liked to point out that the mind can know essences and universals which do not vary with the in-dividual; but Newman always insisted that essences mean little for life. He preferred to go by individual, concrete fact. And so well did he succeed that even his most formidable English opponent, Father Harper, declared with admiration: "Never, we believe, have the manifold and all but contradictory complex-ities of the human mind been treated with such unscrupulous reality." [7] In an age when England was empirically agnostic and atheistic, he would be empirically theistic. As Aquinas was the embodiment of the deductive rationalism of the thirteenth century, Newman would ally himself with the inductive temper of the nineteenth.[8]

b. *The Notional and the Real*

Hence it is that Newman reverses the trend taken by the great scholastic philosophers. Starting with Aristotle's theory of universal ideas, these philosophers had long ago won their victory over the nominalists (for whom universals were but names), establishing, in the philosophy of Aquinas, the validity of universals. Ever since this triumph in the Middle Ages, the scholastic system has constantly been seeking the universal idea, the cause, the law that governs any set of concrete phenomena. Newman, without denying the validity of this effort, maintains that the stress on the abstract and conceptual leads to the neglect of something equal to, if not more important than, the universal, namely, the concrete and the real. This, says Delattre, is "the distinctive originality of Newman . . . the sincere and daring realism of his thought." [1] When he comes to treat of assent, he will make "real assent" the key to his entire grammar of faith and knowledge.

Assent he will define as "the absolute acceptance of a proposition without any condition"; it will be "real" when it involves "the whole man," not merely the faculty of abstraction, which gives only a "notional assent." [2] Besides being either notional or real, assents may be either simple or complex, and their grounds either implicit or explicit. For example, Newman had long given a real and simple assent to the proposition that "Great Britain was an island." [3] His assent was *real* in so far as he did not regard the island's concrete existence as something yet to be theoretically proved. Newman's assent was *simple* in that it was the result of multitudes of apprehensions, statements, imaginative acts, and thoughts which "passed through his mind in long succession without his observing them" (he assented simply); its ground was *implicit* because he had never laid out the recognizably valid reasons for believing Great Britain to be an island. Most of his, and our, assents in everyday life, and in the great crises of our experience, are of this nature — *not* abstract and complex. On the other hand, if Newman had proved or demonstrated, merely through reading or through other intellectual acts, that Great Britain was an island, his assent would have been merely *notional*.   As his demonstration increased in elaborateness of reasoning and concluding, it would have become increasingly *complex*, and its ground progressively *explicit*.   There are times when it is our duty to make a survey of our assents, to render their grounds more cogent and clearly revealed.   The result is a new assent, a complex one that is "an assent to an assent, or what is commonly called a conviction" or a formal certitude.[4] In matters of religion, this means a strengthening of belief, not by skeptical "inquiry" but by "investigation," by the reviewing, and completing the grounds of belief, analyzing and arranging them, yet with no more doubt of the outcome than a schoolboy has in working out a demonstration in geometry.[5]   In Newman's opinion, one ought not only to believe, but also to know what he is doing when he believes.

To return to the subject of assent, we note that in all cases it is preceded by inference.   In what ways do assent and inference differ?   The answer is that the act composed of argument and conclusion is called inference, while the final assertion is termed assent.   Inference draws conclusions, and is therefore always conditional.   Assent accepts the conclusion and abandons the argument, and is ready to act unconditionally.   It requires also that we have some intelligent apprehension of the terms; inference does not.   Thus in algebra, we cannot assent to $x = z$ until we know something about the terms.   But we can *infer* that if $x = y$ and $y = z$ then $x = z$, whether we know the meaning of x and z or not.[6]   One can readily see that Newman is strongly attracted by the characteristics of assent: its unconditionality, its concreteness, its stimulus to action.   Thus he says that

"an act of assent . . . is the most perfect and highest of its kind, when it is exercised on propositions, which are apprehended as experiences and images, that is, which stand for things; and, on the other hand, an act of inference is the most perfect and highest of its kind, when it is exercised on propositions which are apprehended as notions, that is, which are creations of the mind. . . The paradox is true, that, when inference is clearest, assent may be the least forcible [we may feel the reasonableness of an argument for doing a good deed, but some element of self-interest may prevent the final assertion which is called assent], and, when assent is most intense, inference may be least distinct [we may be ready to act on a belief (social, patriotic, or religious) long before we have all the intellectual grounds for action]" [7]

If, for Newman, real assent is superior to notional, as being stronger, more vivid and forcible, and as stimulating the emotions and the will to act, nevertheless notional assent is important and frequent enough in our behavior to warrant Newman's discussing it under five headings, which reveal at once his power of observation and his bold and not altogether happy departure from the terminology of the schools.   He thus discusses (i) *"profession,"* which is an "assent made upon habit and without reflection," as when a man calls himself a Tory or a Liberal, or accepts a theory in higher mathematics, merely because others do, and he is expected to; (ii) *"credence,"* which means "having no doubt" about a proposition, such as one finds in the greater part of morality, politics, or social codes; (iii) *"opinion,"* which is an assent to a proposition as "probably true, independently of the premisses," as when one says "I am of the opinion that we shall have a fine hay-harvest this year" (overlooking the condition, "if the present weather lasts"); (iv) *"presumption,"* which is really "assumption" or "postulate," as in the assent to the propositions with which we start in reasoning on any given subject matter, *e.g.* "there are things existing outside us"; and (v) *"speculation,"* which is the "contemplation of mental operations and their results as opposed to experience, experiment, or sense," as shown in our assent to all reasoning and its conclusions, to all general propositions, rules of conduct, proverbs, aphorisms, and the like. Such are the forms of notional assent, distinct from inference by being unconditional, and from real assent by the absence of that force and directness of apprehension which accompanies our knowledge of particular things and images.   In notional assent the mind contemplates its own creations instead of things, whether they be an unreasoned "opinion" or a mathematical "speculation." [8]

But the perfect course is when such notional assents pass into the real. And Newman asserts that such is the case in daily life. He illustrates by citing the boy at school who acquits himself poorly, and who later, as a man, engages in some particular work; much that had been theory to the boy, rapidly takes on concreteness, and the man becomes highly successful. There are also, he says, numerous truths, practical or ethical, which seem to "float" on the surface of society; they are admitted by all *notionally*, but await some concrete incident to bring them home, *by real assent*, to individuals. Thus the slave trade flourished long after the conscience of Europe was aware of its iniquity; but Wilberforce's organized agitation against it so affected the imagination of men that active efforts were made to stamp it out. Notional beliefs, convictions, certitudes are necessary, but it belongs to *real* assents "to form the mind out of which they grow . . . They create, as the case may be, heroes and saints, great leaders, statesmen, preachers, and reformers . . . They have given to the world men of one idea, of immense energy, of adamantine will, of revolutionary power." [9] On the other hand, the notional assents and inferences with which *science* deals are inadequate to conduct the mind to the belief and the action which *religion* desires. It is in treating this subject that Newman levies on his Tamworth Reading Room letters: "We are so constituted that faith, not knowledge or argument, is our principle of action . . . Science gives the grounds or premises from which religious truths are to be inferred; but it does not set about inferring them . . . [Its] deductions have no power of persuasion . . . First shoot round corners, and you may not despair of converting by a syllogism . . . To most men argument makes the point in hand only more doubtful, and considerably less impressive." [10] It is imperative, then, that knowledge and conviction leave the merely notional state if men are to *live* rather than suspend action in inconclusive abstractions.

Newman's next step — the final one in Part I of the *Grammar* — is to apply his theory of apprehension and assent to "the matter of religion." He will try, for example, to answer these questions: Can I attain to any more vivid assent to the Being of a

God than a merely notional one?   Can I rise to an imaginative apprehension of it?   Can I believe as if I saw?   He believes *real assent* in this matter to be possible.

His method is an extremely interesting and adroit adjustment of the empiricism of Locke, the Platonism of Alexandria, the eighteenth-century psychology of "taste," and his own (and Butler's) doctrine of conscience as an organ of knowledge.   We shall limit ourselves to an examination of his method as applied only to "Belief in One God," the most striking section of Chapter V.   He begins by saying that if we cannot "see" God, neither can we truly "see" His creatures; we have merely a discernment of their phenomena or "outside appearances."   The visible world is, to use his own language, a "picture."   Newman accepts Locke up to the point where the senses deliver knowledge of the outer world (empiricism); but he refuses to accept Locke's further notion that this knowledge tells us the *truth* — it can give us only an *image* of the world (Platonism), which we receive by some "instinct," which it would be a waste of time to try to explain.   This picture-knowledge of the world is "true as far as it goes."   In the same way, "the intellectual and moral objects which are brought home to us through our senses" are known to us by "instinct." [11]   Thus we could not possibly confuse the work of Dr. Johnson and a passage from St. Chrysostom; "so of any great man whom we may have known: that he is not a mere impression on our senses, but a real being, we know by instinct."   Now the thought of God, as entertained by Theists, is not gained by any instinctive association of His presence with any sensible phenomena.   But just as the senses point to a partly knowable external world (Nature), so certain of "our mental phenomena" point to a Creator.   Newman now sums up this thought in a carefully balanced sentence:

"As from a multitude of instinctive perceptions, acting in particular instances, of something beyond the senses, we generalize the notion of an external world, and then picture that world in and according to those particular phenomena from which we started, *so* from the perceptive power which identifies the intimations of conscience with the reverberations or echoes (so to say) of an external admonition, we proceed on to the notion of a Supreme Ruler and Judge, and then again we image Him and His attributes in those recurring intimations, out of which, as mental phenomena, our recognition of His existence was originally gained." [12]

Newman reminds us at this point that he is not trying to "*prove* the existence of God*," but to "explain how we gain an image of God and give a real assent to the proposition that He exists." We must start from first principles, and one of these, he believes, is "that we have by nature a Conscience." Further, he assumes "that Conscience has a legitimate place among our mental acts," as much so as reasoning, imagination, or "the sense of the beautiful." [13] In the "special feeling" consequent on doing right or wrong "lie the materials for the real apprehension of a Divine Sovereign and Judge." This feeling, according to Newman, is twofold: it is a moral sense, and it is a sense of duty. It has a critical office, testifying that there *is* a right and a wrong, though its promptings are not in all cases correct. And it has a judicial office, not as a rule of right conduct, but as a *sanction* of such conduct, ever forcing on us by threats and by promises its primary and most authoritative aspect. To some extent, it occupies in human nature a place parallel with that of the "sense of the beautiful," "good sense," "sense of honor." But conscience goes further, in being concerned primarily with persons, in not reposing on its own evidence (as does taste) but in reaching vaguely forward beyond self toward a living object. Conscience arouses feelings of responsibility, shame, fear, which inanimate objects cannot; hence "this implies that there is One to whom we are responsible, before whom we are ashamed." Thus out of the data of conscience, Newman derives an "instinctive" knowledge of God, just as out of the data of the senses he derives an "instinctive" (configurated, or patterned) knowledge of nature. God becomes an object of real assent, not a principle or a cause but a person. Newman concludes that when men begin and end all their works with the thought of God, living according to the admonitions of Conscience,

"they are brought into His presence as that of a Living Person, and are able to hold converse with Him, and that with a directness and simplicity, with a confidence and intimacy, *mutatis mutandis*, which we use towards an earthly superior; so that it is doubtful whether we realize the company of our fellow-men with greater keenness than these favoured minds are able to contemplate and adore the Unseen, Incomprehensible Creator." [14]

It will be observed that the word "real" has, in all this discussion, a highly individual significance. For Newman a thing or person is real when *experienced*, not necessarily when merely seen or heard. It was not hard for him to have a real apprehension of God if for him nature was real, not in her color and shapes and sounds but in her *life* "behind" her veil of matter, time, and space. What he was trying to do was to rescue the reality of God from the logicians, as the Alexandrian Platonists had rescued nature from the pagan materialists. The "real" becomes the moral, the spiritual, the living. Hence Newman's great repugnance for a materialized religion (superstition) as well as for a religion of abstraction (philosophy, issuing in skepticism). Real assent to the existence of God is possible, according to Newman, if we believe that that alone is real which is moral.

c. *From Probability to Certitude*

Part II of the *Grammar of Assent* opens with a question: How can inference, which is conditional, lead, as it does, to assent, which is unconditional? How is it, for example, that a proposition such as "I shall die," which is not and cannot be demonstrated, but only inferred, is nevertheless assented to with unqualified adhesion? In answering this question, Newman, as we know, takes issue with Locke, who had held that there are *degrees* of assent, and that the test of truth is "the not entertaining any proposition with greater assurance than the proofs it is built on will warrant." [1] Yet even Locke admits, says Newman, that we assent to certain inferences or propositions "as firmly as if they were infallibly demonstrated," and that we do so because "probabilities [may] rise so near to certainty that they [may] govern our thoughts as absolutely . . . as the most evident demonstration." [2] Thus Locke seems to be guilty of a contradiction, at least in view of the way men do actually think; and "his assents [if they admit of degrees] are only inferences." [3]   In fact, concludes Newman, "Locke's theory of the duty of assenting more or less according to degrees of evidence is invalidated by the testimony of high and low, young and old, ancient and modern"; men infer, and hold a conclusion tentatively, and men assent, and hold a conclusion unconditionally.   The two acts are, for Newman, quite distinct.   What allows conditional inference to pass into unconditional assent is the weight of the *probabilities* involved.   We shall note a little later how this factor of probability will operate toward certitude.   It is sufficient here to observe its place in the passage from inference to assent, and to remark that nowhere does Newman acknowledge his real debt to Locke's chapter "On Probability," in which the terminology and even the illustrations reveal the extent of Newman's borrowing.[4]

The next step in Newman's argument is to show that "assents may and do change; certitudes endure . . . Without certitude in religious faith there may be much decency of profession and of observance, but there can be no habit of prayer, no directness of devotion, no intercourse with the unseen, no generosity of self-sacrifice." [5]   What is certitude?   Newman defines it as "the perception of a truth, with the perception that it *is* a truth," expressed in the assertion, "I know that I know."   Its main characteristic is the confidence that "it will last, that even should it fail, the thing itself, whatever it is, of which we are certain, will remain just as it was, true and irreversible." [6]   It is accompanied with a feeling of satisfaction, of self-congratulation, of intellectual security, of finality.   And this, Newman feels, is not an unusual or rare experience: "certitude is a natural and normal state of mind"; without it, any wholehearted act would be impossible.   But how is certitude attained, and how do we attain the *indefectibility* of certitude which Newman says is the mark of genuine belief? The answer takes him back to Bishop Butler's *dictum* that "Probability is the guide of life." [7]   In human affairs, says Newman, we are ever directed by probabilities, "but they are probabilities founded on certainties."   There is nothing improbable about the dictates of sense and memory, of our "intellectual instincts," of the moral sense, and of the logical faculty; the generalizations of science and of history are, for Newman, "certain truths."   In all concrete reasoning, in preparing for an act, we are moved to believe by a "cumulation of probabilities, independent of each other, arising out of the nature and circumstances of the particular case which is under review; probabilities too fine to avail separately, too subtle and circuitous to be convertible into syllogisms, too numerous and various for such conversion, even were they convertible." [8]   Reasoning concretely, then, *i.e.*, from the certainties of sense, of logic, of moral experience, as distinct from reasoning abstractly, one parallels the method employed by Newton "in the celebrated lemma with which he opens his 'Principia' ": that is, arguing by convergent probabilities toward a proof which we finally accept is similar to arguing that a regular polygon inscribed in a circle, its sides being continually diminished, will tend ever to become that circle, though never quite reaching it.   A sure divination that a conclusion, of which the lines of reasoning do not actually put one in possession, is nevertheless inevitable, is what Newman means by a proposition being "as good as proved."   It amounts to a proof, inasmuch as "a proof is the limit of converging probabilities." [9]   This is the basis for a life of action rather than of introspection and doubt.   Both great and little actions are constantly being taken on grounds that cannot be analyzed into more than a group of probabilities.   Even Newman's severest critics — such as Leslie Stephen — acknowledged the cogency of this line of reasoning.   It is, as Newman intimates, a more rigorous form of argument than the "*greater probability*" argument of the theologian Amort: "I prefer," says Newman, "to rely on that of an *accumulation* of various probabilities. . . From probabilities we may construct legitimate proof, sufficient for certitude." [10]   One might add that Newman is not concerned merely with the grounds for action; he also is concerned with the *reasonableness* of his method.   Keble had argued that "the living power of faith and love," not probability, gives firmness to assent.[11]   This struck Newman as beautiful but not logical, and Newman wished to urge the "logical cogency of faith."

The certitude toward which "convergent probabilities" tend has, according to Newman, three conditions.   *First*, it must follow on investigation and proof; it must be the final form of that complex assent which, though not doubting, has nevertheless analyzed, consciously and deliberately, the grounds and proofs involved. *Second*, it must be accompanied by a "specific sense of intellectual satisfaction and repose." And *third*, it must be irreversible. "If the assent is made without rational grounds, it is a rash judgment, a fancy, or a prejudice; if without the sense of finality, it is scarcely more than an inference; if without permanence, it is a mere conviction." [12]

The instrument or *organon* by which converging probabilities effect a complete certitude is called by Newman "the Illative Sense." But before he can pass from his discussion of certitude to his definition and illustration of the illative sense, he must deal finally with inference — (a) formal, (b) informal, and (c) natural inferences, and their place in the passage from the conditional state of mind to the unconditional. It is here that Newman appears to lay himself open to the charge of holding a contempt for logic. On certain grounds the charge is valid. Considered as (a) *"formal inference,"* logic does appear to Newman to be a static, descriptive, merely abstract method of reasoning; its "inferential exercises [are] always conditional"; as such it strips words of all "connatural senses," it drains them of "that depth and breadth of associations which constitute their poetry, their rhetoric, and their historical life"; it starves each term down till it becomes the ghost of itself. Its abstractions can only conduct to the abstract, whereas, according to Newman, "we have need to attain by our reasonings to what is concrete." Its conclusions are only probabilities, whereas we need certainties. In this world of sense, Newman says, we have to do with things far more often than with notions or abstractions: "Let units come first, and (so-called) universals second; let universals minister to units, not units be sacrificed to universals. John, Richard, and Robert are individual things, independent, incommunicable"; the common measure between them may be called "man," but "man" is only a name, not an independent reality.[13] (At this point, Newman's opponents level an additional charge, that of nominalism.) Moreover, like science, logic is too simple and exact, from the nature of the case, to be the measure of fact. And its chain of conclusions hangs loose at both ends — "it comes short both of first principles and of concrete issues." At its best it fails to represent adequately the sum-total of considerations — remote, hidden, personal, delicate, circuitous, and intricate — which determine an individual's judgment of things. Our most natural way of reasoning is not from proposition to proposition but "from things to things, from concrete to concrete, from wholes to wholes" — and "every one who reasons, is his own center." [14] To be sure, adds Newman, logic has its just uses: it catalogues knowledge, corrects mistakes, brings order into our thinking, teaches us the *direction* in which truth lies, and points to the probable fields of experiment and observation. But in matters of concrete thought and action, logic is but "an accessory after the fact." Since its function is to correct and "check-up," we must not be surprised if, in thinking "with the whole man," the inferential method is at times set aside. Indeed in the chapter on "Natural Religion," after having discoursed at length on the evidences in the world of a superintending Providence, Newman pauses and, as if looking at the reader with calm defiance, adds: "should it be objected that this is an illogical exercise of reason, I answer . . . if logic finds fault with it, so much the worse for logic"! [15]

In "concrete thought," in reasoning "from wholes to wholes," Newman maintains that we are employing what he calls (b) "informal inference" and (c) "natural inference." In (b) *inferring informally* we reach conclusions not by any verbal enumeration of all the considerations involved, but by "a mental comprehension of the whole case, and a discernment of its upshot, sometimes after much deliberation, but, it may be, by a clear and rapid act of the intellect, always, however, by an unwritten summing-up, something like the summation of the terms *plus* and *minus* of an algebraical series." [16] This kind of inference, though still a form of logic, is no longer abstract, but laden with the substance and the momentum of a mass of probabilities which carry it out into the realities of life; it is also more or less implicit, not reasoned out consciously; and it is still dependent on premises. This is the kind of inference which leads to Newman's certainty about "Great Britain being an island." He is certain without proof or demonstration, without fact or experience leading him to the belief; his certitude is rational, supported by good sense, yet it cannot be satisfactorily analyzed. He has grasped the full tale of premises and conclusion by "a sort of instinctive perception of the legitimate conclusion in and through the premises, not by a formal juxta-position of propositions." [17] In such informal, concrete reasoning, Newman's criterion has been, not the manipulation of propositions, but his entire intellectual and moral nature. In a religious problem, it would be his "moral state." In such a case he must (to use Butler's words) "be as much in earnest about religion, as about [his] temporal affairs, capable of being convinced, on real evidence, that there is [for instance] a God who governs the world, and feel [himself] to be of a moral nature and [an] accountable creature." [18] Different men will regard different things as "probable"; according to Newman, it is their moral natures which determine which "probability" will appear the most "probable."

Much of what we have just said is true also of (c) *natural inference*, that unconscious, implicit transition from one known thing to another, as illustrated in the weather-wise farmer who knows it will rain tomorrow but can assign no intelligible reasons for his conclusion. His mode of reasoning, says Newman, is really the one in which we all do most of our thinking — "dealing with things directly, as they stand, one by one, in the concrete, with an intrinsic and personal power." [19] This "faculty of spontaneous reasoning" is attached to definite subject matters, and varies with individuals; the shrewd businessman may be a bad arguer in philosophical questions; Priestley, great in electricity, was a poor ecclesiastical historian. This "unscientific reasoning" is akin to genius, and at its greatest, *is* genius. Newton once formulated a "rule for ascertaining the imaginary roots of equations" which was useful to mathematicians, though it was "demonstrated" only a century and a half later. Napoleon had acquired the power of judging quickly and accurately the strength and disposition of his enemy's forces, and could calculate just when and where their attack would occur. This faculty Newman finds it hard to avoid calling "instinct," since it is "a perception of facts without assignable media of perceiving." In any case, it leads him to prefer to trust *persons* rather than "logical science," the "whole man" rather than any one of his faculties. He is thus led to show how the sole and final judgment on the validity of an inference in concrete matters is committed to the personal action of the ratiocinative faculty. The perfection or virtue of this faculty — reasoning acting under the weight of the whole personality — he calls the illative sense.

d. *The "Organon" of Informal Inference: the Illative Sense* [1]

Newman begins the penultimate chapter of the *Grammar of Assent,* with an attempt to answer the question, Can we attain certitude in the concrete? We again note how practical is his method. For actually he aims not at establishing how we *can* be certain, but how we *are* certain. It is common knowledge that we are certain of many concrete facts; how do we arrive at such an assent? Newman approaches the problem inductively: first, he considers the *sanction* actually given by our minds to that assent; then from this experienced sanction, he argues the existence of a faculty, the illative sense, and studies its *nature*; and finally, he explores the *range* of its action. Throughout his discussion he opposes the two schools of Locke and Kant, the former of which held that "since experience leads by syllogism only to probabilities, certitude is ever a mistake" or a delusion, while the latter has recourse to "the hypothesis of intuitions, intellectual forms, and the like." [2]

The *sanction* of the illative sense, according to Newman, lies in the fact that the human mind is so constituted as to judge by its own right, by its own powers. We are born equipped with such powers, and it is fruitless and vain to complain about their limitation; our first disobedience is to be impatient at what we are, to aspire to what we cannot attain. "There is no ultimate test of truth besides the testimony born to truth by the mind itself, and . . . this phenomenon, perplexing as we may find it, is a normal and inevitable characteristic of the mental constitution of a being like man on a stage such as the world." [3] Moreover, argues Newman, the laws of mind are the expression not only of constituted order but of God's will. These laws throw a reflex light upon themselves, and for resignation to his duty, Newman will "substitute a cheerful concurrence in an overruling Providence." [4]   If the path of thought is rugged and circuitous, disappointing and dark, the discipline inflicted on one's mind will promote reverence, humility, devotion; and it will point once again to the fact which, Newman says, has always perplexed men's minds: "Verily Thou art a *hidden* God."

What, then, is the *nature* of the illative sense? It may be defined, as we have seen, as the instrument or *organon* by which the mind discovers certitude in a mass of converging probabilities. It is the mind in its perfection, judging and correlating at the highest point of any given individual; it concerns itself with principles, doctrines, facts, memories, experiences, testimonies, in order to attain insights too delicate and subtle for logical analysis. It draws its conclusions from premises of which it is only partly explicitly conscious, and judges those conclusions to be warranted. Its minute, continuous, experimental reasoning shows badly on paper, but "drifts silently into an overwhelming cumulus of proof, and, when our start is true, brings us on to a true result." Newman considers the illative sense to be somewhat like Aristotle's *phronesis,* or prudence, except that whereas in the *Nicomachean Ethics* the term was applied to *conduct* in contingent or concrete matters, the illative sense is applied by Newman to attaining *truth* in the same field.[5] As such it is a branch of the architectonic faculty, or judgment in all concrete matter. This faculty of the mind, Newman continues, is peculiarly personal; each individual uses it in his own way, just as he exercises the parallel faculties of "good sense," "common sense," and "sense of beauty." As each person follows his own conscience, or judges in the fine arts by his own taste, so in judging the truth of concrete things, each is guided by his own illative sense. This sense varies with individuals, from the intuitions of genius to the biased and self-regarding judgments of the ignorant man.[6] Moreover, the same man may excel in one field and fail in another: "a good man may make a bad king; profligates have been great statesmen." [7] In Aristotelian fashion, Newman further holds that there is a separate *phronesis* for each virtue; hence there are different illative senses in men according to their search for concrete truth, different in law, history, morals, religion. Finally Newman considers the nature and claim of the illative sense in four respects: (a) its exercise is "one and the same in all concrete matters (*e.g.* geology, religion, history). . . We proceed as far indeed as we can by the logic of language, but we are obliged to supplement it by the more subtle and elastic logic of thought"; (b) it is attached, as we have seen, to definite subject matters; an individual may possess it in science and not in religion; (c) its method, as was noted earlier, is to reason from what, in strictly logical demonstration, is a converging cumulation of probabilities, yet it arrives at assent or material certitude, a method similar to that used in the theory of limits in mathematics; and (d) it is the "ultimate test of truth and error" in all our concrete reasoning, whether in experimental science, history, or religious investigation.[8]

In no way does the illative sense exclude logic; on the contrary, it supplements it. Its influence operates throughout the entire process of real, concrete ratiocination — "in the beginning, middle, and end of all verbal discussion and inquiry" — in assuming first principles, in carrying out an argument, and in drawing a conclusion.[9] Its first principles, for Newman, are *not* elementary truths prior to reasoning, but really conclusions from particular experiences, abstractions from fact. Newman's idea of "first principles" is of capital importance in one's understanding of his doctrine at this point; "no [other] key," as Juergens observes, "will open to the student the heart and mind, the personality of England's greatest Catholic thinker."[10] Surprisingly to some of us, Newman holds that first principles, though numerous, are far from being universally received, because they vary with the persons who reason. Being so intimately *personal*, they cannot be measured by logic. They "are half the battle in the inference with which the reasoning is to terminate."[11] For example, a reasoner may choose a "point of view," "scientific" objectivity; then he may begin with Descartes' strategy of doubt, and include of necessity his own character-bias of "independence." Now it will be vain for Newman to argue with him from his own "point of view" — "our hoping is a proof that hope, as such, is not an extravagance"; then to proceed on the assumption that he

"would rather have to maintain that we ought to begin with believing everything . . . than it is our duty to doubt of everything"; and finally to include of necessity his own character-bias
of a sense of "dependence," need for authority, sense of the Unseen.[12]   Newman and his opponent would remain forever poles
apart, because of their first principles.   That is why Newman
has said that "it is as absurd to argue men, as to torture them, into
believing"; [13] their first principles are too personal.   Unless such
principles coincide, there can be no argument, and if they coincide,
argument is superfluous, agreement is, in the end, complete.
"When men understand each other's meaning, they see, for the
most part, that controversy is either superfluous or hopeless." [14]
Hence it is, too, that Newman regards logic as of very limited use
in religion — not to bring about belief, which it rarely does, but to
clarify and illuminate and enlarge the belief already attained by
other than merely logical means.   Hence, finally, his habit of
using logic somewhat ruthlessly as an inferior tool, to be dis-
carded when it cannot minister to belief.

But the illative sense not only assumes first principles, it also
"conducts the argument" and concludes.   It selects a "point of
view"; it chooses or discards testimony; it determines which kinds
of arguments really tell in an inquiry.   "With facts alone," says
Juergens on Newman at this point, "authors would come to no
conclusion; it is the 'tacit understandings,' the assumed starting
points, the 'critical feeling,' the 'antecedent reasonings' and such
like personal, collateral aids which are used by the illative sense
that make possible conclusions one way or the other."   In addition, the illative sense draws the conclusions in all concrete
ratiocination, as we have seen in examining "informal inference."
As Juergens puts it, "the illative sense masses the body of proof,
which consists in a cumulation of converging probabilities, the
only kind of arguments available in concrete matters, and concludes by a simple assent, which is also called 'moral certitude.' " [15]

If we wish to observe Newman applying his principle of the
illative sense by way of illustration, we need only turn to the final
chapter of the *Grammar of Assent*.   Here he discusses "Infer-

ence and Assent in the Matter of Religion," both Natural and Revealed.   He reminds us, at a strategic point in his discussion, that in mathematics or in the exact sciences we are wholly justified by the "dictate of nature" in withholding our assent from a conclusion which has not yet received a strict logical demonstration, but that we are *not* justified, in the concrete reasoning involved in religious inquiry, in waiting until we have such complete logical demonstration.   On the contrary, says Newman, we are bound by *conscience* to "seek truth, and to look for certainty by modes of proof" which will fall far short of formal exactness or completeness, but which will nevertheless lay absolute claim to our belief.[16]   This is because we are dealing not with some matter of only a relative importance — a theory, a merely secular problem — but with the eternal and infinite nature of man's destiny, which demands action.   Long ago Newman had declared, aphoristically: "Religion is for practice, and that immediate." [17]

One of our "first principles" will be that the existence of God is at least "probable," from the intimations of conscience.   When we turn to the various "probabilities" which Newman finds valid in pointing, further, to the "divinity of Christianity," we note, interestingly enough, that they do not involve miracles, strictly so called, but what Newman calls "those [historical] coincidences and their cumulations, which, though not in themselves miraculous, do irresistibly force upon us, almost by the law of our nature, the presence of the extraordinary agency of Him whose being we already acknowledge." [18]   He cites, for example, Napoleon's disastrous Russian campaign due to bitter cold, after he had retorted to the Pope's excommunication with scorn: "Does he suppose the arms will fall from the hands of my soldiers?" Within two years, in the retreat from Moscow, as two writers tell Newman, "famine and cold tore their arms from the grasp of the soldiers." [19]   Thus a varying number of such coincidences is sufficient for Newman's own illative sense to produce "moral certitude," just as circumstantial evidence in a law court may convince a jury of a man's guilt or innocence.   The last pages of the *Grammar* are devoted to showing by way of illustration what *kinds* of coincidences in the history of Christianity appeal most to Newman himself, and create within him the certitude of its divinity. He examines the remarkable history of the Hebrew nation, the Mosaic religion, the Messianic prophecies and their fulfillment in Christianity, the power which the early Christians drew from their real, living "Image of Christ." And all this mass of historical "probabilities" converges and combines to make Newman conclude that Christianity "has upon it *primâ facie* signs of divinity. . . . Either Christianity is from God, or a revelation has not yet been given to us." Newman assures us that these are the "probabilities" which most affect *him*; [20] they are also merely *sketches* of proofs, merely specimens or symbols of the real grounds of his true, living reason for believing. He further asserts that even when all the "proofs" are assembled and expressed, they still could be much stronger and clearer than they actually are. This is because Christianity, in so far as we approach it from the side of reason, belongs to history; and no historical fact can be mathematically or metaphysically demonstrated. Yet, says Newman, it is the duty of all men to assent to the divinity of Christianity as if it were so demonstrated, in obedience to their conscience. Their illative sense readily unites the antecedent probabilities of a revelation, drawn from "natural religion" (belief and moral insights prior to a revelation), and the external proofs (or historical probabilities), to render the divinity of Christianity as convincing to the individual as is to a reader of Newton the proof that the sides of a polygon inscribed within a circle may progressively approach that circle as a limit.

Newman concludes his *Grammar* by observing that Christianity

"addresses [the mind] both through the intellect and through the imagination; creating a certitude of its truth by arguments too various for direct enumeration, too personal and deep for words, too powerful and concurrent for refutation. . . One and the same teaching is in different aspects both object and proof, and elicits one complex act of inference and assent . . . [It is] the counterpart, so to say, of ourselves, and is real as we are real."

Then come the words of the Fourth Gospel, words which reveal once more, as Wilfrid Ward has pointed out, that the expression *Cor ad cor loquitur* sums up the essence of Newman's doctrine of knowledge and faith: heart speaks to heart — it knows its own. "I am the Good Shepherd, and I know Mine, and Mine know Me. My sheep hear My voice, and I know them, and they follow Me . . ." [21]

III. EXCURSIONS IN
CRITICISM AND CONTROVERSY

CHAPTER VII

LIBERALISM AND ANGLICANISM

Although one seldom thinks of Newman as a critic, it is nevertheless fruitful to approach certain of his writings as if they were in fact essays in criticism as well as in controversy, for which he is more widely famous.   His excursions into criticism took him not only into religion but also into history, biography, and literature. Of course, he never attempted criticism in its purest forms; as we have noted, he believed firmly in the virtues of "occasional" writing.   Considering himself a literary artist only incidentally, he was content to write for the day, to help in the struggle.   Hence it is characteristic of him to say to Bishop Ullathorne, in his dedication to *Difficulties of Anglicans*, "It is a better deed to write for the present moment than for posterity." [1]   Yet it is amazing to observe the numerous passages of stylistic beauty and power scattered throughout many otherwise undistinguished and now nearly forgotten pieces in the *Via Media*, the *Essays Critical and Historical*, the *Discussions and Arguments*.   In dealing with Newman's critical efforts we shall thus be examining many of his essays of which the general reader is totally unaware.   And we shall discover in them a remarkable degree of vitality.

i.   *The Anti-dogmatic Principle: Liberalism in Religion*

We must begin by realizing that the Liberalism against which Newman was a lifelong foe was not at all the political and economic Liberalism of Gladstone, John Bright, or John Stuart Mill. Newman was at war with a Liberalism which was virtually a continuation of the deistic spirit of the seventeenth century.   He had been horrified by the possible return of that spirit when he observed the tendencies of the Noetics of Oxford, who, after the manner of the Deists (Toland, Collins, Tindal), wished to banish the mysterious and the irrational from religion. This kind of Liberalism, said Newman, consisted in a "pride of reason," a "false liberty of thought, or the exercise of thought upon matters, in which, from the constitution of the human mind, thought cannot be brought to any successful issue, and therefore is out of place." For Newman, such matters are first principles of whatever kind. When thought is applied to these principles, then contradictions and paradoxes spring up; the mind is dazzled with its own powers, and takes delight in doubting. This, declares Newman, is disastrous when the first principles involved are "the most sacred and momentous . . . the truths of revelation." Thus Liberalism, as Newman understands it, is "the mistake of subjecting to human judgment those revealed doctrines which are in their nature beyond and independent of it, and of claiming to determine on intrinsic grounds the truth and value of propositions which rest for their reception simply on the external authority of the Divine Word." [1] Liberalism is the "anti-dogmatic spirit," which fails to sense the life and objective reality and authority inherent in dogma. As we have seen, Newman had been a steady advocate, from the very first, of what is called dogmatic Christianity, that is, Christianity which is not "a formless and gelatinous mass of vague sentiment, but which springs from a deeply-planted seed of revealed doctrine." [2] All around him, however, the Liberal party in the English Church was flourishing; it finally grew to such proportions that it leaped the bounds of party and embraced the educated lay world. The unwillingness of the Liberal mind to acknowledge the supernatural, the mysterious, the *revealed* in religion resulted at length in the unbelief of such men as Clough, Jowett, and Matthew Arnold. It put forth books like two which Newman himself reviewed, Milman's *History of Christianity* and Erskine's *Internal Evidence*. It produced *Essays and Reviews* (1860), by Mark Pattison, Jowett, Wilson, Williams, Powell, and Frederick Temple. Soon the barriers of public opinion were down. By 1860 the intellectual attack on revealed religion, so eagerly desired by the secular mind, had been greatly promoted by churchmen.

It is possible to charge Newman with ignorance of the total pattern and significance of that modern movement of enlightenment of which "deistic Liberalism" was but a part. That is why such critics as Fairbairn bitterly lament Newman's failure to recognize the possibilities for good in that movement. Newman's world had behind it, as fresh moral stimulus, the spirituality of transcendentalism, the passion for freedom in Byron and Shelley, the immanentism of Wordsworth, the fusion of speculative and creative reason in Coleridge. It had seen, in politics, old dynastic and despotic ambitions fall before the uprisen peoples; it now had a new sense of brotherhood, a longing for ordered freedom, for justice, for security. When the new Liberal spirit knocked at the door of the English Church, says Fairbairn, the eye of the Church should have "read its heart, seen the probabilities of danger, but [also] the infinite possibilities of good — its hatred of wrong, its love of justice, its desire for sweeter manners, purer laws, its purpose to create a wealthier, happier and freer state. And the spirit that so discerned would have helped by bringing Religion into 'Liberalism' to make 'Liberalism' religious." [3] Now Newman may have been unaware of the rich texture of the modern liberal movement, and of its wide-ranging potentialities for good; but even if he had known it in its entirety, his hostility would have been no less implacable. For him the meaning of history was not to be found by human reason, or in human technology and civilization; on the contrary, he saw history moving to a supernatural and divine goal, a goal attainable not by "the march of mind" or "the progress of civilization and science" but "by the fostering of a divine seed which will bear an eternal flower." [4] The aim of religion, as he saw it, was not to make men "good citizens" in a "wealthier, happier and freer state," but, frankly, to make men saints. And any attempt to "bring Religion into Liberalism" would, in his mind, result only in the triumph of Liberalism over religion. Far from holding, like Coleridge, Carlyle, Strauss, or Renan, that the Christian revelation must be reformed in the light of modern thought, he held that modern thought needed reform in the light of the Christian revelation. In short, he took the great Christian dogmas to mean precisely what they say; once having accepted revelation as an objective fact, on the authority of Scripture, Creed, and Church, he could make no compromise with the modern effort to interpret religion symbolically, subjectively, and rationally.

This is not to say, however, that Newman was in no sense a liberal himself.   Actually he was a steady foe of dogmatic tyranny; he always maintained that private conscientiousness is the first step toward orthodoxy.   Indeed, as Hutton well puts it, "he received his Cardinal's hat because he had contended so boldly against any attempt to invade freedom of conscience in the Church." [5]   He regarded any form of coercion as not only ill-advised, but immoral.   He rested his religious belief upon personal experience, and developed from it a new theory of religious knowledge, a theory which was essentially individualistic, *i.e.* liberal.   Though he emphasized the ministry of the Church and the communion of saints, he yet saw the Church as a channel of divine grace only by virtue of her sacraments and her discipline; and her priest as but an intermediary.   Newman was a liberal also in his insistence that the Church had nothing to gain by an alliance with the state; this lesson he had learned from Protestant Erastianism.   Finally, Newman was a liberal in his resistance to ultramontane and bureaucratic sacerdotalism; he stood at the antipodes of Mgr. Talbot and of Manning, who minimized the part of the layman and magnified the part of the clergy in the administration of the Church.   A liberal through the influence of his early Protestant surroundings, through the teaching of his personal experience, a liberal in his conception of religion and of the sacerdotal ministry, Newman held so firmly to the belief in the inviolability of the religious conscience that, as Sarolea declares, one may "conclude that Newman was a liberal Catholic in the highest sense of the word." [6]

Newman's utterances on Liberalism occur of course throughout all his works, but for our purposes it will be sufficient to glance at those writings in which he is specifically analyzing or attacking it.   We note, at the outset, that these writings include three of the *Tracts for the Times,* "The Introduction of Rationalistic Principles into Revealed Religion" (1835), "Holy Scripture in

Its Relation to the Catholic Creed" (1838), and "The Patristical Idea of Antichrist" (1838); two review-articles for the *British Critic*, "The Fall of La Mennais" (1837) and "Milman's View of Christianity" (1841); a review of Seely's *Ecce Homo* for *The Month* (1866); a series of letters to *The Times*, "The Tamworth Reading Room" (1841); an essay on "Private Judgment" (1841); the Note on "Liberalism" in the *Apologia* (1864); and finally the "Biglietto speech" which Newman delivered at Rome on becoming a cardinal (1879). For nearly half a century, therefore, Newman was engaged directly or indirectly in waging war on the "Liberal" spirit.

Sometimes, as in the first of the three tracts we have noted, he identifies it with rationalism. Discussing Thomas Erskine's *Internal Evidence for the Truth of Revealed Religion* and Jacob Abbott's *Corner Stone*, he points out the rationalist's tendency to view faith, with reference to its object, as never more than an opinion, never an active principle apprehending definite doctrines, but merely the fruit of past diligence, independent inquiry, dispassionate thought. The rationalist, says Newman, has difficulty in thinking of divine truth as objective; he cannot "throw himself forward upon what we have but partially mastered or made subjective"; any attempt to do so, through symbols or creeds, "seems to the rationalist superstitious and unmeaning." He is unwilling to postulate Mystery as of the very essence of reality, as does the believer (explicitly or implicitly); he wishes to make all plain, to systematize, to know. Yet by the very nature of a *Revelation* there must be mystery, since the limitations of the human intellect will always leave such Revelation incomplete and unsystematic. The Church Catholic has always insisted on the existence of Mysteries in religion, "facts revealed to us, not of this world, not of time, but of eternity, and that absolutely and independently," not merely "manifested" to us through nature and history. The rationalist, on the other hand, seeks to find hints of the divine in the laws of the universe, and ends with the conviction that only nature is real, that the supernatural is the product of superstitious minds.[7]

This denial of the supernatural is strikingly analyzed in Newman's review of Milman's *History of Christianity*.[8] After contrasting nature and supernature, in three pages of splendid writing, Newman proceeds to condemn Milman for "paring down the supernatural facts" of Christianity, for "disguising Scripture facts and persons under secular names [Milman had called Abraham an Emir and a Sheik]," and for coolly explaining away many Church doctrines by referring to their origins in Platonism, Essenism, Orientalism. The basic evil in Milman's work, according to Newman, is "the disallowing of the supernatural," the reduction of religion to nature and reason, and the accounting for "miracles" by the use of "the more subtle and fastidious intelligence of the present times." Newman is acutely conscious of the fate of Christianity if the Liberal principle is allowed, namely, "that a sufficient account is given of an opinion, and a sufficient ground for making light of it, as soon as it is historically referred to some human origin." "What will be left to us?" asks Newman in alarm. "Will Revelation have done more than introduce a *quality* into our moral life world, not anything that can be contemplated by itself, obeyed and perpetuated? . . . If we indulge [Mr. Milman's views], Christianity will melt away in our hands like snow; we shall be unbelievers before we at all suspect where we are." [9] Christianity will have been a past event, an idea, a movement which gave a certain direction and tone to government, social life, philosophy, literature; a great boon to the world, but, after all, only a natural force, no more supernatural than an earthquake.

The Liberal minimizing of the objective and the supernatural in Christianity in terms not only of pious rationalism, as in Milman, but also of sentiment and emotion, receives from Newman an interesting treatment in his review of John Robert Seely's *Ecce Homo*, a book which, while not attacking orthodox Christianity, laid great emphasis on Jesus as a man. Newman here writes, of course, as a Roman Catholic — Seely's book appeared in 1865 — and his strictures against the author are firmer and more dogmatic than usual on such occasions. Although Newman probably never heard of Albrecht Ritschl, there are pages of Newman's review which read as if written as a direct attack on "Ritschlianism," that "theological peril of the hour" some fifty

years ago. The Ritschlian theologian spoke of Christian doctrines as bearing a "religious value" quite apart from any historical truth they might have; he distinguished between "judgments of fact" and "judgments of worth," and declined to discuss
miracles as historical events.[10] Similarly, in Newman's generation there was a large body of men who were neither skeptical
Liberals nor genuine Anglo-Catholics; they could not give up
tradition, yet were loath to shut the door to progress. They
"loved the conclusions of Catholic theology better than the proofs,
and the methods of modern thought better than its results."
Wishing to believe, they "acquiesced in what is called a practical
belief." It was for these that Seely wrote *Ecce Homo*. Here
they found an argument for Christianity which pleased their
minds and consoled their feelings, a picture of Jesus as a man,
which appealed to the imagination without demanding belief in
Jesus as a supernatural deliverer. To Newman, for whom Christianity is an organic unity, compounded of the natural and the
supernatural, this effort of Seely's savors of intellectual dishonesty. He indignantly rejects the argument as arbitrary,
obscure, and capricious, and concludes coldly with the admonition: "Take Christianity, or leave it; do not practice upon it;
to do so is as unphilosophical as it is dangerous. Do not attempt to halve a spiritual unit . . . You dishonestly pick and
choose . . ."[11] Newman discerns that Seely's eclectic treatment
of the life of Jesus made its greatest appeal to the emotions.
Exactly thirty years before, in a postscript to Tract LXXIII, he
had observed the spread of Schleiermacher's influence, in the
revival of "religious *feeling*," which was producing the "spurious
Christianity" of Liberalism. Schleiermacher's identification of
religion with "the feeling of absolute dependence on God" suggested that "the Christian Revelation was intended only to stir
the affections and soothe the heart." Such a doctrine dispensed
with creeds as impediments to religious growth, stumbling-blocks
to the reason, and shackles to the affections; it could also suggest, not altogether faithfully to Schleiermacher, that the Christian dispensation "contains nothing which is unintelligible to the
intellect."[12] Thus Newman sees in Liberalism the paradoxical

union of rationalism and sentimentalism, a union which is the foe
to the Catholic concept of religion.

Another form of Liberalism which Newman distrusted was
that which was illustrated in the great French Catholic, De Lamennais, who, together with his disciples, De Montalembert,
Lacordaire, and Maurice de Guérin, organized a movement to
encourage the Pope to "place himself at the head of the democratic movement throughout Europe," and to free the Church
from civil domination.   In the end, De Lamennais' policy was
condemned in the encyclical *Mirari vos* (1832), and his journal,
L'Avenir, suspended.   Newman could readily agree with De
Lamennais' arguments against the alliance of the Church with
the state, but he vigorously condemned the French Liberal's
faith in "the gradual and constant advance of the species, on the
whole, in knowledge and virtue."   It is not surprising, says
Newman, that De Lamennais "should practically quite discard
the doctrine that the 'many are always bad'; he seems to consider
them only mistaken."   The "fall of De Lamennais" may be
attributed to the elementary error of not recognizing that rebellion is of the nature of evil.   The power of the Church, adds
Newman, has always "consisted in asceticism," not in ministering to the economic and social "progress" of the people.   In short,
De Lamennais illustrates the temptation among sensitive and
well-meaning believers to make religion a mere instrument for
social amelioration, to subject the Church to the authority of
society.[13]

Liberalism becomes the very spirit of Antichrist in certain
pages of Tract LXXXIII, "The Patristical Idea of Antichrist,"
and eventually in the Biglietto speech.   Here we find Newman
summarizing the nature of a "heresy" virulent both in the fourth
century and in his own day, which held that a nation has nothing
to do with religion, that religion can and should be eliminated
from education, that all forms of religion might well be put
together inasmuch as all are equally valid or equally false, that
temperance and other virtues may be more effectively encouraged by social organizations than by a Church (with utility as
the great measuring rod), and that the truth is to be ascertained

by consulting majorities instead of by a divine authority. Indeed, Newman is persuaded that with these notions the Evil One
himself is seducing the modern world, promising it civil liberty,
equality, wealth, reform, "knowledge, science, philosophy, enlargement of mind." With these promises, "[Satan] shows
you how to become as gods. Then he laughs and jokes with you,
and gets intimate with you; he takes your hand, and gets his
fingers between yours, and grasps them, and then you are his." [14]
It is this spirit which supplies the subject matter for Newman's
speech forty-one years later. On receiving the *biglietto,* Newman replied with a summary of modern Liberalism, against which
he had fought so long. He reminded his audience that this
movement teaches that "there is no positive truth in religion,"
that all forms of religion are merely matters of taste or personal
preference, without objective reality, without power to bind society into a unity, without authority. It teaches, further, that
universal and secular education must take the place of religion,
in inculcating such ethical virtues as benevolence, veracity, justice, sobriety. Newman admits that "there is much in the Liberalistic theory which is good and true"; in fact, its excellences
blind one to its really threatening character, *i.e.* its determination
to "block out religion" and to supersede it. Thus Newman declares, with quiet horror, "There never was a device of the Enemy
so cleverly framed and with such promise of success." The danger of secularism does not, however, strike Newman with very
deep fear; he is certain that Christianity will triumph over its
present foe as it has triumphed over numerous earlier foes.[15]

No doubt the most telling arraignment of Liberalism which
Newman ever composed is the series of letters which make up
The Tamworth Reading Room. In these letters to *The Times,*
in reply to an address by Sir Robert Peel on the establishment
of a library and reading room at Tamworth, Newman argued
with great stylistic informality and wit against Peel's assumption that secular education might become a substitute for religion.
Newman holds that "secular knowledge" — a liberal and non-
religious education — can in no way supply a principle or a means
or an antecedent for moral improvement; nor can it afford a

principle of social unity, or of action.   Without personal religion,
secular knowledge tends simply to unbelief.   It is in these letters
that we find some of Newman's choicest epigrams:

"Who was ever consoled in real trouble by the small beer of literature
or science?" . . . "There are two ways of reading Nature — as a
machine and as a work.   If we come to it with the assumption that it
is a creation, we shall study it with awe; if assuming it to be a system,
with mere curiosity."

At a time when Carlyle was declaring *wonder* to be the essence of
religion, Newman tersely reminds his readers that "Wonder is
not religion, or we should be worshipping our railroads."   He
sums up his position in the end, as follows:

"I consider, then, that intrinsically excellent and noble as are scientific
pursuits, and worthy of a place in a liberal education, and fruitful in
temporal benefits to the community, still they are not, and cannot be,
the *instrument* of an ethical training; that physics do not supply a
basis, but only materials for religious sentiment; that knowledge does
but occupy, does not form the mind; that apprehension of the unseen
is the only known principle capable of subduing moral evil, educating
the multitude, and organizing society; and that, whereas man is born
for action, action flows not from inferences, but from impressions, —
not from reasonings, but from Faith." [16]

Throughout all his study and indictment of "the Liberalistic
theory," Newman remembered his vision of the primitive Church.
No modern winds of doctrine, however enchanting to the intellect or affections, could prevail over his severely patristic conception of religion. To the end he was conscious of the warfare
between the Church and the world, between the City of God and
the City of Man, between nature and grace.   Thus he wrote:

"What we want, is to understand that we are in the place in which the
early Christians were, with the same covenant, ministry, sacraments,
and duties; — to realize a state of things long past away; — to feel
that we are in a sinful world, a world lying in wickedness; to discern
our position in it, that we are witnesses in it, that reproach and suffering are our portion . . ." [17]

ii. Defining the "Via Media": Newman and Anglicanism

Contrary to the impression in many quarters, Newman's discussions of the Anglican position have a remarkable vitality and a relevance to our own day. This is attested by statements made by Catholics and non-Catholics alike. Newman's definition of the *Via Media*, in the judgment of Frank Leslie Cross, continues to be "a magnificent apologia for what may be termed the Anglican ethos." A Roman Catholic judgment, that of Christopher Dawson, reaches the same conclusion: Newman's work "still remains the best justification for the essential Anglican position." And Geoffrey Faber, commenting on Pusey's taking over the *Via Media* after Newman departed, remarks that even now, long after Pusey's generation, "it must be admitted that, after a fashion, it is working still." [1] Thus we are justified in looking carefully into at least three of Newman's major Anglican works, the *Lectures on the Prophetical Office of the Church* (later called the *Via Media*) (1837), the *Lectures on Justification* (1838), and Tract LXXXV, "Holy Scripture in Its Relation to the Catholic Creed" (a work originally consisting of eight lectures) (1838). There is warrant also for glancing into some of Newman's essays and reviews, published in the *British Magazine* and the *British Critic* between 1836 and 1842: "Home Thoughts Abroad," "Palmer's View of Faith and Unity," "The Theology of St. Ignatius," "Prospects of the Anglican Church," "The Anglo-American Church," "The Catholicity of the Anglican Church," "The Reformation of the Eleventh Century," and "Private Judgment." In these writings we find notable passages expressing some of the ideas, aspirations, and ideals of present-day Anglo-Catholicism, whether British or American, and of the "High Church" Episcopalianism peculiar to the United States.

The *Lectures on the Prophetical Office of the Church* grew out of a controversial correspondence with the Abbé Jager, a learned French priest, at a time when Newman was considering the comparative weakness and strength of Roman and Anglican Catholicism. We know very little about this correspondence, but apparently the French priest was attempting to persuade Newman to consider the possibility of a union of the Anglican with the Roman Church. At any rate, Newman used his letters as a basis for the series of lectures which, as we have seen,* he delivered in Adam de Brome's chapel. As they now appear in Volume I of the *Via Media* these lectures group themselves according to three or four general topics: after an initial lecture on the nature and ground of Roman and Protestant errors, there are chapters on Rome as neglectful of Antiquity, on the doctrine of Infallibility considered morally and politically, on the use and abuse of private judgment, on the indefectibility of the Church Catholic, on the essentials of the Gospel, on Scripture as a record of faith and teachings and as the document of proof in the early Church, and, finally, on the fortunes of the Church. Three basic themes inform the book as a whole: institutional authority, scriptural authority, and private judgment. The three themes are indeed one: What is the *seat* of religious authority?

Newman's attitude toward the Roman Church in 1836–37 was, in some ways, a new one. He had started, as he tells us in the *Apologia,* with the common Protestant belief that the Pope was Antichrist, and that the whole Roman system was so patently unsound as to need no further examination. The great struggle over Catholic Emancipation had not softened his feeling; nor had his growing dissatisfaction with ordinary Protestantism. But as his friendship with Hurrell Froude developed, and as he observed the Roman Catholic system during his Mediterranean journey, he came to believe that, while it harbored a "wretched perversion of the truth," it nevertheless soothed the heart and promoted piety. On his journey home he wrote poetically of Rome:

> "O that thy creed were sound!
> For thou dost soothe the heart, thou Church of Rome,
> By thy unwearied watch and varied round
> Of service, in thy Saviour's holy home." [2]

Moreover, in his own thinking, and in his reading of the great English divines, he slowly arrived at the conviction that what-

* Cf. Chap. II, ii, p. 35.

ever might be said against the modern Roman Church, with all her corruption and error, she still was a teacher of "the Christian creed and hope." Like the English Church, she still retained her title to be a part of that historic body which connects the present with the day of the Apostles; and she also had a strong and consistent theory with which to oppose her assailants or to explain or justify popular traditions. So far as her constitution, doctrine, traditions, and spirit reflected the ancient undivided Church, there could be no quarrel with her. Yet in so far as the Roman Church interpreted her claims as the witness and suffrage of antiquity solely at her own convenience and by her own authority, she could hardly expect the submission of the English Church. This was especially true in respect to the claims of infallibility and supremacy. Though Newman in 1836–37 felt that Rome should no longer be regarded as being Babylon or Antichrist, he still believed that her arrogant assertions and her highhanded claims would generate resistance in every Anglican; neither union nor submission was possible. Such was the general state of Newman's mind when he composed the lectures in 1836; it reflected a line of thought in English divinity from Andrewes to Wake. But it was new in its reasonable caution, its avoidance of abuse or insult, its moderation, and its recognition that the Roman Church had a just case which Newman was prepared to defend fearlessly in the face of strong popular prejudice. He was ready to show Englishmen how little they knew of the real Christianity in the Roman Church; how ancient, Catholic, and edifying were many elements in her which were commonly called "Popish"; how discreditable and dangerous were loose and uncritical allegations against her; and how urgent was the need for discarding slovenly prejudices and for appraising Rome with objective reasoning and with a knowledge of the technical points and the minutiae of a highly scholastic subject. Newman's arguments were all the more potent at the time because their clearness matched their sternness, coming from one who did not disguise his feeling that there was much in the Roman system to be preserved, admired, and emulated.

Since the central theme of the lectures is the question of religious authority, it is natural that Newman should choose for his

point of assault the Roman doctrine of Infallibility. To this
question he subordinates his discussion of private judgment, the
Scripture, and the nature of the Church. Against the Roman
claim of infallibility, he levels two main objections. In the first
place, the present Roman Church, in her assumed infallibility,
seems to override and supersede, at least to be neglectful of, the
historical evidence of antiquity to doctrine, namely, the "consent
of the Fathers." Newman reviews the great Roman Catholic
theologians, and examines the conclusions of the great Councils,
and finally concludes: "We have her own avowal that the Fathers ought to be followed, and again that she does not follow
them." [3] The other objection is characteristic of Newman. He
subjects the Roman claim to the test of practical human experience: he sees the inherent contradiction between the notion of
infallibility and the actual limitations of human knowledge.
From Bishop Butler he has learned the folly of trying to "round
off into finished and pretentious schemes our fragmentary yet
certain notices of our own condition and of God's dealings with
it." [4] He has come to prefer *moral evidence* to rational demonstration, and he seems to see that the former points toward
authority, not to infallibility. Following the great Anglican
divines, he notes that the historic Church possessed, in varying
degrees, a true authority, trustworthy and supreme on the most
fundamental points of religion, clear and weighty on many other
questions, but inadequate to decide everything. Hence the
Church is, not "infallible," but *prophetic* in her office. Newman
has made an appeal to the facts of history; and he has found that
in the early undivided Church there was such a thing as authority,
and there was no such thing as infallibility.

If Newman is hostile, in his lectures, to the Roman Catholic
doctrine of Infallibility, he is no less so to the Protestant doctrine
of Private Judgment. Three of the best-written chapters in the
Via Media deal with its use and abuse. Newman insists, with
great force and eloquence, on the absurdity of treating private
judgment as an invaluable privilege, of thinking of it as a setting
out in life without any guidance. Again following the empirical
method, Newman reminds his reader that few men ever act
solely on private judgment, that from the first we are forced to

rely on one authority or another. In religious matters, it becomes important whether we trust absolutely in an "infallible" Church, or in each individual's ability to be his own guide, or in some intermediate course. For Newman, the proper use of private judgment begins with the *habit* of obedience to those who have "natural authority" over us, no matter who they are; we thus cultivate a "teachable temper" before we venture to cavil or scrutinize. Self-conscious private judgment, which says, "I am examining, I am judging freely," is like a person who exults in grief, saying, "I am weeping, I am overcome." [5] From Newman's view, true judging is like true thinking — half-unconscious or implicit, and morally submissive. In short, private judgment is at its best when working in a spirit of reverence and humility, not when seeming to sit in magisterial superiority. If this is so, then the just conditions of the right exercise of private judgment in religion are present only in a Church which has authority but which does not overstrain that authority, in a Church which follows the *via media* between authoritarianism and anarchic individualism. The Anglican Church, Newman concludes, wields a comparatively gentle authority which elicits and even cultivates the spirit of freedom in its adherents, but also curbs that spirit and will not permit it to go beyond a certain point, either in opinion or in practice.

If Newman is asked what is the subject matter of Anglican authority, he replies that it lies in the Creeds and the Articles and the interpretation of the Scripture. Here the Church draws "the line between essentials and non-essentials . . . without imposing any yoke . . . She allows for a defect in the evidence [which her children] have received of her full doctrine . . . She exacts the great rudiments of the Gospel from all." Much discussion is devoted by Newman to just what these rudiments are,[6] but we may observe here only his statement of the general differences between the Anglican and the Roman "theory of religion," which will indicate the nature and scope of Anglican authority, and which will show further the degree to which Newman's lectures describe the present position of Anglicanism in relation to the Roman Church:

"Both we and the Roman Catholics," says Newman, "hold that the

Church Catholic is unerring in its declarations of faith, or saving grace; but we differ from each other as to what is the faith, and what is the Church Catholic.   They maintain that faith depends on the Church, we that the Church is built on the faith.   By Church Catholic we mean the Church Universal, as descended from the Apostles; they those branches of it which are in communion with Rome.   They consider the see of St. Peter to have a promise of permanence, we the Church Catholic and Apostolic.   Again, they understand by the Faith, whatever the Church at any time declares to be faith; we what it has actually so declared from the beginning.   We hold that the Church Catholic will never depart from those outlines of doctrine which the Apostles formally published; they that she will never depart in any of her acts from that entire system, written and oral, public and private, explicit and implicit, which the Apostles received and taught; we that she has a gift of fidelity, they of discrimination.

"Again, both they and we anathematize those who deny the Faith; but they extend the condemnation to all who question any decree of the Roman Church; we apply it to those only who deny any article of the original Apostolic Creed.   The creed of Rome is ever subject to increase; ours is fixed once for all.   We confine our anathema to the Athanasian Creed; they extend it to Pope Pius's.   They cut themselves off from the rest of Christendom; we cut ourselves off from no branch, not even from themselves.   We are at peace with Rome as regards the essentials of faith; but she tolerates us as little as she tolerates any sect or heresy.   We admit her Baptism and her Orders; her custom is to re-baptize and re-ordain our members who chance to join her." [7]

If the lectures on the *Via Media* attempted to find a sound compromise on the subject of authority, the *Lectures on Justification* (1838) sought to find a "middle way" on the subject of the "attainment of righteousness."   These lectures are much less interesting than *The Prophetical Office of the Church,* and many critics, such as Hutton, have found them "somewhat straw-chopping and dry."   It is very difficult, if not impossible, as Hutton adds, for a layman of the present day to enter into the controversy between the Lutheran and the Catholic on justification. [8] Few ordinary readers today care to dwell on the distinction between "imputed" and "infused" righteousness, between "making a man just" and "*accounting* him just."   Newman's lectures, their themes and their language, seem to belong to an age which spoke a language quite different from our own. Yet so able a writer on the Anglican Revival as Yngve Brilioth declares that these lectures "form perhaps the chief theological document of the Oxford Movement." [9] They deserve therefore a few moments' attention if we are to have a complete picture of Newman's Anglican labors.

We may begin by remembering that in theological literature the word "justify" means to "make acceptable to God," as righteous or worthy of salvation. Precisely how this was done, by what particular process, had long been a chief point of contention between Catholics and Protestants. The Roman Catholics, who believed in "justification by obedience," held that "justification consists in love, or sanctity, or obedience, or 'renewal of the Holy Ghost.' " [10] The "substance" of justification was sanctification, a mingling of faith and love, manifesting itself in "good works," or penance. Inasmuch as, in Catholic theology, baptism cleanses the soul of guilt, justification is rather by baptism than by faith; for guilt incurred after baptism the offender must make satisfaction (do penance), without which the merits of Christ are of no avail.[11] On the other hand, the Lutherans, holding to the doctrine of "justification by faith," maintained that the faith which justifies imparts its gift "without the exercise or even the presence of love." [12] Luther wished to extirpate all notions of human merit, to drive home the idea that man cannot save himself, that acceptance and justification must come from God and cannot be earned by men. Put briefly, the Lutheran doctrine means that man is forgiven and accepted by God simply in response to faith, and in no sense because he has discharged a debt, or in some way earned pardon, by any form of good works or penance.

Now between these two doctrines of Justification — the Catholic one of obedience and the Lutheran one of faith — Newman attempted a *via media* of justification by baptism. He regarded the Lutheran doctrine as distinctly faulty, the Catholic doctrine as merely incomplete. Only when the latter is present in a one-sided way, as in the later Roman Church (to which the inward renewal revealed in obedience is the *unica formalis causa* of justification), is it in conflict with the Anglican position. Its main

features are accepted by Newman as true, and it is referred to
with great warmth and eloquence in expressions derived from St.
Augustine.[13]   Besides the Augustinian basis for Newman's doctrine, there was for Newman, as there could not be for the Protestants, a basis in the witnesses of both Testaments, instead of in
one or two books, as with Luther.   From psalmist, prophets, and
apostles came the same promise and announcement, "the gift of
righteousness, not a shadow but a substance, not a name but a
power, not an imputation but an inward work." [14]   This doctrine,
Newman believes, has behind it the whole witness of the Christian Church.   The Lutheran doctrine, on the other hand, is a
novelty with only three centuries behind it.   Hence, in very
vehement language, Newman dismisses it as private, arbitrary,
modern, barren, and dead.   His own doctrine, to put it briefly in
Brilioth's words, was that justification "consists in a something, a
quality, a substance, which comes into and changes man, and makes
him acceptable"; [15] it makes man a temple of the Holy Ghost,
raises him from a state of nature to a state of grace, which bears
fruit in holiness and obedience.   But the presence of the Spirit
is only a form or means of the presence of Christ.   At this point
in Newman's doctrine we find ourselves confronted with sacramental mysticism: it is the sacraments which impart this presence
of Christ; they are the means of justification — not merely faith,
as with the Lutherans, not merely obedience and good works as
with the Roman Catholics.   It is the mystical efficacy of the sacraments that protects Anglicanism from the presumptuous assurance
of salvation which appears in the Lutheran, and from the ex-
ternalism and incompleteness which appear in the Roman Catholic.   Thus, to conclude, Newman is again applying the conception
of the *via media*: here he arrives at the idea that justifying faith
is the organ by which the soul appropriates the working of outward means.   It is balanced exactly "in relation to Baptism,
which brings new birth; to the Eucharist, which is the source of
new life; and to obedience, which is 'the atmosphere in which
faith breathes.' " [16]   The Lutherans had laid stress on confidence, the Catholics on obedience; Newman now looks to the
Anglican homilies for the union of the two.   From that he assures himself that faith will grow out of obedience, and, through

the ministry of the sacraments, will "make its venture," grasp the paradox of the Gospel and find itself confirmed by further obedience, winning ultimately the crown of justification.

It is noteworthy that Newman concludes his book with a violent attack on the subjectivism of popular Evangelical preaching. Since he has been charged with wishing to divide man from God by rites and dogmas and laws, he now counters by inverting the charge: it is the opposite side which separates man from God by overstressing the emotions, by aggravating one's tendency to self-analysis, and by giving the chief place in religious worship to preaching and exhorting. Once more we see Newman affirming his convictions as to the objective, dogmatic, institutional character of the Church. His book ends with a memorable attack on Luther, who, he says, "found Christians in bondage to their works and observances; [who] released them by his doctrine of faith; and [who] left them in bondage to their feelings." [17]

A much more interesting work than the lectures on justification is Newman's series of lectures on *Holy Scripture in Relation to the Catholic Creed*. Here we find Newman explaining the difficulties of founding one's faith either on a literal adherence to the Biblical text or on tradition. The English Church, according to these lectures, avoids Latitudinarianism on the one hand and Romanism on the other, by following a policy of interpretative selection in Scripture, and a faith in the abilities of the early Fathers. By Latitudinarianism Newman means the view that it is not important what doctrine a man holds, so long as he honestly holds it and lives up to it conscientiously. To combat this view many had had recourse to Scripture, only to be disappointed at not finding the "Church system of doctrine" explicitly set forth therein. Newman attempts to show such inquirers that there is no more difficulty in proving from Scripture the Church doctrines he was preaching than there was in proving from Scripture the doctrine of the Trinity, and much less than in proving the authenticity of the canon. In so doing he shows a remarkable advance in his thinking over that of most of his ecclesiastical contemporaries. As J. A. Froude later noted, he "seems to have recognized earlier than most . . . that the Bible was not a single book, but a national literature, produced at intervals, during many hundred years, and under endless varieties of circumstances." [18]   He was also acutely aware that just as the Creed was now everywhere under assault, so in time would be the Canon of the Scripture, unless it were understood and interpreted in a fashion quite different from that dictated by "the spirit of the age."   He was sure, he said, "that the way which the Age follows cannot be right, for it tends to destroy Revelation altogether."   Such a way must be evil which, when pursued, "destroys Church, Creed, Bible altogether, — which obliterates the very Name of Christ from the world." [19]

Newman tries to meet the problem of scriptural authority for the Catholic Creed by examining first the difficulties in scriptural proof of that Creed and also of Latitudinarianism, then by analyzing the structure of the Bible antecedently considered and in matter of fact, and by turning finally to the external and internal difficulties of the Canon and the Creed.   It is not necessary to follow Newman's detailed and technical argument; much of it is no longer fresh or even tenable.   But there are certain passages which make Tract LXXXV stimulating reading to the present day, especially those passages on the structure and style of the Bible.

"The structure of Scripture is such," declares Newman, "so irregular and immethodical, that either we must hold that the Gospel doctrine or message is not contained in Scripture (and, if so, either that there is no message at all given, or that it is given elsewhere, out of Scripture), or, as the alternative, we must hold that it is but indirectly and covertly recorded there, that is, under the surface."

This confusion in the text has a bearing on the "inspiration of the Bible"; and Newman is prepared to say that "though the Bible is inspired, and therefore, in one sense, written by God, yet very large portions of it, if not far the greater part of it, are written in as free and unconstrained a manner, and (apparently) with as little apparent consciousness of a supernatural dictation or restraint, on the part of His earthly instruments, as if He had had no share in the work."   But, argues Newman, as God "rules the course of the world, yet men conduct it, so He has inspired the

Bible, yet men have written it." Its writers had definite objects in view, were influenced by circumstances, purposely omitted or introduced certain matters, leaving other matters incomplete. It bears the marks of dialect and style and the effects of the times as does any other book.   And yet, says Newman, "I insist . . . [that] it has in it the Spirit and the Mind of God."

Even so, as we have noted, Newman is far from considering the Bible to be *one* book:

"It is a great number of writings, of various persons, living at different times, put together into one, and assuming its existing form as if casually and by accident.   It is as if you were to seize the papers or correspondence of leading men in any school of philosophy or science, which were never designed for publication, and bring them out in one volume.   You would find probably in the collection so resulting many papers begun and not finished; some parts systematic and didactic, but the greater part made up of hints or of notices which assume first principles instead of asserting them, or of discussions upon particular points which happened to require their attention.   I say the doctrines, the first principles, the rules, the objects of the school, would be taken for granted, alluded to, implied, not directly stated.   You would have some trouble to get at them; you would have many repetitions, many hiatuses, many things which looked like contradictions; you would have to work your way through heterogeneous materials, and, after your best efforts, there would be much hopelessly obscure; and, on the other hand, you might look in vain in such a casual collection for some particular opinions which the writers were known nevertheless to have held, nay to have insisted on." [20]

The Scriptural writings are, in like manner, those of men who had already been introduced to a body of divine knowledge, in this case "a knowledge of the unseen world and the society of Angels, and who reported what they had seen and heard."   Such men's writings are full of allusions to a *system* with which they are all familiar.   It is therefore highly unlikely that all of that system will be represented in their "occasional" writings — for, as Newman insists, these men wrote on the occasion of some particular error, or to stir the minds of their brethren, or to answer questions, or to give directions for conduct.   Thus, for Newman, it is "very improbable that the Bible [as we have it] should contain

the whole of the Revealed Word of God." [21]   They who insist
to the contrary have the burden and the duty of proving the point.
On the other hand, as regards matters of *faith*, the Bible "contains all that is necessary for salvation . . . The early Church
thought so, and the early Church must have known." [22]   As for
a complete code of *morals*, or systematic statement of Church
government, or of *rites*, or of *discipline*, the early Church seems
to have found none of these in Scripture.   As for the doctrines of
the faith, considering all the circumstances involved, "the wonder is, that they are *all* there . . . they are there by a sort of
accident" — as by some divine interposition.[23]

So much for the structure of the Bible antecedently considered,
and examined for matters of fact.   Newman's next consideration,
of scriptural style, is aimed at answering why a doctrine is sometimes not introduced when there is an actual call for it, and why
when it is introduced it should so often be obscurely mentioned.
Two attributes of the Biblical style will, Newman thinks, account
for these facts: simplicity and depth.   "Simplicity leads a writer
to say things without display; and depth obliges him to use inadequate words."   Moreover, depth of thought may lead a
writer to verbal contradictions, to paradoxes, "and it is a property
of simplicity not to care to avoid them."   When a writer is
"deep," his half-sentences, parentheses, clauses, even his individual words, may have a meaning in them independent of the context, and admit of exposition.   He is simple, puzzlingly direct,
careless of systematic presentation, unable to communicate the
full burden of his message.[24]   Thus the style of the Bible is
"plain and colourless, as regards the relation of facts"; its facts,
like its texts, "need a comment — they are evidently but a text *for
a comment*." [25]   The same is true of its statements of doctrine:
their simplicity and depth, accorded a figurative or sacramental
style characteristic of Oriental teaching, require a comment or an
interpretation.   And the early Church, as Newman viewed it,
always considered Scripture to contain recondite meanings and
mysteries; in fact the early Church half-concealed many of her
doctrines from the uninitiated, observing a great secrecy, for example, concerning the Trinity and the Eucharist.   Now, con-

cludes Newman, "if the early Church had reasons for concealment, it may be that Scripture has the same, especially if we
suppose . . . that the system of the early Church is a continuation of the system of those inspired men who wrote the New
Testament." [26]

Here again we observe Newman, as an Anglican in the late
1830's, pursuing his quest for authority. Since there is a great
deal beneath the letter of the Bible, which is only an apparently
miscellaneous collection of writings, and since, furthermore, the
early Church had sifted it out and believed these writings to be
the authentic collection (though why these books were accepted
and others rejected we do not know), Newman feels compelled
to regard the Church as the authority in interpreting Scripture and
in verifying the "Church system of doctrine" which an individual's "searching of the Scripture" can never adequately succeed in
doing. There is, for Newman, something in the apparently accidental and miscellaneous nature of the Bible analogous to the
apparently accidental and miscellaneous character of human life.
"The Church reveals a hidden unity and purpose within Scripture,
just as Scripture reveals a hidden unity and purpose in human
life." [27] The true Christian, according to Newman, is obliged to
choose between accepting this hidden unity and purpose under the
guidance of the Church, on the one hand, and, on the other, of entering upon a course of private judgment and criticism which must
end in breaking down a belief in revelation itself, leaving nothing
of value in the content of faith. Without a humble trust in the
Church, and in her credentials as verified in the proper places of
Scripture, those individuals who seek the truths of the Bible will
be confronted with incoherent and capricious meanings, bewil-
deringly varying with the minds of those who undertake the disappointing task.

We must forego the reader's possible desire to trace Newman's
further arguments as he carries his discussion into the external
and internal difficulties of the Canon and the Creed. Here his
thought and his methods have less freshness and vitality than we
have observed in his analysis of the structure and style of the
Bible as illuminating the basis of the Catholic Creed. We may

say, on the whole, that Tract LXXXV contains some of the most epigrammatic and intellectually fascinating passages in all of Newman's writings.

Let us conclude our study of Newman's Anglican criticism by turning to various pertinent remarks scattered through the other essays and tracts. They show, in varying degrees, the spirit and aim of much in Anglo-Catholicism which persists even today. For example, in "How to Accomplish It," Newman hopes for a reconstruction of the Anglican Church on the principles of Laud. He looks for materials for that reconstruction (which will make the Church again attractive to the masses) in the ordination service, in the sacraments, in a revitalization of the celebration of festival days and the solemnization of fast days, in a recovery of "the legitimate priesthood," and in a revival of "religious Sisterhoods." [28]   Newman also expresses Anglo-Catholic willingness to accept the high sacramental language of St. Ignatius, who cried, "I have no pleasure in corruptible food . . . I would have *God's bread . . . which is the flesh of Jesus Christ,*" instead of the bread and wine as symbols only. [29]   Newman further expands the "Catholic" outlook by examining the early Fathers' actual use or interpretation of such key-words as "altar," "sacrifice," "liturgy," "heresy," "perfect man," "the Mother of God," especially as employed by St. Ignatius, one of the very earliest of the Christian Fathers, who was bishop of Antioch from about A.D. 69 to 107. [30]   In so doing, Newman believes that he is returning to the uncorrupted beginnings of the faith, and that he is there finding something quite other than modern Protestantism or Church-of-England Evangelicalism. He believes he is finding a religion more severe, otherworldly, and authentic than the varieties of Christianity he sees flourishing about him.

Anglo-Catholic also are his remarks about the Church, about her intellectual grounds, about her "Notes," and about certain pitfalls lying in wait for the convert. He mourns that the Anglican Church has so "few large systematic treatises . . . no ecclesiastical historian [like] Fleury or Mosheim, no fully furnished polemic [like] Bellarmine, and no dogmatic writer [like] Petavius or Vasquez." [31]   The unlearned condition of the Church has fostered the growth of ultra-Protestantism, with its key-doctrine of Private Judgment, and its corollary that "there is nothing which individuals might not find out for themselves, that in fact there is no real body of doctrine . . . but either an internal feeling on the one hand, or a good life on the other." [32]   Present-day Anglo-Catholics lament in like fashion that their position has suffered from the lack of vigorous theologians since the death of Bishop Gore.   Newman, we note further, is distressed over the seeming lack, or the weaknesses, of the "Notes" of the Church. Historically the Church has been One, Holy, Catholic, Apostolic; but now, he observes, her children "have substituted political and civil watchwords" — they talk not of "the Catholic Church," but of the "Church of England," "the National Religion," which is not Apostolic but "by law established."   They speak of "the Episcopal Church," "Protestantism," "the glorious memory," "Martin Luther," "civil and religious liberty all over the world."   To Newman all these expressions are infinitely repugnant.   What seemed to his bustling, optimistic, liberal contemporaries as enlightened, freeing, and full of promise, was to Newman the essence of low-mindedness.   Such people, he concludes acidly, "have taken tavern toasts for the Notes of the Church." [33]

Newman also admits certain surface blandishments awaiting the convert.   In his article on the "Prospects of the Anglican Church," he acknowledges that, since "the Church system [is] beautiful in idea," ritual, and symbol, persons susceptible to sentiment and romance may accept Anglo-Catholic doctrine on inadequate intellectual grounds.   However, he adds, "we see no harm in persons obeying the higher perceptions and impulses of their minds," even when they are romantic or emotional, "provided always that they are ready to go on with what they have begun, to acquiesce in consequences when they come upon them, to take up with a course as a whole." [34]   They will be safe, Newman further adds, if they go to the Fathers and to the seventeenth-century English divines.   The former, unlike the modern practical religious writers, were contemplative, mystical, subtle, find-

ing truth not in separate verses of the Bible but "hid under the
tenor of the sacred text as a whole," and therefore using the
Bible not as a foundation but as "an organ of the truth."

Another danger awaiting the potential convert lies in the social
snobbery connected, in many minds, with the externals of the
Anglican system. This is dealt with in a memorable but
now little-read essay of Newman's on "The Anglo-American
Church." Here we find a devastating analysis in 1839 of some
of the vices of American Episcopalianism. A commercial nation,
Newman says, produces a social class — "the opulent merchants
and traders in towns" — who desire

"a religion which neither irritates their reason nor interferes with their
comforts . . . They need nothing to fill the heart, to feed upon, or to
live in; they despise enthusiasm, they abhor fanaticism, they persecute bigotry. They want only so much religion as will satisfy their
natural perception of the propriety of being religious. Reason teaches
them that utter disregard of their Maker is unbecoming, and they
determine to be religious, not from love and fear, but from good sense."

Such persons will shun the sectarian churches as "enthusiastic" or
vulgarly emotional, and the Roman Catholic Church as "despotic." In the Anglo-American Church, they will find "moderation, rationality, decency, order." As they are increasingly
admitted, "a sleek gentlemanlike religion will grow up within
the sacred pale, with well-warmed chapels, softly cushioned pews,
and eloquent preachers. The poor and needy, the jewels of the
Church, will dwindle away; the clergy will sink in honour, and
rich laymen will culminate." There will be churches "which
rather resemble splendid drawing-rooms than houses of worship,
and in which the poor man could hardly feel himself at home."
Newman, in these last words, is quoting an American account,
which proceeds: "At Chillicothe [in Ohio] the Episcopal Church
contains many of the wealthier and more refined families, but
has not established itself in the preference of the great mass of
the religious people, who are principally, as in other parts of
Ohio, Methodists, Presbyterians, and Baptists." [35] On this account of the vices of the Anglo-American Church, Newman
makes the acid comment: "we think . . . that pews, carpets,

cushions, and fine speaking are not developments of the Apostolical Succession." Then he addresses the American Church directly, bidding it throw away the luxurious appurtenances of worship, to open the Church to all, to return to severe and holy simplicity.[36] Later in the essay, as a further effort to correct American notions, he pours scorn on the term "Episcopalian." "We are," he says, " 'of the Church,' not 'of the Episcopal Church'; . . . to call ourselves Episcopalians is to imply that we differ from the mass of dissenters mainly in Church government and form . . ." In conclusion, Newman adds that far from being "a genteel and fashionable communion for the rich and happy" — the "Episcopal Church" as he saw it in England and America — the true Church is One, Holy, Catholic, and Apostolic, earnestly encountering "the realities of human life, need, sickness, pain, affliction, sin, doubt, despair, [which] it was sent into the world to overcome." [37]

Elsewhere in Newman's Anglican essays we find his preoccupation with the exalted authority of the Church Catholic. At times, as in his essay on the "Catholicity of the Anglican Church," he accepts the "branch theory" of Palmer, which he at one time had rejected,[38] and feels that "the Roman, Greek, and English are [the Universal Church's] three great portions . . . the English Church is . . . the Catholic Church in England." [39] In this sense, the Anglican Church shares with the Roman and the Greek the final spiritual authority. Looking back on the past of the Church Catholic, Newman is impressed not merely by the reforms which it called forth but more often by its amazing triumphs over the temporal power. In his article on the "Reformation of the Eleventh Century," he surveys all the ecclesiastical evils of that time, yet emerges with a strong sympathy for Gregory VII, who kept Henry IV waiting barefoot in the snow at Canossa. Admitting, in the language of understatement, that "it was an uncomfortable thing," Newman reminds us that "Henry III, the king's father, would habitually, before presenting himself in royal robes upon his throne, submit in private to a self-imposed scourging." [40] As Newman observes the history of the Church Catholic, he remembers his early conviction that the Pope was Antichrist. Now he comes to the belief that the charge of being Antichrist is almost a "Note" of the Church, and that, properly considered, the charge places the Anglican and the Roman Churches in the same class. This observation occurs in his essay on "The Protestant Idea of Antichrist." Here, we may note in passing, Newman attacks one of the favorites of his youth, Thomas Newton, whose *Dissertations on the Prophecies* had implanted in him the doctrine of the Pope as Antichrist. Nowhere in Newman's writings is there a more scathing and merciless portrait, in this case a portrait which is intended to show that only "a man so idolatrous of comfort, so liquorish of preferment," could have propounded such a doctrine.[41]   Finally, we note in these essays frequent considerations of the doctrine of "Private Judgment," to which Newman gives special attention in an essay with that title. By way of championing the authority of the Church, he points out the heavy responsibility attendant on judging privately. He also points out, as we have noted elsewhere, that it is in fact an extremely rare act: "few men have time to scrutinize [and judge] accurately." [42]   Then with the consummate skill characteristic of his portraits of types of men, he illustrates how a convert, in one case a servant in a family, may pass from Anglicanism to Presbyterianism, or from Unitarianism to Evangelicalism, under the impression that private judgment underlay all the decisions involved. The truth is, according to Newman, that such conversions, indeed all important decisions, are made under the influence or guidance of other *persons*, never merely in the private recesses of the individual's mind. Newman notes that in the Bible, "conversions . . . are brought about in a very marked way through a *teacher*, and *not* by means of private judgment: . . . if an appeal *is* made to private judgment, this is done in order to settle who the teacher is, and what are his tokens, rather than to substantiate this or that religious opinion or practice." [43]   The implications for the Newman of the late 1830's and early 1840's are obvious: private judgment in matters of religion should be confined to ascertaining the credentials of the Church as a teacher, and, once convinced of her "Notes," it should submit to her as a divine *authority*.

So strongly at this time does Newman feel the need of Anglican authority being genuinely exercised that he inserts into his essay on "Private Judgment" various passages of warning which have never been profitably utilized by those writers who have traced his progress toward Rome. For example, though he is still, in 1841, convinced that his Church is "the divinely appointed teacher," [44] he nevertheless deeply regrets the lack of Christian unity in Great Britain under the Archbishop of Canterbury. "The time is come when so great an evil, as this, cannot stand its ground against the good feeling and common sense of religious persons." Then, almost as if looking forward to the climactic year of 1845, he adds: "Unless the proper persons take it into their very serious consideration, they may look for certain to undergo the loss, as time goes on, of some whom they would least like to be lost to our Church." [45] There can hardly be any doubt that he has himself in mind. His essay on "Private Judgment" appeared in July; Tract CX had appeared in February and had been condemned in March. There is thus considerable significance in the final lines of the essay; they warn the Anglican Church not to "own itself Protestant," and not to persecute the "Ancient Truth." "If," concludes Newman, "our own communion were to own itself Protestant . . . if the profession of Ancient Truth were to be persecuted in our Church, and its teaching forbidden, — then doubtless, for a season, Catholic minds among us would be unable to see their way." [46] We have already seen that Newman indeed was "for a season" — between 1842 and 1845 — "unable to see his way." The problem of authority was ultimately solved, for him, by submission to Rome.

CHAPTER VIII

DEFENDING ROME

Newman's critical and polemical efforts in behalf of Rome took the form of two sets of lectures, the *Difficulties of Anglicans* (1850) and *The Present Position of Catholics in England* (1851); portions of the *Apologia* (1864); two epistolary polemics, the *Letter to Dr. Pusey* (1866) and the *Letter to the Duke of Norfolk* (1875); and one of the most unusual Prefaces ever penned, the Preface to the third edition of the *Via Media* (1877). All these works show us Newman the controversialist; all abound in brilliant rhetorical passages; all demand our attention if we wish to complete our impression of Newman's mind and methods.

i. *An Appeal to Anglicans*

On March 8, 1850, there occurred the celebrated decision in what came to be known as "the Gorham case." The Bishop of Exeter had refused to install G. C. Gorham in the vicarage of Bramford Speke because he had denied the doctrine of baptismal regeneration. The bishop's refusal had been confirmed by the Court of Arches. Now the Privy Council overruled the bishop's refusal. At once there was great excitement in the newspapers and magazines and among Anglicans in general. Here was a glaring case of the civil power asserting its supremacy over the Church, even to dictating what was, and was not, orthodox doctrine, and making its decision in a flagrantly Latitudinarian spirit. Many Tractarians, such as Hope-Scott, Manning, and Allies, who had been near the eve of conversion to Rome, were now nearer than ever. Here was an opportunity for some persuasive Catholic controversialist to show wherein Anglicanism contained ineradicable difficulties, and wherein Catholicism met the needs of wavering Tractarians. Newman was persuaded, much against his will (he preferred to let the Gorham case speak for itself), to deliver twelve lectures on the problems of Anglicanism. In the first seven of his lectures he shows how the Oxford Movement, in his opinion, must issue legitimately in communion with the Church of Rome. He tries to indicate that the Movement had been "foreign to the National Church"; that it had not really derived its strength from that Church; that its "Providential course" was in the direction neither of that Church, nor any party in it, nor any "branch Church," nor any sect. It is clear that Newman is trying to block off all paths but that which leads to Rome. These seven lectures are chiefly negative, but negative in a brilliant and persuasive way. The next five lectures are devoted to removing the difficulties in accepting the communion of Rome as One, Holy, Catholic, and Apostolic. They recognize the popular Victorian conception of Roman Catholics, of their Church, and of their social state. They try therefore to show that the Church's sanctity — the Church as Holy — is not in fact prejudiced by either the social or the religious state of Catholic countries; that her unity — the Church as One — is not prejudiced by the differences among Catholics; that her Catholicity is not prejudiced by her heretical and schismatical bodies; and, finally, that her Apostolicity is not prejudiced by her ecclesiastical history. These lectures, like the first seven, are negative, but, again, negative in a seductive way, for Newman disarms his critics by stating their objections more forcibly than they could themselves. Others of Newman's books are of greater value and substance, but no other work, except *The Present Position of Catholics*, so well exhibits the full range of his oratorical power. Though we have classified the work as a critical effort in behalf of Rome, still that effort took the form of brilliant rhetoric which left an unforgettable impression on such an Anglican as R. H. Hutton, who has described Newman's manner and method as a lecturer.[1] "His exposition of the weakness of the Anglican position," says another and later critic, "is devastating, and yet it arouses no unnecessary antagonism. There is no unfairness, no cheap sarcasm, no empty rhetoric." [2]

Few listeners could resist the fine rhetorical tact of the opening lecture, with its apology for what might seem an attempt to weaken a religious institution which, Newman admitted, forms a defense against those forces "which carried the Reform Bill and

Free Trade, and [which] may make short work with ortho-
doxy." [3] Yet few Anglicans could sit without squirming while
Newman described the growth of his disillusionment with the
Church of England, and concluded by saying:

"We look in amazement on what we thought so unearthly, and find
so commonplace or worthless. Then we perceive that aforetime we
have not been guided by reason, but biased by education, and swayed
by affection. We see in the English Church, I will not merely say,
no descent from the first ages, and no relationship to the Church in
other lands, but we see no body politic of any kind; we see nothing
more or less than an establishment, a department of government, or a
function or operation of the State — without a substance, — a mere
collection of officials, depending on and living in the supreme civil
power. Its unity and personality are gone, and with them its power
of exciting feelings of any kind. It is easier to love or hate an abstraction than so commonplace a frame-work or machinery." [4]

In the fourth lecture, the dialogue between a Tractarian and the
state is one of Newman's most effective pieces of irony. Newman has the Tractarian urge, among other tenets of his school,
that the Church is no mere creation of the state — "Did the State
make us? Can it unmake us? Can it send out missionaries?
Can it arrange dioceses?" To which the state, in cold super-
ciliousness, simply announces: "William the Fourth, by the
grace of God of the United Kingdom of Great Britain and Ireland, King, Defender of the Faith, to all to whom these presents
shall come, greeting; we having great confidence in the learning,
morals, and probity of our well-beloved and venerable William
Grant Broughton, do name and appoint him to be Bishop and
ordinary pastor in the See of Australia." [5] And so the ironic
dialogue proceeds for several pages. This whole lecture struck
Hutton as being "one of the most powerful attacks ever opened
on the Anglican theory of the Church as independent of the
State." [6] Nor was the fifth lecture less powerful, in its delineation of the collapse of the Anglican theory of the Church when
applied in practice.

But it is in the second series of lectures, especially in lectures
VIII and IX, when Newman abandons technicality, that he
reaches the summit of his persuasive eloquence. He is here

dealing with objections grounded on the actual social and religious conditions of Catholic countries. Newman does not hesitate to outdo the shocked English tourist in describing the apparent irreverence of the continental Catholic populace, or the mechanical way in which it seems to regard the supernatural. But he insists that its very casualness, its superstitions, testify to a hold on the supernatural, on the unseen world, which is denied to many a religious non-Catholic. In a passage which so offended Kingsley that fourteen years later Newman was challenged to defend it, and which really should not be read apart from its context, he drew a memorable contrast between the spiritual potentialities of "a mere beggar woman, lazy, ragged, and filthy, and not over-scrupulous of truth" and "the State's pattern-man, the just, the upright, the generous, the honorable." The former, says Newman with rhetorical audacity, "if she is chaste, sober, and cheerful, and goes to her religious duties . . . will in the eyes of the Church, have a prospect of heaven, quite closed and refused" to the pattern English gentleman if he is what he is, "not from a supernatural power." [7] As to the social objections of non-Catholics, Newman replies in some of his finest prose, on the radical contrast between the "Church" and the "world." Catholic countries are charged with being unprogressive. To this Newman answers that such countries place the spiritual values of the Church above the "supreme worship of comfort, decency, and social order," which are the "worldly" values of the Protestants. Then follows the well-known passage, in which he acknowledges that the Church, being "in warfare" with evil, must ever be making a new beginning, must always seem inefficient and old-fashioned in the eyes of the "world":

"The Church aims not at making a show, but at doing a work. She regards this world, and all that is in it, as a mere shadow, as dust and ashes, compared with the value of one single soul. She holds that, unless she can, in her own way, do good to souls, it is no use her doing anything; she holds that it were better for the sun and moon to drop from heaven, for the earth to fail, and for the many millions who are upon it to die of starvation in extremest agony so far as temporal affliction goes, than that one soul, I will not say should be lost, but should commit one single venial sin, should tell one wilful untruth, though it harmed no one, or steal one poor farthing without excuse. She considers the action of the world and the action of the soul as simply incommensurable, viewed in their respective spheres; she would rather save the soul of one single wild bandit of Calabria, or whining beggar of Palermo, than draw a hundred lines of railroad through the length of Italy, or carry out a sanitary reform, in its fullest details in every city of Sicily, except so far as these great national works tended to some spiritual good beyond them." [8]

It was passages of such strength and force as this which made the *Difficulties of Anglicans* a "landmark in Newman's history as a Roman Catholic," and which caused it to be "the first book of Newman's generally read amongst Protestants" who might wish to measure his full literary power.[9]

ii. *Fighting the "No-Popery" Spirit*

The nine lectures on *The Present Position of Catholics in England* (1851) were occasioned by the formal re-establishment of the Catholic hierarchy in England. The uproar which immediately resounded throughout England, on the announcement of this re-establishment, was intensified when Archbishop Wiseman published a pastoral letter in which it appeared that the Catholic Church was about to "govern" England. Though Wiseman tried to make amends by publishing his "Appeal to the English People," all classes "from the Queen to the Infant School" were aroused, and the old cry of "No-Popery" was again heard everywhere. Wiseman and the Pope were burned in effigy on village greens up and down the kingdom; Parliament passed an Act (which at once became a dead letter) making it illegal for Catholic bishops to take their titles from English towns; the Lord Chancellor made an excited speech in the Guildhall. Newman himself was distressed by the uncritical zeal of the Roman "aggressors"; he preferred education to bishoprics in such turbulent times, and would have been glad to see the new hierarchy abandoned. But he accepted the facts, and decided to give a course of popular lectures on the "protestant Tradition" as it was in 1851, showing how it caricatured the true nature of the Roman Church. In some respects these lectures are the most amazing work that Newman ever produced. By nature extremely reticent, aristocratically fastidious and self-restrained and aloof, he nevertheless let himself go with brilliant effects in irony, broad humor, sarcasm, parody, scathing satire, and dramatic appeal. So great was the humor at times that peals of laughter were audible even outside the building.[1]

Newman's lectures, delivered in the Corn Exchange in Birmingham in the summer of 1851, are not, however, memorable merely as specimens of literary form. As J. Elliot Ross has put it, "they are still an important contribution to an understanding of the relations between Catholics and Protestants in the English-speaking world. The same prejudices, the same slanders that Newman dealt with in the England of 1851 are to be met with to-day in the United States." [2]   Newman himself regarded these lectures affectionately, not only as highly successful efforts in defense of his Church but also as, in his opinion, "the best written of all his works." [3]   Of them it may be said, on the other hand, that they make little effort to be fair or objective; and they might have been strengthened by a few passages here and there, pointing out the extravagances of some Catholics, or discussing the statistical aspects of the Catholics of his time — "their number, their geographical and racial distribution, their social and economic status, their influence, if any, in politics." [4]   Yet Newman was hardly a statistician or social historian, and we cannot scold him for not doing what he did not intend to do.

Early in the first lecture Newman sets the tone of his work. After suavely saying that he "but proposes to investigate how Catholics come to be trodden under foot, and spurned by a people which is endowed by nature with many great qualities, moral and intellectual," he wonders if an indictment similar to the one leveled at Rome might not plausibly be framed against some other institution of parallel greatness and power, such as the British Constitution.   He will suppose a vast mob of Russians assembled in Moscow; they have never seen a member of parliament, a policeman, a queen, or a London mob, and have never read English history, philosophy, law, ethics, or poetry.   They are addressed by "a member of a junior branch of the Potemkin family," who has indeed dipped into Blackstone and several English writers, and has picked up facts at third or fourth hand, together with a good deal of falsehood and nonsense. Then follows a passage too long to quote in its entirety, but one that has become a classic in satire and parody. The British Constitution, says the spell-binding Russian, is "aggrandizing itself in East, West, and South"; yet it is a "crazy, old-fashioned piece of furniture," symbolical of the "atheistic tenets and fiendish maxims of John-Bullism." The speaker holds up a book, "Blackstone's Commentaries," and from it reads and expounds to the astonished angry mob some of its passages — "The King can do no wrong," the sovereign "is never bound in justice to do anything," yet does acts of reparation and restitution "as a matter of *grace*"; "the power of Parliament is . . . transcendent and absolute"; "Queen Elizabeth . . . once said to one of her Bishops: 'Proud Prelate, I made you, and I can unmake you.'" The speaker, of course, omits context and historical explanation. He then goes on to quote adherents to John-Bullism; one Alexander Pope called Queen Anne a *goddess*! Such are the rubbish and blasphemies of the John-Bullites. Their present Queen Victoria is actually mentioned in the Book of Revelation as having the number of the beast! — "You recollect that number is 666; now, she came to the throne in the year thirty-seven, at which date she was eighteen years old. Multiply then 37 by 18, and you have the very number 666 . . ." Newman piles charge upon charge, luxuriating, like a seventeenth-century anti-popery fanatic, in vituperation, name-calling, gross inaccuracies, scrambled logic, and inapposite quotations until "the cheers become frantic, and drown the speaker's voice . . . [and] one half of the meeting is embracing the other half" in a delirium of fanatical fear and joy. They break the windows of the British residents, form a great procession, and (the managing committee having provided the paraphernalia), they burn John Bull in effigy, as well as "a lion and unicorn, and a Queen Victoria." Then, their fury spent, they disperse, "and the silver moon looks down in untroubled lustre on the city of the Czars." [5]

Such, in unfortunately condensed form, is Newman's brilliant and amusing satire on the old British "no-popery" views of the Catholic Church and her "superstitions," "aggressions," her status as "Antichrist" and "Babylon," her persecutions, her mysterious and hidden vices, her presumptuous claims and her hopelessly intricate and unsubstantial theology. But this passage is only one of a number of unforgettably vivid or droll or burlesque-filled passages which attest to Newman's astonishing range of literary power. Never before or after did he use that power to its limit. In other places in the lectures he examines "tradition" (in literature, wealth, respectability, virtue, enlightenment) as the source of misconception of the Catholic Church; in others he looks into the "fables" or rumors, into the logical inconsistencies, into the prejudices and assumed principles and mere ignorance, which have gone into the making of the "no-popery" tradition.

Not altogether amusing (since Newman unflinchingly paints the whole picture) is the passage dealing with the "Awful Disclosures" of Maria Monk as to the sexual vice and infanticide allegedly prevalent in Roman Catholic convents. Nowhere does Newman show more courage and skill. He follows what to him must have been a deeply revolting narrative: one "poor victim," says Maria Monk, is brought to the bishop because she had refused to commit "crimes which she detested." "It was easy to perceive . . . her fate to be sealed." Having refused to "murder harmless babes," she hears the bishop then say: "That is enough, finish her." " 'Two nuns instantly fall upon the woman . . . they gag her and throw her on the bed . . . another bed is thrown upon her. One of the priests springs like fury upon it with all his force. He is speedily followed by the nuns, until there are as many upon the bed as can find room . . . After a lapse of fifteen or twenty minutes . . . the nuns cease to trample upon her, and step from the bed. All is motionless and silent beneath it. They then begin to laugh,' etc." On this narrative Newman comments to his audience: "But I surely need not continue trash such as this, which is as stupid as it is atrocious." [6]

Elsewhere Newman lets the facts speak without comment; he himself remains almost inhumanly neutral. For example, in narrating the Catholic martyrdoms under "bloody Elizabeth," he writes with a chilling terseness of one Mr. Maine who "was hanged, cut down alive, falling from a great height, and then quartered . . . John Wilson, while they tore out his heart, said, 'I forgive the Queen, and all that are the cause of my death.' Edward Campion was cruelly torn and rent upon the rack divers times. Before he went to the rack, he used to fall down at the rack-house door, upon both knees, to commend himself to God's mercy; and upon the rack he called continually upon God, repeating the holy name of Jesus. His keeper asked him the next day, how he felt his hands and feet, he answered, 'Not ill, because not at all.' He was hanged and embowelled at Tyburn.' Ralph Sherwin came next; the hangman, taking hold of him with his bloody hands, which had been busy with the bowels of the martyred priest who preceded him, said to him, thinking to terrify him, 'Come, Sherwin, take thou also thy wages.' But the holy man, nothing dismayed, embraced him with a cheerful countenance. and reverently kissed the blood that stuck to his hands; at which the people were much moved. He had been twice racked, and now he was dealt with as his brother before him . . ." [7]

In the memorable fifth lecture Newman paints the appalling picture of Dr. Achilli, "the incontrovertible proof," cries Newman sorrowfully, "that priests may fall and friars break their vows." [8] Newman uses the offenses of which the papal government believed Achilli guilty as illustrations of the sources from which grew much of the conventional Protestant attitude toward the Catholic faith. Achilli denied the charges, sued Newman for libel, and, in spite of much outraged Catholic and non-Catholic opinion, won his case. More important for Newman and for his fellow-Catholics was the final lecture on the "Duties of Catholics Towards the Protestant View." Here Newman urges Catholics to make themselves known for what they truly are, to live up to the highest level of their religion, to let the daily press alone, to work modestly but zealously in their local neighborhoods. Then, he feels, "Popular Protestantism" will lose its fear and hatred of "popery." This final lecture, however, is not without its flourish, which appears in a passage perfectly exemplifying rhetorical exaggeration, parallelism, antithesis, pithiness, and climax. At the end of section 1, Newman summarizes triumphantly:

"Such, then, is Popular Protestantism, considered in its opposition to Catholics. Its truth is Establishment by Law; its Philosophy is Theory; its Faith is Prejudice; its facts are Fictions; its reasonings Fallacies; and its security is Ignorance about those whom it is opposing. The Law says that white is black; Ignorance says, why not? Theory says it ought to be, Fallacy says it must be, Fiction says it is, and Prejudice says it shall be." [9]

iii. *An Instrument Suited to the Need*

We shall elsewhere consider Newman's next great Catholic work, the *Apologia*, from the standpoint of autobiography and literature. Here we shall look at one or two pregnant and eloquent passages which parallel and supplement much of the argument in the preceding works. It will be recalled, by readers familiar with the *Apologia*, that in the final chapter Newman is concerned with defining the position of his mind since 1845, in other words the *Catholic* position of his mind. He points out, for instance, how he as a Catholic can believe in transubstantiation, because "Catholic doctrine leaves phenomena alone" — the substance of the bread and wine in the Eucharist, and any transformation which may occur, are mysteries of which the greatest philosophers know nothing.[1] Newman next justifies his belief in his Church as a divine interposition in "the anarchical condition of things" in this world, an institution "invested with the prerogative of infallibility in religious matters," an "instrument suited to the need" of "smiting hard and throwing back the immense energy of the aggressive, capricious, untrustworthy intellect." Newman arrives at this point in his discussion by summarizing, in one of his most justly famous passages, the horrible and futile "human situation," as he sees it:

". . . Starting then with the being of a God (which, as I have said, is as certain to me as the certainty of my own existence, though when I try to put the grounds of that certainty into logical shape I find a difficulty in doing so in mood and figure to my satisfaction), I look out of myself into the world of men, and there I see a sight which fills me with unspeakable distress. The world seems simply to give the lie to that great truth, of which my whole being is so full; and the effect upon me is, in consequence, as a matter of necessity, as confusing as if it denied that I am in existence myself. If I looked into a mirror, and did not see my face, I should have the sort of feeling which actually comes upon me, when I look into this living busy world, and see no reflection of its Creator. This is, to me, one of those great difficulties of this absolute primary truth, to which I referred just now. Were it not for this voice, speaking so clearly in my conscience and my heart, I should be an theist, or a pantheist, or a polytheist when I looked into the world. I am speaking for myself only; and I am far from denying the real force of the arguments in proof of a God, drawn from the general facts of human society and the course of history, but these do not warm me or enlighten me; they do not take away the winter of my desolation, or make the buds unfold and the leaves grow within me, and my moral being rejoice. The sight of the world is nothing else than the prophet's scroll, full of 'lamentations, and mourning, and woe.'

"To consider the world in its length and breadth, its various history, the many races of man, their starts, their fortunes, their mutual alienation, their conflicts; and then their ways, habits, governments, forms of worship; their enterprises, their aimless courses, their random achievements and acquirements, the impotent conclusion of long-standing facts, the tokens so faint and broken of a superintending design, the blind evolution of what turn out to be great powers or truths, the progress of things, as if from unreasoning elements, not towards final causes, the greatness and littleness of man, his far-reaching aims, his short duration, the curtain hung over his futurity, the disappointments of life, the defeat of good, the success of evil, physical pain, mental anguish, the prevalence and intensity of sin, the pervading idolatries, the corruptions, the dreary hopeless irreligion, that condition of the whole race, so fearfully yet exactly described in the Apostle's words, 'having no hope and without God in the world,' — all this is a vision to dizzy and appall; and inflicts upon the mind the sense of a profound mystery, which is absolutely beyond human solution.

"What shall be said to this heart-piercing, reason-bewildering fact?" [2]

Clearly, for Newman, if there is a Creator, then man "is implicated in some terrible aboriginal calamity." What will deliver him from his predicament? Education? Economic comfort? Freedom from war? In Newman's opinion nothing on earth "will afford a fulcrum" for moving or arresting the hand of fate. No book, such as the Bible, can make a stand "against the

wild living intellect of man." Only *from outside nature* can
there be a deliverance from "the passion and the pride of man."
And Newman saw in the Roman Catholic Church the "direct,
immediate, active, and prompt means" to meet man's need.
Her claim to infallibility in faith and morals; her constant treatment of man as a rebel needing to learn the peace of submission;
her "renovating grace," which, together with "certain outward
provisions of preaching and teaching," enabled her "to rescue
human nature from its misery" — all this persuaded Newman
that she was a *divine instrument*, "a suitable antagonist" for mili-
tantly opposing "the intensity of the evil which has possession
of mankind." [3]

The *Apologia* is noteworthy also for Newman's skillful handling of the doctrines of Infallibility and the Immaculate Conception, which, he says, have come to be defined because they were
long since believed, not believed because they have recently been
defined. "Be large-minded enough to believe," he begs his hostile Victorian public, "that men may reason and feel very differently from yourselves." [4] He admits, however, that on another
subject there "*is* a great trial of the Reason" when it is confronted
with the claims of the Church, namely, her animadversions on
secular matters which bear on religion, on matters of science, literature, philosophy, history. She does censure books, silence
authors, forbid discussion. Granting that his Church has erred
grievously at times, as have many Protestant communities, Newman insists that, with scientific theories rising and falling so be-
wilderingly, it would "be very undignified for a Catholic to commit himself to the work of chasing what might turn out to be
phantoms." [5] The Church is in no hurry. She is of eternity.
Under the proper conditions she permits, and even encourages,
scientific and intellectual controversy, until "the question has
been ventilated and turned over and over again . . . and authority is called upon to pronounce a decision, which has already
been arrived at by reason." [6] The reader of course remembers
the case of Galileo. "Here," says Newman, " 'exceptio probat
regulam'; for it is the one stock argument." Newman's conclusion is that the infallibility of his Church has not in fact "destroyed the energy of the Catholic intellect." [7]

iv. *An Olive Branch from a Catapult*

Newman's next notable polemic was *A Letter Addressed to the Rev. E. B. Pusey, D.D., on Occasion of His Eirenicon* (1866). This little book has the smallest literary interest of all Newman's Catholic works. His friend Dr. Pusey, laboring hard in the interests of Anglican reunion with Rome, published in 1865 the first of three parts of his *Eirenicon,* a book designed, as its title indicated, to promote peace between the two communions. So unfairly did Pusey seem to represent certain Catholic doctrines, notably the doctrine of the Blessed Virgin, that Newman felt obliged to reply. He wished also to show that the extravagances of Catholic faith and devotion referred to in the *Eirenicon* were those of a *party* in the Church — of certain Oxford converts like W. G. Ward, and Frederick William Faber — and not those of the central Catholic tradition. Further, he wished, characteristically, to show that the recognized Catholic doctrine and devotion were natural and legitimate developments from beliefs already visible in patristic days. Though his book had none of the rhetorical splendor or adroitness of his other works, it nevertheless, by virtue of its timeliness, made a tremendous stir. The public, which had just seen Newman brilliantly overthrow Charles Kingsley (the *Apologia* was now selling widely in book form), admiringly beheld Newman, with delicate and at times icy rhetoric, matching his mind with that of the great Dr. Pusey. The press, which had ignored him for twenty years, now accorded him the fullest attention. *The Times* published an article seven columns long, on March 31, 1866, reviewing Newman's book and giving it national importance.[1]

Admirers of Newman's unexpected stylistic climaxes no doubt chuckled over the first few pages, in which gently and suavely the author manifests the deep affection between himself and Pusey, then swiftly shows the woeful gap between them. Pusey's book has "wounded those who love him well but love truth more . . . We give you a sharp cut," says Newman, "and you return it . . . But we at least have not professed to be composing an Irenicon, when we were treating you as foes. There was one of old time

who wreathed his sword in myrtle; excuse me — you discharge
your olive-branch as if from a catapult." [2]

But Pusey has been guilty of another fumble with words.   If
his *Eirenicon* is too belligerent to be an offering of peace, his quotation from Newman in the *Apologia* — that the English Church
is a *bulwark* against doctrinal errors — is equally misleading.
Just as the careless Kingsley found himself tangled up in Newman's swiftly woven web of words and arguments, so Pusey here
finds himself caught in one of Newman's deft distinctions between
words which *almost* mean the same thing.   Pusey is reminded
that Newman said "serviceable *breakwater*," not "bulwark."
"A bulwark," Newman explains, "is an integral part of the thing
it defends" — Anglicanism as a "breakwater" does indeed protect Catholic truth, but like all breakwaters is really *external* to
the thing it protects.   Here, again, Newman had made a telling
blow at the Anglican Church and her pretension to "Catholic
truth." [3]

The ordinary reader will find in Newman's *Letter to Dr.
Pusey* a number of passages of considerable vitality.   If he
wishes, for instance, to know precisely what is the "great rudimental teaching of Antiquity" concerning the Blessed Virgin, he
can find no simpler, more lucid, or attractive account than Newman's.   Standing on the authority of the Fathers — "as to the
Blessed Virgin. . . ," he says, "the Fathers are enough for me"
— Newman will tell the reader that

"She is the Second Eve . . . In that awful transaction [in the Garden
of Eden], an event was announced for a distant future, in which the
three same parties were to meet again, the serpent, the woman, and
the man; but it was to be a second Adam and a second Eve, and the
new Eve was to be the mother of the new Adam.   'I will put enmity
between thee and the woman, and between thy seed and her seed.'
The Seed of the woman is the Word incarnate, and the Woman, whose
seed or son He is, is His mother Mary." [4]

Newman now adduces passages from the earliest Fathers — St.
Justin Martyr, Tertullian, St. Iranaeus — to show Antiquity's
conviction that the Blessed Virgin was not "a mere physical in-

strument of our Lord's taking flesh, but . . . an intelligent, responsible cause of it." [5]   What Eve lost, Mary was to restore —
"Death by Eve, life by Mary," said St. Jerome.   More Fathers
and authorities are brought forward — St. Cyril of Jerusalem,
St. Ephrem Syrus, St. Epiphanius, St. Peter Chrysologus, St.
Fulgentius, all flourishing before A.D. 533.   Newman then proceeds to discuss the inferences of their "rudimental doctrine":
first, Mary's *sanctity,* which involves a consideration of the Immaculate Conception, and of the Catholic doctrine of *Original
Sin* as distinguished from the Protestant doctrine; and second,
Mary's *dignity.*   Newman reduces the doctrine of the Immaculate Conception to its simplest terms:

"If Eve had [a] supernatural inward gift given her from the first
moment of her personal existence, is it possible to deny that Mary too
had this gift from the very first moment of her personal existence?
I do not know how to resist this inference: — well, this is simply and
literally the doctrine of the Immaculate Conception . . . It has no
reference whatever to her parents, but simply to her own person." [6]

In her, added to the nature inherited from her parents, there was
a superadded fulness of grace, from the first moment of her existence — thus she was addressed by the angel, "Hail, Mary,
full of grace."   She was born without *original sin,* because that
term, in Catholic thought, merely means deprivation of supernatural unmerited grace, the grace lost by Adam and Eve, who
then passed their loss on to their children.

On the Blessed Virgin's "dignity" Newman is somewhat less
striking.   He turns to the twelfth chapter of the Apocalypse,
and points to the vision of the woman and the child and the serpent, reminiscent of the meeting in the Garden of Eden.   Is the
vision an allegory?   "Scripture," says Newman, "is not fond of
allegories."   If, according to ecumenical council, Mary is "the
Mother of her Creator . . . what dignity can be too great to
attribute to her who is as closely bound up, as intimately one,
with the Eternal Word, as a mother is with a son?"   Thus the
term *Theotocos,* as ascribed to her, goes back as far as Origen
(185–254), and her "dignity" as the Mother of God is asserted

as early as St. Ignatius (d. 106) ("Our Lord was carried in the womb of Mary").[7]

The rest of Newman's book is devoted to the belief of Catholics in the Blessed Virgin's intercessory power, their exuberant devotion to her, and to Anglican misconceptions of the excesses of that devotion. Before we leave the book, let us note a few memorable passages. The Blessed Virgin, says Newman, "is the great exemplar of *prayer* in a generation which emphatically denies the power of prayer *in toto,* which determines that fatal laws govern the universe, that there cannot be any direct communication between earth and heaven, that God cannot visit His own earth, and that man cannot influence His providence." [8] Admitting that doctrines may be abused, Newman adds, "I prefer much wherever it is possible, to be first generous and then just; to grant full liberty of thought, and to call it to account when abused . . . I would not give much for that love which is never extravagant, which always observes the proprieties." [9] Religious devotions may, in the privacy of the heart, go to extravagant lengths. Like the emotions of love, Newman continues, they may get written down, "sometimes they get into the newspapers," and "make a melancholy exhibition when served up cold for the public eye." When religious devotions, in a parallel case, get written into formalized meditations or exercises, they may be "as repulsive as loveletters in a police court." In fact, concludes Newman honestly,

"the religion of the multitude is ever vulgar and abnormal; it ever will be tinctured with fanaticism and superstition. . . . A people's religion is ever a corrupt religion, in spite of the provisions of Holy Church. If she is to be Catholic, you must admit within her net fish of every kind . . . You may beat religion out of men, if you will, and then their excesses will take a different direction; but if you make use of religion to improve them, they will make use of religion to corrupt it."

Nor is reason or logic a safeguard against excesses or corruptions: "Theology both uses logic and baffles it; and thus logic acts both for the protection and for the perversion of religion." [10] Here, in these passages, we see once more how readily Newman utilizes a specific occasion or topic as an opportunity to utter words of universal interest and appeal. He is not here the mere arguer for belief in the Catholic doctrine of the Blessed Virgin; he is also a kind of religious philosopher, who sees the remotest implications of his subject and asserts various truths or propositions which every Catholic and non-Catholic alike can ponder with interest and enlightenment.

By the end of the book Newman has dismissed a long list of attributes and powers which uninstructed Protestants had long since ascribed to Mary — that, for instance, God has resigned into her hands His omnipotence, that it is safer to seek her than her Son, that her Son is subject to her commands, etc., etc. A full list of these is given in Ward's *Life of Newman*; they attest to the widespread misconception, even among learned men like Pusey, of the true nature of the doctrine. If, on the other hand, one wants a glimpse of the *ethos* of Roman Catholicism, exemplified in relation to that doctrine, one might well turn to the following passage:

"He who charges us with making Mary a divinity, is thereby denying the divinity of Jesus. Such a man does not know what divinity is. Our Lord cannot pray for us, as a creature prays, as Mary prays; he cannot inspire those feelings which a creature inspires. To her belongs, as being a creature, a natural claim on our sympathy and familiarity, in that she is nothing else than our fellow. She is our pride, — in the poet's words, 'Our tainted nature's solitary boast.' We look to her without any fear, any remorse, any consciousness that she is able to read us, judge us, punish us. Our heart yearns towards that pure Virgin, that gentle Mother, and our congratulations follow her, as she rises from Nazareth and Ephesus, through the choirs of angels, to her throne on high, so weak, yet so strong; so delicate, yet so glorious; so modest and yet so mighty." [11]

v. *Tilting with an Orator: Newman vs. Gladstone*

In one of his memoranda for the year 1874, Newman is startled "that in the last 15 years he [had only written] two books, the 'Apologia' and the Essay on Assent — of which the former was almost extempore." He queries in alarm: "What have I been doing with my time? though I have never been idle." In the same passage he notes that his habit had always been "of not writing and publishing without a *call* . . . I *cannot* write without such a *stimulus*." [1] Such a call came very soon. Gladstone had in 1874 retired from the leadership of his party, and had been employing his new leisure in writing a strong attack on the Vatican decrees of 1870, and on the *Syllabus Errorum* and the encyclical *Quanta Cura* of 1864. There had long been an active party in the Catholic Church known as the ultramontanes, who held extreme views favoring papal supremacy. In France this party's great organ was the periodical *L'Univers,* under Louis Veuillot; in England its most vocal exponents were William George Ward (father of Newman's definitive biographer) and Henry Edward Manning, Archbishop of Westminster since 1865. Ward had said that he would like a daily infallible document with his morning *Times* at breakfast. Manning, together with Ward and Faber, favored the "maximizing" of Catholic doctrine — an adding of significance to doctrine — rather than, as Newman preferred, a "minimizing." The maximizers were convinced that there was an unbridgeable chasm between the Church and everything modern; anything "Liberal" became to them the equivalent of heretical. Newman's tendency had always been to proceed cautiously in determining just what one had to hold as a loyal Catholic. He feared that the extravagances of the ultramontanes and the maximizers — in England they were usually converts from Anglicanism — would alienate many individuals and otherwise prove a danger to the Church. He also preferred to leave such doctrines as Infallibility undefined until time provided the proper occasion.

However, in 1870 the Vatican Council decreed the infallibility of the Pope. Actually, in its quite moderate terms, it was a defeat for Veuillot, Ward, and other extremists; though the fact that the decree passed at all was to some extent the work of Manning. But while the decree was in fact moderate, the extremists had alarmed the British people, who thought, for example, that it meant the supremacy of the Pope over all temporal sovereigns, even the power of deposing the king of England or the president of the United States. Its true meaning may be summed up as follows: that under certain conditions the decrees of the Pope are "irreformable," and have the same authority as that which, according to Catholic belief, Christ wished the Church to have. These conditions are: (i) that the Pope should speak not only to a portion of the Church but to the whole world; (ii) that his words should come not as from a private theologian but as from the supreme head of the Church; (iii) that he should pronounce on questions of faith or morals, as revealed in Scripture or tradition; and (iv) that he should indicate clearly his intention of using his infallible prerogative.[2] From these conditions it can be seen that papal infallibility does not mean that the Pope is inspired, that he cannot sin or err, that he exacts a loyalty inconsistent with loyalty to a civil state.

Yet this was more or less the inference drawn by Gladstone, who, in November, 1874, published his attack under the title, *The Vatican Decrees and Their Bearing on Civil Allegiance.* In this work Gladstone made much of Manning's recent lecture, *Caesarism and Ultramontanism,* in which extreme emphasis was put on the undying struggle between the Pope and the civil power. Gladstone's general method was much the same as that which Macaulay had long ago, in a devastating review, described as "darkening and perplexing the logic which it would illustrate." Newman was of course familiar with this review, and with Macaulay's further observations, that Gladstone's mind showed "no want of light, but a great want of what Bacon would have called dry light. Whatever Mr. Gladstone sees is refracted and distorted by a false medium of passions and prejudices." [3] There is a hint of Newman's recognition of this fact on the last page of the postscript to his *Letter to the Duke of Norfolk,* in which he answered Gladstone; there we read: "If Mr. Gladstone is merely haranguing as an Orator, I do not for an instant quarrel with him or attempt to encounter him; but if he is a controversialist, we have a right to look for arguments, not mere assertions." [4] This is worth noting because Newman's reply to Gladstone was not merely a counterargument to the great statesman's attack but also, and more importantly, a statement for the benefit of Manning. "We can speak against Gladstone," wrote Newman to Lord Blachford, "while it would not be decent [as a fellow-Catholic] to speak against Manning." [5] Thus it was that, as with Kingsley and Pusey, Gladstone's pamphlet gave Newman a chance to defend his Church and to impale his opponent on the delicate point of his rhetoric. In this case, also, he could give a back-handed slap at Manning and the maximizers. It was a situation ideally suited to Newman's talents, though he had long since thought he was through with controversy — "I thought I should be in peace for the remainder of my life," he wrote mournfully to Dean Church, "and now I am in controversy again." [6]

Newman's *Letter to the Duke of Norfolk,* now a part of the second volume of *Difficulties of Anglicans,* is really a book of two hundred and seven pages. Its importance may be judged by the comment of one Catholic biographer of Newman, who considers the book as

"remaining to this day the best answer in English to the charges of civil disloyalty brought against Catholics . . . Nothing can at all compare in thoroughness and persuasiveness with Newman's treatment of the question. In the half century that has elapsed since the appearance of Newman's book, it has held the field without competition. And it does not seem that anything better will be produced in the future." [7]

But it is also a brilliant example of Newman's controversial methods. He might have lashed out at Gladstone with the feline fury he inflicted on Kingsley, since Gladstone was alleged to have written in chagrin at the defeat of his Irish University Bill. Newman was not so unsubtle. He would not ridicule Gladstone, or impugn his motives. He would try to convince Gladstone of his errors, and bring the British public to look calmly on the papal claims as they actually were. In his dedicatory note to the Duke of Norfolk he deplores not merely Gladstone's "extraordinary severity," but also, and much more, "those [Catholics] among us . . . who for years past have conducted themselves as if no responsibility attached to wild words and overbearing deeds; who have stated truths in the most paradoxical form, and stretched principles till they were close to snapping." In fact, "Catholics may in good measure thank themselves, and no one else, for having alienated from them so religious a mind" as Gladstone's. "The English people," he continues, "are sufficiently sensitive to the claims of the Pope,

without having them, as if in defiance, flourished in their faces."
The present excitement, he adds, is "caused partly by the chronic
extravagances of knots of Catholics here and there." [8]   One wonders whether blushes of embarrassment and fury did not pass, at
least momentarily, over the faces of Faber, Manning, and Ward.

With this tactful nod toward Gladstone, and this dry rasp at
the Catholic extremists, Newman begins his task.   Gladstone, in
his headlong fashion, has written that "Rome had substituted for
the proud boast of *semper eadem* a policy of violence and change
in faith," and that after the Vatican decrees, "no one could become her convert without renouncing his mental and moral freedom, and placing his loyalty and duty at the mercy of another."
Rome, he said, "had equally repudiated modern thought and
ancient history." [9]   The main question, however, as Newman
saw it, was simply: "Can Catholics be trustworthy subjects of
the State?"   Round this question his whole book revolves.   He
is therefore led into a brief history of the rise of the papal power
and of the doctrine of Infallibility, together with an exposition
of the doctrine's real meaning as applied to faith and morals.
He considers the problem of "divided allegiance"; he analyzes
and exalts conscience as "the aboriginal Vicar of Christ" in a passage equaling in style and penetration the great passage in the
Grammar of Assent; he expounds the true meaning of the Encyclical of 1864 and the *Syllabus Errorum*; and he concludes by
discussing the Vatican Council and its definition.   With his characteristic discernment Newman says early in his *Letter* that Gladstone might better have chosen another issue for attack than the
Pope's special power; "it is not the existence of a Pope, but of a
Church, which is his aversion" — a Church which "wields the
weapons of St. Ambrose and St. Augustine."   This statement
proves to be a veiled barb — Gladstone's Anglican Church is not
really a Church! — and this is made plain when Newman asks
a few lines further on what would happen if politicians had to
deal not with one Church but with 1800 of them, each following
its own polity; "it would be," says Newman dryly, "the Anglican
theory made real." [10]   However, Newman keeps to the point
selected by Gladstone, and in consequence does not discuss the
general question.

On the problem of "divided allegiance," Newman points out that the Pontiff's claim to "supreme direction" over Catholics does not mean "minute supervision," and that the Pope is supreme over them only as civil law is supreme, in no way interfering with one's comfort or conscience. Further, says Newman, the Pope's real aim, in exacting the "regimen and discipline" of the universal Church, is to combat that modern scourge, nationalism. He seeks to unite all souls in "one and the same structure of laws, rites, rules of government, independency, everywhere." Yet he is in no sense hostile to the civil power as such. And the possibilities of disobeying that power in order to serve the Pope are extremely remote. But for the sake of the argument, Newman poses an example in which he *would* obey the Pope: if an Act of Parliament was passed bidding Catholics to attend Protestant service every week, he would "obey the Pope and not the Law." On the other hand, supposing an extremely hypothetical case, if Newman were a soldier or sailor in Her Majesty's service, engaged in a just war, and if the Pope suddenly bade all Catholic soldiers and sailors to retire from the service, "here . . ." says Newman, "taking the advice of others, as best I could, I should not obey him." [11] In short, there may arise circumstances under which conscience may come into collision with the word of a Pope. Indeed, "the Pope is not infallible in that subject-matter in which conscience is of supreme authority," because conscience "is a messenger from Him, who, both in nature and in grace, speaks to us behind a veil . . . a prophet in its informations, a monarch in its peremptoriness, a priest in its blessings and anathemas. . ." [12] In support of his claims for the authority of conscience, Newman cites the Fourth Lateran Council, St. Thomas, St. Bonaventure, Cajetan, and several other theologians of note, including the famous Jesuit, Busenbaum, the Spanish Franciscan Antonio Corduba, the French Dominican Natalis Alexander. He had already cited the great Jesuit defender of the papacy, Cardinal Bellarmine, who wrote: "As it is lawful to resist the Pope, if he assaulted a man's person, so it is lawful to resist him, if he assaulted souls, or *troubled the state* . . ." [13] Of course Newman is assuming that the individual in question is already teachable and loyal. Here Newman gives, incidentally, his notion of the irreligious person: "that mean, ungenerous, selfish, vulgar spirit . . . which, at the very first rumour of a command, places itself in opposition to the Superior who gives it, asks itself whether he is not exceeding his right, and rejoices, in a moral and practical matter, to commence with skepticism." [14]   The adjectives in this sentence suggest much about Newman's own religious nature; for him, religion was not merely lowliness and sacrifice, but something choice, aristocratic, select.   He ends his section on "Conscience" with an often-quoted passage: "If I am obliged to bring religion into after-dinner toasts, (which indeed does not seem quite the thing) I shall drink — to the Pope, if you please, — still, to Conscience first, and to the Pope afterwards." [15]

Though the Vatican decree of infallibility had been the occasion of Gladstone's attack on Catholic loyalty, his real ammunition had been taken from the Encyclical of 1864 and the *Syllabus Errorum*.   In discussing these documents Newman has little difficulty in showing that Gladstone either did not understand them or misrepresented them.   According to Gladstone, the Pope had condemned "free speech, free writing, a free press, toleration of non-conformity, liberty of conscience."   Now, says Newman, "is not this accusation of a very wholesale character?   Who would not understand it to mean that the Pope had pronounced a universal anathema against *all* the liberties *in toto*, and that English law, on the contrary, allowed those liberties *in toto*, which the Pope had condemned? . . . The Pope has done no such thing." Newman then shows that what *has* been condemned is the idea that liberty of conscience and worship is the *inherent right* of all men, proclaimable in *every* rightly constituted society; a right to *all sorts of liberty*, not to be curbed by any ecclesiastical *or civil* authority, so far as public speaking, printing, or other manifestations of opinion are concerned.   "Now," says Newman, "is there any government on earth that could stand the strain of such a doctrine?"   What if a man's conscience "demands" that he embrace the duty of regicide? infanticide? free love?   One may ask "why the Pope should take the trouble to condemn what is so wild?"   Newman answers simply: "But he does: and to say that he condemns something which he does not condemn, and then to inveigh against him on the ground of that something else, is neither just nor logical." [16] Gladstone's error was to treat papal utterances, which are technical documents, as if they were Catholic propaganda-pamphlets. It should be added that Newman sees in the encyclical and in the *Syllabus* a determination of the Pope not to "come to terms with 'progress, liberalism, and the new civilization.'" Newman reminds his readers that the modern world has long since departed from the age of Blackstone when severe punishments were meted out by the state for denying the Holy Trinity, for attacking Christianity, even for "absenting oneself from divine worship." Newman himself laments that the state no longer has a conscience. He therefore accepts the encyclical and the *Syllabus* as the Church's official statement of its repudiation of the secular and godless modern spirit.

It was the *Syllabus Errorum*, rather than any encyclical, which in Gladstone's time, proved, as it does in ours, to be a source of consternation to non-Catholics and to all non-religious persons. This compilation of eighty propositions, so easily accessible, has misled not only the general reading public (such as have seen it) but also careful and scholarly men, who have failed to understand the nature of the *Syllabus*. It is in fact a *résumé*, as Newman points out, a sort of table of contents or index, of propositions contained in various documents issued by Pius IX. Gladstone, like many who followed him, made the error of quoting the *Syllabus* without determining the exact meaning of the particular proposition. This is like quoting the summary in an analytical table of contents, and then attributing some condensed statement to the author, without consulting the text. Newman observes that the *Syllabus* has no mark or seal of the Pope on it; that it is really anonymous and impersonal; that it is not in fact an official act, because it is not signed. He then takes up several typical "errors" condemned in the *Syllabus*, and shows how easy it is to misinterpret it. We have room for only one illustration. "For instance," says Newman, "take [Gladstone's] own 16th [the 77th of the 'erroneous Propositions'], that 'It is no longer expedient that the Catholic Religion should be established to the exclusion of all others.' When we turn to the Allocution, which is the ground of its being put into the *Syllabus*, what do we find there? First, that the Pope was speaking, not of States universally, but of one particular State, Spain," and, second that he was primarily protesting against the breach of the concordat by the Spanish government, and, further, that he was neither proposing nor condemning anything, but was in fact expressing "his wonder and distress." [17]

Newman attempts, before he ends his discussion, to explain why the *Syllabus* caused such widespread alarm. He attributes the alarm to two facts: (i) that so many "errors," seemingly harmless one at a time, were brought all together, thus impressing the European mind with its own low spiritual condition and with the possibility of the Catholic Church attempting to found a new world "in opposition to the social principles of the 19th century"; and (ii) that, though the *Syllabus* "was intended for the Bishops, who would be the interpreters of it, as the need arose, to their people . . . it got bodily into English newspapers even before it was received at many an episcopal residence," [18] and thus was subjected to a hasty and ill-informed interpretation. He might have added a third cause for alarm, if not disappointment, namely, the peremptory and blunt wording with which the *Syllabus* ends: "It is an error to believe that the Roman Pontiff can and ought to reconcile himself to, and agree with, progress, liberalism, and contemporary civilization."

Newman's *Letter* was a great success in both Catholic and Protestant circles. To be sure there were rumblings of discontent among the extreme ultramontanes; and Cardinal Franchi, then Prefect of Propaganda, wrote to Manning that Newman's book contained censurable propositions. But Manning, an astute statesman of the Church, recognized the dangers in a situation involving so powerful a political leader as Gladstone; so he took a cautious line and curbed the journalistic tendencies of the maximizers. We end our consideration of Newman's *Letter* with a second reference to Franchi. It seems that there was one statement of Newman's which, said Franchi in a second letter, was especially *troppo irreverente* to the Roman See. It happens to be one of the finest of Newman's witticisms, more barbed than usual, and perhaps for that reason unforgettable: "The Rock of

Peter on its summit enjoys a pure and serene atmosphere, but there is a great deal of Roman *malaria* at the foot of it." [19]

vi. *A Preface to One's Dead Self*

Nowhere in Newman is there a more amazing critical performance, a greater feat of icy objectivity, than in the Preface to the third edition (1877) of the *Via Media*. Those lectures which he had delivered just forty years before, in the heydey of his power at Oxford, Newman looks upon with grief and chagrin in 1877: "Gladly would I obliterate them," he says in the Prefatory Notice. However, since they doubtless will be reprinted, he thinks it wise to equip them with a Preface and with explanatory footnotes "in behalf of the Catholic religion." What makes that Preface so unlike any other that readily comes to mind is the fact that Newman refers to himself throughout in the third person, as if the Newman who lived before 1845 were indeed dead, or at least as if he were another individual altogether. He begins by explaining wherein each of the lectures is Catholic or anti-Catholic, or wherein a particular lecture may be, in various passages, either one or the other. At least one-half the volume, as he sees it, is wholly sympathetic to Catholic principles and doctrines. As a controversialist he pauses to distinguish between the three main elements which constitute controversial writings: truths and facts, and the deductions from them; the free use of hypothesis, in the absence of direct proof, appealing primarily to the imagination (as he believes) and not admitting of logical refutation; and, finally, formal argument.

It was in handling the second element, hypothesis, that Newman believes "the Author" (as he calls his dead Anglican self) to have erred most grievously. The *Via Media*, he says, with a pitying glance at "the Author," was but a dressing up of an hypothesis; it was indeed a congeries of hypotheses "as expedients for successive emergencies," at once without consistency or substance. "The Author" had desiderated both "a broad, intellectual, intelligible theory, and a logical and historical foundation for that theory; and he was content to attempt the former, taking the latter for granted." [1] As an example of pure and unfounded theory, Newman cites the fifth lecture, on "Private Judgment," which "is scarcely more than a gratuitous hypothesis from beginning to end." [2]   Later, in arguing the "indefectibility of the Church," Newman the Anglican had been curiously "more intent on distinguishing between the Roman and Anglican teaching . . . than on proving the Anglican to be true."   Newman the Catholic does not even grant that Newman the Anglican wanted to prove his case!   Throughout the preface, the Catholic Newman is stern and cold toward his former self, politely pitiless about the "coarse rhetoric of hard names and sweeping imputations in advance of proof" which that unwary self had carelessly indulged in.   As if reproving an inferior opponent, Newman observes: "In controversy one has no right to complain of strong conclusions, but to assume them on starting is the act of a pleader or advocate, not of a theologian . . . This arm in polemical attack . . . may without scruple be ignored and passed over by a respondent."   Its methods of special pleading have "their proper place in public meetings or the Courts of Law, [but] when disjoined from argument, they are as unworthy of ecclesiastics as they are easy and seductive." [3]   We need not believe that Newman had forgotten that he had used these very methods himself, not long before, in the *Difficulties of Anglicans* and the *Present Position of Catholics in England.*   However, in these lectures he had spoken in "public meetings," not as a theologian but frankly as "a pleader and advocate."   The *Via Media,* on the other hand, was to be regarded, according to Newman in 1877, as the work of a *theologian,* who had stooped to unworthy instruments.   Thus Newman the Catholic confesses plainly: "I wish these Lectures did not furnish instances of this reprehensible polemic."   He regrets the "calling of names" — Romanism, Romanist, Romish.   But "worse than the use of these words are the vague charges, and random reproaches, and scornful epithets indulged in by the Author, keenly alive as he was to the vulgarity of the Exeter Hall eloquence of the day."   Newman regrets also that "the Author goes out of his way to aim a side-blow at Rome." [4]   Anglicans to the present day, of course, can point to the numerous and often highly painful "side-blows" which Newman gives their Church when he appears to be absorbed in quite another subject.

In fact, Newman is a master of the unexpected, deftly aimed sideswipe at an opponent's tenderest spot.

Having disposed of the errors, blunders, and stupidities of the unfortunate author of the *Via Media*, Newman now addresses himself, in the second part of the preface, to a defense of his Church by answering two broad charges which he had made against the modern Church of Rome in his lectures of forty years ago. The first charge was that modern Catholicism had long since lost vitalizing contact with the primitive Church. Since Newman has already answered this charge, to his own satisfaction, in his *Essay on Development*, he proceeds at once to reply to the second charge, namely, that there is too great a difference between Rome's formal teaching (in the Breviary, the Roman Catechism) on the one hand, and her popular and political manifestations, on the other, as in the "spirit and tone of various manuals of Prayer and Meditation and of the Sermons or Addresses of ecclesiastics in high position." [5] In making his reply, Newman candidly states something that all readers of his works could profitably remember: "I am not here addressing those," he says, "who unhappily find themselves unable to profess Christianity." He then describes, incidentally, those numerous people for whom the Catholic Church has an attraction, but who cannot become Roman Catholics:

"They see in the Catholic Religion a great substance and earnest of truth; a depth, strength, coherence, elasticity, and life, a nobleness and grandeur, a power of sympathy and resource in view of the various ailments of the soul, and a suitableness to all classes and circumstances of mankind; a glorious history, and a promise of perpetual youthfulness; and they already accept without scruple or rather joyfully feed upon its solemn mysteries, which are a trial to others; but they cannot, as a matter of duty, enter its fold on account of certain great difficulties which block their way, and throw them back, when they would embrace that faith which looks so like what it professes to be." [6]

To the second charge, then, that the modern Church of Rome shows a painful difference between her formal teachings and her popular and political activities, Newman replies in one of his most impressive passages, in which he shows his admiration for her structure, his veneration for her long history, and his pride in her "majesty and divinity." Here his style is simple, dignified, at times a bit Augustan, and informed with a spirit of absolute certainty:

"When our Lord went up on high," he says, "He left His representative behind Him. This was Holy Church, His mystical Body and Bride, a Divine Institution, and the shrine and organ of the Paraclete, who speaks through her till the end comes. She, to use an Anglican poet's words, is 'His very self below,' as far as men on earth are equal to the discharge and fulfilment of high offices, which primarily are His.

"These offices, which specially belong to Him as Mediator, are commonly considered to be three; He is Prophet, Priest, and King; and after His pattern, and in human measure, Holy Church has a triple office too; not the Prophetical alone and in isolation [as Newman's lectures on the *Via Media* maintained] . . . but three offices, which are indivisible, though diverse, viz. teaching, rule, and sacred ministry."

After a short passage on the Pope as "the Vicar of Christ," the "visible head" of the Church, and the "chief part" of it, Newman proceeds to define Christianity from the Catholic-historical point of view:

"Christianity, then, is at once a philosophy, a political power, and a religious rite: as a religion, it is holy; as a philosophy, it is Apostolic; as a political power, it is imperial, that is, One and Catholic. As a religion, its special centre of action is pastor and flock; as a philosophy, the Schools; as a rule, the Papacy and its Curia.

"Though it has exercised these three functions in substance from the first, they were developed in their full proportions one after another, in a succession of centuries; first, in the primitive time it was recognized as a worship, springing up and spreading in the lower ranks of society, and among the ignorant and dependent, and making its power felt by the heroism of its Martyrs and confessors. Then it seized upon the intellectual and cultivated class, and created a theology and schools of learning. Lastly it seated itself, as an ecclesiastical polity, among princes, and chose Rome for its centre.

"Truth is the guiding principle of theology and theological inquiries; devotion and edification, of worship; and of government, expedience. The instrument of theology is reasoning; of worship, our emotional nature; of rule, command and coercion. Further, in man as he is, reasoning tends to rationalism; devotion to superstition and enthusiasm; and power to ambition and tyranny." [7]

Newman readily admits that the exercise of these duties, especially "when taken in combination," is extremely arduous and involves the modification of each other in scope, direction, interests, influence. " 'Who,' in St. Paul's words, 'is sufficient for these things?'" Newman himself asks, quite frankly, "What line of conduct, except on the long, the very long run, is at once edifying, expedient, and true?" [8] The Roman Church, he grants, cannot show, in this respect, an impeccable record. However well she may perform her duties on the whole, her enemies will always find it easy to make a case against her, well founded or not, simply from

"the action or interaction, or the chronic collisions or contrasts, or the temporary suspense or delay, of her administration, in her three several departments of duty, — her government, her devotions, and her schools, — from the conduct of her rulers, her divines, her pastors, or her people.

"It is this difficulty lying in the nature of the case, which supplies the staple of those energetic charges and vivid pictures of the inconsistency, double-dealing, and deceit of the Church of Rome, as found in Protestant writings, and in particular in [the author of *The Prophetical Office of the Church*]." [9]

The rest of the Preface is devoted to the problem which the Roman Church has always had in adjusting her formal teachings to widely differing peoples in widely differing circumstances at widely differing levels of comprehension. In the province of religion, Newman holds, the "principle of popular edification" is just as powerful as truth, especially inasmuch as men are keenly sensitive to "the chance of scandal." Thus "to the devotional mind what is new and strange is as repulsive, often as dangerous, as falsehood is to the scientific. Novelty is often error to those who are unprepared for it." Popular ideas on religion, even when erroneous or excessive, will therefore be allowed to have their way so long as the particular truth involved is not of vital or primary importance. Thus "in a religion which embraces large and separate classes of adherents, there always is of necessity to a certain extent an exoteric and esoteric doctrine." [10] Nowhere has this been more remarkably illustrated than in the cases of men of science, and the impact of their theories upon "the popular religious sense." The stock example, of course, is Galileo. Galileo was right in his conclusions, Newman observes, but "there was nothing wrong in censuring [his] abrupt, startling, unsettling, unverified disclosures, if such they were, disclosures at once uncalled for and inopportune, at a time when the limits of revealed truth had not as yet been ascertained." We are now, says Newman, accustomed to the universe of Galileo, but we should be charitable toward the ecclesiastical authorities who were "shocked and scared" by "Galileo's truth." In short, says Newman, "All I say is, that not all knowledge is suited to all minds" — he cites Jesus and St. Paul as warning "against scandalizing the weak and unintellectual." Thus while there is a time to speak out, there is also a time for concealment, or "economy," in the dispensing of fact and truth.

We should not leave the third edition of the *Via Media* without a glance at some of the footnotes which accompanied the Preface. In them one observes how Newman treats his old Anglican self the way a rather short-tempered schoolmaster corrects a pupil's essay. At one point in Lecture II, he interrupts the text with a footnote saying curtly, "All this is true, but not to the purpose," and proceeds to give the correct accoutn. Farther on, where the Anglican Newman has unwittingly connected infallibility with "systematizing," the Catholic Newman, in a footnote, asks, as if irritated, "What has infallibility to do with systematizing? . . ." Still later, in Lecture III, at the end of a passage describing devotion in "the Roman system," Newman adds a terse footnote: "This is plausible, theoretical, and untrue." [11] Throughout the notes, of course, he alludes to himself as "the Author." At the end of Lecture V, he begins a footnote in what seems a reproachful tone: "Is this Lecture written in the tone of 'Antiquity'?" [12]

Truly the Preface and the footnotes are, in a remarkable way, addressed not only to the reader but to the dead self which Newman left behind him in Littlemore in 1845.

CHAPTER IX

HISTORY AND BIOGRAPHY

i. *Was Newman a Historian?*

Whether Newman may be properly regarded as a historian and biographer may be open to some dispute. Professor Reilly has written a very engaging chapter on "Newman as Historian," and Denys Gorce, in his charming little study, *Newman et les pères*, declares that Newman is a historian "in the fullest sense of the term." [1] The Abbé Brémond likewise has celebrated Newman's "unfailing historical sense," and, like Gorce, admires his ability to naturalize himself in the Age of the Fathers.[2] Nevertheless, there is no evidence that Newman regarded himself as other than a kind of amateur in historical and biographical writing. One may gather this from the very title of the three volumes representing his effort in that field: the *Historical Sketches* are precisely what their title suggests — *sketches*, making no claim to originality or completeness or objectivity. They are informed with Newman's ever-present moral sense, and are critical and polemical from first to last. Everywhere we find the touch of the gifted "amateur." In the Preface to *The Turks*, he frankly admits that he has drawn on "materials which are to be found in any ordinarily furnished library," and is merely grouping old facts in his own way.[3] At no time is he concerned with historical fact as intrinsically interesting. Indeed, in *The Northmen and Normans in England and Ireland*, after finishing a vigorous account of the Northmen's overrunning England in Alfred's time, he pauses to remind us: "Let not the reader suppose that we are referring to this history for its own sake." [4] His *Church of the Fathers*, he tells us, took on a deliberately polemical character, "as being directed against certain Protestant ideas and opinions." [5]

Yet it remains true that, regardless of the moral or polemical aims in these essays, Newman's historical writings hold our interest as narratives. His psychological insight, his philosophic spirit, his concern with great historical figures, his sense of the mystery of man's actions, the attraction — sometimes the enchantment — of Newman's style, which varies from essay to essay — all make the *Historical Sketches* one of the finest portions of Newman's entire works. Though they are in fact outlines of larger works which he never had time to write, they nevertheless have a certain finish. What is more, they are among the most spontaneous works Newman ever produced. Most of them were written when he was a misunderstood Roman convert, withdrawing into his study, and writing on subjects of his own choosing. Unhappily, as Brémond observes, the general public knows nothing of these essays; "but," he adds, "of those who really know Newman's writings well, no one makes a mistake about it. We there find the true Newman, much more than in his better known works, in the joy of a work which he loves." [6] If he is content with secondary sources, if he falls short of present-day standards of historiography, it is because he is, after all, like his much-maligned contemporary, James Anthony Froude, a scholar of the transitional school, literary rather than learned, interpretative rather than merely factual in his treatment of history, yet gifted with infallible literary taste.

His shortcomings as a historian soon become obvious. He is wholly unimpressed by sheer fact, in contrast to Carlyle, or by the pageantry of history, in contrast to Macaulay. He is, for a historian, appallingly deficient in historical sense. Lacking the critical training which Milman received, Newman remained to the end as unhistorical in his outlook as the Oxford Noetics of the 1830's. Thus, as Brilioth observes, he is unable to see the past as a process of uninterrupted growth; "epochs of history are to him homogeneous units, with something of the timeless character of philosophical categories." [7] This is most amusingly pointed out by Professor Reilly, who shows how in *The Rise and Progress of Universities*, Newman has a hypothetical freshman come to ancient Athens to study. For Newman, Athens seems never to have changed; he has his freshman hear either Lysias or Demosthenes pleading in the Agora — though Demosthenes was but three years old when Lysias died. Newman's freshman arrives at the Ceramicus, where he may hear Pericles pronouncing a funeral oration — though this could only have happened a century later. The freshman saunters on and soon finds himself in the presence of Plato in the groves of Academe — though Plato was unborn when Pericles died. Thus we note how unreal for Newman is the passing of historical time. He seems unable to realize that conditions in Athens or Rome varied enormously from Cicero's day to that of Marcus Aurelius, or from Aurelius' day to that of Gregory. Dates mean as little to him as do the physical facts about a man and his environment which would bring him vividly before our eyes. We never get a concrete picture of Basil, of Anthony, of Chrysostom. Yet Newman strives ever for accuracy. And if he is deficient in a "time sense," he is strangely meticulous in matters of geography. His "geographical sense" may well be seen in his careful tracing of the itinerary of the exiled Chrysostom. Two reasons may be given for Newman's shortcomings as a historian, though others are no doubt conceivable. In the first place Newman always approaches history with his mind made up and solidly established on principles which, for him, throw light on everything and are indeed truer and more real than historical facts. Thus he explains the facts in accordance with a philosophy which appears to him much clearer than the facts themselves. In the second place, as we shall note later in connection with the *Church of the Fathers*, Newman is less interested in a great man's outward appearance, habits, and peculiarities than he is in the man's *mind*. Each of the biographical essays is an attempt to present "the *picture* of a mind." That is why, as a historian, Newman leaves a good deal to be desired. History, as we now think of it, records the inner life partly through revealing the outward show and drama.

For Newman, then, historical writing involved philosophy and psychological insight. He is at his best when, as in writing of Chrysostom or Theodoret, he indulges in a "psychography" which is far in advance of his time, at least in England. Brémond, like all admirers of the Introduction to "St. Chrysostom," grows ecstatic over Newman's achievement in this *genre*:

"I do not think," he says, "that such a hymn has ever been sung before in praise of psychological biography . . . Kindred masters in the opposite camp, a Sainte-Beuve, a Renan, would have gladly put their name to this lively, joyous, and confident preface; and, if they had read the 'Chrysostom' or the 'Theodoret' of the 'Historical Sketches,' they would have saluted in Newman one of their equals." [8]

ii. *Early Efforts*

We have already noted that when Newman was only in his twenties, he contributed two articles to the *Encyclopaedia Metropolitana* — the essays on "Cicero" and "Apollonius of Tyana" (1824).* For the most part, they are painstaking, plodding, honest pieces of writing. Yet both show that even in 1824 Newman was capable of exactness of style, of penetrating insight, and of an unusual mental poise and a wariness against extravagant intellectual enthusiasms into which the young writer is sometimes seduced. Of the two essays, that on Cicero shows Newman both as critic and historian. Though much of it is simple, straightforward writing, there are times when Newman's enthusiasm for the age of his favorite classic author imparts memorable distinction to his style. The reader tends to pause and re-read Newman's account of the rise of the New Academy, of the teachings of Arcesilas and Carneades, and of the spread of Pyrrhonism. One notes how early the young Newman had encountered those very skeptical arguments which he was to expound and attack in the *Grammar of Assent*. One notices the familiar vocabulary — "probability," "assent," "opinion." Throughout, there is that unmistakable Augustan style to which Gibbon had contributed so much. Early in the essay Newman writes, for example, of Cicero's rise to power: "the integrity of his public life was only equalled by the correctness of his private morals; and it may at first sight excite our wonder that a course so splendidly begun should afterwards so little fulfil its early promise." [1] But what is perhaps most notable of all is that in describing Cicero's rhetorical methods in his famous orations, Newman unconsciously but prophetically describes the rhetorical strategy of *The Idea of a University*. Cicero, he says, opens his case with a profession of

* See Chap. I, ii, p. 10.

timidity and diffidence, endeavoring to conciliate his hearers; he entreats the patience of his judges; he drops some generous popular sentiment; he states the plan of the oration. All goes so smoothly, everything is accounted for so naturally, every detail tells so happily, objections are so adroitly converted in confirmation of his argument "that it becomes impossible to entertain a question on the truth of his statement." But this is not all. Like Newman, Cicero "goes round and round his subject; surveys it in every light; examines it in all its parts; retires and then advances; turns and re-turns it; compares and contrasts it; illustrates, confirms, enforces," until his hearers wonder at having doubted a single point of his argument.[2] This was the technique used in Dublin in 1852; this was the technique of the *Difficulties of Anglicans,* of the *Letters* to Dr. Pusey and to the Duke of Norfolk — formal, sinuous, supple, persuasive. Finally, one long remembers the closing sections of the essay in which Newman, with the skill of a practised literary critic, compares the genius of the Latin tongue with that of the Greek, awarding the palm to the latter, then ending with a few swiftly damning sentences describing the literary taste of post-Ciceronian Rome. The essay had begun with the mechanical formality of an encyclopedia article; it ends with the sparkle and verve of literary art.

The *Arians of the Fourth Century* (1833), which we have already considered from the point of view of doctrine and dogma,* stands as Newman's only substantial achievement as a historian. We know that he slaved at it until nearly fainting from exhaustion, and that he scrupulously labored with original sources in order to give his work authentic stature. However, in the *Arians* Newman is not concerned primarily with history but with doctrine. Hence we look in vain for portraits of such great figures as Athanasius or Arius, for Eusebius of Nicomedia, the adroit politician, or for that other Eusebius, of Caesarea. Only the great *shadow* of Athanasius walks through Newman's pages. Instead of historical figures we have two or three hundred pages devoted to the tracing and the analysis of all the protean changes into which Arianism dissolved in that strange and turbulent fourth century. In spite of the sedateness of Newman's prose,

---

* See Chap. III, iii, p. 61.

we catch glimpses of the terrible ecclesiastical and civil strife consequent on the heresy, a strife which surged into the palace of bishop and emperor, swept both the East and West into waves of hatred and recrimination, and nearly rent the Church itself asunder. Arianism was not merely a religious heresy; it was also the occasion for unscrupulous ambition in Church and state, for riot and turmoil, revenge and murder. It is impossible to believe that Newman is completely indifferent to the historic drama he is presenting; too often does he fall into pure Gibbonian narrative, and we know that he is luxuriating in that far-off, stately world of the *Decline and Fall*. Moreover, we cannot miss his evident enthusiasm when he describes that ancient Church to which he spiritually belonged — the Church of Alexandria, with its doctrines of "economy" and the *disciplina arcani,* its allegorical method, its neo-Platonism. Chapter II, which follows some pages later, may be said to reveal Newman in his spiritual home; dealing with the teachings of the Ante-Nicene Church in its relation to the Arian heresy, it shows Newman completely at home (in 1833) with the doctrines of Apostolical Tradition, of the "Christian Mysteries," of the Trinity viewed scripturally and ecclesiastically. Newman ends the chapter, after explaining the Arian heresy, with a startling justification for persecution. The heretic, says the young Anglican clergyman, "should meet with no mercy"; he is embodied evil. "To spare him is a false and dangerous pity. It is to endanger the souls of thousands, and it is uncharitable towards himself." [3] This sounds indeed like Gregory IX or Innocent IV. On the whole, however, the *Arians* is an unexciting and highly complicated theological narrative and exposition. Even the historical passages are colorless; there are few dates; and at times chronology seems to be either ignored or confused. Newman's friends considered the *Arians* a great disappointment. Most of it was merely laborious, detailed, scholarly, and dull. Never again (except, curiously enough, in writing about the Convocation of Canterbury and about mediaeval Oxford) was Newman to be so hopelessly unexciting.

During this same year (1833) Newman published in the *British Magazine* a series of sketches later brought together under the title of *The Church of the Fathers*.   Here, again, he is attempting "neither the grand outlines, nor the living details of the [fourth] century, but some scenes or passages which chronologically or morally belong to it." [4]   Newman's method is informal, loose, "journalistic," sometimes surprisingly uninspired. His chronology and his transitions are frequently indeterminate, and the general organization of the sketches lacks the tightness and symmetry given to his greater works.   Between a third and a half of the work consists of passages presented from the letters and documents of Basil, Gregory of Nazianzus, Antony, Augustine, St. Martin, and Demetrias (a fifth-century Roman lady who renounced the world and helped St. Leo after Genseric's sack of Rome).   However, Newman's skill in selection, together with his admirable touches of portraiture, gives on the whole an authentic and vivid impression.   In his very choice of the people he delineates, he reveals much about himself.   He finds a kindred spirit in Basil, the retired and thoughtful student, elevated and single-minded of purpose, yet able when called at length into active life, to conduct himself with firmness, zeal, and integrity, ready of wit, negligent of men's applause.   We note that like Newman, St. Basil was sensitive, anxious, affectionate, somewhat reserved, and thus thought proud.   On the other hand, there was Gregory, playful and enthusiastic, humorous and whimsical, loving and buoyant.   Like Newman and Hurrell Froude, these two were great in friendship, and at one in having a "profound sense of the world's nothingness."   Both had been pupils at Athens, had classical tastes, were champions of the Catholic creed, excelled in rhetoric and debate, and had enjoyed for a time the acquaintance of one of the greatest of the Roman gentlemen, Julian, "since of evil name in history as the Apostate."   The mere reading of Gregory's and Basil's letters, as assembled by Newman, serves to show us some of the deepest sources for his convictions about the world's "hollow blessedness," the idea of a gentleman, the beauty of the monastic life, and the ideal which both saints embodied, that "Christian humanism" which combined the virtues of the monk and the man of affairs.   Basil became exarch of Caesarea, and Gregory, after many bitter years, patriarch of Constantinople.   Newman was especially drawn to

Gregory, we may be sure, because of his belated recognition: on the partition of Cappadocia, Basil the exarch, sent his friend Gregory, not yet advanced in the Church, to the see of Sasima, which proved a tortuous exile and estranged the two men for some time. Like Newman, "Gregory was nothing till he was almost an old man." [5] Only the last three of his sixty years were ecclesiastically successful, in the patriarchal throne of Constantinople.

One does not have to ask why Newman chose such varied types for *The Church of the Fathers*, or what Basil has to do with Demetrias, or Augustine with St. Martin. All these figures had suffered, like Newman, the bitterness of misunderstanding and of spiritual perplexity. It is not merely that Antony's discussions of faith — "Faith," says Antony, "which operates, is better and surer than your subtle syllogism" — are strikingly like those of Newman. It is not merely that Augustine's conversion occurred, like Newman's, in an age of irreligion, and in spite of almost insuperable obstacles. All the people in *The Church of the Fathers* had fought for their integrity: St. Martin had heroically resisted the blandishments of the crafty Maximus, the usurper of Britain, Gaul, and Spain; Demetrias resisted the appeal of the fifth-century Roman aristocracy to which she belonged, and devoted herself at Carthage to a single life, and later, after the sack of Rome, gave of her great wealth to build the Basilica of St. Stephen; Antony had fought against the "open assaults of Satan"; and Augustine struggled with both the perversities of the intellect and the lusts of the flesh. Lest we forget, incidentally, that all these figures are treated as thoroughly human, we should note that in quoting passages from St. Augustine's *Confessions*, Newman does not omit the confessor's famous plea to God: "Give me chastity and continence, but not at once." [6] But above all, there were Basil and Gregory, men of culture and refinement, theologians, preachers, who had their trials and prevailed in the end. Basil's leadership evoked contention from the emperor Valens; Gregory's came bitterly late and was soon cut off by death. Truly the age of Gregory, Basil, Antony, and Augustine was, as Gorce has well put it, the home and kingdom of Newman's soul. [7]

Brief mention should here be made of two papers which Newman published in 1834-35 and 1838 — the *Convocation of Canterbury* and *Medieval Oxford* — in the *British Magazine* and the *British Critic*, respectively. The former essay is a dull and legalistic inquiry into the historical basis of the "supremacy" and "jurisdiction" of the king as head of the Church. Its aim is to clear the air of 1834-35, when the Tractarian Movement was at its height, and to show wherein the royal supremacy has no power in the Church, *e.g.*, in ministering the sacraments, in bestowing ministerial commissions. Later events showed Newman to what extent he was wrong, and he capitalized on his knowledge, as we have seen, in his *Difficulties of Anglicans*. In *Medieval Oxford* Newman finds an occasion for pleasant browsing in the interesting antiquities of the university, and also an opportunity to come out boldly in defense of Oxford's "conservatism" — "Oxford never shows so well as when resisting innovation and rallying round an ancient principle." Indeed, Newman (in 1838) is sure that the university "has, and ever has had, what men of the world will call a Popish character." [8] Both these papers belong to the least enduring of Newman's writings. As one reads them, says Professor Reilly, one's strongest feeling is of gratitude that Newman was never again as dull as in these dreary pages. [9]

iii. *Newman and the "Terrible Turk"*

In October, 1853, Newman delivered in the Catholic Institute of Liverpool a course of lectures on *The History of the Turks in Their Relations to Europe*, which drew considerable attention partly because they preceded the outbreak of the Crimean War by only a few months. As history they were frankly unoriginal, borrowing words and phrases from easily accessible authorities, and aiming frankly at a temporary purpose — to influence public opinion against any alliance of England with Turkey. So rapidly were the lectures put together, and so dependent were they on well-known histories that Newman did not intend, in the first instance, to publish them at all. But they now appear in the first volume of the *Historical Sketches*, and because they are at times so poetic in treatment, so interesting in their occasional digressions, and so truly a product of Newman's genius, the reader is glad that Newman allowed them to be printed.

Like his other historical writings, they show his weaknesses as a historian. The old problem of chronology again lifts its embarrassing head. There are almost no dates; historical figures are brought together in one sentence though their lives were separated by a hundred years; battles, invasions, conquests, kings and generals and dynasties pass across Newman's pages in confused pageantry. It is all a series of magnificent but shadowy scenes. And through it all, as Newman narrates it, is the hand of Providence, sending Attila as the "scourge of God," and tipping the balance of history in favor of the Church in the great battle of Lepanto. There is thus no attempt at what we today would call "objective history." But Newman excels in many a passage of description, or analysis, or narrative. We feel his delight in going back over the times of Zingis and Timour and Attila; they no doubt shocked and fascinated him as they had when he used to read of them in Gibbon. We feel it especially when he gives us his detailed description of the outward appearance of the Huns, with their shrill voices, their broad shoulders, their flat noses, and "their eyes black, small, and deeply buried in their head." Newman adds that "they had little hair on their skulls, and no beard," and reports the Gothic belief that they were the "detestable progeny of evil spirits and witches in the wilds of the East." [1]

For Newman, the Turkish menace goes back into antiquity. Making no attempt at a scientific distinction among the races, he says simply that when the Turks "first appear in history they are Huns or Tartars, and nothing else." These terrible people have from the first been the "enemies of God and persecutors of His Church." [2] The year 1048 he singles out as a critical date for Christendom, for then it was that the savage hordes poured down from the north upon Khorasan, and into Syria, Egypt, and the Holy Land. "In vain was the power of [the Turk] overthrown by the Crusaders; in vain do the Seljukians disappear from the annals of the world; in vain is Constantinople respited; in vain is Europe saved." Christendom in arms still had centuries of struggle before it.³   Though Newman grants that the Turks gained much from Islamism — a military aim, a political principle, a social bond, and a sense of responsibility — "Tartar still is the staple of their composition," and their very gifts make them a deadlier foe to civilization.   Though he grants that the Mahometan faith is a great improvement on paganism, he laments that the Turks, at the critical moment of their history, while standing between "Christ in the West and Satan in the East," chose, partly under the circumstances of the time, to oppose themselves not to paganism but to Christianity.   This, for Newman, was all the more tragic in that during the "miserable period" of the fifteenth and sixteenth centuries, the Turkish menace came at a time when the internal history of the Church was "most disastrous and melancholy." ⁴   The rise of the Ottomans almost coincides with the rise of heresies throughout Europe; and the weakened Church was unable to cope successfully with either the Turks or the Protestants.   Moreover, Newman observes, the increase in national wealth in these centuries disinclined the nations to continue the war against the infidel Turk, though it drove them to war among themselves.   However, on October 7, 1571, came the great battle of Lepanto which, in Newman's eyes, was the death grapple between barbarism and civilization, between Christ and Satan.   Rome had got a saint as Pope, Pius V.   The struggle at Lepanto reminds Newman of the history of Leo and the Hun — the power of a meek and praying Pius V against the remorseless Ali Pasha.   In one of the greatest of naval battles in history, the Christian League, led by Don John of Austria, thoroughly defeated the Turkish fleet.   "Such," concludes Newman, viewing the victory as a manifestation of divine clemency, "was the catastrophe of this long and anxious drama; the hosts of Turkistan and Tartary had poured down" like the Huns of old, and were now, as then, "reversed by an old man," by the "heroic obstinacy" of St. Pius.

In the last three lectures, in discussing the prospects of the Turks, Newman takes up the distinction between barbarism and civilization, and makes some of the most penetrating observations in the whole work. Civilization he holds to be the triumph of mind over imagination and passion; it is marked by some indwelling principle or idea which is developed by consistent habits and actions. Civilization is constantly achieving its own existence, not as an established state of things but as a point in a career. Hence it has a history. Barbarism, on the other hand, "has no individuality, it has no history"; it is "a principle, not of society, but of isolation," ignorant, purposeless, complacent, and stagnant. While civilization develops art out of nature and self-government out of passion, barbarism does not improve talents or fix motives, or control impulse. For a time, a barbarian horde may rise to power, but not from some inner principle; their success springs from some able or determined leader. Having no inner principle of social life, this power is always precarious and unproductive; when it is attacked and swept away, it leaves behind it no monuments of its soul. On the other hand, civilization has its own weaknesses, too. In a passage remarkably like something out of Spengler, Newman describes how a civilization, once mature, begins to decay — reason dissipating political greatness, institutions losing their sacred character, opinion taking the place of conviction, social unity becoming merely unanimity, classes pitting themselves against each other, morals becoming corrupt in proportion to material prosperity, responsibility being avoided by the individual, until the nation "dies a natural death, even though some Alaric or Genseric happens to be at hand to take possession of the corpse. And centuries before the end comes, patriots may see it coming." [5] Newman analyzes the slow ruin of a civilization with all his characteristic calm and detachment, with an objectivity which sometimes makes one gasp.

Newman's final word on the Turks reminds us that he is speaking from the middle of the nineteenth century. Today the Turks are no formidable menace to civilization and Christianity; other menaces of far greater stature have arisen. Nor is Newman correct in denying to the Turks the power of adapting themselves to the modern world. Of the people of Kemal Ataturk it can no longer be said: "One thing is inconceivable — that the Turks should, as an existing nation, accept of modern civilization." [6]

iv. *"The Rise and Progress of Universities"*

Newman's next historical writing was the natural outgrowth of his rectorship of the Catholic University in Dublin. We have already noted * that he supplemented his lectures on the *Idea of a University* with a series of papers, published in the *Catholic University Gazette* (1854), on the rise and growth of universities. Having defined the scope and function of an ideal university in his lectures, he now seeks to justify his own conception of such an institution from the historical point of view, and thus to persuade the Irish that, in setting up a real university — a *Studium Generale* — they have a long and powerful tradition behind them. The writing of these papers was undoubtedly very congenial to Newman. They permitted him once more, in that famous essay, "What is a University?" to luxuriate in definition, and in that equally famous essay on the "Site of a University" and in the two succeeding papers, to live again in one of the favorite kingdoms of his mind, the age of the Athenian academies and of the Sophists. They were the occasion also for distinguishing between the great virtue of the Athenian schools, which was *influence* (the "action of personality"), and the virtue of the Macedonian and Roman schools, which was *discipline* (the rule of "law," and organization). They allowed him once more to ruminate over the downfall of the Graeco-Roman world before the onrush of the Goth, the Hun, and the Lombard. He narrates, in his peculiarly quiet tone, how the great library of ancient Alexandria, "noblest of dynastic monuments," was burned by the Saracens; how the twenty-nine public libraries of Rome were destroyed by the Lombards; how at Constantinople, under the barbarian scourge, "ten thousand persons are said to have died daily." He traces the flight of learning, limping from the devastated world of the Mediterranean in the sixth and seventh centuries, to "the Isles of the North," where England and Ireland "opened to the lovers of learning and piety a welcome asylum." [1] Then he follows the course of learning through the Middle Ages, notably under Gregory the Great and the Schoolmen. There

* See Chap. V, i, p. 97.

are chapters on the University of Paris, on Oxford, on "the ancient University of Dublin," and finally a chapter on "L'École des Hautes Études," in which he hopes to discern the beginnings of a revival of great Catholic universities.   Everywhere there are the typically Newman touches — the poetic descriptions, the wonderful definitions, the limpid eloquence, the adroit pleading, the penetrating insight, the well-managed argument.

To readers of these papers perhaps nothing is more memorable than Newman's sketch of Abelard.   Doubtless this surpasses, for many of us, the papers on the nature and the ideal site of a university.   Abelard represents, for Newman, the strength and the weakness of "communicating knowledge for its own sake," which he calls "the University principle."   Abelard's devotion to the "new philosophy," coupled with his devouring intellectual ambition, led him to undervalue the ancient classics and the Seven Arts, led him also to mix up spiritual matters with temporal, and to aim at a bishopric through the medium of his *logic*.   Newman follows him sorrowfully through his period of dazzling popularity, watches people gather from all parts of the world to hear his marvelous eloquence, sees him take up his abode with an old ecclesiastic whose niece was the fateful Eloisa.   Then comes a characteristic Newman passage, incisive, compact, and understanding: "A more subtle snare was laid for him than beset the heroic champion or the all-accomplished monarch of Israel [*i.e.* either Samson or Solomon]; for sensuality came upon him under the guise of intellect, and it was the high mental endowments of Eloisa, who became his pupil, speaking in her eyes, and thrilling on her tongue, which were the intoxication and the delirium of Abelard." [2]   Abelard is judged, and punished.   He has passed through two phases of his career, as logician and lover.   There is yet a third: we find him at the Abbey of St. Denis "languidly rising from his dream of sin," soon urged by the abbot to lecture again.   Once more his school is thronged with students.   But again his ideas take heretical directions: he moves from place to place — in the Champagne, in lower Brittany, and into the presence of two Councils.   He has to burn his book, and he starts toward Rome to make his peace.   He does not arrive, but dies, in the year 1142, having retracted what had given scandal in his writings. For Newman, Abelard is a great intellect "miserably thrown away." But the account of Abelard's rise and fall makes one of the climaxes in the third volume of the *Historical Sketches*.

Throughout *The Rise and Progress of Universities* there is, of course, many an arid stretch, as when Newman distinguishes between the college and the university, the one a sphere of "influence" under men of magnetic intellectual attraction like Scotus or Aquinas, the other the sphere of "law," which sleeplessly guards its universality and cosmopolitan scope against the "nationalism" and the disintegrating tendencies of the colleges. But aridity is not the only weakness of these papers. There is, once more, almost no chronology. Moreover, Newman presupposes a great amount of knowledge, on the part of the reader, regarding the origins and the various types of early universities. The uninformed reader is at times confused or misled. But three virtues redeem these papers for all readers of Newman: the occasional descriptions, as of "Athens, the city of the mind"; [3] the re-creation of the spirit of the old seats of learning, Rome, Athens, Paris, Oxford; and the flashes of epigrammatic insight or wisdom — "The Romans deified Law, as the Athenians deified the Beautiful," "the love of the Beautiful will not conquer the world, but like the voice of Orpheus, it may for a while carry it away captive," "in this world no one rules by mere love; if you are amiable, you are no hero." [4]

Not long after his sojourn in Ireland, and while he was for a short time editor of the *Rambler*, Newman published in that magazine during May and July, 1859, two papers on *The Northmen and Normans in England and Ireland*. Their chief purpose was to attempt, with all the tact which Newman could summon to his aid, "to investigate the policy of the Holy See in the twelfth century, in annexing Ireland to the English crown," [5] and to justify the Anglo-Norman expedition to Ireland under "Strongbow." What interests us today is not Newman's cautious historical narrative, but his study of the Northmen and the Normans. He regards both as playing, in those early centuries, a Providential role as bearers of order to confused and stormy England, and a little later to an even more chaotic Ireland.

Newman is clearly enjoying himself as he describes the North-men, their sea kings, their *berserkirs,* their marauding expeditions, restlessly roving from the German Sea to the Mediterranean.   He is also evidently at home when he describes the "ordinary course of barbarian invasion," and shows how a barbarian horde — even the Northmen, "cradled in surge and storm" — gradually assimilates the civilization it has attacked, until "the wild Scandinavian . . . changes into the chivalrous Norman."   He sees in the Northmen the noble, stern, gigantic, and untamed heroes of the romantic tales of Fouqué, of whom he was a fond reader.   He admires in both the Northmen and the Normans their warlike heroism: "War was their life; it was almost their *summum bonum;* good in itself, though nothing came of it."   In the Norman this trait is softened into knight-errantry:

"His very worship was to do battle; his rite of sacrifice was a passage of arms.   He couched his lance to prove . . . that his lady was the beautifullest of all conceivable women; he drew his sword on the blasphemer to convince him of the sanctity of the Gospel; and he passed abruptly from demolishing churches and burning towns to the rescue of the Holy Sepulchre from the unclean infidel." [6]

Newman's account of the Northmen and Normans ends abruptly, with a footnote stating that it is "but a fragment, in consequence of the author's suddenly retiring from the editorship of the *Rambler* magazine."   Just what Newman had originally planned to do with his subject, it is difficult to say.   We remember it, however, for its proof once more that Newman admired vigor and action; we here see him dwelling with admiration on the heroic character of the Norman knights.   We also remember it for its occasional digressions, some of them very striking or challenging.   In dealing with the low level of civilization in twelfth-century Ireland, in spite of its great seats of learning, he observes: "A University does great things; but this is just one of the things it does not do: it does not intellectualize its neighborhood." [7]

v.   *Newman and the Benedictines*

In 1858–59 Newman published two papers in the *Atlantis* — an uncontroversial Catholic periodical which he had helped to launch — on *The Mission of St. Benedict* and *The Benedictine Schools*. These papers were intended to be part of a larger work showing in the rise and growth of monasticism the element of "poetry" in the Benedictines, the "scientific" element in the Dominicans, and the "practical" element in the Jesuits. The two latter studies were never completed. We have, however, in the papers on the Benedictines, an admirable contribution to the history of educational progress from the break-up of the Roman Empire until the time of Anselm, a great Benedictine but also the first of the Schoolmen. There are, of course, scores of passages revealing again Newman's power as an analyst, a describer, and a definer.

Newman sees the early Benedictines as frankly in "flight from the world, and nothing else." They found themselves in "an old, decayed, and moribund world . . . Society was in the slow fever of consumption. . . It was powerful, however, to seduce and deprave." It was a world crazed with paganism, heresy, and violence. Early monachism therefore sought a life "free from corruption in its daily work, free from distraction in its daily worship; and it sought employments as contrary as possible to the world's employments" [1] — tasks that would mortify not only the flesh but the reason, that would bring rest and peace through simple, unthinking action, through prayer, fasting, meditation, study, manual labor. Newman loves to visualize the early Benedictines in the mountains, deep in the forests, or in the woody swamps, digging, clearing, and building — "wherever they came, they converted the wilderness into a cultivated country." [2] It is true that they often chose a beautiful spot for their dwelling, such as Beaulieu Abbey in Hampshire, but this was not from any sentimental love of "melancholy winds and purling rills, and waterfalls and nodding groves"; it was from their "poetic" aim to live simply, in "admiration, enthusiasm, devotion, love," and from their ability to find poetry in the hard work and hard fare which went into the founding and building of their abbeys. St. Benedict's direct object, of course, in setting his monks to such labor was "neither social usefulness nor poetry, but penance." [3] Nevertheless a great indirect product resulted — "the woody swamp became a hermitage, a religious house, a farm, an abbey, a village, a seminary, a school of learning, and a city"; from the simple, silent, hard-working monks there rose a civilized community. Then, says Newman as quietly as when relating the sack of Alexandria, down came the invader:

"The Hun succeeded to the Goth, the Lombard to the Hun, the Tartar to the Lombard; the Saxon was reclaimed only that the Dane might take his place.   Down in the dust lay the labor and civilization of centuries, — Churches, Colleges, Cloisters, Libraries, — and nothing was left to [the monks] but to begin all over again; but this they did without grudging, so promptly, cheerfully, and tranquilly, as if it were by some law of nature that the restoration came." [4]

The Mission of St. Benedict concludes with two very beautiful passages.   One shows how "to the monk heaven was next door; he formed no plans, he had no cares"; he lived for the day, ploughing, sowing, praying, meditating, clearing a way into the forest and building his dwelling with "a wild, irregular beauty." When he read the Fathers, it was without regard to system or logical analysis, but with the simple Benedictine desire to reflect "as a faithful mirror, the words and works of the Almighty." The other passage illustrates this Benedictine simplicity by quoting St. Cuthbert's account of the death of St. Bede.

More academic and less poetic is Newman's paper on *The Benedictine Schools*.   Yet he succeeds in interesting us in the way the Benedictines coped with the social complexities of the Middle Ages.   The political revolutions consequent on the rule of Charlemagne made new demands upon an order which had long sought its peace and labor "in the lonely wood or the silent mountain top."   Once so withdrawn from the world, "the lonely Benedictine rose from his knees and found himself a city . . . Europe was new mapped, and the monks were the principle of mapping.   They had grown into large communities, into abbeys, into corporations with civil privileges, into land-holders with tenants, serfs, and baronial neighbors"; they were the centers of education, religion, and politics — "they found themselves priests, rulers, legislators, feudal lords, royal counsellors, missionary preachers, controversialists." [5]   The solitude of St. Anthony now seemed impossible.   The Benedictines, brought by necessity from the cloister into the political world, solved their problem by becoming the educators of their times while still remaining faithful to Benedictine conservatism and simplicity. It was in their *schools* that they now served both the Church and the world. They admitted lay boys on an equal footing with novitiates, and opened up the old books and subjects which they accepted from the pagan schools. To the study of Scripture they added Latin poetry and prose, and, in the true Benedictine tradition, training in the manual arts. Their schools, Newman reminds us, were infant schools and grammar schools; higher education, in that day of bloodshed and revolution, could scarcely be said to exist. Nor were the Benedictines innovators: "they cared little for knowledge even theological, or for success, even though it was religious"; they were contented, resigned, patient, incurious. The Benedictine did not analyze; he marveled; he related all objects and events immediately to "the First and Supreme Cause." [6] Hence, while the Benedictine schools were admirable defenses and retreats in an age of barbarism, they eventually yielded their supremacy to other orders. As universities sprang up, as heresies arose, and as bolder intellects came to the front in the Church, a new type of champion was needed. As Aquinas developed his philosophy, and united the resources of ancient thought with his own, the Benedictine period gave way to the Dominican.

vi. *Newman and Two "Ancient Saints"*

In the year following the publication of the papers on the Benedictines, Newman brought out in the *Rambler* two biographical studies which took him back to the early Fathers. They were intended to form part of a volume to be entitled *Ancient Saints*, which was planned to include studies of St. Ambrose, St. Jerome, and perhaps St. Athanasius, as well as those he completed, on St. John Chrysostom and Theodoret. He prefaces his essays with an unforgettable introduction which, because in it Newman confesses his delight in personal and concrete details about the saints, leads at least one writer to say that it gives "the most intimate glimpse of John Henry Newman as a man of letters which he ever deigned to give." [1] Newman expresses repugnance for official hagiography which "chops up a saint into chapters of faith, hope, charity, and the cardinal virtues," which omits those telling details which make a saint a man, and which ignore too often the "conflict which is waging in the soul between what is divine and what is human." [2]   He roundly condemns "the endemic perennial fidget which possesses us about giving scandal."   What he wants is the saint's "real life," a narrative which will convey "the idea of moral unity, identity, growth, continuity, personality," preferably through letters.   And Newman exults in realizing that the world still has four hundred of St. Basil's letters, about two hundred and forty of St. Chrysostom's, and a hundred and forty-six of Theodoret's.   He is so especially attached to the saints of the third and fourth centuries, he says, because they have left so much of their history in those "goodly folios" in which he may "trace and study the real, hidden but human life, or the *interior*, as it is called, of such glorious creations of God."   He realizes that saints, as other men, differ from each other, and he wants a living narrative about them.   Church histories, such as Mosheim's, are as dry and unfruitful for Newman as Robertson and Hume were for Carlyle.[3]

From this very informal and human Introduction, we are led to expect vivid portraits and realistic background studies.   But we are disappointed.   The backgrounds of St. Chrysostom and Theodoret are hopelessly vague.   There is only an occasional date.   Too many pages are given to digressions on the Isaurians and on the geography of Asia Minor.   Too little is offered to explain the relentless hatred of St. Chrysostom's enemies.   In fact there is too little straightforward *narrative*; in its stead we have numerous letters, and a curiously static, or slow-paced, treatment of Chrysostom's and Theodoret's vicissitudes.   And yet, in spite of these shortcomings, Newman's biographical studies of these two saints stand out as among the most charming of his writings. The reason is not far to see.   Both men suffered, like Newman, misunderstanding and exile.   Chrysostom's exile was a literal banishment by a synod at Constantinople to the wild desert of Pityus on the coast of the Black Sea; Theodoret's exile was more like Newman's — he was bishop of Cyrrhus, an isolated, uncultured, and unresponsive bishopric, no more attractive to Theodóret than Birmingham was to Newman. Both Theodoret and Chrysostom were men of high gifts, of sensitive intellect and feeling, of charm united to great strength of purpose. In writing of Chrysostom Newman's thoughts went back to Basil, with his "tenderness, gravity, self-possession, resignation, penance," and to Gregory, with his innocence, amiableness, inward peace, and self-resource. And some of their charm and lucidity enter into Newman's style as he presents their letters and tells their heroic story.

We follow with Newman the story of Chrysostom's separation from his bishop's throne in Constantinople by the Empress Eudoxia whom he had offended with his reforming zeal. The saint was nearly sixty when he took his way toward the place of exile, Cucusus, which failed, however, to prove severe enough to kill him and thus satisfy his enemies. He was therefore forced to travel across a far wilder country and to a remote town on the eastern coast of the Euxine Sea. Here Newman digresses a bit into one of his often quoted descriptions:

"The Euxine! strange mysterious sea, which typifies the abyss of outer darkness . . . the Black Sea has ever been on the very outskirts of the habitable world, and the scene of wild unnatural portents; with the legends of Prometheus on the savage Caucasus, of Medea gathering witch-herbs in the moist meadows of the Phasis, and of Iphigenia sacrificing the ship-wrecked stranger in Taurica; and then again, with the more historical, yet not more grateful visions of barbarous tribes, Goths, Huns, Scythians, Tartars, flitting over the steppes and wastes which encircle its inhospitable waters." [4]

"I am going to take some rest," Chrysostom said, so calling his exile. Old and ill, he trudged through wild country and remote towns, managing not to fall into the hands of the Isaurians who had just descended from their mountain-holds and had spread panic and terror throughout the interior of Asia Minor. Pausing at Caesarea, he writes letters to his friends, Olympias and Theodora. Later, in his exile, he writes many others — to Evethius, Paeanius, Diogenes. These letters Newman presents with suitable comment. The saint is obliged to move farther into more inhospitable regions. "He is to die by inches; want of sleep, want of rest, want of food and medicine, and the collapse certain to follow, are to extinguish the brave spirit which hitherto has risen superior to all sorrows." [5]   He never reaches the end of the journey, but dies at Comana, A.D. 407.   Newman's narrative is, as usual, quiet and suggestive, touched here and there with poetry and wonder, never with pity or literary "sentiment."

The Trials of Theodoret makes exciting reading.   Newman is here dealing with a man whom he admired but whose temper and bad judgment lost him canonization.   Theodoret got himself tragically entangled in the controversies and machinations of both laymen and ecclesiastics; he placed himself in a hostile position, first wrongly, then rightly, against Egypt and Alexandria; he came into collision with the third Ecumenical Council held at Ephesus; he discovered the nascent heresy of Eutyches, and then got himself shut up in a monastery as a turbulent busybody; he was later deposed by the second great Ephesian Council, and was at length vindicated by St. Leo at Chalcedon.   This was truly a stormy career.   And Newman obviously throws himself wholly into the narrative about Theodoret and the Council of Ephesus — a story he had seen told in masterly fashion in Gibbon's great forty-seventh chapter.   He looks on in grief and wonder at the tremendous struggle between St. Cyril and Theodoret, and though he tries to condemn Theodoret and justify Cyril, his heart is with Theodoret.   At one point in the story his emotions flame up: Cyril had been a party to the persecution of Chrysostom, had even called him a Judas.   Then Newman turns to the reader: "Cyril, I know, is a Saint"; then he adds, with a slight rasp in his voice, "but it does not follow that he was a Saint in the year 412." [6]   Seldom does Newman let the bars down quite that far.   And it is noteworthy that his feelings are wrought up over a man who had been dead over fifteen hundred years.   Such was the power of Newman's imagination: Theodoret was as real to him as John Keble.

It grieves Newman that such a great bishop and writer as Theodoret should have played so violent a part in those meetings and altercations.   He should have remained a priest; he was made a bishop too young, and then sent off to uncongenial surroundings.

"Had he been kept back at Antioch for half a dozen years," Newman muses mournfully, "he might have followed Chrysostom to Constantinople, and have been placed on its patriarchal throne, instead of the unhappy Nestorius. Then the Church would have been spared the scandal and the misery of the Nestorian heresy, controversy, and schism, of the strong acts of St. Cyril and of the Fathers of the third Ecumenical Council." [7]

One wonders just why Newman writes so at length, and at times with such passion, about a man so unlike himself, and so different from the gentle, patient, and gracious Chrysostom. The answer is, as we have intimated, that he identified himself with Theodoret. Who was the arrogant and domineering Cyril of Newman's acquaintance? In the dark years between 1850 and 1864 it was probably Henry Edward Manning.

Newman follows the unhappy, warmhearted Theodoret to the end of his story: at last Theodoret and Cyril are reconciled; Rome vouches for Theodoret's orthodoxy; and death comes in the peaceful retirement of the monastery in which, forty years before, he had prepared himself for his career. In *The Trials of Theodoret* we see again Newman's historical and biographical methods; they issue in the end, not in a picturesque or dramatic impression, but in precisely what he aimed to achieve: a "picture of the mind." On finishing a reading of the *Historical Sketches* we have the feeling of having moved among great personalities; we know little of their outward garments, but we know what they thought, how they suffered, what they wrote to their friends, how they struggled, and how they died.

CHAPTER X

LITERATURE

There are sufficiently numerous critical *dicta* scattered throughout Newman's writings to justify one in regarding him, to a certain extent, as a literary critic. Thus a French scholar, Mlle. Fernande Tardivel, devotes a whole chapter of her study of Newman's literary personality to *Newman critique littéraire.* More recently Alvan S. Ryan and L. G. Miller have examined Newman's conception of the nature and function of literature.[1] The general subject of Newman's relation to criticism is complicated by the fact that his critical opinions and standards changed from time to time. It is further complicated by his wide range of literary interest, by his fondness for both classical and nonclassical writers, and by the degree in which English Romanticism afforded a congenial background for the Oxford Movement. Because of this last factor, any discussion of Newman and literature is soon involved in the question of whether Newman was, or was not, a Romantic.

i. *Newman the Romantic*

There are undeniable affinities between Newman's mind and the mind of almost any of the great Romantics. We remember his defense of a nonrational, or intuitive, approach to religious faith; we recall that he "fled to the past"— not to the Middle Ages, to be sure, but to the Patristic Age. We also remember his literary preferences, especially Scott and Southey. In fact, it is sometimes easy to forget Newman's love for Cicero, the Greek dramatists, Johnson, and Burke, and to conclude hastily, with Professor Stanley Williams, that "every literary preference of Newman's proclaims him, directly or indirectly, a romanticist."[1] It is also possible so to broaden the term "Romantic" that, with Sister Mary Kiener, we see nothing but Romanticism in Newman's love for natural beauty, his interest in the past (even though he went back to the fourth century for dogma rather than for thrills), his aspiration, idealism, and sensitive affections.[2] Finally, one may err with both Sister Mary Kiener and the Abbé Brémond by quoting indiscriminately and uncritically from Newman's early and late utterances on literature, and thus neglect to notice that Newman's views on poetry as expressed in the essay on Aristotle and those set forth in the *Idea of a University* represent the difference between an immature and a mature conception.[3]

That Newman was to some extent a Romantic needs no further evidence. It is sufficient merely to indicate at this point in what respects he belongs to the Romantic school, and to observe which of his writings most clearly serve that school. We have noted that in childhood and youth, Newman devoured the novels of Scott and Jane Porter, the Gothic romances of Mrs. Radcliffe, and the poetry of Southey. But two forces tended always to counteract the Romantic influences of his early years, and to render his Romanticism a constantly ambiguous element in his nature and his work: namely, the Evangelical piety of the Newman home (morally severe, and nonaesthetic), and Newman's classical studies at Oxford. We should not therefore be surprised to find a curious ambiguity, a vein of paradox, in one of his earliest publications, the essay on "Poetry, with Reference to Aristotle's Poetics" (1829).

Filled as he is with Aristotle and the Greek dramatists, the young critic nevertheless calls into question the basic idea of Aristotle's *Poetics*, the importance of plot, or the "imitation of human action." Moreover, while ignoring throughout the essay the famous Aristotelian doctrine of *katharsis*, Newman proceeds to treat Aristotle's concept of tragedy in a Romantic rather than in a classical manner. The merit of the Greek tragedies, says Newman, lies not so much in plot — "the Greek tragedians are not generally felicitous in the construction of their plots" — as in "the characters, sentiments, and diction." [4] Indeed, the suggestive power of a single word seems to Newman more able "to convey a world of information to the imagination, and to act as a spell upon the feelings" than the most brilliantly constructed plot. Aristotle, continues Newman, erroneously treated dramatic composition as an exhibition of ingenious workmanship; Newman prefers to think of it as the "free and unfettered effusion of genius." Very clearly, the young critic is in the company of Wordsworth, who thought of poetry as "the spontaneous overflow of powerful feelings," and of Coleridge, whose dramatic criticism singled out character rather than plot for special emphasis. He is with them also in preferring suggestiveness, irregularity, vagueness above Greek clarity and form. And he is with them in exalting personal expression and genius over law and pattern, even denying that Aristotle ever attempted to tell us what the laws and patterns of Greek tragedy actually *were,* only what they should be.[5] If we compare Newman's Romantic, if not sentimental, view of Greek poetry with that set forth by Matthew Arnold in the Preface to his *Poems* (1853), we are struck at once by the extent to which Newman misinterprets the Greek idea of poetry. Arnold's Preface, justly famous as true to the general spirit of Greek art, holds that the Greek dramatists placed "the poetical character of the action itself" — the plot — above all other considerations, whereas the modern — or Romantic — tendency is to fix the attention "mainly on the value of separate thoughts and images." We treasure the "graceful and felicitous words and images" of Keats' *Isabella,* and are undisturbed by the fact that the action in the poem is "so feebly conceived" as to be "absolutely null" in its poetic effect.[6] Newman, in prizing "characters, sentiment, and diction," was reflecting in 1828–29 that Romantic view of poetry which later culminated in the cult of Keats, and which Arnold so vigorously attacked in the 1850's.

Equally Romantic is Newman's treatment of Aristotle's doctrine of ideal imitation. He grants that the doctrine is "most true and philosophical," but, as Ryan points out, "he gives it a turn that can hardly be justified by passages in the *Poetics* itself. Newman's emphasis is upon the ideal conceived in a Romantic pseudo-Platonic fashion as a realm of perfection, and not upon the imitation of those elements in human character and action that are most typical or universal."[7] For Newman, "the poetical mind is one full of the eternal forms of beauty and perfection" — a statement which is clearly an appeal to the Platonic doctrine of ideas.[8] Throughout the essay, as Ryan observes, we see re-

flections of the Romantic view of poetry current at the time of
its composition. Quite un-Aristotelian — in fact quite Words-
worthian — is Newman's conviction that "opinions, feelings,
manners, and customs are made poetical by the delicacy or splendor with which they are *expressed* . . . Facts are made new by
the coloring of a poetical imagination." [9] A few pages before,
however, Newman had been classical enough to demand that the
artist treat his subject "independently of the accidents of attitude,
dress, occasional feeling, and transient action," and that he "depict the *general* spirit of his subject." [10] Thus we note the uncertainty, the ambiguity, in Newman's mind as he composed his
essay. He was doubtless in sharp recoil from the rationalism
of Whately, perhaps also from his labors on Whately's *Logic,*
as well as from the current neoclassical canons of criticism.
Though his mind was Aristotelian, his heart was Romantic-
Platonic. Like Wordsworth, Coleridge, and Shelley, he was
seeking a more emotional and imaginative conception of poetry.
In the end, his exaltation of the poet's spontaneity ("the effusion
of genius"), his stress on the single word as sometimes being more
poetic than a well-constructed plot, and his high evaluation of the
"sentiments and diction" of the Greek plays over the action as a
whole, are all typical of precisely that kind of Romanticism
against which Irving Babbitt fulminated in *Rousseau and Romanticism.*

Newman's views of poetry and literature matured greatly by
the time he composed the Dublin lectures. But as late as 1849
he uttered in a lecture, "On the Characteristics of True Poetry,"
some opinions which were strangely superficial, sometimes sentimental, and moralistically narrow. We have only an auditor's
notes of this lecture, and no doubt we should be critical in accepting them as an accurate reflection of Newman's ideas. Mlle.
Tardivel, however, has valued them highly enough to reprint
them from *The Tablet* (July 21, 1849) in an Appendix to her
critical study of Newman's literary achievement. Here, as in
the essay on Aristotle, Newman is the classicist with Romantic
leanings. He prefers Goldsmith's description of the alehouse
to Wilkie's picture of the Village Festival, because Goldsmith
has "poetized" the "coarse, rough, yet true features" of the sub-

ject.   He is uneasy about Milton's having made Satan the hero
of *Paradise Lost* — he is the "most poetical person in the poem"
— and "this is wrong."   The same is true of Byron's *Cain*: "the
first murderer is made a beautiful one."   On the other hand,
the Romantic in Newman promptly adds that, even so, "this only
proves the assertion that poetry is the perception, and the poetical
art is the *expression* of the beautiful." [11]   Mention of the beautiful leads Newman to expatiate on its general nature, as comprised
of harmony, proportion, poetic justice.   This last element of
beauty tempts Newman into a complete rejection of tragedy:
since evil is not adequately punished at the end of the play, the
principle of poetic justice "will militate against tragedy, which,
by terminating with horrors, violates the idea of poetical justice."
Titus Andronicus is cited as "a peculiarly painful instance."   Nowhere else in Newman's writings do we find an amplification of
this view of tragedy.   In the present lecture, Newman passes on
to a Platonic consideration of artistic beauty as the "reflection of
the beauty of God," and to a glowing account of Southey's *Thalaba*.   One is strikingly reminded of Coleridge at this point.
Newman tells how a witch in Southey's poem is converted from
evil in precisely the same way as the Ancient Mariner: by suddenly admiring the beauty of nature — the Mariner blessing the
beautiful watersnakes, the witch succumbing to the spell of "the
sky, the stars, the beauty of everything around her."   Newman's
passage, his acceptance of Southey's principle, is an excellent example of that "sentimental morality" which Wordsworth and
Coleridge had popularized in the early years of the nineteenth
century.[12]   Apparently Newman had toyed with the idea that
aesthetic experiences may, under certain circumstances, pass into
moral impulses.   The lecture notes close with some arresting but
arbitrary generalizations — "Virgil was the poet of nature, Homer of man; in our own day, Wordsworth was a true poet of
nature, Southey was a poet of society."   "Milton knew but little
of human nature."   True poetry may express melancholy, "but
never misanthropy."

It would thus seem, from a study of Newman's earlier utterances on literature, that he not only held certain Romantic views,
but also held them in some confusion, and without completeness.

Mr. Ryan penetratingly attributes some of Newman's Romanticism to his "failure to break free of the nineteenth-century empirical tradition." This means that Newman was essentially a nominalist in his philosophy — only concrete things and experiences are real; all else — general ideas, principles — are but "names." "It is the same doubt about the ability of the reason to get at universals that makes him emphasize the fictional and the personal elements in literature instead of the universal," and hence makes him, to that extent, a genuine Romantic. "Furthermore," adds Mr. Ryan, "Newman always associates poetry with *lyrical* expression rather than with dramatic or narrative writing. His own poetry is a rendering of his own soul states, never an imitation in the Aristotelian sense. As poet, Newman is 'expressor,' not 'maker.' " [13]

ii. *Newman the Un-Romantic*

Although the lecture of 1849 shows Newman at forty-eight to be at heart considerably a Romantic, there had nevertheless occurred in him a definite transition away from his earlier position. He already was firmly anchored in his admiration for such un-Romantic eighteenth-century writers as Addison, Pope, Gibbon, and Crabbe. And his deep fondness for Cicero continued to the end of his life; in fact he seldom let a day pass without translating at least a sentence from his great Latin master.[1] But the profoundest alteration of his early Romanticism came not from a literary, but from a religious source. This source was the early Fathers of the Church, notably St. Augustine and his doctrine of man. Newman had already been prepared for the Augustinian view of man by his early reading in Milner's *Church History,* and by the Calvinism which he absorbed at home and which he did not abandon until about 1823. Traces of Calvinism appear in Newman's early sermons even after he had come under the influence of Whately and the Liberals. It is Newman's Calvinistic view of human nature which prevents him from being a genuine Romantic. We see this very clearly when we examine a few of his sermons, and portions of *The Tamworth Reading Room.*

In addressing the cultivated minds of his Oxford congregation, Newman constantly emphasizes the difference between the philosopher's sense of imperfection and the Christian's sense of sin and corruption. Cultivated people, he says, too often regard Christianity, when viewed in its basic teachings, as "a slavish system . . . prejudicial to the freedom of thought, the aspirations of genius, and the speculations of enterprise"; they think of it as "unnatural," or even "pernicious," as unfitting men for normal life in this world.[2] Newman vigorously fights these notions by frequently distinguishing between *nature* and *grace,* and by reminding his hearers that as Christians they are supposed to be convinced that "they are rebels in the sight of God, breakers of the fair and goodly order which the Creator once established."[3] He reminds his congregation that the learned men of his day are so often defective Christians because they fail to see that "ability of mind is a *gift,* and faith is a grace,"[4] and that no amount of brilliant mental endowment can of itself make one wise in religion. Nor is this all. Newman is aware of the tendency of the day to seek in literature, especially in poetry, those special insights and consolations, and that spiritual sustenance formerly sought only in religion. It was a time, of course, of "religious philosophy" — of Coleridge's and Carlyle's transcendentalism, of Wordsworth's nature-mysticism. But Newman, far from accepting these Romantic doctrines, undeviatingly cautions his hearers that the "refinement which literature gives is that of thinking, feeling, knowing, and speaking right, not of *acting* right." Even "certain *religious* novels" are harmful; "they lead men to cultivate the religious affections separate from religious practice." Newman adds, with characteristic severity, that even poetry and music are "likely to make us unmanly, if we are not on our guard," since they so often excite our feelings without insuring a corresponding act.[5] Spiritual emasculation may even occur through reading religious poetry or hearing eloquent preaching, if this is an indulgence in emotion for its own sake. Quite clearly, all this points to Newman's favorite themes — man "must be born again"; "The World is Our Enemy"; refinement is one thing, holiness quite another.[6]

Newman the un-Romantic, Newman the austere preacher at St. Mary's, will have no part in early nineteenth-century Romantic immanentism, that widely popular view of nature as suffused with deity, and of man as essentially good, or at least perfectible. The increasing tendency of the day was to turn away from the supernatural, or to find it implicit in nature (Carlyle's "natural supernaturalism"), and to assume that man could save himself unaided. The idea of "grace" was rapidly passing out of the minds of thinking men. But for Newman it remained as real and fresh as it was to the primitive Christians of Antioch or Jerusalem, as it was to St. Augustine in the fourth century. In fact, as he steadfastly held to the orthodox view of man's need of grace, he was in some respects doing again the work of Augustine. Thus Erich Przywara, in *A Monument to St. Augustine*, sees Newman as reading the same lesson from the face of the world as did the great Bishop of Hippo: "Newman saw man, the world, and history from the already almost prophetic perspective revealed to him by that final struggle between Christ and Antichrist legible on the countenance of the modern world. He is thus the peculiar and unique *Augustinus redivivus* of modern times." [7]

Newman is thus an un-Romantic insofar as he fought the implicit or explicit Pelagianism of his day. Modern men, like the heretical Pelagius of the fifth century, were convinced of the innate goodness of human nature, of the beauty of the "noble savage," of the potential improvement of man and his world until an earthly paradise should be attained. Their great prophet, of course, had been Rousseau; and "Rousseauism," in one form or another, was spreading throughout England and the continent. To Newman, as to Augustine before him, this doctrine seemed to be a complete and dangerous misreading of history, and a fatal misconception of human nature. Newman was willing, however, in his doctrine of "natural and revealed religion," to grant that the natural man, even without Christianity, has a measure of the divine in him. Indeed, following his beloved Clement of Alexandria, he held that no nation or race had ever been without some dispensation of its own. Thus the Greek poets and sages, under the "Dispensation of Paganism," were at times gifted with a more than natural "inspiration." The work of Aristotle thus recommends itself as urging on natural grounds what religion teaches as a divine message. But, Newman adds, once Revelation has been given, nothing short of Christianity will really change man or the world.   Newman can never hold, as did Matthew Arnold, that poetry alone can do what religion has done, "interpret life for us . . . console us . . . sustain us." [8]   In *The Tamworth Reading Room*, Newman brilliantly and roundly attacks this fallacy: "if we attempt to effect a moral improvement by means of poetry, we shall but mature into a mawkish, frivolous, and fastidious sentimentalism . . . You must go to a higher source for renovation of the heart and will. You do but play a sort of 'hunt the slipper' with the fault of our nature, till you go to Christianity." [9]   To be sure, the early Church cultivated heathen literature, but never as a substantial improvement of our moral nature, only "in order, if it were possible, to lead [non-Christian philosophers] into the truth." [10]

We may note, finally — and repeat what is too often forgotten — that Newman's turning to the past was neither Romantic nor un-Romantic; it was simply, as we have seen earlier, an attempt to find what he considered permanent religious truth. Mr. Ryan has well summed up that attempt: Newman's search was "not a search for the mere glamor and atmosphere of the past.   His love of the Pagan, Patristic, and Medieval past was not Romantic — they were for him the way to this permanent and living truth.   Whereas the extreme Romanticists broke with two traditions, the classical and the Christian, Newman broke with neither, but tried to recapture both." [11]

iii.   *Newman the Literary Critic*

In view of the nature and origins of Newman's writings, we need hardly observe that throughout his collected works there is not a single essay devoted exclusively to literary criticism. The nearest approach which he made to such writing occurs in the essay on John Keble, in which he considers the religious value and significance of Keble's *Lyra Innocentium* (1846), especially in connection with the possible continuance of the Oxford Movement, and in regard to the poet's "blameless Donatism" and its Church of spiritual children.[1]   None of Keble's poems receives purely literary attention.   If, then, we are to look for Newman's performance as a literary critic we must turn to certain of his

major works in which he throws out suggestive and often penetrating observations.   We must look into *The Idea of a University*, the *Historical Sketches*, various of his sermons, and even
The Grammar of Assent.   Our principal source for Newman's
mature conception of literature is in fact *The Idea of a University*.   Evidently English Catholics in the 1850's, when the hierarchy had been restored and many unhistorical enthusiasts expected almost daily that England would be converted, were
hoping for an "English Catholic literature," one, probably,
which would be "without sin," an exalting, poetical voice of the
Church.   Newman is obliged to warn his Dublin audience
against any "such vain enterprise as that of reversing history."
He himself "has no dream of Catholic Classics as still reserved
for the English language."   Indeed, classical authors, he insists,
not only are national but belong to a particular age of a nation's
life.   And Newman wonders whether the age of great writers is
not passing away.[2]   English Catholics must reconcile themselves
to living with a largely Protestant literature, and should derive
from it whatever benefit and pleasure it may legitimately give
them.   Newman's further purpose in the Dublin lectures was to
justify giving the study of literature a prominent and influential
position in the university's curriculum.   To accomplish these two
purposes, Newman discussed the nature of literature and language, style, the vocation of the author, the relation of literature
to religion and education, in such lectures as "Duties of the
Church towards Knowledge," "Christianity and Letters," "Literature," and "Catholic Literature in the English Tongue."

Newman defines literature first in terms of man's nature, second in terms of linguistic expression.   Literature "is the Life
and Remains of the *natural* man, innocent or guilty."   It stands
related to man as science stands to nature; it is man's history; it
is, in Newman's view, "in some sort what autobiography is to the
individual."   And this literature — indeed *all* literatures considered as one voice — must be regarded as the voice of man as
he is, of "man in rebellion." [3]   If literature (to put it differently) is the study of human nature, then, says Newman with
some audacity, considering his clerical hearers, "you cannot have
a Christian Literature.   It is a contradiction in terms to attempt

a sinless Literature of sinful man." [4]   "Man's work will savor
of man; in his elements and powers excellent and admirable, but
prone to disorder and excess, to error and sin.   Such too will be
his literature; it will have the beauty and the natural fierceness,
the sweetness and the rankness, of the natural man."   It will inevitably offend the senses of those who "in the Apostle's words,
are really 'exercised to discern between good and evil.' "   It will
exhibit "the leapings and the friskings, the plungings and the
snortings, the sportings and the buffoonings, the clumsy play and
the aimless toil, of the noble, lawless savage of God's intellectual
creation." [5]   In fact it will, says Newman, know this lawless
savage so well as occasionally to constitute a hazard.   For if natural science presents the danger of ignoring moral evil, "literature
is open to the more grievous imputation of recognizing and understanding it too well." [6]   Newman never amplified this last
statement, but we may be sure that he was referring to the possibility of literature dwelling excessively or morbidly upon evil,
or condoning it on the grounds of its being *natural*, or presenting
it "objectively," as hopeless, or as "not mattering."

Characteristically, Newman regards the writing of literature
as a highly *personal* experience, one which expresses subjective
rather than objective truths.   In a passage which is at once antiquated and quite up to date, he asserts, on the one hand, that
science deals with things while literature deals with thoughts,
and also holds, on the other hand, a view of language which is
remarkably in harmony with that of present-day students of se-
mantics.   What keeps Euclid's *Elements* a work of science is not
only that it "relates to truths universal and eternal," but also the
fact that *its words do not constitute language* but are merely
symbols.   According to Newman, for words to make language
they must become the vehicle not of mere things but of events
within the mind.   Indeed, a word becomes a word only where
personality has given it its true being.   "Science uses words
merely as symbols," says Newman, "but literature uses language
in its full compass, as including phraseology, idiom, style, composition, rhythm, eloquence . . . Literature is the personal use or
exercise of language." [7]   The many use language as they find it;
the man of genius bends it to his will, injects new meanings or

nuances into worn-out words, indeed creates his language as he
writes, insofar as he is original in thought and expression. Here,
again, we see the familiar stress which Newman gives to the individual. Just as his doctrine of assent emphasized the concrete
and the individual, so his conception of literature and of composition is highly individualistic and personal.

It follows that Newman's theories of literary style will emphasize expression and spontaneity rather than organization and
rules. For him, matter and expression are indissolubly one, and
style becomes a mere "thinking out into language." It is this
language, as a living garment of the writer's thoughts, which is
literature — not things, nor verbal symbols of things, nor even
mere words, but thoughts conveyed in inevitable utterance.
Newman recalls to us the Greek word which expresses the special prerogative of man over "the feeble intelligence of the inferior animals." He finds that the Greek word *logos* designates
precisely what he thinks literature stands for: "it stands for *reason* and for *speech*, and it is difficult to say which it means more
properly. It means both at once." When we can separate light
and illumination, life and motion, the convex and the concave of
a curve, then, says Newman, the intellect will be able to "re-
nounce its own double, its instrument of expression." [8] This
austere view of style allows no more room for ornament, added
from without, than do the theories of Flaubert or Pater; there
must be no "surplusage." On the other hand, Newman is so
wedded to his doctrine of the *personal* nature of the creative act
that he readily allows an elaborateness of style if it genuinely reflects the author's mind. "That pomp of language, that full and
tuneful diction" which delights us today in Sir Thomas Browne,
or in *The Seven Pillars of Wisdom*, or in Shakespeare, Newman
would regard as "nothing else but the mere habit and way of a
lofty intellect." Such a mind fertilizes its simplest ideas, and
germinates into a multitude of details, and prolongs the march of
its sentences, and sweeps round to the full diapason of its harmonies. "A narrow critic may call it verbiage, when really it is a sort
of fullness of heart." [9]

Newman is no less original in the remarks which he throws
out here and there in the *Idea* about the vocation of the author,

especially in relation to language. A great author, Newman observes, "takes his native language, masters it, partly throws himself into it, partly moulds and adapts it" to his purposes. Great writers may be, in great measure, the creatures of their own times, but, like Spenser in the sixteenth century, they may also be "in a far higher sense the creators of their language," which "virtually did not exist till they gave it life and form." Newman is sensitively aware of the degrees in which the English language was given strength, grace, precision, and harmony by "certain masters of composition" — Shakespeare, Milton, the translators of the Jacobean Bible and Prayer Book, Hooker, Addison, Swift, Pope, Hume, Goldsmith. Their phraseology and diction, he notes, have become "the very idioms of our familiar conversation." [10] Originally, however, to write was like crossing a country before roads were made; the authors of any early age deserve to be called classics, says Newman, "both because of what they do and because they do it." At such a time, it requires the courage and the force of great talent to compose in the language at all. However, unfettered by precedent, and gifted with the power of expression, the early pioneering author writes with spirit and freshness. He and his successors are "masters of the two-fold Logos, the thought and the word, distinct, but inseparable from each other." Newman notes also, in a characteristically Augustan sentence, that the true author "writes passionately, because he feels keenly; forcibly, because he conceives vividly; he sees too clearly to be vague; he is too serious to be otiose; he can analyze his subject, and therefore he is rich; he embraces it as a whole and in its parts, and therefore he is consistent; he has a firm hold of it, and therefore he is luminous." But, even more important, this master of language is, in Newman's conception of literature, one of "the spokesmen and prophets of the human family" — bringing the secrets of the heart into the light, relieving the mind of pain and grief, imparting wisdom, and drawing the people into unity, so that "national character is fixed, [and] a people speaks." [11]

Newman does not leave his subject without a few comments on the "tame" language of any advanced culture. As a literary man himself he seems to have considered the English language as too decadent and exhausted to be an instrument of the highest creativity. He traces the ordinary growth of a language and literature, as ideas find their fit expressions, roots expand, phrasal variety develops, and separate professions, pursuits, and provinces of literature gain their own conventional terminology. Original vivid metaphors have become dull. Criticism rises to the level of an art, and it is difficult for a writer to be original in his mother tongue without being offensive to overcultivated ears. The author is tamed down to the loss of his individuality. It is "not a day for great writers, but for good writing, and a great deal of it." But Newman is certain "we have well nigh seen the end of the English classics." Admirable writers there may be, but "what they lack is that individuality, that earnestness, most personal yet most unconscious of self, which is the greatest charm of an author." [12]

iv. *Insights, Limitations, and Preferences*

Along with Newman's frequent and casual pronouncements on literature in general, on writers, and on style, we find occasional passages of unusual literary insight, at least for his own day. Some of these are hidden away in his lesser-known volumes. At a time when the prestige of Byron was at its height, when most readers were still so enchanted by *Childe Harold* that a really critical view of him was extremely rare, Newman perceived that Byron, far from being a truly great poet, simply "did not know how to make poetry out of existing materials." This judgment Newman delivers in his essay on Aristotle in 1828–29. He adds that so long as Byron is allowed to declaim, he is fluent and able; "but if interrogated on principles of nature and good sense, he is at once put out and brought to a stand." This is very close to the well-known *dictum* of Goethe (whom Newman seems never to have read), that when Byron thinks, he is a child. Moreover, Newman anticipates a later generation in placing a high value not so much on *Manfred* or *Cain* as upon *Sardanapalus*. He is also in advance of a great many of his contemporaries in regarding the poetry of Byron as, for the most part, eloquent rhetoric. "It is the fault of the day," he asserts, "to mistake mere eloquence for poetry."

On the subject of poetry itself, Newman drops some remarks (again in the essay on Aristotle) which show that in an age when rhetorical and intellectually transparent poetry was the mode, he nevertheless wishes justice done to the "obscure" poet. Newman nowhere discusses Donne or Browning, but we may be sure that he would have approached their work — and we may add that of Gerard Manley Hopkins — in a highly sympathetic spirit. For he maintains that "the poet's habits of mind lead to contemplation rather than to communication with others." This is a startlingly "modern" statement. Most readers even today insist that the poet's first *concern* is communication. Probably the *personal* element in Newman's theory of poetry accounts for his position. At any rate, he holds that the poet will be inevitably obscure, to some extent, either because of the "particular style of poetry he has adopted" or "from the depth of his feelings." Obscurity will occur less, he feels, in epic, dramatic, or narrative compositions, more so in the shorter, and more subjective forms, the lyric, the ode, the elegy. Further, the poet's obscurity will rest not only on the depth of his feelings but on their acuteness, which, Newman adds with admirable understanding, "shrinks from any normal accuracy in the expression of them." Again, the poet may fail in adequate communication owing to "the carelessness of genius," or to some "natural deficiency in the power of clear and eloquent expression." Some poets, one infers, while highly proficient in clearness and eloquence are nevertheless second-rate poets. For Newman insists that "eloquent expression" — as in Byron's or Shelley's more flamboyant poems — "is a talent distinct from poetry, though often mistaken for it." However, poetical eloquence, in the technical sense of the term, is regarded by Newman as "manifestly more or less necessary." It consists not only of the power to organize or arrange an extended poem, and the mastery of language, but also and primarily "in the power of illustration." By this Newman evidently means that the *image* is the basic element in poetry, "as the sole outlet and expression of intense inward feeling." It is a "spontaneous power of comparison." [1] And it is never merely ornamental. Indeed, if one were to follow out Newman's brief observations to their logical implications, one would doubtless arrive at the "metaphysical" view of the image as being at once the illustration and the expression of the poet's thought. It is hazardous to press Newman's few brief sentences beyond what they were intended to say; but one is at least justified in admiring those insights into the nature of poetry which came to him, as it were, obliquely, while his main attention was focussed on another field.

On the other hand, the limitations of Newman's critical outlook are illustrated by a singular passage in "The Mission of St. Benedict," in which, like the rash young Macaulay in his essay on "Milton," Newman maintains that "as science makes progress in any subject-matter, poetry recedes from it." The winding bridle path is more poetic to Newman than the "straight railroad." Poetry and science are forever incompatible, and Newman could not say, with Wordsworth, that "poetry is the breath and finer spirit of all knowledge," or see, with Sandburg, the flowering of beauty in a deserted brickyard at dusk. Indeed, we must be as children if we are to be fully aware of the poetic beauty around us, aware of something "vast, immeasurable, impenetrable, inscrutable, mysterious," something "we should look up to" without "fancying that we can comprehend" it.[2] For Newman, then, poetry is not a way of knowing; it is an experience of the imagination and the affections, an intimation from a Platonic supersensible realm of being. We may call this view of poetry limited in that it leaves out of account so much of the world's genuine poetry. It is, in short, *one way* to conceive of poetry and the poetic experience.

Yet in spite of his Platonic tendencies, there are times when Newman speaks as though the poet can never rise to the level of the universal. There is, as Mr. Ryan has pointed out, a highly enigmatic passage in the *Idea* which one wishes Newman had seen fit to carry out in its fullest implications. He has just spoken of how scriptural passages at times — *e.g.* in portions of the four Gospels — rise to the "grandeur, the majesty, the calm, unimpassioned beauty of Science" and hence "are in no sense Literature, [since] they are in no sense personal." Then follows the "enigmatic" conclusion:

"Did time admit I could show you parallel instances of what I am speaking of in the Classics, inferior to the inspired word in proportion as the subject-matter of the classical authors is immensely inferior to the subjects treated of in Scripture — but parallel, inasmuch as the classical author or speaker ceases for the moment to have to do with Literature, as speaking of things objectively, and rises to the serene sublimity of Science.   But I should be carried too far if I began." [3]

Here, quite clearly, Newman is denying to literature that power of grasping universal and objective realities which Matthew Arnold saw in the best of the world's great writers.   Here Newman's conception of literature is comparatively narrow.   Arnold sought in these writers a universal ethical pattern, based on their deepest insights and on their highest moments of vision.   Newman was profoundly familiar with those insights and those moments, but his native subjectivity prevented him from according them any sovereign universality or authority.   Had he given us a body of literary criticism in which the greatest achievements of poetic insight were treated as "a way of knowing," as an "enunciation of eternal things," and had he then called them "the great moments of the world's literature" or "the great tradition," instead of designating them "Science" (with a mystical suggestion), then we might well link Newman with Arnold among the humanists. [4]   As it is, Newman's subjectivism and his nominalism prevent him from seeing literature as other than personal and mundane.   For him, reality is suprapersonal; it is the realm of *science*, not in our ordinary sense of the term, but absolute knowledge, beyond image, sound, or reason, hence beyond the lowly powers of literature, the record of "sinful man."

That Newman did not sense the full potentialities of literature as a discipline is evidenced by the fact that he constantly stresses its effect on the intellect rather than upon the moral character. To be sure, he does not do what he criticized Abelard for doing: subordinate literature to theology or recommend its banishment from the schools. [5]   He wants it placed, as we have said, in the center of the curriculum.   But its services are to be primarily for the natural man.   It will cultivate his taste, strengthen his judgment, impart poise and grace to his mind, and release him from prejudice and provincialism. [6]   As the Autobiography of Humanity it will remind us of the "greatness and littleness of man." Whatever may be those insights it provides into the real nature of the world and its destiny, into man and his calling, into religious objects and experiences, Newman regards them as indirect, fragmentary, and unreliable. For him, of course, such insights more properly and authoritatively come through the Church.

The literary preferences of such a mind as Newman's are not difficult to ascertain. Indeed we have already noted a few of them; so definite are they, in fact, that it is hard to understand J. Connop Thirlwall's statement that it is "extremely difficult to find any direct mention of Cardinal Newman's favorite authors in anything that has been published of his" and that his range of literary taste is "not found or suggested in any of his works or . . . letters." [7] On the contrary, Newman's delight in the Greek and Roman classics and in certain English authors is evident in numerous passages in his works. In addition to this source of our information, however, we have the testimony of Father Ignatius Dudley Ryder, contemporary of Newman at the Oratory, and of Professor Williams.[8] We may say, on the whole, that while Newman was ardently devoted to Cicero and the Greek dramatists, he never seems to have felt any great admiration for the English neoclassic writers, except Addison.[9] Though he quotes occasionally from Cowper, he generally ignores those poets commonly known as the "Pre-Romantics." He loved Crabbe, not for anything "classical" or "Romantic" about him, but for "the firm realistic touches of his descriptions of scenery and character" and for the moralizing which recommended itself to Newman as "the legitimate outcome of common-sense humanity." [10] He admired Dr. Johnson's learning, but was offended by "Johnsonese" — "his style often outruns the sense and the occasion." [11]

Among the English Romantics, Newman apparently most admired Scott, Southey, and Byron. Obviously fond of the *romantic* in modern literature, he was attracted to Scott not only by the enchantment of the world of the Waverley novels but also by the manifestation in both the novels and the poems of Scott's benevolence and firm moral fibre. Scott's manliness, humorous sanity, and cheerful conservatism appealed to something deep in Newman.   Next to Scott came Southey, especially *Thalaba*, and this for a characteristic reason: "*Thalaba*," says Ryder, "was particularly attractive to Cardinal Newman as the picture of a life-long vocation, with its mysterious isolation ever at war with the social instincts of the hero; . . . its asceticism; . . . [and] the tremendous catastrophe in which the hero dying achieves his victory, without earthly recompense.   It was his picture of what he trusted the [Oxford] Movement and his share in the Movement would have been." [12]   Newman loved the color, the onward movement of the poem in spite of its "grave Oriental quietude"; but he also identified himself with the hero and saw his own struggle poetically symbolized.   There is thus an admixture of the personal and the sentimental in Newman's faithful love for Southey's now more than half-forgotten poem.   We have already noted some of Newman's opinions about Byron, of whom, on the whole, he disapproved both as man and poet.   Yet Ryder heard him speak with enthusiasm of the third canto of *Childe Harold*, with an "O si sic omnia."   And there can be no doubt that Newman as a master of rhetoric took keen delight in Byron's flowing eloquence, even while he looked on him with "moral disapprobation," and lamented the absence of true poetry in some of Byron's most impressive and popular poems.   The other Romantic poet whom Newman read, though with qualified approval, was Wordsworth.   Ryder tells us that when he himself was as yet a boy and was recovering from an illness, Newman came to him and read the ode on "Intimations of Immortality": "there was a passion and a pathos in his voice that made me feel that it was altogether the most beautiful thing I had ever heard." [13]   Yet Newman never took cordially to Wordsworth.   He was offended by the Lake Poet's pantheism, his excessive deliberateness, his "almost sacerdotal pretensions."

Of the poetry and fiction of Newman's own Victorian period he knew comparatively little.   His younger friends induced him to read Tennyson, and he seems to have been attracted to a few of Tennyson's poems, greatly admiring, with his more sentimental and Romantic side, "Mariana," in her moated grange.   So far as we know, the only Victorian poet whom he read beyond the opening pages was William Morris, whose "Earthly Paradise" and "Life and Death of Jason" captivated his imagination. Of Victorian novelists he was a devoted admirer of Mrs. Gaskell; he is said to have read everything that Anthony Trollope wrote; and he read faithfully all of Thackeray's works down to the last fugitive pieces in the *Cornhill Magazine*. On Thackeray's death he wrote to a friend about "the piercing sorrow" he felt; he had never met the novelist, but "saw in his books the workings of his mind." For Newman, Thackeray was "himself the greatest instance of the text of which he was so full: 'Vanitas vanitatum, omnia vanitas.'"[14] Evidently Newman admired Thackeray's insight into human pride and frailty. However, his admiration must have been based upon more than that, for he felt little or no attraction to the novels of George Eliot, whose insights were expressed in un-Thackerayan heaviness of style. On the other hand, while he admired the stylistic felicities of Jane Austen, he was repelled by the lack of substance and the lack of the "romantic" in her novels.[15]

Among the non-fiction prose writers of his time, he has nothing to say of Ruskin, Matthew Arnold, or Pater. He knows his Macaulay thoroughly, but offers no critical comment on him as a writer. We have, however, a very interesting critical response to Carlyle's *French Revolution* in two letters written in 1839 and 1840. His response is mixed, and it is of course less literary than philosophical. In the first letter he recommends Carlyle's book to Mrs. J. Mozley, as "a queer, tiresome, obscure, profound, and original work. The writer has not very *clear* principles and views, I fear, but they are very deep." The other letter we have already noted on another occasion;[16] it was written during a gloomy hour when Newman despaired of the English Church and of his age. Carlyle strikes him as "a man of first-rate ability . . . and quite fascinating as a writer. His book on the 'French Revolution' is most taking (to me)." This from a lover of Ciceronian and Addisonian prose is evidence of considerable catholicity of interest. But Newman is disturbed by Carlyle's point of view: "I had hoped he might have come round right, for it was easy to see he was not a believer; but they say he has settled the wrong way. His view is that Christianity

has good in it, or is good *as far as it goes*" — a view which shocks
Newman as a picking and choosing among what he himself re-
gards as the elements of an organic whole, Revealed Religion.[17]
This appears to be the last reference to Thomas Carlyle.

Such then are the chief literary preferences of Newman.   It
has been noted by critics, such as Professor Williams, that he
quotes comparatively little of Shakespeare; and that he seems
to have known little or nothing of the other Elizabethan writers.[18]   There are a few references to Milton, Jeremy Taylor,
George Herbert.   On the whole, Newman's literary enthusiasms
seem largely and singularly bounded by the ancient classics and
a few English novelists and Romantic poets.

IV. NEWMAN AND HIS ART

CHAPTER XI

NEWMAN AS LITERARY ARTIST

i. *Newman's Aesthetic Temperament*

The artist in Newman was nourished by that sense of the concrete and the real which we have had numerous occasions to observe. It played so great a part in his thought as well as in his literary methods that some of his critics, notably Baudin and Grandmaison, have declared that it vitiated much of his teaching.[1] It appears with splendid vitalizing effect in his sermons, as the power of "realizing" — and of making his audience or reader "realize" — the actuality of whatever he is discussing. As Brilioth says, "it is the poet and the literary artist, as much as the preacher," that we find in those memorable descriptions and observations scattered throughout the *Plain and Parochial Sermons*.[2] This aesthetic side of Newman's nature is most abundantly evident in his earlier years, and manifests itself, curiously enough, not so much in his poetry as in his letters, notably those written just before and during his Mediterranean tour. In the Long Vacation of 1831, while visiting Hurrell Froude at Dartington, he wrote enthusiastically to his mother about the sensuous glories of the countryside in Devonshire:

"What strikes me most is the strange richness of everything. The rocks blush into every variety of colour, the trees and fields are emeralds, and the cottages are rubies. A beetle I picked up at Torquay was as green and gold as the stone it lay upon, and a squirrel which ran up a tree here just now was not the pale reddish-brown to which I am accustomed, but a bright brown-red. Nay, my very hands and fingers look rosy, like Homer's Aurora, and I have been gazing on them with astonishment. All this wonder I know is simple, and therefore,

267

of course, do not you repeat it.   The exuberance of the grass and the
foliage is oppressive, as if one had not room to breathe, though this is
a fancy — the depth of the valleys and the steepness of the slopes increase the illusion — and the Duke of Wellington would be in a fidget
to get some commanding point to see the country from.   The scents
are extremely fine, so very delicate yet so powerful, and the colours
of the flowers as if they were all shot with white.   The sweet peas
especially have the complexion of a beautiful face.   They trail up the
wall mixed with myrtles as creepers.   As to the sunset, the Dartmoor
heights look purple, and the sky close upon them a clear orange.
When I turn back and think of Southampton Water and the Isle of
Wight, they seem by contrast to be drawn in Indian ink or pencil.
Now I cannot make out that this is fancy; for why should I fancy?   I
am not especially in a poetic mood.   I have heard of the brilliancy
of Cintra, and still more of the East, and I suppose that this region
would pale beside them; yet I am content to marvel at what I see,
and think of Virgil's description of the purple meads of Elysium.
Let me enjoy what I feel, even though I may unconsciously exag-
gerate." [3]

Similar descriptions abound in his letters during the tour, descriptions of the Portuguese coast near Torres Vedras, with its
"greenish-reddish-brown" rocks passing before his vessel "like
a pageant"; of Gibraltar, with its "long, whitish, handsome
buildings" and its orange trees and its enormous geraniums; of
Malta, a "literal rock of yellowish brown"; of Zante, Patras,
Parnassus, Ithaca, Corfu.   Every moment seems to have held a
riot of the senses.   Yet at the same time, Newman was filled
either with religious reflections or with memories of home or
childhood.   As his vessel, the *Hermes,* passed within half a mile
of Ithaca, he "gazed on it by the quarter of an hour together," but
thought less about Ulysses and Argus and the Cyclopes than
about Ham, the London suburb near Richmond, and his sister
Harriett's birthday.[4]   And almost daily he composed a poem, a
lucid, wistful, sometimes sentimental religious lyric, later to be
published in the *Lyra Apostolica.*
     A comparatively "unpoetical" but highly expressive account
of seasickness makes Newman's Mediterranean letters more than
an interesting record of sensibility.   He gives his sister Harriett

what to many knowing readers will seem to be virtually a classical description:

"A strange feeling came over me; the heaving to and fro of everything seemed to puzzle me from head to foot, but in such a vague, mysterious way, that I could not get hold of it, or say what was the matter with me, or where. On I ate: I was determined, for it is one of the best alleviations. On I drank, but in so absurdly solemn a way, with such a perplexity of mind, not to say of body, that, as I have said, I laughed at myself. How I wished dinner over! Yet, on I sat, heaving up and down, to and fro, in an endless, meaningless motion; a trouble without a crisis; the discomfort of an uneasy dream. I went upstairs and got better. Then I lay down and was well. Got up at eleven at night, walked about, and was better again — went to bed and slept soundly. Sunday morning I was languid and qualmish; lay down on the deck and got well, but was afraid to stir. We had great difficulty to read the service. Archdeacon Froude was very bad and in bed. R. H. F. was getting well, but I did not like to let him try by himself. However, he read, and I was able to respond. I was better and worse all day, and after bed-time had no more trouble up to this time, when I eat and drink, loll about, read and write as usual." [5]

Memorable also is his description of a tourist's accommodations aboard a "peculiarly convenient" sailing vessel a hundred years ago. He is getting reconciled to his berth, he tells his sister, but it is "more like a coffin than a bed." Then he bids her imagine his daily experience:

"First, think of the roll of the vessel to and fro. The first night my side was sore with the rub, rub of the motion. Then fancy the swinging, the never-ended swinging — you knock your head, you bruise your arms, all the while being shelved in a cupboard five feet from the floor. Then the creaking of the vessel; it is like half a hundred watchmen's rattles mixed with the squeaking of the Brobdingnag pigs, while the water dashes, dash, dash against the side. Then overhead the loud foot of the watch, who goes on tramping up and down for more or less the whole night. Then in the morning the washing of the deck; rush comes an engine-pipe on the floor — ceases, is renewed, flourishes about, rushes again: then suddenly half a dozen

brooms, wish-wash, wish-wash, scrib-scrub, scratching and roaring
alternately.   Then the heavy flump, flump of the huge cloth which is
meant to dry the deck as a towel or duster.   Last, and not least, the
smell.   In spite of airing it, the berth will smell damp and musty; at
best it is close; there is no window in it; it opens into the cabin, which
at night is lighted with oil.   Added to this, the want of room for
your baggage, and your higgledy-piggledy state; and you will allow
I have given you enough of discomfort.   Yet one day like yesterday
outweighs them all; and, in fact, they are vanishing fast.   To be sure,
a valetudinarian could not bear it.   I think that it would quite have
knocked me up a year or two since: and as for those who, in advanced
stages of consumption, are sent abroad, it must be a martyrdom: yet,
I repeat, our vessel is a peculiarly convenient one." [6]

This is first-rate reporting, and we readily understand why
certain critics have lamented not only the poet but the journalist
that was lost in Newman.   He had the poet's quick and sensitive
eye.   Thomas Mozley tells us that

"his eye quickly caught any sudden glory or radiance above; every
prismatic hue or silver lining; every rift, every patch of blue. . .
His admiration of the beauties of earth and sky, his quickness to observe
changes overhead, and the meaning he put into them, sometimes taxed
the patience of a dull observer.   Flowers, especially certain flowers,
he was as fond of as a child could be." [7]

However, Newman was never dependent upon external beauty;
he "carried his scenery with him."   He never caught the contemporary craving for a change of residence, for mountains and
lakes: "he never made a tour for pleasure sake, for health sake,
or for change sake." [8]   This man who was passionately fond of
Sicilian scenery, who loved bold and barren tracts of land, and
who likened such rugged landscape to the music of Beethoven,
occupied, as a tutor at Oxford, merely an undergraduate's lodging, meager, almost bare in its furnishings, and cluttered with
boxes of books for which he had too little shelf space.[9]   The
truth was, of course, that in Newman, the moralist, was fiercely
at war with the poet.   And the moralist won.   While on that
visit at Dartington in the summer of 1831, Newman explicitly
stated in a poem, "The Pilgrim," that a "vow had bound him"
not to yield to the allurements of Nature's beauty:

"There stray'd a while, amid the woods of Dart,
　　One who could love them, but who durst not love.
A vow had bound him, ne'er to give his heart
　　To streamlet bright, or soft secluded grove.
　　'Twas a hard humbling task, onwards to move
His easy-captured eyes from each fair spot,
　　With unattach'd and lonely step to rove
O'er happy meads, which soon its print forgot: —
Yet kept he safe his pledge, prizing his pilgrim-lot." [10]

Newman indeed kept his pledge; his "easy-captured eyes" were
never permitted the poet's freedom. As Mlle. Tardivel tell-
ingly points out, the moralist in Newman was enriched by the
despoilment of the poet in him — deepening his insight into
human nature and equipping him with a splendid mastery of
language [11] — and the wan remains of the poet in him account
for Newman's having written so little genuine poetry. Both by
his moralistic minimizing of himself as a poet, and by his depreca-
tory view of his own poetry, he — some will say unnecessarily —
condemned himself to an inferior rank among English poets.

ii. *Newman as a Poet*

It is one of the ironies of the Oxford Movement that its poetry
should have been so feeble. Unfortunately, Tractarian poets
seem to have felt that the graceful versifying of approved sentiments, ornamented with metaphor and some eighteenth-century
"poetic diction," was a satisfactory method of writing religious
poetry. In a letter to his friend Rogers in 1833, Newman revealed his strangely limited notion of poetry as merely the art
of rhetoric in metrical shape: "Ten thousand obvious ideas become impressive when put into a metrical shape; and many of
them we should not dare to utter except metrically, for thus
the responsibility (as it were) is shoved off of oneself . . ." [1]
Though there is some theoretical truth in this view, Geoffrey
Faber is doubtless right in saying of it that "there could not be a
better, nor a more damning, description of the art of poetry as it
was practised by Keble as well as Newman." [2] We have seen,
on the other hand, that Newman could apply high critical stand-

ards to the work of other poets.* His own poems he regarded
as a form of relaxation, written with great ease, certainly without the slavish care he gave to perfecting his prose. Of the
Mediterranean verses, he wrote: "When I was most qualmish
[with seasickness] I solaced myself with verse-making." [3] It is
easy to understand, as Mlle. Tardivel points out, that Newman's
best poetry is in his best prose; [4] nothing in his verse equals the
closing paragraphs of the *Apologia*.

The volume which contains Newman's poems appeared in
1868, under the unpretentious title *Verses on Various Occasions*.
More than half of the poems had already appeared in a little volume called *Lyra Apostolica*, published in 1836, and consisting
of poems contributed to the *British Magazine* by Newman and
five of his Tractarian friends, Hurrell Froude, Keble, Bowden,
Robert Wilberforce, and Isaac Williams. These lyrics attempt
little more than to give verse form to the aspirations and sentiments of the Oxford Movement. Some critics, like Christopher
Dawson, regard them as "perhaps the most remarkable literary
product" of that Movement.[5] Others, like Geoffrey Faber, dismiss them as genuinely "bad poetry," written "to order" as religious propaganda.[6] The truth lies somewhere between these
extreme views; for, in spite of Newman's failure to think of his
poetry as a form of artistic expression, rather than as versified
propaganda, he nevertheless does at times achieve real poetic
effect. The *Verses on Various Occasions* contains, besides some
eighty-five Mediterranean verses, a few hymns composed at
Littlemore, some translations from the Roman and the Parisian
Breviary, some technically "occasional" verse, and the poem
which finally gave him major stature in the Victorian mind, "The
Dream of Gerontius."

Most of the Mediterranean verse shows Newman looking
upon the world and himself as lying under the "burden of sin,"
awaiting deliverance. He feels his own unworthiness as an instrument of the Divine; he looks about him and within him, and
writes poems on "Temptation," "Absolution," "The Brand of
Cain"; he thinks of the great Biblical leaders, and writes poems
on "Moses," "Jeremiah," "Melchizedek," "The Call of David."

* See Chap. X, p. 249.

But only a few of the poems achieve distinction. The following stanza from "Reverses" is typical of Newman's more successful attempts:

> "When mirth is full and free,
> Some sudden gloom shall be;
> When haughty power mounts high,
> The Watcher's axe is nigh.
> All growth has bound; when greatest found,
> It hastes to die." [7]

Here we see the characteristics of much of Newman's poetry: its lack of force or color, of "hidden music" or of passionate expression. Sometimes, as in "Progress of Unbelief," he makes a promising beginning:

> "Now is the Autumn of the Tree of Life;
> Its leaves are shed upon the unthankful earth." [8]

But the succeeding lines fall back into *clichés* — "The cheerful hearth," "comely gear," "choicest scent and hue" — and into unavoidable Biblical allusion. More successfully maintained are the tone and force of "Waiting for the Morning," which begins

> "They are at rest:
> We may not stir the heaven of their repose
> With loud-voiced grief, or passionate request,
> Or selfish plaint for those
> Who in the mountain grots of Eden lie,
> And hear the fourfold river, as it hurries by." [9]

Sometimes there is a curious angularity, occasionally almost Browningesque, in Newman's verses. This is very striking in the last stanza of "Warnings." After stating that heaven sends presentiments of sorrow, and that science fails to bear us to the hidden springs of life, he asks, in an unusual stanza-pattern and in deliberately difficult cadences:

> "Are such thoughts fetters,
> While Faith disowns

> Dread of earth's tones,
> Recks but Heaven's call,
> And on the wall
>   Reads but Heaven's letters?" [10]

Two of the Mediterranean poems are far superior to all the others, and in the opinion of many readers, surpass any other poem in *Verses on Various Occasions*. They both show what Hutton calls an "exquisite and almost Aeschylean genius," and reveal, in the words of J. M. Flood, that Newman, at least momentarily, "possessed the Greek spirit to a degree scarcely ever shown by any other English poet." [11]   The first poem is a "tragic chorus" entitled "The Elements," which bears comparison with one of the great choruses in the *Antigone*:

> "Man is permitted much
> To scan and learn
> In Nature's frame;
> Till he well-nigh can tame
> Brute mischiefs, and can touch
> Invisible things, and turn
> All warring ills to purposes of good.
> Thus as a God below, he can control,
> And harmonize what seems amiss to flow
> As severed from the whole
> And dimly understood.
>
> But o'er the elements
> One Hand alone,
> One Hand has sway.
> What influence day by day
> In straiter belt prevents
> The impious Ocean, thrown
> Alternate o'er the ever-sounding shore?
> Or who has eye to trace
> How the Plague came?
> Forerun the doublings of the Tempest's race?
> Or the Air's weight and flame
> On a set scale explore?

Thus God has willed
That man, when fully skilled,
Still gropes in twilight dim;
Encompassed all his hours
By fearfullest powers
Inflexible to him;
That so he may discern
His feebleness,
And e'en for earth's success
To Him in wisdom turn,
Who holds for us the keys of either home,
Earth and the world to come." [12]

The other poem, also a "tragic chorus," is entitled "Judaism,"
and draws a weird analogy between the Jewish people and Oedi-
pus Coloneus. "Would not Aeschylus himself," asks Hutton,
"if he had lived again in our generation, have been proud to have
written the following on the Jewish race?"

"O piteous race!
Fearful to look upon;
Once standing in high place,
Heaven's eldest son.
O aged blind,
Unvenerable! as thou flittest by,
I liken thee to him in pagan song,
In thy gaunt majesty,
The vagrant king, of haughty-purposed mind,
Whom prayer nor plague could bend;
Wronged at the cost of him who did the wrong,
Accursed himself, but in his cursing strong,
And honoured in his end." [13]

The Aeschylean effect of these lines leaves us wholly unprepared for another side of Newman's poetic talent. Strangely
enough Newman's readers, including his most careful critics,
have failed to recognize in him an astonishing gift for "light
verse." Indeed, he had not a little of that talent which distinguished Charles Stuart Calverley. One does not ordinarily
think of Cardinal Newman, the author of "Lead, Kindly Light,"

as the sort of man who could have, in 1829, written "Opusculum:
for a Very Small Album," of which the following are the first
two of its six stanzas:

> "Fair cousin, thy page
> is small to encage
> the thoughts which engage
> the mind of a sage
>   such as I am;
>
> 'Twere in teaspoon to take
> the whole Genevese lake,
> or a lap-dog to make
> the white Elephant sac-
> -red in Siam." [14]

In the same year, and possibly for the same cousin, he wrote a
fifteen-stanza poem entitled "Monks: for Another Small Album
(With Lines on Hinges to Fit It)." Here are the opening
lines —

> "Why, dear Cousin,
>   why
> Ask for verses,
> when a poet's
> fount of song is
>   dry?
>
> Or, if aught be
>   there
> Harsh and chill, it
> ill may touch the
> hand of lady
>   fair." [15]

Conventional as are the diction and tropes and Biblical allusion
in the *Lyra Apostolica*, Newman obviously had the capacity for
stanzaic invention, for the playful wit of "society verse." That
this gift did not desert him in his later years is clear from a letter
of thanks, written in 1863 to J. W. Bowden's niece, Charlotte

Bowden (whose nickname was "Chat"), in acknowledgment of some cakes baked by herself:

> "Who is it that moulds and makes
>   Round, and crisp, and fragrant cakes?
>   Makes them with a kind intent,
>   As a welcome compliment,
>   And the best that she can send
>   To a venerable friend?
>   One it is, for whom I pray,
>   On St. Philip's festal day,
>   With a loving heart, that she
>   Perfect as her cakes may be. . .
>   Here's a rhyming letter, Chat
>   Gift for gift, and tit for tat." [16]

"The Dream of Gerontius" was composed, singularly enough, in the midst of the Kingsley controversy. Perhaps because of the strain imposed by the writing of the *Apologia*, perhaps because of medical information, Newman was seized with a vivid apprehension of impending death. Though feeling quite well, he actually wrote a memorandum headed "Written in Prospect of Death," dated Passion Sunday, 1864, 7 o'clock A.M., in which he made a formal commitment of his soul to the Most Holy Trinity, to particular saints, and to his Guardian Angel. After the Kingsley affair was over, and when the abandonment of the Oxford scheme gave him leisure for it, he set down "on small bits of paper" a dramatization of the vision of a Christian's death, on which his mind had been dwelling. Beginning on January 17, 1865, he finished the poem within three weeks, with scarcely an erasure, then put it aside, and dismissed it from his mind. According to Aubrey de Vere, when a magazine editor wrote to him asking for a contribution, Newman looked into his papers for suitable theological material, and, not finding any, he wrote to the editor that he had come upon some verses which, if the editor desired them, would be sent at his request. Thus it was that "Gerontius" appeared in the April and May numbers of the Jesuit periodical, the *Month*:[17] The middle decades of the Victorian era were highly sensitive to the poetry of death; in the 'forties and 'fifties, Bailey's

Festus, a philosophical drama of the supernatural, somewhat suggestive of Goethe's *Faust,* was widely popular; and Tennyson's *In Memoriam* (1850) had become a classic statement of the enigmas of death and the "longings for immortality" in the intellectual non-Catholic world. Newman's poem came at the culmination of this interest and its lucid and ghostly beauty won it immediate recognition as a masterpiece of its kind. Later, even Swinburne, whose temperament was so unlike Newman's, admired the "force, the fervor, the tense energy" of Newman's best lines. And General Gordon, at Khartoum, while awaiting the relief that never came, read and reread his underlined copy of "Gerontius." [18]

The poem should be read as an account of a *dream,* a dream of supersensible things. Knowing Newman, one will not expect much visual appeal in its imagery, though there is considerable appeal to the ear and to the emotions. In fact, the greatest success of the poem lies in its psychological penetration, its presentation of the mind of a dying man.

Gerontius, lying on his deathbed, feels a "strange innermost abandonment," an "emptying out of each constituent and natural force," as though he were "no more a substance now," but about to drop into "that shapeless, scopeless, blank abyss, that utter nothingness, of which [he] came." He can still hear the assistants in the room, chanting the litany of the dying. Rousing himself to fuller consciousness, he makes a declaration of faith. Then there returns

> "That sense of ruin, which is worse than pain,
> That masterful negation and collapse
> Of all that makes me man; as though I bent
> Over the dizzy brink
> Of some sheer infinite descent;
> Or worse, as though
> Down, down for ever I was falling through
> The solid framework of created things,
> And needs must sink and sink
> Into the vast abyss. And, crueller still,
> A fierce and restless fright begins to fill
> The mansion of my soul. And, worse and worse,

> Some bodily form of ill
> Floats in the wind, with many a loathsome curse
> Tainting the hallow'd air, and laughs and flaps
> Its hideous wings . . ."

Gerontius prays for help. The assistants continue their slow chanting of prayers for the dying, and gradually peace steals over the dying man, weary with pain:

> "Novissima hora est; and I fain would sleep.
>   . . . Into thy hands,
> O Lord, into thy hands. . ."

While the priest utters his prayers ("Proficiscere, anima Christiana, de hoc mundo . . ."), Gerontius dies, and the first part of the poem comes to a close.

The second part begins with the Soul of Gerontius aware of "a strange refreshment" after a sleep; he "hears no more the busy beat of time," and can but faintly remember "a priestly voice cry 'Subvenite' " and the thin accents of the assistants. He cannot be sure whether he is alive or dead.

> "So much I know, not knowing how I know,
>   That the vast universe, where I have dwelt,
>   Is quitting me, or I am quitting it . . .
>   Yet . . . is this peremptory severance
>   Wrought out in lengthening measurements of space,
>   Which grow and multiply by speed and time?
>   Or am I traversing infinity
>   By endless subdivision, hurrying back
>   From finite towards infinitesimal,
>   Thus dying out of the expansive world?"

The Soul of Gerontius is now aware of someone holding him fast "within his ample palm," bearing him upward, and singing a "heart-subduing melody." It is his Guardian Angel, who, calling him "child and brother," tells him that they are "hurrying to the Just and Holy Judge," and that less than a "million-million-millionth part" of a moment has passed since Gerontius heard the "Subvenite." There is no fear in Gerontius's Soul, as they near the judgment-court, though they are aware of a "sullen howl" from the demons who assemble there:

> "It is the middle region, where of old,
> Satan appeared among the sons of God,
> To cast his jibes and scoffs at holy Job."

At this point in the poem, Newman attempts to reproduce, not altogether successfully, the "sour and uncouth dissonance" of the hungry demons, who

> "Like beasts of prey, . . . caged within their bars,
> In a deep hideous purring have their life."

In contrast to the three demonic songs, in irregular and harsh rhythm, and in short clacking lines, there are five Angelical Choirs, whose songs always begin with the same graceful quatrain:

> "Praise to the Holiest in the height,
> And in the depth be praise:
> In all His words most wonderful;
> Most sure in all His ways!"

These choirs surround Gerontius and his Guardian Angel as they soar above the blasphemous laughter and wailing of the demons, and approach "the stairs which rise towards the Presence-chamber," where the Angels of the Sacred Stair hymn the

> "Father, whose goodness none can know but they
> Who see [Him] face to face."

Gerontius is warned that the sight of God will at once "kindle his heart" and "pierce him to the quick," moving him to slink away as unworthy but also to wish to "dwell forever in the beauty of [God's] countenance." These two pains will be his "veriest, sharpest purgatory."

At last the Guardian Angel announces to Gerontius:

> "Thy judgment now is near, for we are come
> Into the veilèd presence of our God."

Gerontius again hears the prayers of his friends around his bed, who are saying the "Subvenite" with the priest — so little time has passed since the early "dream." But these prayers are not unattended: the Angel of the Agony, "the same who strengthen'd Him" in Gethsemane,

> "That Angel best can plead with Him for all
> Tormented souls, the dying and the dead."

The Soul of Gerontius, however, "with intemperate energy of love," flies from his Guardian Angel directly to the "feet of Emmanuel":

> "But ere it reach them, the keen sanctity,
> Which with its effluence, like a glory, clothes
> And circles round the Crucified, has seized,
> And scorch'd, and shrivell'd it; and now it lies
> Passive and still before the awful Throne . . .
> Consumed, yet quicken'd, by the glance of God."

The last utterance of the Soul of Gerontius now occurs in one of Newman's most delicate lyrics; the Soul sings of its longing for the lake of purification:

> "Take me away, and in the lowest deep
> There let me be,
> And there in hope the lone night-watches keep,
> Told out for me."

The Guardian Angel commits the Soul to the Angels of Purgatory, whereupon we hear, most appropriately, in rhythmical prose, a song by the Souls in Purgatory — a selective paraphrase of the Ninetieth Psalm. The poem ends with the Guardian Angel addressing the soul of Gerontius:

> "Softly and gently, dearly-ransom'd soul,
> In my most loving arms I now enfold thee,

> And, o'er the penal waters, as they roll,
>   I poise thee, and I lower thee, and hold thee.

> And carefully I dip thee in the lake. . .

> Farewell, but not forever! brother dear,
>   Be brave and patient on thy bed of sorrow;
> Swiftly shall pass thy night of trial here,
>   And I will come and wake thee on the morrow."

"The Dream of Gerontius" has a simple, sometimes a severe, beauty which is easily lost on the "common reader." To recognize the artistry of the poem one must examine its stanzaic variety, the occasional, almost Miltonic, grandeur of its blank verse, its skillfully managed contrasts, its boldness of imagination. Its contrasts alone are evidence of Newman's admirable grasp of his subject: the chant of the assistants, for example, follows, solemn and hopeful, on Gerontius' despairing sensation of collapse, then on his desperate effort to cling to consciousness, and, later, on his anguished prayers for aid when he senses the nameless evil "tainting the hallow'd air." The Angelical Choirs are all the more majestic after the clattering blasphemies of the demonic songs. And even "on the threshold of the Eternal Presence where all is joy and peace, the plea of the Angel of the Agony conjures up the anguish of Gethsemane and stirs us with an almost overwhelming sense of sadness." [19] Newman shows his artistic shrewdness when, with Gerontius in the arms of the Angel, he makes no attempt to depict to the eye the grandeurs and mysteries of heaven; as Professor Reilly has noted, he prudently turns to the Church's teachings, and "transforms the psychological drama into a spiritual one," levying upon the doctrines and the ritual of the Church — "the Litany of the Dying, the Act of Faith, the ascent to immediate judgment, the Guardian Angel, the demons hungering for human souls, intercessory prayer, Purgatory." [20] These are all handled with skill and consistency, and with an appeal to the emotions and to the ear. Although the sacrifice of visual effect leads to a loss of interest and tension in the central part of the poem, this loss is retrieved at the end where Newman's own *feeling* creates some of the most moving lyrics in the whole work. Newman realized to what extent he had depended on hearing, and thus proposed that "Gerontius" might well be set to music; those who have heard Sir Edward Elgar's oratorio will know the justness of Newman's suggestion. On the whole, "The Dream of Gerontius" is not only what a very unsympathetic critic has admitted, "one of the subtlest of modern religious poems" [21]; it is also the culmination and summary of Newman's poetic achievement, the fruit of many years of thought and experience. "Had he been asked," writes Professor Reilly, "how much time he had spent on *Gerontius*, he might truthfully have answered, not 'A few weeks,' but rather, 'All my life.' " [22]

iii. *Newman as a Novelist*

Newman's attempts at fiction are represented by two novels, *Loss and Gain, the Story of a Convert*, published in 1848, and *Callista, a Sketch of the Third Century*, published, at first anonymously, in 1856. Like his poetry, they were the by-products of his genius, and like all his works they were evoked by an occasion and by some pressing sense of obligation. *Loss and Gain* was intended, as Newman tells us in the Advertisement, as a "suitable answer" to a "wantonly and preposterously fanciful" tale which had been directed against converts to the Catholic faith in the summer of 1847. Early in the spring of the same year that *Loss and Gain* was published, Newman also began what was to become the subplot of *Callista*, writing a "great part of Chapters I, IV, and V, and sketching the character and fortunes of Juba." [1] A year later, in a letter of February 28, 1849, he expresses a desire to "bring out the ἦθος of the Heathen from St. Paul's day down to St. Gregory," to show "what conversion *was* in those times," in "that world of sin [and] the sophistries of philosophy." [2] Though the general idea of what became the main plot of *Callista* seems to have taken some shape in his mind, Newman did nothing more with the story until the summer of 1855, when he suddenly resumed it and completed it in a few months. In 1853 Charles Kingsley's historical novel, *Hypatia*, had offended Roman Catholics and the Catholic party in the Church of England by its sympathetic treatment of pagan life and thought, and by its attack on monasticism among the early

Christians.[3]   Possibly with such a novel in mind, Newman declared his opposite intention, in the Advertisement of the first edition of *Callista*, to "imagine and express, from a Catholic point of view, the feelings and mutual relations of Christians and heathens at the period to which it belongs."   Both *Callista* and *Loss and Gain* are stories of conversion, both show Newman chiefly interested in the inner drama of a change of faith by the central character of the story, and both reflect Newman's own religious development and conversion.

Of the two novels, *Loss and Gain* is more argumentative in its dialogue and less successful in its plot.   Charles Reding, son of an old-fashioned Anglican clergyman, is sent to Oxford where his attendance at courses of lectures, and his acquaintanceship with men and groups of various religious opinions, stir up difficulties in his mind.   He becomes interested in Catholicism; he finds the Thirty-nine Articles extremely perplexing.   His doubts about the Articles reach the vice-principal, who questions him on justification and the invocation of the saints; Charles' answers do not sound sufficiently orthodox, and he is summarily sent home from college.   This unexpected exile does not prevent his coming up for his examinations later, but the distractions of religious uncertainty cause him ultimately to fail them.   Among the men who contribute to his uncertainty are Dr. Brownside, the Liberal divine, for whom Revelation "instead of being the abyss of God's counsels, with its dim outlines and broad shadows, [is] a flat sunny plain, laid out with straight macadamized roads"; Freeborn, the Evangelical, who thinks theology a mistake; Vincent, a junior tutor, an oracular, "no party," "safe" man; Sheffield, the rationalist; White, who toys with the idea of going over to Rome, but who is finally "reclaimed to be a devoted son and useful minister of the Church of England"; Bateman, a young Oxonian, recently ordained, interested in "restoring" chapels; Campbell, an intelligent, tactful, and traveled clergyman of the Anglican Church; and Willis who has "gone over" to the Church of Rome. Reding is anxious to resolve his difficulties and to remain in the Church of his father.   From none of his friends and acquaintances does he receive much help; neither Bateman nor Campbell, who make the most effort, succeeds in curbing his drift away from his Church, while Willis, with his infectious enthusiasm for Rome, only adds to Reding's confusion.   Charles postpones taking his B.A., and for two years lives with Campbell as his mentor, and reads the great English divines and apologists in an effort to plant his roots deeper in the English Church.   The effort is fruitless.   At last he takes leave of his saddened mother and of the patient Campbell, and sets out for Oxford, to see it for the last time before his final step.   Then he proceeds to London, where he is received into the Roman Church at the House of the Passionists.

Like *Loss and Gain*, the story of *Callista* stems from the author's own experiences while he was still an Anglican, and reflects his inner conflicts while passing from a semiconscious to a fully conscious acceptance of "primitive Christianity."   Laid in the third century, in the reign of the persecuting emperor Decius, the plot contains elements of the historical romance, the familiar "saint's life," and also something of the psychological study which matured in later Victorian fiction.   Though less so than *Loss and Gain*, the novel is likewise a series of arguments.   Callista, a beautiful pagan Greek girl, lives in Sicca in northern Africa with her brother Aristo, whom she aids in modeling statues and idols.   She is beloved of Agellius, a Christian farmer who hopes to convert her and marry her.   Agellius' uncle Jucundus favors the marriage but not the conversion, and indeed hopes that the marriage will reconvert Agellius to Callista's paganism.   However, Callista has begun to sense a vision of truth beyond her Greek idealism, and has become interested in Christianity.   Before she learns much about the new religion, a plague of locusts ravages the country; and the ignorant populace, in the days of starvation and riot which follow, lay the blame for the visitation on the magistrates who had failed to carry out the recent imperial edicts against Christians.   A great mob, shouting "Christianos ad leones," sweeps through Sicca in search of Agellius.   Though it fails to find him, it plunders and murders without check, and finally through some mistake it captures Callista, and flings her into prison.   Meanwhile Jucundus has spirited Agellius away to safety.   In her dark and noisome cell, Callista reads the secret parchment given to her by Agellius' friend, Caecilius, exiled

Bishop of Carthage; it is a transcript of the Gospel of St. Luke.
She broods over her predicament, as she is drawn to, yet repelled
by, the doctrines of Christianity. A few days earlier, when
brought before the authorities, she had denied being a Christian,
yet had refused to offer incense to the Roman gods; her brother
had become alarmed, her friends dumb with surprise. Aristo
had even induced the popular pagan philosopher of the day,
Polemo, to visit her and persuade her out of her repulsive and
dangerous delusions, but in vain. Now, as she studies the parchment Gospel, she becomes convinced of the truth of Christianity, and is baptized by Caecilius, who somehow succeeds in
gaining entrance to her cell. The news of her conversion spreads
through Sicca; her brother abandons her in anger and despair;
her friends among the magistrates and tribunes — notably Cal-
phurnius, who looks upon her with aesthetic as well as with sensual desire — are unable to secure her release, because of red
tape and departmental jealousy. At last, to end the deadlock,
and to satisfy the authorities at Rome, Callista is tried, and put to
torture on the rack, where, in her exhaustion from imprisonment,
she quickly dies. Agellius, torn with grief, recovers her body,
which soon begins to work miracles, curing the madness of Juba,
brother of Agellius, who had been under the evil influence of
their mother, the sorceress Gurta. The novel ends with St.
Cyprian celebrating at Callista's burial.

Clearly we have here a far better novel than *Loss and Gain*:
the characters are successfully individualized; the dialogue is
more appropriate to each speaker; the psychology — motivation,
reaction, development — is far more searching and subtle. But
both novels suffer from very serious defects, which prevent a
quick and interested response by the present-day reader who is
not already thoroughly informed about the Oxford Movement
and third-century Roman life and Christianity. Both novels are
of course intended as instruments of propaganda, and therefore
fail from the very start in giving us a complete feeling of reality.
Only in certain situations or episodes does Newman show his
potential ability as a novelist. Starting with his assumptions, he
could hardly produce fiction of any marked dramatic quality.
For him there is really no conflict in Reding and Callista, only a

gradual enlightenment as to their direction. As Professor Baker has pointed out, Newman's

"belief that the most important event in life is not any measurable success nor even human failure, but the attainment of a certain subjective attitude, assent, communion with the true Church, this belief makes itself manifest in the choice of incident and the management of each story, and is present in the climax. . . It permits dialogue that is quite undramatic, [and] reflects merely intellectual steps along the way to conversion, not emotional reaction of man on man. . . Newman, vividly conscious of being in the hand of God, shows us not the consequences of acts of will, but the stages in the path along which the soul is led by a divine power quite independent of time, place, circumstance, and personal inclination. [Though Newman does not deny free will] the important thing is the act of grace, not the act of will. Newman's chief characters do not exhibit a conflict of desire and duty. They are eager to obey if only they may learn what is right." [4]

There can therefore be no real conflict or suspense; from the first we can see what is coming. We miss in Newman's novels any real struggle of will against will, of character against circumstance, any real influence of one character upon another. The dialogue, especially in *Loss and Gain*, serves merely as a medium for discussing religious problems, and is usually no more like genuine fictional dialogues than those of Plato.

Moreover, Newman continually breaks into the narrative and speaks *in propria persona*, either to comment or to pull his story together, sometimes artlessly, as when in *Loss and Gain* (the opening of Chapter XI) he says: "No opportunity has occurred of informing the reader that, during the last week or two, Charles had accidentally been a good deal thrown across Willis." Objectionable also are those passages — sometimes whole chapters — in which Newman writes as an essayist rather than as a novelist; this is true of the historical and topographical beginning of *Callista* and of the opening of the second chapter, "Christianity in Sicca." The beginning of *Loss and Gain* is equally lacking in prompt appeal to what we now call "reader interest." Here Newman fails to exploit the very real possibilities of the setting, "the city of the dreaming spires." Instead we have a long soliloquy by Charles' father on the advisability of sending the boy to Oxford. Since Newman's aim in both novels is to depict a mind gradually accepting a new religious position, he naturally neglects or omits the element of the "love story" in his plots: "*Loss and Gain*," says Professor Baker, "is as devoid of a love story as is any biography of its author." [5]　When Agellius declares his love to Callista, he is covered with confusion when she rebukes him for courting her like an ordinary man instead of converting her like the superior man, the Christian, which she has always thought him.　This is not necessarily a blemish in Newman's technique, but it does constitute a real limitation; his characters are not seen "in the round."　If the creation of fully rounded characters is an ultimate test of a novelist's skill, then we must conclude that Newman fails to meet that test; his delineation of character is severely confined within the bounds of his religious position.　So long as he is giving us prototypes of himself, in Reding or Callista, he succeeds fairly well; as soon as he depicts characters who are neither Romanist nor High Anglican, he resorts either to caricature or to melodrama.　In *Loss and Gain*, Dr. Brownside, Vincent, and the Evangelicals (some of whom are merely referred to as No. 1, No. 2, No. 3!) are simply caricatures; in *Callista*, the characters of Juba and his mother Gurta are drawn with touches which remind us of "Gothic" drama and romance.　On the whole, Newman's characters are shadowy outlines; they are given very few physical traits, in some cases none at all; he was content that they remain primarily spiritual types.　Thus, as Reilly says, "you would never recognize any of Newman's characters if you met them in the street." [6]

In smaller ways Newman's novels are equally deficient.　He is careless about names.　One notes that the parsonage of Reding's father is never described; it is not even named until the thirteenth chapter.　Willis, one of the more important secondary characters, is not clearly named until page 37.[7]　Details of appearance are, as we might expect, minimized or delayed; we have to search through all of *Callista* to find her age to be nearly eighteen, her hair auburn, her voice sweet and thrilling, her features "expressive."　Inconsistencies of characterization bring the reader up with a start.　Bateman in the opening pages of *Loss and Gain* is introduced by Newman as a "bore," but nowhere does he really behave like one, judging from the other characters' acts and remarks.   Indeed Newman asserts: "The reader . . . must believe this upright Mr. Bateman to be, what otherwise he might not discover, and thank us for our consideration in not proving as well as asserting it." [8]   Thus lightly does Newman flout one of the basic canons of artistic narrative.   Reding puts his trust in Carlton, though nothing that Carlton has said or done prepares us for Reding's attitude.   We are equally unprepared for Charles' decision in favor of the celibate life, for his rapid turning toward the Roman Church, for his sister Mary's sudden realization that he might become a Catholic.   Charles is drawn to the Roman Church, yet Newman admits on page 269 that his hero had "never seen a Catholic priest . . . ; never, except once as a boy, been inside a Catholic church; he only knew one Catholic in the world [Willis]."   By the end of Part I, Charles' father has died; Charles himself has become sick of all religious controversy, and appears to be a changed person: "he had left Oxford a clever, unformed youth; he returned a man." [9]   But throughout Part II Charles remains much the same as he was, and engages again in religious argument.

One may well ask why, in view of all their patent defects, Newman's novels are still reprinted and still read with considerable interest.   It is not only because they are of unusual historical and biographical value; it is because they contain passages of memorable beauty, or drama, or psychological understanding.   For the reader who is reasonably familiar with the events and principles of the Oxford Movement there are delightful surprises in *Loss and Gain*.   One wonders how a man so preoccupied, as was Newman, with religious doctrine and with "the life of the soul in the Unseen," could even momentarily turn off a bit of humorous or realistic dialogue.   For example, Charles and his friends are having lunch in Bateman's room:

" 'But what do you say to Rubrics and the Calendar?' insisted Bateman.   'They are not binding,' answered Campbell.   'They *are* binding,' said Bateman.   A pause, as between the rounds of a boxing-match.   Reding interposed: 'Bateman, cut me, please, a bit of your capital bread — home-made, I suppose?'   'A thousand pardons!'

said Bateman: — 'not binding? — Pass it to him, Willis, if you please. Yes, it comes from a farmer, next door. I'm glad you like it. I repeat, they *are* binding, Campbell.' " [10]

This has the ring of perfectly natural conversation. Victorians in the 1850's must have been amused, also, at the conversation between Willis and White and "the pretty Miss Boltons," two Catholic-minded young ladies who have been making a cope for the new bishop. "It will take four years to finish," says Charlotte.

" 'Four years!' cried White; 'we shall all be real Catholics by then; England will be converted.' . . . 'How different all things will be [muses one of the young women]; yet I don't quite like, though, the idea of a cardinal in Oxford. Must we be so very Roman? I don't see why we might not be quite Catholic without the Pope.' 'Oh, you need not be afraid,' said White sagely; 'things don't go so apace. Cardinals are not so cheap.' " [11]

Readers of *Loss and Gain* do not soon forget certain passages, memorable either for their humor, or their eloquence, or their satire; the picture of Oxford as a place of "intellectual fashions," as typifying "academic life" almost everywhere, and as embodying (in Newman's early years) a comfortably worldly notion of religion; the charming domestic scenes at Hartley; Willis's remarkable account of the Mass; the discussions of Gregorian music and Gothic architecture; Charles' dismissal by the Rev. Joshua Jennings, and his final visit to his old principal, Dr. Bluett, who refused to let him remain until Easter: "What! remain here, sir, with all the young men about?" asked Dr. Bluett, with astonishment. When Charles could not conceive why he was unfit company for the gentlemen of the college, "Dr. Bluett's jaw dropped, and his eyes assumed a hollow aspect":

" 'You will corrupt their minds.' Then he added in a sepulchral tone, which came from the very depth of his inside, 'You will introduce them, sir, to some subtle Jesuit — to some subtle Jesuit, Mr. Reding.' " [12]

Perhaps the most poignant passage in the entire novel is that in which Charles took his last look at Oxford:

"He had passed through Bagley Wood, and the spires and towers of the University came on his view, hallowed by how many tender associations, lost to him for two whole years. . . There lay old Oxford before him, with its hills as gentle and its meadows as green as ever. At the first view of that beloved place, he stood still with folded arms, unable to proceed. Each college, each church, he counted them by their pinnacles and turrets. The silver Isis, the grey willows, the far-stretching plains, the dark groves, the distant range of Shotover, the pleasant village where he had lived with Carlton and Sheffield — wood, water, stone, all so calm, so bright, they might have been his, but his they were not." [13]

It was on a misty, frosty morning a few days later that he took his actual farewell:

"The leaves flitted about; all was in unison with the state of his feelings. He re-entered the monastic buildings, meeting with nothing but scouts with boxes of cinders, and old women carrying off the remains of the kitchen. He crossed to the Meadow, and walked steadily down to the junction of the Cherwell with the Isis; he then turned back. What thoughts came upon him! for the last time! There was no one to see him; he threw his arms round the willows so dear to him, and kissed them; he tore off some of their black leaves, and put them in his bosom. 'I am like Undine,' he said, 'killing with a kiss. No one cares for me; scarce a person knows me.' " [14]

Here is an obvious identification of Newman and Reding: both always felt misunderstood and isolated. There are, however, other resemblances. Both men failed to take honors in their university, though for different reasons; both accepted their failure with unwounded pride. Ironically enough, Newman makes Reding, who is so like him, a hater of "party men," though he himself was known throughout the British Isles as the leader of the "Tractarian party." Both men were retiring and over-sensitive, lovers of music, especially of "Gregorians"; both early felt called to the celibate life; both delayed their entrance into the Roman Church until sure they were under no delusions. Indeed, on the very eve of his departure from Oxford, Charles is assailed by the very doubts which Newman in the *Apologia* says attacked him:

"Why could he not leave well enough alone?   Better men than he had lived and died in the English Church.   And then, what if . . . all his so-called convictions were to vanish just as he entered the Roman pale . . . ?" [15]

Even Reding's estrangement from Sheffield is paralleled by New-man's from Frederick Rogers; like Reding and Sheffield they had roomed on the same staircase at Oxford.[16]   Finally, as Reilly has pointed out, "the 'Father Dominic,' a Passionist born in Italy, who received Reding into the Church, was the same even to the name and antecedents, as he at whose feet Newman himself made his submission . . ." [17] On the other hand, in some ways Reding is not Newman at all: he is not the leader of a Movement; indeed *Loss and Gain* gives us very little of the party strife, the politics, the action of corporate bodies, the leader-ship, and the efforts to influence public opinion, which were all a part of the Tractarian Movement.   Yet Pusey and Puseyism are occasionally mentioned, and even Newman is indirectly re-ferred to — White has been to hear him and thinks him "very injudicious or worse."   In Chapter IV, with the affair of Tract XC still fresh in his mind, Newman must have written with dry irony the report which Sheffield makes to Reding:

"Have you heard the news? . . . The kitchen man was full of it as I passed along. . . I don't know what it means, but Oxford has just now a very bad inside.   The report is, that some of the men have turned Romans . . . The Dons have met several times; and several tutors are to be discommoned, and their name stuck up against the buttery-door." [18]

Callista differs from *Loss and Gain* not only in being a histori-cal novel but also in conveying to the reader a clearer sense of character, and of the "spirit" of an age.   One does not soon for-get Jucundus, the old image maker, hearty and gruff, impatient of scruples and sensibilities, fond of the "good life" of pagan Rome.   He and Aristo and Cornelius discuss the two great dan-gers of the empire, the Goths and the Christians.   Cornelius ecstatically tells of the Secular Games of the foregoing years, and praises the beauty and majesty of Rome; Aristo, who has heard that the Christian "superstition" may yet be her salvation, still feels that Christians as a sect will probably fade away instead of spreading:

" 'Spread?' cried Jucundus, . . . yes, they 'll spread. Yes, grow like scorpions, twenty at a birth. The country already swarms with them . . . the air breeds them like flies . . . No one 's safe; any one may be a Christian; it 's an epidemic. Great Jove! *I* may be a Christian before I know where I am." [19]

"All confidence is gone," he says; one goes to his tailor, and finds him a changed man — "a Christian dressed up like a tailor." Later in the evening, the party breaks up; Jucundus returns to his table, and, somewhat flown with wine, addresses one of his absent guests in what Newman probably intended to be a summary, partly ironical, of the pagan view of life, with all its delight in the senses, its acute recognition of life's transiency and sadness, its profound frustration:

" 'Jove 's the god for me; a glorious, handsome, curly god — but they are all good, all the gods are good. There 's Bacchus, he 's a good, comfortable god, though a sly, treacherous fellow . . . There 's Ceres, too; Pomona; the Muses; Astarte, too, as they call her here; all good; — and Apollo, though he 's somewhat too hot in this season . . . He gave me a bad fever once. Ah! life 's precious, most precious; so I felt it then, when I was all but gone to Pluto. Life never returns; it 's like water spilt . . . Ah! there 's something more there than I can tell; more than all your philosophers can determine . . . Enjoyment 's the great rule . . . Oh, if I had now to begin life again how many things I should correct! . . . Those abominable pears! . . . All is vanity,' he continued with a slow, grave utterance, 'all is vanity but eating and drinking . . . What 's fame? what 's glory; what 's power? smoke. I 've often thought the hog is the only really wise animal . . . Hogs keep the end of life steadily in view; that 's why those toads of Christians will not eat them . . . Quiet, respectable, sensible enjoyment . . . Life is short.' " [20]

But probably the most successful passages in the whole novel are those which narrate two catastrophes which befall Sicca: the invasion of the locusts, and the rioting of the mob. Whether by intention or not, Newman contrives to have each event announce itself by a distant noise, just as an important dialogue is coming to a close. First we have Agellius, Juba, and Caecilius arguing about Juba's scorn of Christianity; the words of Caecilius irritate Juba beyond further speech:

" 'There,' said Juba [pointing to a tiny cloud of insects over the distant marsh], 'is what will tell more against you than imperial edict, informer, or proconsular apparitor; and no work of mine.'

"He turned down the bank and disappeared. Agellius and his guest looked at each other in dismay. 'It is the locusts,' they whispered to each other, as they went back into the cottage." [21]

All three had heard the telltale "harsh and shrill sound, a whizzing or a chirping," which announced the arrival of a plague for which the Christians would be blamed. The other dialogue is between Callista and Caecilius, in Agellius' cottage. "I am a child of Greece," she tells the old bishop; while Christianity "seems too beautiful to be anything else than a dream," some of its dogmas are "too dismal, too shocking, too odious to be believed. They revolt me." Caecilius resorts to self-confession in order to show how "the Mighty Power" had changed him from a man of pleasure to a lowly Christian. Callista, in her pagan simplicity, is as shocked at this revelation of the bishop's humanity as she was at Agellius' declaration of love; she wonders if Caecilius can be any better than "those base hypocrites, priests of Isis or Mithras."

"Here her speech was interrupted by a hoarse sound, borne upon the wind as of many voices blended into one and softened by distance . . . 'Dear father,' [Callista] said, 'the enemy is upon you.' " [22]

The plague of locusts, says Newman, extended from the Atlantic to Ethiopia, from Arabia to India, from the Nile to the Red Sea:

"Like the Harpies," he continues, "they smear every thing that they touch with a miserable slime, which has the effect of a virus in corroding, or, as some say, in scorching and burning it. And then, as if all this were little, when they can do nothing else, they die; — . . . and create a pestilence . . .

"The swarm to which Juba pointed grew and grew till it became a compact body, as much as a furlong square; yet it was but the vanguard of a series of similar hosts, formed one after another out of the hot mould or sand, rising into the air like clouds, enlarging into a dusky canopy, and then discharged against the fruitful plain. At length the huge innumerous mass was put into motion, and began its career, darkening the face of day . . . Thus they advanced, host after host, for a time wafted on the air, and gradually declining to the earth, while fresh broods were carried over the first, and neared the earth, after a longer flight, in their turn. For twelve miles did they extend from front to rear, and their whizzing and hissing could be heard for six miles on every side of them. The bright sun, though hidden by them, illumined their bodies, and was reflected from their quivering wings; and as they heavily fell earthward, they seemed like the innumerable flakes of yellow-colored snow. And like snow did they descend, a living carpet, or rather pall, upon fields, crops, gardens, copses, groves, orchards, vineyards, olive woods, orangeries, palm plantations, and the deep forests, sparing nothing within their reach, and where there was nothing to devour, lying helpless in drifts, or crawling forward obstinately, as they best might, with the hope of prey . . . The poor peasants hastily dug pits and trenches as their enemy came on; in vain they filled them from the wells or with lighted stubble. Heavily and thickly did the locusts fall; . . . they choked the flame and the water . . . and the vast living hostile armament still moved on . . .

"They come up to the walls of Sicca . . . they climb up the wood or stucco, they surmount the parapet, or they have entered in at the windows, filling the apartments, and the most private and luxurious chambers . . . They dim the bright marbles of the walls and the gilding of the ceilings . . . They move along the floor in so strange an order that they seem to be a tasselated pavement themselves . . . Onward, they go, to the market, to the temple sacrifices, to the bakers' stores, to the cookshops, to the confectioners, to the druggists; nothing comes amiss to them; wherever man has aught to eat or drink, there they are, reckless of death, strong of appetite, certain of conquest." [23]

This description has struck some critics as being too much like a "set piece" for inclusion in the fabric of a novel; indeed the chapter in which it occurs begins more like an essay in *Historical Sketches* than a passage organically united to the rest of the narrative. But it is one of the things for which *Callista* is most vividly remembered.

The great mob scenes of the novel begin, appropriately enough, when a hungry and angry crowd in Sicca's forum is stirred to fury by the arrogance of a young half-drunk legionary. A scuffle ensues; two or three fellow soldiers try to rescue him, are attacked by the crowd, and barely escape into the temple of Esculapius. The priest is a shrewd man in this hour of danger: he rebukes the mob for its impiety, shows the absurdity of believing bread to be present in the temple, and reminds them of a baker's shop at the other end of the forum. "A slight impulse," says Newman at this point, "determines the movements of an excited multitude." The mob rushes to the baker, and in a moment has destroyed his house and seized his supplies. A man mounts an African ass, and rides round the forum, picking up in his train all the riffraff of Sicca; the crowd swells. Quietly, without delay, the prudent servants of the great families, shopkeepers, and officials vanish from the scene of action. The cry of "Africa!" goes up — signal that mischief is in the wind.

"Suddenly, as they march on, a low and awful growl is heard. It comes from the booth of a servant of the imperial court. He is employed as a transporter of wild beasts from the interior to the coast, where they are shipped for Rome; and he has charge at present of a noble lion, who is sitting majestically, looking through the bars of his cage at the rabble, who now begin to look at him . . . It was at this moment, while they were closing, hustling each other, staring at the beast, and hoping to provoke him, that a shrill voice cried out, 'Christianos ad leones!' . . . A sudden and dead silence ensued, as if the words had struck the breath out of the promiscuous throng. An interval passed; and then the same voice was heard again, 'Christianos ad leones!' This time the whole Forum took it up from one end to the other. The fate of the day, the direction of the movement, was decided; a distinct object was obtained . . . 'Long live the emperor! long live Decius! He told us this long ago. There's the edict; it never has been obeyed. Death to the magistrates! To the Christians! to the Christians! Up with great Jove, down with the atheists!'" [24]

Seizing the ass, the roaring throng "dresses it up in tawdry fin-ery," and sets out to force every Christian to sacrifice to it.   Soon the mob becomes so threatening to the peace of Sicca that the magistrates shut themselves up for their own safety; the small body of Roman soldiery reserve their strength for their own de-fense; numerous Christians hang out "heathen symbols" to avert the storm; the priests of Jupiter, the hierophants of Isis, of Mi-nerva, Juno, Esculapius, and Mercury, all shut their gates in terror and disgust.   The vast crowd now seizes upon the sacristan of a Christian chapel, drags him into the street, and forces him to worship the ass, and then the "genius of the emperor"; still lust-ing for blood, they throw him to the ground, where he is crushed to death by thousands of feet.   By nightfall the wild mob has seized and killed a Tertullianist, a Greek cook and perfumer, and some of the children of a "well-connected" Christian lady — the other children being handed over to the priestesses of Astarte and the "loathsome votaries of Cybele."   Meanwhile the authorities at the capitol seek to divert the crowd's attention and to lure it out of the city.   Thus it happens that, with the cry, "Agellius to the lions," the mob rushes through the southwest gate, and to Agel-lius' cottage, where it finds not Agellius but Callista and, in its indiscriminate lust for vengeance over the plague of locusts, falls upon her as better prey than nothing.

Most readers will admit that, in spite of Newman's rather old-fashioned and slow-moving narrative methods, he does build up the solid effect of reality; his mob behaves like a mob.   Even when he makes the now unpardonable fictional blunder of in-voking the "magic pen of Sir Walter," right in the midst of the mob scenes, one still may feel the hot breath and hear the name-less noise of the rioters.

There are other memorable incidents in the novel which rise well above the amateur level which Newman as a novelist did not mind occupying.   There is Juba, a "tall, swarthy-looking youth," flaunting his arrogant independence before both the holy Cae-cilius and, later, before his sorceress mother Gurta.   In a rather lurid and stilted chapter devoted to her, Newman shows her rage at her son's rejection of her "religion":

" 'You 're a bloodthirsty old hag!' says Juba. 'Yes, *I 've* seen your secret doings. Did not I catch you the other day, practising on that little child? You had nailed him up by hands and feet against the tree, and were cutting him to pieces at your leisure, as he quivered and shrieked the while. You were examining or using his liver for some of your black purposes. It 's not in my line; but you gloated over it; and when he wailed, you wailed in mimicry. You were panting with pleasure.' " [25]

Gurta glares at her son with intense malignity, and "utters a low piercing whistle"; a moment later, while Juba talks on and sings defiantly, "an animal of some wonderful species" — Newman does not identify it, but it would seem to be a cat — creeps forward, and Gurta takes and fondles it for a while, then suddenly flings it at her son, saying, "Take that." Whereupon Juba falls under her curse and, possessed of a demon, rushes madly through the countryside for several days and nights until exhausted. It is only near the end of the novel that he is rescued, and in a most melodramatic fashion: he is brought by Agellius and some exorcists to the dead body of Callista, and is made to touch her feet with his hands:

"Immediately he screamed fearfully, and was sent up into the air with such force that he seemed discharged from some engine of war: then he fell back upon the earth apparently lifeless . . . [Later] after the mass, his attendants came to him; he was quite changed: he was quiet, harmless, and silent; the evil spirit had gone out; but he was an idiot." [26]

Though there is something of the stereotyped "horror story" in this part of *Callista*, there is enough evenness of technique, and sureness of touch, to make one realize that Newman was more than the author of delicate religious lyrics and gently rhythmical prose; he was capable, through his creative imagination, of sounding some of the depths of evil and depravity, and of setting them forth in not implausible artistic form.

However, not all of *Callista* is represented by locust plagues and mob scenes and devil worshiping. With competent realism, Newman gives us glimpses of Roman life and manners: Jucundus explaining to Agellius certain kinds of Roman marriage which would leave him free to desert Callista if she did not prove a satisfactory mate; Polemo, "the friend of the great Plotinus," discoursing to Callista on the greatness of Rome, "the perfect state of human society," the dominion of one empire over all the nations; the trial of a Christian before the proconsul and the magistrates of Sicca; the imprisonment of Callista in the state prison, first in the hot and airless inner prison, the *lignum*, then in the *barathrum*, "nothing short of the public cesspool," beneath the floor of the *lignum*; the martyrdom of Callista on the rack, outside the walls of Sicca, while the rabble looks on, first in curiosity, then in amazement and fear, and finally in a "strange pity and reverence" which, says Newman, nearly moved them to worship. These are memorable scenes. In others there are notes of deep irony, as when Caecilius finds his new convert rushing far ahead of him toward martyrdom:

" 'Alas, my child!' said Caecilius, 'that feeble frame, ah! how will it bear the strong iron, or the keen flame, or the ruthless beast? My child, what do *I* feel, who am free, thus handing you over to be the sport of the evil one?' " [27]

In the portrait of Callista we see Newman's idealism, his groping for peace and satisfaction, his longing for sympathy in the midst of his spiritual isolation, and, indeed, his almost feminine sensibility. The fundamentally autobiographical nature of both novels explains in large part their lack of dramatic quality, their too infrequent realism. But obvious as are their defects, and uninviting and old-fashioned as are some of Newman's narrative methods, both novels continue to appeal by virtue of their author's psychological insight. As fiction they belong to that very large group of works composed by the gifted amateurs of Newman's day, when clergymen like Charles Kingsley and statesmen like Disraeli found time in their busy lives to write long, competent, at times brilliant, and always leisurely novels.

CHAPTER XII

AUTOBIOGRAPHY: THE APOLOGIA

In previous chapters we have touched on the importance of the *Apologia* as a record of Newman's gravitation toward the Roman Church, and of his critical efforts on her behalf.* We have now to consider it as a superb piece of controversial writing, a literary work of high excellence, and, as even one of his most hostile critics calls it, "a masterpiece of autobiography and a powerful defence of Catholicism." [1] So striking and compelling was its revelation of John Henry Newman that from its very first appearance it was hailed as ranking with the greatest autobiographies of the past:

"As a specimen of mental analysis, extended over a whole lifetime," wrote an early reviewer, "the 'Apologia' is probably without a rival. St. Augustine's Confessions are a purely religious retrospect; Rousseau's are philosophical; Dr. Newman's psychological." [2]

1. *The Bludgeon and the Rapier: Kingsley vs. Newman*

One day late in December, 1863, someone placed in Newman's hands a copy of the current number of *Macmillan's Magazine*, in which he found a review by Charles Kingsley of Volumes VII and VIII of J. A. Froude's *History of England*. In the review, which included one of Kingsley's characteristic attacks on Roman Catholicism, there occurred a passing allusion to "Father Newman":

"Truth for its own sake had never been a virtue with the Roman clergy. Father Newman informs us that it need not be, and on the whole ought not to be; that cunning is the weapon which Heaven has given to the saints wherewith to withstand the brute male force of the wicked world which marries and is given in marriage. Whether his notion be doctrinally correct or not, it is at least historically so."

* See Chaps. I, II, and VIII, pp. 15, 51, 201.

Newman, who did not yet know the author of this insult — only Kingsley's initials were given — wrote at once to the publishers, not with any controversial purpose but merely to "draw their attention, as gentlemen, to a grave and gratuitous slander." Kingsley immediately wrote to Newman, and acknowledged the authorship of the review, adding that he regarded his words to be justifiable from passages in Sermon 20, "Wisdom and Innocence," in *Sermons on Subjects of the Day*. When Newman reminded him that that sermon had been published when the author was an Anglican, twenty years before, and that it did not fairly bear any such interpretation, Kingsley made no reply. Later, in the course of their correspondence, however, Kingsley wrote that the *tone* of Newman's letters convinced him that he had mistaken the Catholic priest's meaning, and that he was enclosing a proposed apology to appear in *Macmillan's*. The "apology," a highly ingenuous letter which showed Kingsley's true *animus*, ran as follows:

"To the Editor of Macmillan's Magazine.
"Sir,
"In your last number I made certain allegations against the teaching of the Rev. Dr. Newman, which were founded on a Sermon of his, entitled 'Wisdom and Innocence.' . . .
"Dr. Newman has, by letter, expressed in the strongest terms, his denial of the meaning which I have put upon his words.
"No man knows the use of words better than Dr. Newman; no man, therefore, has a better right to define what he does, or does not, mean by them.
"It only remains, therefore, for me to express my hearty regret at having so seriously mistaken him; and my hearty pleasure at finding him on the side of Truth, in this, or any other, matter.
                    (*Signed*)   CHARLES KINGSLEY."

Newman naturally took exception to the third paragraph and to the second half of the last sentence in the letter, with their insinuation about Newman's cleverness with words against the cause of truth. Kingsley withdrew them. The letter, thus altered, was printed in the February number of *Macmillan's*. But the gist was that Newman had explained away his own words, though in fact Kingsley had not confronted him with any words at all. Newman remonstrated in a letter dated January 17, 1864, that Kingsley's *amende honorable* would be misinterpreted by the reading public, and he placed in parallel columns the four paragraphs of the original "apology" and the "unjust, but too probable, popular rendering of them." To Kingsley's careless and impetuous mind, this seemed like irritable hairsplitting; he replied that he "did not think it probable that the good sense and honesty of the British Public [would] misinterpret [his] apology, in the way in which [Newman] expected." He concluded: "Having done this, and having frankly accepted your assertion that I was mistaken, I have done as much as one English gentleman can expect from another." [1]

Throughout this correspondence one notes that Kingsley is conscientiously trying to live up to the standards of the gentleman. He had written in an early letter (January, 1864) that the course which Newman demanded of him — the published apology — was "the only course fit for a gentleman." Now that the apology, conventional as it was, would appear in *Macmillan's*, he evidently felt that he had done the handsome thing. Indeed as Mrs. Thorp, a comparatively recent biographer of Kingsley, points out,

"The Kingsley-Newman *rencontre* displays, more completely perhaps than any single incident on record, the limitations of that conception of the gentleman which was so important a Victorian axiom. To Kingsley, as to most of his contemporaries, and to a large fraction of the British race today, the concept of the gentleman was the fundamental philosophy of life . . . Throughout his combat with the Roman priest he was totally unable to conceive that Newman was concerned with issues so large that gentlemanliness melted into air." [2]

Before the controversy ended neither protagonist behaved like one who (to use Newman's phrase) "never inflicts pain." But of the two, Kingsley followed the fixed Victorian pattern: he left the reality of his charge against Newman untouched, and took refuge behind a conventional letter of apology which merely accepted Newman's disclaimer of having meant what he seemed to mean. As soon as Newman saw that there was no hope of bringing Kingsley to comprehend the nature of his offense, he knew that he must vindicate before all the world not only his own integrity but also that of the Roman priesthood. The gentleman in Newman now yielded to the practised and deadly controversialist. "He struck, without malice but without mercy." He did the unexpected and the crushing thing: he published the whole correspondence between Kingsley and himself in a shilling pamphlet, entitled *Mr. Kingsley and Dr. Newman: a Correspondence on the Question Whether Dr. Newman Teaches That Truth Is No Virtue?* ³ and ended it with a witty caricature of Kingsley's argument which has now become a classic in irony. Under the heading, *Reflections on the above*, it runs as follows:

"Mr. Kingsley begins then by exclaiming, 'Oh, the chicanery, the wholesale fraud, the vile hypocrisy, the conscience-killing tyranny of Rome! We have not far to seek for an evidence of it! There's Father Newman to wit: one living specimen is worth a hundred dead ones. He a Priest, writing of Priests, tells us that lying is never any harm.' I interpose, 'You are taking a most extraordinary liberty with my name. If I have said this, tell me when and where.' Mr. Kingsley replies, 'You said it, Reverend Sir, in a sermon which you preached when a Protestant as vicar of St. Mary's, and published in 1844,* and I could read you a very salutary lecture on the effects which that Sermon had at the time on my own opinion of you.' I make answer, 'Oh . . . *Not*, it seems, as a priest speaking of priests; but let us have the passage.' Mr. Kingsley relaxes: — 'Do you know, I like your *tone*. From your *tone*, I rejoice, greatly rejoice, to be able to believe that you did not mean what you said.' I rejoin, '*Mean* it! I maintain I never *said* it, whether as a Protestant or as a Catholic.' Mr. Kingsley replies, 'I waive that point.' I object: 'Is it possible? What? Waive the main question? I either said it or I didn't. You have made a monstrous charge against me — direct, distinct, public; you are bound to prove it as directly, as distinctly, as publicly; or to own you can't!' 'Well,' says Mr. Kingsley, 'if you are quite sure you did not say it, I'll take your word for it, I really will.' My *word*! I am dumb. Somehow I thought that it was my *word* that happened to be on trial. The *word* of a Professor of lying that he does not lie!' But Mr. Kingsley reassures me. 'We are both gentlemen,' he says; 'I have done as much as

* The sermon on "Wisdom and Innocence," in *Sermons on Subjects of the Day*, was first published in the preceding year, 1843.

one English gentlemen can expect from another.' I begin to see: he thought me a gentleman at the very time that he said I taught lying on system. After all, it is not I, but it is Mr. Kingsley who did not mean what he said. *Habemus confitentem reum.*"

This withering burst of irony left Kingsley completely dumbfounded. He had acted up to his code. His opponent had rejected the principles of that code. A less rash or a less courageous man than Kingsley would now have dropped the subject; but he felt himself deeply injured, and his anger at what seemed to him rhetorical double-dealing led him to return to the attack. Urged on by Froude, though Macmillan advised silence, he published a reply, entitled *What, Then, Does Dr. Newman Mean?* "I am answering Newman now," he wrote to a friend, "and though of course I give up the charge of conscious dishonesty, I trust to make him and his admirers sorry that they did not leave me alone. I have a score of more than twenty years to pay, and this is an instalment of it." [4]   Kingsley's pamphlet was obtuse and ill-tempered, yet shrewdly aimed to arouse the old Protestant prejudices against Newman and his Church. It bore all the marks of that "steeplechase fashion in which," as Hutton had already remarked, "[Kingsley] chose not so much to think as to *splash up* thought — dregs and all"; it reminded one that the subtitle of one of Kingsley's books was *Loose Thoughts for Loose Thinkers.* [5]   Moreover, it brought forth fresh charges: the Puseyite "Lives of the Saints," edited by Newman in 1843, were flagrantly untruthful; Newman's belief in such miracles as that of St. Januarius' blood revealed that "while he tried to destroy others' reason, he was, at least, fair enough to destroy his own"; Newman was accused of fatuous Mariolatry, of justifying equivocation, the low estate of Catholic countries, and the precedence of the Church over the Bible. The whole pamphlet tended to support Kingsley's conclusion that Newman was a fool if he believed, and a knave if he did not believe, some portions of his own teaching. Unfortunate as were Kingsley's manners throughout, his two greatest errors were his failure to make the least effort to understand Newman's mentality, and his willingness to hit below the belt. Doubtless a certain feminine strain in Newman's complex character repelled him, and this, together with his mistrust of his opponent's argumentative subtlety, led him to say the unpardonable, as in the following:

"I am henceforth in doubt and fear, as much as an honest man can be, concerning every word Dr. Newman may write. How can I tell that I shall not be the dupe of some cunning equivocation, of one of the three kinds laid down as permissible by the blessed St. Alfonso da Liguori and his pupils even when confirmed with an oath, because 'then we do not deceive our neighbor, but allow him to deceive himself.' " [6]

By publishing so indiscriminating an attack, Kingsley had in fact overreached himself; he was destined, as a writer in the *Quarterly* put it, to go down in history as "the embedded fly in the clear amber of his antagonist's apology." [7] For Newman now saw his opportunity for a hearing which would vindicate his whole lifework. While the influential journals, such as the *Spectator*, were showing their disapproval of Kingsley, and while the British public was awakening to a realization that fair play and simple justice were long overdue for Newman, he hit upon the happy plan of issuing his reply in weekly parts, instead of in a long book which comparatively few would read. The first part, which came out on April 21, 1864, is devoted to an expert analysis of "Mr. Kingsley's Method of Disputation," and to an admirably dignified plea for a fair hearing in view of the circumstances of Newman's religious development. After reminding his reader that Kingsley's method will make anything Newman says about him sound suspicious, he declares his intention not to deal with his opponent but with his opponent's charges:

"And now I am in a train of thought," concludes Newman, "higher and more serene than any which slanders can disturb. Away with you, Mr. Kingsley, and fly into space. Your name shall occur again as little as I can help, in the course of these pages. I shall henceforth occupy myself not with you, but with your charges." [8]

The next part, published on April 28, was devoted to the "True Mode of Meeting Mr. Kingsley," namely, by giving a plain history of Newman's religious opinions, and by letting his readers judge of his sincerity.   By the time this pamphlet was before the public, Newman's friend, Sir Frederick Rogers, wrote to him in some alarm that the author's severe sarcasm, his personal strictures on Kingsley, and the appearance of personal sensitiveness might alienate his readers.   Newman recognized the justness of Rogers' criticism, and, though determined to "go through with it," he declared that he had "no intention of saying another hard word against Mr. Kingsley." [9]   This decision happily fixed the fate of the *Apologia*: it was to be no mere feat of retaliation, however brilliant, but a spiritual autobiography in which the name of Charles Kingsley is conspicuous for its absence.   In the second edition of the book Newman removed the portions which friends had questioned, relegated other segments of the first two Parts to the "Preface," and omitted about half the original Appendix, while retaining the rest in the form of Notes.[10]

In the third part, or pamphlet, which now constitutes the opening chapter of the *Apologia,* Newman begins the story of his change of religious opinions, from childhood influences and experiences until his final submission to Rome in 1845.   The act of reliving some of the most delightful and some of the most painful years of his life, the physical strain of consulting innumerable letters and other papers, the frequent correspondence, and the amazing speed in writing by which he succeeded in producing "the longest book [he] ever wrote [562 pages] in ten weeks" — all this made the spring of 1864 the most grueling period in Newman's life.   The marvel is that a work of enduring literary quality could have been produced at all under such circumstances.   He had, however, the help of Rogers, Church, Copeland, and Keble, who could insure accuracy in the narration of the events of the Tractarian Movement, and who, we should note, were Anglicans and therefore the last to give a Roman Catholic color to facts and testimony.   He had also the wisdom and persistence of his publisher, Longman, who urged prompt action and an unbroken weekly series of Parts.   "Had I delayed a month," Newman wrote to Church, "I should not have done [the book] at all" [11] — which means, evidently, that without the touch of a sagacious publisher we might never have had the *Apologia.*   Newman wrote "from morning to night, hardly having time [for] his meals." "Excuse my penmanship," he wrote to the printer; "my fingers have been walking nearly twenty miles a day." In his diary he recorded working one day on Part 3 "for sixteen hours at a stretch," and on Part 5 "for 22 hours running." From fatigue and from emotional strain he was sometimes found, while writing through the night, "with his head in his hands crying like a child over the, to him, well-nigh impossibly painful task of public confession." [12] It was all, he said, like "ploughing in very stiff clay" — "moving on at the rate of a mile an hour, when I had to write and print and correct a hundred miles by the next day's post." [13] At last, however, on June 25, the Appendix was published, and the long labor was completed. With enormous relief he wrote to a Dominican sister: "It is a prodigious, awful marvel that I have got through it and that I am not simply knocked up by it." [14]

The *Apologia,* both as a serial and as a book, had an instant and immense success. It wrought a veritable revolution in Newman's life and reputation; his fame had a "second spring" almost without parallel in the annals of authorship. Within a few brief weeks he soared from menial obscurity to national attention, and to honor among Catholics and non-Catholics. His autobiography made him a front-page figure. His writings now received more attention than they had ever obtained before. Although he held no official position in his Church, his opinion was increasingly sought on any seemingly controversial point in Catholic teaching. The public now saw him no longer merely as a seceder from the Establishment, dwelling in a much-deserved obscurity, but as at once the greatest religious genius of his time and "one of the finest masters of the English language." [15] Certain sections of his own Church, however, were still unfriendly: "Singularly interesting; it is like listening to the voice of one from the dead," said Manning, whose name, one critic notices, "had not been mentioned in the *Apologia* from the first page to the last." [16]

Only one seriously adverse criticism remained long in the public mind — that Newman, in his rapier-like replies, had been unduly severe toward Kingsley. Newman and Kingsley, unfortunately, never met. But, if we are to take Newman's word for it, he never harbored a personal grudge against his bludgeon-wielding opponent.   On Kingsley's death, he wrote to Sir William Cope (February 13, 1875):

"I never from the first have felt any anger towards him. . . It is very difficult to be angry with a man one has never seen.   A casual reader would think my language denoted anger, — but it did not. I have ever found from experience that no one would believe me in earnest if I spoke calmly . . .

"As to Mr. Kingsley, much less could I feel any resentment against him when he was accidentally the instrument, in the good Providence of God, by whom I had an opportunity given me, which otherwise I should not have had, of vindicating my character and conduct in my 'Apologia.' . . . I have always hoped that by good luck I might meet him, feeling sure that there would be no embarrassment on my part, and I said Mass for his soul as soon as I heard of his death." [17]

ii. *The "Apologia": Its Method and Art*

Newman's autobiography is one of the most carefully planned of all his works, and also the only one in which he takes his readers into his confidence and explains to them his objectives and his methods.   In all of his controversial writing he is ever conscious of confronting not only a series of explicit or implicit arguments but also a delicate psychological problem in his readers.   In his *Present Position of Catholics*, in his *Difficulties of Anglicans*, in his *Letter to the Duke of Norfolk*, he employs all the arts of persuasion without once stating his method or commenting on the difficulties of his problem.   In the *Apologia*, however, he provides a Preface which admirably wins his readers by setting forth the prejudices he must counter, the various possibilities in his mode of attack, the precise considerations which will ultimately determine his choice of approach, and the elaborate plan which underlies and controls his sometimes apparently desultory discussion.   According to Ryder, the original structure of the *Apologia* was first sketched as a whole; then the principal heads of narrative and argument and the general plan of ·the work were all written up in their order in large letters, and were placed on the wall opposite Newman's desk.[1]   This, of course, was the book's architectural plan.   Its *psychological* plan can best be seen if we turn to the unaltered Part 2, the pamphlet of April 28, "True Mode of Meeting Mr. Kingsley." [2]

There we find that Newman considers his task to be the destruction, not of Kingsley's arguments, but of "the bias of the court" — the immense barrier of prejudice which holds that "when much is imputed, something must be true." It will be vain to answer the charges point by point through interminable pages, each point forgotten as soon as a new one is taken up. However, all of Kingsley's charges illustrate one and the same imputation:

"He called me a *liar*," says Newman bluntly, "a simple, a broad, an intelligible, to the English public a plausible arraignment. . . What I needed was a corresponding antagonist unity in my defence. . . . My Accuser asks, 'What then, does Dr. Newman mean?' . . . I reflected, and I saw a way out of my perplexity.

"Yes, I said to myself, his very question is about my *meaning* . . . He asks what I *mean*; not about my words, not about my arguments, not about my actions, as his ultimate point, but about that living intelligence, by which I write, and argue, and act. He asks about my Mind and its Beliefs and its Sentiments; and he shall be answered. . ." [3]

Newman's task is thus greatly simplified. He will answer Kingsley for the sake, not of Kingsley or himself, but of all well-wishers and lovers of fair play. With this quiet but irresistible appeal to his British public's sense of honor, Newman says that his perplexity as to method "did not last half an hour."

"I must, I said, give the true key to my whole life; I must show what I am. . . False ideas may be refuted indeed by argument, but by true ideas alone are they expelled. I will vanquish, not my Accuser, but my judges. . . I will draw out, as far as may be, the history of my mind. . ." [4]

He will indeed answer his accuser's charges and criticisms, but in an Appendix; his chief method will be to show what external suggestions, accidents, influences, books, doctrines, and friends contributed to make him John Henry Newman, the Roman Catholic. He will consult "an abundance of letters from friends," and copies or drafts of his own. His intention is to be "simply personal and historical," not doctrinal, to explain *himself*, his opinions and his actions. He may be accused of stressing little things, of giving scandal, of being egotistical. He shrinks from laying bare his inmost thoughts "to every shallow or flippant disputant."

"But," he says, with one final gesture of indignation, "I do not like to be called to my face a liar and a knave: nor should I be doing my duty to my faith or to my name, if I were to suffer it. I know I have done nothing to deserve such an insult; and if I prove this, as I hope to do, I must not care for such incidental annoyances as are involved in the process." [5]

Two facts about the controversial strategy of the *Apologia* become quite clear. Being a "history of his mind," it will not be an autobiography in the ordinary sense of the word. Very little of Newman as a man, as a human being who ate in the common room, grieved over the death of his sister, and suffered from nearsightedness — very little of this man will appear in the book. Secondly, although the *Apologia* is to be a powerful and successful effort at persuasion, argument will have but a very subordinate position. One critic will in time observe that "of the 289 pages of the *Apologia*, only the last 15 pages are devoted to the actual refutation of Kingsley's charges: the preceding 274 pages are all indirectly persuasive, and simply prepare the way for the final defence." [6] Persuasion with as little argument as possible — this is Newman's daring strategy; self-revelation, intensely personal in tone and in some matters of fact, arrestingly concrete and dramatic, sincere and dignified in look and bearing — this is his method. Logical argument will give coherence to his discussions, to his transitions from point to point in his theological development. Occasionally, when the questions or ideas become complicated, he will resort to numbered propositions, and will carry on his discussion with all the precision of the practised dialectician. But it will not be the logical ordering of theory which will give the book its most telling quality; the *Apologia* will compel by its embodiment of a *life*. And its style will be the perfection of colloquial informality, its manner an apparent and attractive desultoriness.

By the time the reader has read Part 2 (or the Preface to the later editions) he is won by its candor and brilliancy, and is ready to enjoy Part 3, or the first chapter of the present *Apologia*. This is no doubt the most interesting and most successful section of the book. In it we learn more about Newman as a man than in any other chapter: we see him under the influence of the Evangelical divines, and later of Whately, Keble, and Hurrell Froude; we are taken briefly into the world of Bishop Butler, and of the Alexandrian Fathers; we see Newman gathering his forces for a fight against "Liberalism" and writing "Lead, Kindly Light," and finally arriving home from the Mediterranean ready for "the religious movement of 1833." The succeeding sections become so highly involved in forgotten controversies and technical theological questions that some readers are soon lost or bored. Yet there are many unforgettable passages for any reader, such as the account of Tract XC in Chapter II; the story of the *Via Media* and of how Newman was "sore about the Anglican divines, as if they had taken him in" (Chapter III); and, of course, the classic passage in Chapter V in which Newman gives the grounds for his belief in a Creator,* illustrating perfectly in 1864 the use of that "Illative Sense" which he was to define six years later in the *Grammar of Assent*. More definitely designed for the immediate occasion are his discussions of the doctrine of Infallibility, of the Church and intellectual progress, of Liberalism, of "economy" and reserve. Everywhere, whether in argument, definition, historical or doctrinal survey, Newman's touch is graceful and deft, his manner gentle, earnest, and appealing. After reviewing the question of duplicity in religious instruction, in terms of St. Alfonso da Liguori, and some Protestant theologians and literary men, and effectively disposing of it, he concludes the *Apologia* with a moving and noble passage, a memorial to all "those familiar affectionate companions and counsellors," Catholic and non-Catholic, who had been loyal to him throughout his trial:

"I have closed this history of myself with St. Philip's name upon St. Philip's feast-day; and, having done so, to whom can I more suitably offer it, as a memorial of affection and gratitude, than to St. Philip's

* See Chap. VIII, Sect. iii, p. 201.

sons, my dearest brothers of this House, the Priests of the Birmingham Oratory, AMBROSE ST. JOHN, HENRY AUSTIN MILLS, HENRY BITTLESTON, EDWARD CASWALL, WILLIAM PAINE NEVILLE, and HENRY IGNATIUS DUDLEY RYDER? — who have been so faithful to me; who have been so sensitive to my needs; who have been so indulgent to my failings; who have carried me through so many trials; who have grudged no sacrifice, if I asked for it; who have been so cheerful under discouragements of my causing; who have done so many good works, and let me have the credit of them; — with whom I have lived so long, with whom I hope to die.

"And to you especially, dear Ambrose St. John; whom God gave me, when he took everyone else away; who are the link between my old life and my new; who have now for twenty-one years been so devoted to me, so patient, so zealous, so tender; who have let me lean so hard upon you; who have watched me so narrowly; who have never thought of yourself, if I was in question.

"And in you I gather up and bear in memory those familiar affectionate companions and counsellors, who in Oxford were given to me, one after another, to be my daily solace and relief; and all those others, of great name and high example, who were my thorough friends, and showed me true attachment in times long past; and also those many younger men, whether I knew them or not, who have never been disloyal to me by word or deed; and of all these, thus various in their relations to me, those more especially who have since joined the Catholic Church.

"And I earnestly pray for this whole company, with a hope against hope, that all of us, who once were so united, and so happy in our union, may even now be brought at length, by the Power of the Divine Will, into One Fold and under One Shepherd."

iii. *The "Apologia" and Some Critics*

Newman had always maintained that "the truest modesty is egotism" — a frank statement of one's *personal* position in any controversial matter; and he wrote to Keble, regarding his sketch covering the years 1833 to 1840, that "it is an egotistical matter from beginning to end.   It is to prove that I did not act *dishonestly.*" [1]   However, in spite of his efforts to be objective, such a reader as Herbert Vaughan, the future cardinal, "read it with a mixture of pain and pleasure," the "egotism" of the book "disgusting" him, the "satire and contempt appealing to one's bad nature, unfortunately." [2]   Even as late as 1890 the Cambridge divinity scholar, F. J. A. Hort, regarded the Newman-Kingsley controversy as "a tragic and shameful business," and the *Apologia* as so "horribly unchristian" as to be "sickening to read." [3]   On this severe judgment, Dean Inge, who has ever been the foe of Catholicism, remarks nevertheless that "unchristian" as New-man's methods may have been, "it is demanding too much of human nature to expect a master of fence, when wantonly at-tacked with a bludgeon, to abstain from the pleasure of pricking his adversary scientifically in the tender parts of his body." [4] More representative of criticism hostile to the *Apologia* is that of Principal Fairbairn, who in 1896 recorded his opinion of it as a cunning idealization of the facts.   He dismisses it as of "the least historical worth," as "neither a biography nor an autobiog-raphy, but simply what it professes to be, a dialectical apology for a life by the man who lived it"; it is "only a history idealized . . . under the transfiguring light of a superlative ratiocinative genius, whose imagination made his successive experiences [seem] like steps in [a] logical process." [5]   Finally, we may note an-other typical charge against the Newman of the *Apologia*.   In 1933 the late Anglican Bishop E. A. Knox, while conceding the book to "rank for all time among the greatest of the world's auto-biographies," nevertheless condemns it as "the work of one of the most self-centred of men . . . written in a passion of self-admiration." [6]   This condemnation, as we shall see, will hardly stand the test of an examination of the *Apologia*.   Newman's *autocentrism* — to use Brémond's term — was certainly not "self-admiration."   However, all of these judgments by critics who were repelled or unsatisfied by Newman's great autobiography may serve as a cross section of a certain persisting opinion current in Newman criticism, namely, that Newman is simply an intel-lectually seductive, self-deluded, self-centered, and dangerously unscrupulous user of the English language.   We shall have oc-casion in a later chapter to consider the whole question of New-man's integrity.   Here we may observe that it is indeed an im-portant question in the study of the nature and literary method of the *Apologia*.

A much more cogent, though still inadequate, criticism is that of Frank Leslie Cross, who reminds us that Newman's conversion to Roman Catholicism — which, after all, is the main theme of the *Apologia* — may have had at least one of three types of nonphysical motivation: intellectual convictions, moral considerations, or "psychological" factors.   More than one of these causes may have operated conjointly, but Cross is convinced that the reasons leading to Newman's conversion were primarily "psychological."   The *Apologia*, says Cross, is no doubt the greatest autobiography in the English language, but to judge it so is not also to pronounce any opinion as to its historical accuracy.   Indeed, according to this critic, the *Apologia*, which appears to set forth "a series of theological discoveries" and intellectual considerations, is in reality "a distinctly misleading account of the chief motives," which were in fact profoundly emotional.   So far as *doctrinal* considerations played their part, the *Apologia* is highly accurate; but the psychological factors were so deep and subtle, so unsusceptible to explanation in words, that Newman's account, consciously or unconsciously, is "fundamentally misleading in its whole staging of the story." [7]   This is an excessively severe judgment, as we shall later see; but it merits further attention before we abandon it.

According to Cross, not until "the period before and round about 1841" were Newman's theological considerations other than academic.   The weight which he attaches in the *Apologia* to many of the events and doctrinal problems prior to Tract XC was probably much less at the time than he later ascribed to it in his autobiography.   Before 1839 Newman was concerned with the problem of Anglican "Catholicity" — i.e. with the "note of Unity" — and with Antiquity as a criterion by which to judge the truth of a doctrine; and in neither of these matters was he fundamentally disturbed.   More serious, says Cross, was his discernment of an adumbration of Anglican weaknesses in ancient heresies; thus, as we have noted, he studied the Monophysite, the Donatist, and the Arian schisms.   Yet here again, in Cross' opinion, Newman probably overstates, in the *Apologia*, their historical importance in his actual thinking in the 1830's.   They had, at the time, very little to do with Newman's progress toward the Roman Church.   We should observe further, with Cross, that Newman, like most Englishmen in the early nineteenth century, "had very little acquaintance, and practically no sympathy, with the specific forms of Roman Catholic devotion until after he had entered the Roman Catholic Church." [8] His knowledge of Roman Catholic "piety" was derived from popular Evangelical commentaries on the Book of Daniel and on the Apocalypse; he probably knew very little of the great Counter Reformation writers on mystical and pietistic theology. His own great problem was simply one of *authority*. And he had solved the problem for himself, fairly well, in the brilliant *Lectures on the Prophetical Office of the Church* (1837). So long as no other authority challenged the authority of his "Pope," the Bishop of Oxford, his attacks on Dissent and on Rome were fundamentally academic; his life in the Church of England could proceed happily and calmly. But with the publication of Tract XC a great change occurred: Newman discovered that his Church was disowning him. The blow to his sensitive feelings, and to his confidence in Anglican "authority," was too much. By nature what Cross calls — using a Nietzschian term — a man of *ressentiment*, one who is temperamentally given to a "sense of injury," Newman was unable openly to seek a victory over his calumniators. Seeing ten years of his labors apparently lost on his Church, he withdrew to Littlemore, and sought to win a victory in another field. According to Cross, this aspect of Newman's conversion — the *psychological* effect on him of the action of his Church in 1841 — is given too little weight in the *Apologia*, and to this extent his account is misleading.

It is not hard to find reasons for Newman's virtual silence on his emotional reaction to the affair of Tract XC. For one thing, as is well known, Newman was temperamentally reserved and shy, aristocratic and aloof. In the *Apologia* he is attempting to appeal to the reader's mind and sense of justice, not to his sympathies and emotions. There can be no Rousseauistic confessions from a man like Newman; he can never tell us, for example, the mental and emotional stages through which he passed to the conviction that he should lead the celibate life. He is not only too reticent and fastidious, he is also too "Victorian." Moreover, even when dealing with a crisis so acute and passionate as that which occurred between 1843 and 1845, Newman naturally falls into his characteristic habit of *intellectual* analysis and persuasion. Thus he is incapable of "staging" the drama of his conversion so that all aspects of it will emerge in due perspective; his story is distinctly personal, even in its predominantly intellectual dress. Cross' contention that the *Apologia* is essentially a rationalization of a psychological experience is therefore only partially valid. If we turn back to Newman's letters of 1843–45, we find that intellectual and moral motives *did* play their part in propelling him toward the Roman Church.   Writing to Manning in 1843, he says that "that wretched Jerusalem Bishoprick affair, no personal [or psychological] matter, revived my alarms."   Ecclesiastical and quasi-ecclesiastical acts had been "keen stimulants" to convictions.[9]   Moreover, other letters, notably those published in 1933 by Gordon Huntington Harper, show that there is far more explicit emotion in the *Apologia* than in his correspondence with William Froude.   Clearly the forces at work in him were confusing; but his letters to William Froude "proceeded along [a] strictly intellectual line . . . slighting the emotional causes which had influenced him."   Indeed, says Harper, "it is the portrayal of these subtle emotional causes at work within him that gives to the *Apologia* [its] poignancy and appeal." [10]   Thus a careful reading of Newman's correspondence between 1841 and 1845 will do much to correct the impression that Newman's account of his change of opinions in the *Apologia* is largely a rationalization of psychological and emotional factors in his conversion to Rome.

Many readers, having heard that this book is a masterpiece of autobiography, are deeply disappointed when they open its pages. It is only later that any reader recognizes in it a remarkable instance of sheer power of style overcoming none too promising materials.   The autobiographical portions are seldom personal in the "human-interest" sense of the term; as we have said, we rarely see Newman the man — indeed as a physical creature he is as shadowy as the characters in *Loss and Gain* and *Callista*. Newman confines himself strictly to the matter in hand, namely, the account of his changes in religious opinions, of the differences between the Anglican and Roman Churches, of doctrines and heresies and of now forgotten or half-forgotten personalities. Much time has passed since some of the incidents, teachings, and personalities of the Tractarian Movement could evoke a vivid response in the reader. Even Newman's very practical purposes do not encourage much general reflection. His conversion itself was so gradual, so almost bookish, that its narration cannot put it in a class with some of the other great conversions, such as St. Augustine's. Yet the *Apologia* holds its place among the greatest autobiographies by virtue of its stylistic charm, its remarkable absence of pose (not common to religious or other autobiographies), its simple dignity as it reveals the intimate self of a very sensitive and reserved man. As the narrative proceeds, its style and method vary with the subject and the mood. Whether in plain narration, or in close reasoning, or in portrayal of mental states, the style is ever under complete control and yields absolutely to the demands made upon it. It is by turns persuasive, scornful, pathetic, indignant, pleading, conversational, and always deceptively simple. As one follows this amazingly fetching style, one agrees with Hutton that "Kingsley never made a greater mistake than when he discerned any tortuousness of mind in Dr. Newman." [11] Not "tortuousness," but subtlety, the utmost refinement of meaning and connotation — these are the marks of Newman's method. To Kingsley as to most readers, to almost all Protestants, Newman seemed unnecessarily, even suspiciously, complex and indirect in his mode of getting at truth in religious matters. But for Newman there was never any simple or easily applied test of such truth, no rough and ready process by which eager and impatient minds might cut their way to it. More important for Newman, in any case, was the feeling that he "ought" to believe. And his first practical conception of what he "ought" to believe was anything inculcated by Scripture; next, anything inculcated by the *catena* of Anglican divines; and, finally, whatever the voice of the Roman Catholic Church imposed upon him. [12] With these facts in mind, one may read the *Apologia* without suspicion, without any perplexity as to motives, integrity, or objectives.

CHAPTER XIII

INSIGHT AND ELOQUENCE: THE SERMONS

i. *The Victorian Sermon*

The Victorian age, which loved oratory, from platform and pulpit alike, produced great preachers and great sermons. We of a later time find considerable difficulty in realizing with what interest the Victorians listened to the sermons of their favorite preacher, and read them when they were eventually published in a handsome and sober volume. "No right-minded Victorian," writes Amy Cruse, "thought his Sunday properly spent unless he heard at least one sermon." [1] And no literate Victorian failed to read a sermon in times of bereavement, or in other specially serious hours. Mary Gladstone followed her father in her fondness for sermon reading, "gloating," as she said, over one preached by Canon Scott-Holland at Winchester on a Good Friday. But sermons were read on other than solemn occasions. Walter Bagehot not only took a volume of sermons with him on his honeymoon, but read a discourse by F. D. Maurice aloud to his bride. Lord and Lady Cavendish read sermons together both before and after their marriage, enjoying, for example, "two fine sermons on *The Subjection of the Creature to Vanity*." [2] Hearing and reading sermons — preferably long ones — was regarded not merely as a duty but as a keen intellectual pleasure and a spiritual and emotional discipline. To be sure, there were low-grade sermons not much different in their effect on readers from that of a third-rate novel; some of these George Eliot attacked in her withering article on Dr. Cumming. But in an age rich in preachers and in pulpit eloquence, the output of excellent published sermons was enormous. Sermons held the place in the public's interest that is now held by fiction.

So great was the market for sermons that successful preachers published their sermons almost as a matter of course. Even

those preachers who were in no sense great, but who had won a
certain amount of popularity with their own congregations and
could expect at least a moderate sale, were eager to see their discourses in print. Amy Cruse, who has made a study of the Victorians and their books, observes that "a congregation could offer
no higher compliment to its pastor than a request that his sermon
or sermons be published." [3] Thus the Reverend John Jenkyns
of Mrs. Gaskell's *Cranford* publishes, "by request," the sermon
which he preached before "My Lord Judge" at the assize, and
finds it necessary to go up to London to see it through the press;
afterwards his portrait is painted, with his hand upon a copy of
the work that has brought him local fame. For even a distinguished preacher, to achieve a published volume of sermons was
the fulfillment of a soaring ambition. This is noteworthy in that
Newman seems to have felt a great reluctance "against divulging
to the world at large what had passed between him and his congregations." [4] But, as we have observed on several occasions,
Newman was unusual in his deep aristocratic reticence.

Of all the eloquent preachers of Newman's day, only six are
regarded by one authority as reaching true greatness: Newman
himself, then Frederick William Robertson of Brighton, Canon
Liddon of St. Paul's, Charles Haddon Spurgeon of Exeter Hall
and the Metropolitan Tabernacle, William Connor Magee (successively Bishop of Peterborough and Archbishop of York), and
William Boyd Carpenter, Bishop of Ripon and Canon of Westminster.[5] To these may be added Newman's friend, Dean
R. W. Church of St. Paul's, Dean Stanley of Westminster, Frederick D. Maurice of Lincoln's Inn Chapel, Charles Kingsley of
Eversley, Thomas Arnold of Rugby, Thomas Binney of the
Weigh House Chapel, and, in the closing years of the era, Canon
Scott-Holland and Bishop Charles Gore. The power and eloquence of these men have long been matters of historical record.
Yet of the six greatest, Newman alone is read widely today as a
master of sermon eloquence. Fashions in pulpit oratory have
greatly changed since the heyday of Victorianism, and since much
of preaching is personality, the Victorian master-preachers must
be accepted purely on the evidence of their contemporaries, so
little do their printed discourses testify to their skill. Spurgeon,

Magee, and Boyd Carpenter were the greatest orators among the top-ranking six, and had to be heard rather than read for their merits to be appreciated. Robertson of Brighton, like Newman, is still read, though certainly not so widely nor with such devotion.

Many of Newman's admirers had the Victorian habit of listening to clergymen of almost every denomination and every shade of opinion — the Low Church Bishop Wilberforce, the Broad Church Dean Stanley, the Free Church Dr. Guthrie, the Presbyterian Dr. Oswald Dykes, Dr. Caird of the Established Church of Scotland, Père Hyacinthe of the Church of Rome. Victorian sermons show, from all reliable accounts, a great variety in subject and method. It was a time of tumultuous debate and soul searching. One might follow, with Sara Coleridge, Dr. Pusey's "rhapsody describing with infinite repetition the wickedness of sin," with "not one of the graces of oratory"; or listen to Binney's thunderous denunciations of the Church of England; or hear James Martineau expound, with great learning, logic, and piety, the doctrines of Unitarianism; or listen, with Alfred Ainger, to Maurice, who, with the voice, the look, and the inspiration of a prophet, preached eloquently but sometimes very hazily about the subtleties of the spiritual life; or shudder at the awe-inspiring Evangelical visions of the great Spurgeon; or be enchanted by the sweet and unassuming manner of Dean Church; or be moved by the hearty and masculine Christianity of Mr. Kingsley. In every case, personality had a great deal to do with the preacher's effectiveness. Gestures and voice and even clothing were a part of his success, or lack of it. Of Boyd Carpenter, Matthew Arnold once wrote, after hearing him in a country church: "There got up into the pulpit a small man in a shabby Bishop's attire, and I thought I wonder what 's coming now? and I never heard anything like what I heard then, and I listened as I had never listened to anything before in my life." [6] The subject matter of Victorian sermons in general was far broader than a reading of Newman's would indicate: besides the conventional analysis of a text or the discussion of a vice or virtue, there were sermons or discourses on economic and social problems (even the erudite and cloistered Dr. Pusey preached on these subjects), on political principles, on sectarian differences, and, in the 'sixties and 'seventies, on the conflict of religion and science.

Newman's sermons, as we shall see, were intentionally confined to certain fields; yet they were popular with Victorians of the most diverse convictions. Thackeray and Edward Fitzgerald both declared them to be the best that ever were written; Dean Stanley ranked the *Parochial and Plain Sermons* as belonging "not to provincial dogma, but to the literature of all time"; Macaulay, the Whig Liberal, knew by heart Newman's great Roman Catholic sermon "The Second Spring," and George Eliot, the positivist, could not quote it without tears. Frederick Robertson, who later won fame for pulpit eloquence, carefully studied Newman's early sermons when he came up to Brasenose College, Oxford, in 1837; and they made so deep an impression on him that he continued to read them with pleasure and profit until the day of his death. The novelist Mrs. Gaskell, wife of a Unitarian minister, wrote in 1842 that she was "taking a course of Newman's sermons"; and Sara Coleridge, daughter of the poet, read them, and, in spite of her High Church sympathies, criticized their "unfair reasonings," and their "notions that appear . . . superstitious." [7] We have already noted what a deep impression Newman's sermons left on such widely differing men as James Anthony Froude, Matthew Arnold, Dean Church, Benjamin Jowett, and Arthur Hugh Clough.* What was the secret of Newman's power? What qualities of method and appeal still linger in his published sermons which preserve them from the oblivion that has overtaken the eloquence of so many of his great contemporaries?

ii. *Newman and the Art of the Sermon*

From what has been said earlier, it is clear that Newman's fame as a preacher does not rest on his ability as an orator. In pulpit eloquence he was never the equal of Spurgeon or Robertson. For the most powerful and finished eloquence, we must in fact turn to France, to Bossuet, Massillon, Bourdaloue, Lacordaire.[1] These great masters did not, like Newman, glide silently into their pulpits, and read from a manuscript in a scarcely audi-

* See Chap. II, ii, 33.

ble voice. Newman's manner in the pulpit has been described by a contemporary writer in the *Dublin Review*:

"Action in the common sense of the word there was none.   Through many of [the sermons] the preacher never moved anything but his head.   His hands were literally not seen from the beginning to the end.   The sermon began in a calm musical voice, the key slightly rising as it went on; by-and-bye the preacher warmed with his subject, it seemed as if his very soul and body glowed with suppressed emotion.   There were times when, in the midst of the most thrilling passages, he would pause, without dropping his voice, for a moment which seemed long, before he uttered with gathering force and solemnity a few weighty words." [2]

The secret of Newman's pulpit appeal lay elsewhere than in gesture, or majestic voice, or dramatic emotion.   We find that secret indicated in large part in his discourse on "University Preaching," published in *The Idea of a University*.   There we learn that the preacher's aim is twofold: (i) "the ministering of some definite spiritual good to those who hear him," and (ii) an intense "earnestness in pursuing it." [3]   Newman dismisses "talent, logic, learning, words, manner, voice, action" as of little importance when not serving some "definiteness of object," the "conveying to others some spiritual benefit." [4]   It was Newman's earnestness and his concentration on a single message which, even when his hands remained at his sides, caused his "very soul and body [to glow] with suppressed emotion," and gave to his voice the thrill and force noted by the writer in the *Dublin Review*.   Furthermore, Newman declares in his discourse that the wise preacher will "select some distinct fact or scene, some passage in history, some truth, simple or profound, some doctrine, some principle, or some sentiment," and bring it home to others as forcefully as he has already brought it home to himself.[5]   Here is one source of the "concretenesss" and singleness of effect in Newman's sermons and discourses.   Here is the reason also, to some extent, for the absence of the "flowers of oratory, fine figures, [and] tuneful periods" in most of them.

Though Newman's address on "University Preaching" is concerned with the proper methods of reaching undergraduates, he realizes that, on the whole, "what is suitable for one audience is suitable for another; all hearers are children of Adam." Though the university preacher will concentrate, he believes, on the problems of the young, on the dangers threatening their virtue and their faith, nevertheless certain great subjects are, in his opinion, valuable above all others, as being comprehensive and permanent. Moreover, adds Newman, special dangers or probable deficiencies or the needs of his hearers should be approached *covertly*, "not showing on the surface of his discourse what he is aiming at":

"I see no advantage in a preacher professing to treat of infidelity, orthodoxy, or virtue, or the pride of reason, or riot, or sensual indulgence. To say nothing else, common-places are but blunt weapons; whereas it is particular topics that penetrate and reach their mark. Such subjects are, for instance, the improvement of time, avoiding the occasions of sin, frequenting the Sacraments, divine warnings . . . and any others, which may touch the heart and conscience, or may suggest trains of thought to the intellect, without proclaiming the main reason why they have been chosen." [6]

In this passage, Newman is consciously or unconsciously revealing one of the sources of his pulpit irony — his habit of appearing to be considering some general subject and at the same time of being about to point to an individual hearer and saying "Thou art the man for whom these words are intended." This feature of Newman's sermons has been noted by more than one listener. It kept the congregation in a nerve-tingling suspense, and sent it inward upon itself in a passion of self-exploration, in a feverish sense of shame. Moreover, Newman's careful avoidance of commonplaces not only put sharper weapons in his hands; it brightened his sentences, and in the end gave to his printed pages the indestructibility of prose which has not rested on the subjects and emotions of a season or a decade. Finally, the "covert" approach to his audience was partly responsible for the appearance of reserve, indirection, subtlety, and refinement in his discourses. And it gave the twofold impression that Newman was extremely impersonal yet uncannily aware of one's deepest personal secrets.

Newman concludes his address by advising the preacher to prepare his sermon in writing (a few persons like Pitt may converse like a book, he says; "others must be content to write and read their writing"), and by summing up the essence of pulpit effectiveness:

"Definiteness is the life of preaching. A definite hearer, not the whole world; a definite topic, not the whole evangelical tradition; and, in like manner, a definite speaker. Nothing that is anonymous will preach; nothing that is dead and gone; nothing even which is of yesterday, however religious in itself and useful. Thought and word are one in the Eternal Logos, and must not be separate in those who are His shadows on earth. They must issue fresh and fresh, as from the preacher's mouth, so from his breast, if they are to be 'spirit and life' to the hearts of his hearers." [7]

Turning to Newman's sermons themselves we find them distinguished for their psychological insight, their imagination, and their literary power. More specifically they are marked by a delicate realism which adjusts them to their particular audience. For example, note how tactfully, with what understanding, he enters into the minds of his youthful audience in the sermon on "Religion a Weariness to the Natural Man," preached at Oxford on July 27, 1828:

" 'Religion is a weariness.' . . . Alas! my brethren, is it not so? Is not religion associated in your minds with gloom . . . ? The very terms 'religion,' 'devotion,' 'piety,' 'conscientiousness,' 'mortification,' and the like you find to be inexpressibly dull and cheerless; you cannot find fault with them, indeed you would if you could; and whenever the words are explained in particulars and realized, then you do find occasion for exception and objection. But though you cannot deny the claims of religion used as a vague and general term, yet how irksome, cold, uninteresting, uninviting does it at best appear to you! how severe its voice! how forbidding its aspect! With what animation, on the contrary, do you enter into the mere pursuits of time and the world! What bright anticipations of joy and happiness flit before your eyes! How you are struck and dazzled at the view of the prizes of this life, as they are called! How you admire the elegancies of art, the brilliance of wealth, or the force of intellect! According to your opportunities, you mix in the world, you meet and converse with persons of various conditions and pursuits, and are engaged in the numberless occurrences of daily life. You are full of news; you know what this or that person is doing, and what has befallen him; what has not happened, which was near happening, what may happen. You are full of ideas and feelings upon all that goes on around you. But from some cause or other religion has no part, no sensible influence, in your judgment of men and things. It is out of your way. Perhaps you have your pleasure parties; you readily take your share in them time after time; you pass continuous hours in society where you know that it is quite impossible even to mention the name of religion. Your heart is in scenes and places where conversation on serious subjects is strictly forbidden by the rules of the world's propriety." [8]

This clear and emphatic recognition of his hearer's difficulties gave Newman's sermons much of their singular power. But this realism extended beyond the understanding of other men's minds; it reached into the supersensible. Most critics of Newman agree that his power of *realizing* for others the actuality of the spiritual world was the most prominent feature of his sermons. In such sermons as "The Greatness and Littleness of Human Life" and "The Invisible World," he is able to make the "glories of nature, the sun, moon, and stars, and the richness and the beauty of the earth" appear as the mere types and figures witnessing to the invisible things of God. [9]

In his later sermons, especially in *Discourses to Mixed Congregations*, this exercise of his imagination manifests itself in some of the most remarkable passages in the literature of sermons, as in the sixteenth sermon on "The Mental Sufferings of Our Lord in His Passion," a sermon "before which," it has been said, "even the richness and wealth of Jeremy Taylor's imagination looks poor in comparison." [10] With extraordinary detail Newman realizes and conceives the various and collective sins and miseries of all humanity as pouring upon Christ in Gethsemane and being so completely absorbed as to be all but His own:

"There, then, in that most awful hour, knelt the Savior of the world, putting off the defenses of His divinity, . . . opening His arms, baring His breast, sinless as He was, to the assault of His foe, — of a foe whose breath was a pestilence, and whose embrace was an agony. There He knelt, motionless and still, while the vile and horrible fiend clad His spirit in a robe steeped in all that is hateful and heinous in human crime, which clung close round His heart, and filled His conscience, and found its way into every sense and pore of His mind, and spread over Him a moral leprosy, till He almost felt Himself to be that which He never could be . . . Are these His lips, not uttering prayer, and praise, and holy blessings, but as if defiled with oaths, and blasphemies, and doctrines of devils? . . . And His ears, they ring with sounds of revelry and of strife; and His heart is frozen with avarice, and cruelty, and unbelief; and His very memory is laden with every sin which has been committed since the fall, in all regions of the earth, with the pride of the old giants, and the lusts of the five cities, and the obduracy of Egypt, and the ambition of Babel, and the unthankfulness and scorn of Israel. . . And adversaries such as these gather round Thee, Blessed Lord, in millions now; they come in troops more numerous than the locust or the palmer-worm, or the plagues of hail, and flies, and frogs, which were sent against Pharaoh. Of the living and of the dead and of the as yet unborn, of the lost and the saved, of Thy people and of strangers, of sinners and of Saints, all sins are there . . . It is the long history of a world, and God alone can bear the load of it. Hopes blighted, vows broken, lights quenched, warnings scorned, opportunities lost; the innocent betrayed, the young hardened, the penitent relapsing, the just over-come, the aged failing; the sophistry of misbelief, the wilfulness of passion, the obduracy of pride, the tyranny of habit, the canker of remorse, the wasting fever of care, the anguish of shame, the pining of disappointment, the sickness of despair; such cruel, such pitiable spectacles, such heartrending, revolting, detestable, maddening scenes; nay, the haggard faces, the convulsed lips, the flushed cheek, the dark brow of the willing victims of rebellion, they are all before Him now, they are upon Him and in Him. They are with Him instead of that ineffable peace which has inhabited His soul since the moment of His conception. They are upon Him; they are all but His own; He cries to His Father as if He were the criminal, not the victim; His agony takes the form of guilt and compunction. He is doing pen-ance, He is making confession, He is exercising contrition with a reality and a virtue infinitely greater than that of all saints and penitents together; for He is the One Victim for us all, the sole Satisfaction, the real Penitent, all but the real sinner." [11]

With the aid of the Fathers of the Church, who had analyzed the mystery of the Passion, and whose analysis and imaginative reconstruction of the scene in Gethsemane he had accepted, Newman is thus able, as it were, to enter into Christ's mind, to conceive with terrible vivacity and intensity, the vast human transgression, gathered out of all lands and all times, piling itself up in the spirit of Christ until He is "all but the real sinner." Never again did Newman allow his imagination to soar to such a height. Only in the sermon on "The Glories of Mary for the Sake of Her Son" did he permit himself an almost equal freedom in describing the death of the Virgin Mary. In both sermons his imaginative flight offends the Protestant's sense of history. But, judged as a feat of literary evocation, as an effort to clothe a dogma with human realism, they rank high among the world's great sermons.

United with Newman's realism is his vivid sense of the truth and the wonder of revelation. He never had the slightest difficulty in accepting as objectively real the dogmas of revealed religion. His singularly strong grasp of the reality of revelation is seen in such sermons as "The Invisible World," "Faith and Sight," "Faith and Experience," "The Mysteries of Nature and of Grace," "Christ upon the Waters." For Newman, it was not the unseen world which played tricks upon the mind; it was the world of the senses: "the world overcomes us," he says, "not merely by appealing to our reason, or by exciting our passions, but *by imposing on our imagination.*" [12] He had little respect for "the religion of the day," which tried to reduce Christianity to the dimensions of the world, to adjust it to modern knowledge, to keep the unseen a matter of morality rather than of dogma. Hence Newman's uncompromising severity and austerity:

"Christianity, considered as a moral system, is made up of two elements, beauty and severity; whenever either is indulged in to the loss or disparagement of the other, evil ensues." [13]

Newman shocked many of his Anglican listeners when, in a sermon on "The Apostolical Christian," preached in February, 1843, he declared:

"If the truth must be spoken, what are the humble monk, and the holy nun, and other regulars, as they are called, but Christians after the very pattern given us in Scripture? . . . Who but these give up home and friends, wealth and ease, good name and liberty of will, for the kingdom of heaven?" [14]

Most of Newman's sermons were preached to well-bred, cultivated, respectable congregations, whose emotions had long lain dormant, whose hearts were cold and complacent, whose minds were affected by modern tolerance and worldliness and liberalism.   It was therefore his task to remind his listeners of the austere and threatening side of Christianity.   He chose moral rather than doctrinal subjects, and treated them so skillfully that they pierced the crust of complacency and sophistication.   Avoiding generalities, he aimed the arrows of his insight at the frivolities and the self-deceptions of his hearers, and discoursed on such subjects as the "Neglect of Divine Calls and Warnings," "The Usurpations of Reason," "Secret Faults," "Unreal Words," "The Individuality of the Soul," "The Religion of the Day."

This practice partly accounts for Newman's frequent appeal to his listener's fear, a practice commented upon by numerous critics.   "A long tremor of restrained fear," says Brémond, "runs through the sermons at St. Mary's." [15]   Contrary to the practice of many Catholic preachers, Newman rarely seems able to end a sermon with an impression of peace and joy.   What Faber calls "the device of fear" was probably an inheritance from Evangelicalism which he never entirely shook off.[16]   But it was also a part of Newman's *natural* approach.   He tells us in his address on "University Preaching," that

"He who has before his mental eye the Four Last Things [Death, Judgment, Hell, and Heaven] will have the true earnestness, the horror or the rapture, of one who witnesses a conflagration, or discerns some rich and sublime prospect of natural scenery." [17]

The man who has constantly before his imagination the Four Last Things will be haunted by the idea of sin and punishment; one's very childhood will be "the hidden sowing-ground of sin." Such a man will be tempted to overstress "the dominion of the law."   Indeed, according to Whyte, who doubtless exaggerates,

"Newman's very heart of hearts never, to the day of his death, got her complete divorce, to use Paul's great word, from the dominion of the law. Newman's Maker and Law-giver and Judge was, all his days, far more self-luminous to Newman than his only Redeemer, with His sin-cleansing blood, and with His sinner-justifying righteousness. . . There is a whole shining chain of Gospel texts that Newman never touches on. . . He never preached a single sermon like John Wesley's famous St. Mary's sermon on the text, 'By grace ye are saved through faith' . . . I never take down Newman's sermons for my recovery and my comfort." [18]

Newman does not, however, like Pusey, indulge in passages describing "The End of All Things" — "this universal burning, and this awful lurid light of a world in flames, crackling, sinking, melting, amid the deluge of the everlasting fire of God." [19] But he does say to us, in "The Immortality of the Soul," and elsewhere: "we must fear and be in sorrow, before we can rejoice," "to be at ease, is to be unsafe," "you must always fear while you hope," "you are not in a safe state — if you were now to die, you would have no hope of salvation," "fearing will secure you from what you fear." [20] Yet we must do Newman the justice of observing that for him "fear" was ordinarily more a "holy awe" at the mysterious and dreadful seriousness of man's destiny, than the mere terror of the possibility of eternal damnation which Evangelicals like Spurgeon exploited with such tremendous effect. Moreover, there are sermons, such as "Keeping Fast and Festival" and "Indulgence in Religious Privileges," in which Newman enjoins the duty of Christian joy: "Gloom is no Christian temper. . . We must live in sunshine even when we sorrow." [21] "Joy in all its forms," he says, was one of the chief graces of primitive Christianity. We should add, too, that listeners like J. A. Froude came away with a feeling not of fear or dread but of compassion. Of the sermons Froude wrote:

"A tone, not of fear, but of infinite pity runs through them all, and along with it a resolution to look facts in the face, not to fly to evasive generalities about infinite mercy and benevolence. . ." [22]

Throughout all of Newman's sermons we note the union of that beauty and severity which he said were the two great features of Christianity as a moral system. But Newman's "beauty" is in itself severe — severe not only in its "passionate reserve"

which Delattre so much admired,[23] but also in its austere intellectuality. "The finer and the more fastidious your mind is,"
says Whyte, "the more you will enjoy Newman's sermons." [24]
There is no attempt to whip up one's emotions or to offer one's
mind vaguely impressive ideas. Though Newman retained to
the end something of the Evangelical's tendency to portray human weakness in grim and mournful colors, there is none of the
"religious enthusiasm," of Romaine, Milner, or Wilberforce.
Religious zeal has been transformed by the academic tradition
which shaped Newman's mind and style. Yet, despite the intellectual refinement of Newman's sermons, they are for the most
part strongly unintellectual, in the usual sense of that word.
They are the work of a man whose theory of religious knowledge
is such that he eagerly embraces every paradox as an expression
of the sovereignty of faith. He sees with joy that "religious
light is intellectual darkness." [25] For him the very "mysterious-
ness" of a doctrine serves as a touchstone to distinguish the hypocritical from the sincere disciple. Paradoxically, this attitude
toward the intellect in matters of faith leads him to the most
splendidly audacious intellectual statements of the inexpressible.
Thus he achieves remarkable effects when he discusses the Incarnation, in "The Humiliation of the Eternal Son," or Christ's
Passion, in "The Incarnate Son, a Sufferer and Sacrifice"; or
when, as in "Peace in Believing," he expounds the doctrine of the
Holy Trinity, or when, as in the remarkable sermon on "Omnipotence in Bonds," he devotes four and a half pages to a definition of God, in terms of His self-dependence.[26]

Everywhere in the sermons there are passages memorable for
their insights, dramatic contrasts, descriptive touches, exhortations. Newman's psychological insight is most strikingly seen
in his gentle but merciless delineations of certain types of men —
the respectably religious man, in "The Strictness of the Law of
Christ"; the young man drifting away from the religion of his
parents, in "Intellect, the Instrument of Religious Training";
the skeptical man, in "Faith without Sight"; the philosopher, in
"The Three Offices of Christ"; the practical worldly man, in
"Faith and the World." [27] In all these delineations there is an
icy pitilessness, a cold calm toward the individual yet an infinite

compassion over the pathos of the world, as Newman probes and explores his listeners' hidden ugliness of soul. Sometimes there is mordant irony, scorn, or hot indignation, as when he attacks complacency and indifference in his sermon on "The Religion of the Day." [28] Elsewhere in the sermons we find individual passages which stand out for their vivid or apt wording: passages, for example, on the elect as constituting the true Church, in "The Visible Church for the Sake of the Elect"; on the nature of the Church, in "The Kingdom of the Saints"; on the conflict of the Church and the World, in "Faith and Experience"; on saintliness, in "Saintliness the Standard of Christian Principle" and in "St. Paul's Characteristic Gift"; on conscience as a voice within the soul witnessing to God's existence, in the sermon on "Dispositions for Faith"; on the career of Savonarola, in "The Mission of St. Philip." [29] There are passages which anticipate certain pages in the *Apologia*, just as the passage on conscience in "Dispositions for Faith" and several of the Oxford university sermons anticipate the *Grammar of Assent*. We read, for instance, in "The Immortality of the Soul," that "To every one of us there are but two beings in the whole world, himself and God." [30] In the sermon on "The Powers of Nature," we find pages that recall to our minds the Alexandrian Platonism which Newman discusses in the first chapter of the *Apologia*. Occasionally an aphorism startles the smooth rhythm of Newman's sentences: "Everything is plain and easy to the earnest; it is only the double-minded who find difficulties"; "Nothing is more common than for men to think that because they are familiar with words, they understand the ideas they stand for"; "Health of body and mind is a great blessing, if we can bear it"; "Nature is not inanimate; its daily toil is intelligent; its works are *duties*"; "Let it be well understood that [pain] has no sanctifying influence in itself; bad men are made worse by it." [31] Thus Newman's sermons are marked by great variety in method and mood, even though he intentionally narrowed the scope of his subject matter. They are eminently readable, and often have the virtues of the essay, one volume of them being entitled *Discourses* rather than *Sermons*.

They are marked too by Newman's genius for the closing paragraph.   Sometimes it is a simple terse reminder, as in the sermon on "God's Commandments not Grievous":

"Any of you, my brethren, who will not take advantage of this considerate providence, if you will not turn to God now with a *warm* heart, you will hereafter be obliged to do so (if you do so at all) *with a cold heart*; — which is much harder.   God keep you from this!" [32]

Very often it is an exhortation or a prayer, or a tissue of Biblical quotations, or all three in skillful combination.   It is frequently couched in measured phrases, balanced or antithetical in rhythm, rising to an impressive rhetorical climax:

"After our soul's anxious travail; after the birth of the Spirit; after trial and temptation; after sorrow and pain; after daily dyings to the world; after daily risings unto holiness; at length comes that 'rest which remaineth unto the people of God.'   After the fever of life, after wearinesses and sicknesses, fightings and despondings, languor and fretfulness, struggling and succeeding; after all the changes and chances of this troubled, unhealthy state, — at length comes death, at length the White Throne of God, at length the Beatific Vision." [33]

The most famous close of all is, of course, that of the great sermon on "The Parting of Friends," which was Newman's farewell to the Anglican communion, a farewell expressed in the simplest of words, yet curiously moving in its mounting rhythms:

"O my brethren, O kind and affectionate hearts, O loving friends, should you know anyone whose lot it has been, by writing or by word of mouth, in some degree to help you thus to act; if he has ever told you what you knew about yourselves, or what you did not know; has read to you your wants or feelings, and comforted you by the very reading; has made you feel that there was a higher life than this daily one, and a brighter world than that you see; or encouraged you, or sobered you, or opened a way to the inquiring, or soothed the perplexed; if what he has said or done has ever made you take an interest in him, and feel well inclined towards him; remember such a one in time to come, though you hear him not, and pray for him, that in all things he may know God's will, and at all times be ready to fulfil it." [34]

iii. *Newman's Sermons and Discourses*

Newman's twelve volumes of sermons fall into three divisions. The first group, the *Parochial and Plain Sermons*, eight volumes, published individually between 1834 and 1843, contains sermons written or preached between January 23, 1825, and April 30, 1843.[1] They are of great value in any analysis of Newman's mind. No reader can form an adequate impression of his personality, his art, or his message, if he leaves these sermons unread. They are exquisitely simple in the literary art with which they give body to abstract argument without seeming to do so, and with which they suddenly concentrate upon some moving illustration. Readers have sometimes found their style too austere, unadorned, even bald. And at first sight it does have this appearance. But its rhetorical art is the kind which conceals itself; the very "baldness" is the studied effect of the carefully phrased and grouped sentences, preparatory to the sudden illumination which one sentence will give to all the rest, one paragraph to the argument which has gone before. The result is the more effective because it approaches so gradually and unobtrusively. This calm, coldly chaste, Anglican style was ideally suited to Newman's purposes, the *troubling* of men into religion, the uncovering of their subtle vices and hypocrisies and self-deceptions. There is nothing topical or ephemeral in these sermons; they are concerned almost entirely with ultimate matters, though never illustrating them with the sort of experiences of which he had little personal knowledge.

However, in dealing with ultimate problems, he is never merely general. Brémond has illuminatingly contrasted Newman's methods with those of Bossuet and Massillon.[2] The great French preachers chose such general subjects as "Justice," "Providence," "Almsgiving"; they next took a rapid survey of the subject to fix its divisions; then they covered this vast ground more slowly, in two or three stages. Newman, as we have already observed, takes just the opposite course: he deals with a particular subject; some of his titles, taken at random, are "Contracted Views in Religion," "The Good Part of Mary," "Chris-

tian Sympathy," "Sincerity and Hypocrisy," "The Church a
Home for the Lonely." One has only to compare the sermons
on "Providence" by Bossuet and Bourdaloue with Newman's on
"A Particular Providence as Revealed in the Gospel," to see that
Newman is not interested in the idea of Providence as a dogma
but in bringing home to his hearers the conviction that God beholds each one of them *individually*. And this leads to a very
typical and often-quoted passage which gives one the true flavor
of these Anglican sermons, so simple and concrete, so personal
and direct:

"How gracious is this revelation of God's particular providence! . . .
God beholds thee individually, whoever thou art. He 'calls thee by
thy name.' He sees thee, and understands thee, as He made thee.
He knows what is in thee, all thy peculiar feelings and thoughts. . .
He sympathizes in thy hopes and thy temptations. He interests Himself in all thy anxieties and remembrances. . . He compasses thee
round and bears thee in His arms. . . He looks tenderly upon thy
hands and thy feet; He hears thy voice, the beating of thy heart, and
thy very breathing. Thou dost not love thyself better than He loves
thee. Thou canst not shrink from pain more than he dislikes thy
bearing it. . . What a thought is this, a thought almost too great
for our faith!" [3]

In this sermon, as in the others, Newman foregoes any temptation
to set up and analyze an abstract idea, whether it be a dogma or a
human type; he prefers what is specific and experienced. Instead of the theological and metaphysical approach employed by
Bossuet or Lacordaire, he prefers the psychological: he probes
the apathy, the indecision, the perplexities of actual men and
women before him. He uses his remarkable insight into their
minds to introduce them to that spiritual world which was so intensely real to him. And through it all he skillfully manages
the endless resources of his seemingly simple style so that we
come with a start upon a sentence or a paragraph which leaps
from its quiet context, such as the following:

"What a truly wretched state is that coldness and dryness of soul, in
which so many live and die, high and low, learned and unlearned.

Many a great man, many a peasant, many a busy man, lives and dies with closed heart, with affections undeveloped, unexercised. You see the poor man, passing day after day, Sunday after Sunday, without a thought in his mind, to appearance almost like a stone. You see the educated man, full of thought, full of intelligence, full of action, but still with a stone heart, as cold and dead as regards his affections, as if he were the poor ignorant countryman. You see others, with warm affections, perhaps, for their families, with benevolent feelings towards their fellow-men, yet stopping there. . . Life passes, riches fly away, popularity is fickle, the senses decay, the world changes, friends die. One alone is constant; One alone is true to us; One alone can be true; One alone can be all things to us; One alone can supply our needs; One alone can train us up to our full perfection; One alone can give a meaning to our complex and intricate nature; One alone can give us tune and harmony; One alone can form and possess us." [4]

Or we may pause over the often-quoted passage which expresses Newman's vivid sense of the unseen:

"Whenever we look abroad, we are reminded of those most gracious and holy Beings, the servants of the Holiest, who deign to minister to the heirs of salvation. Every breath of air and ray of light and heat, every beautiful prospect, is, as it were, the skirts of their garments, the waving of the robes of those whose faces see God in heaven." [5]

The *Parochial and Plain Sermons* are marked with Newman's literal application of scriptural imagery, with the technique of fear and pity, and with his sacramental view of visible phenomena as a veil hiding the glories of the spiritual world. There are remnants of Calvinistic teaching, and the tone is generally one of mystery and awe.

The second group of sermons comprises the *Oxford University Sermons* and *Sermons on Subjects of the Day*, both volumes published in 1843. The former volume is made up of fifteen discourses delivered at various times between 1826 and 1843. Their central theme is the interrelation of faith and reason. Since they were composed primarily for a university audience, they are academic and impersonal in tone, tightly knit and closely reasoned in method.   Here we find a number of memorable type-portraits: the man of the world, the "so-called philosophical Christian," the skeptic.   Here, again, we find obvious anticipations of the *Grammar of Assent*, in such discourses as "The Usurpations of Reason," "Faith and Reason Contrasted as Habits of Mind," "The Nature of Faith in Relation to Reason," "Implicit and Explicit Reason," and "Wisdom as Contrasted with Faith and with Bigotry."   As we have noted earlier,* the final sermon gives us a preliminary sketch of the *Essay on Development*.   Less frequently observed, however, is the foreshadowing of a passage of *The Idea of a University* by five pages of the sermon on wisdom contrasted with faith and bigotry, in which Newman discusses various desirable and undesirable ways of "enlarging the mind."   The unity of the *Oxford University Sermons*, as a volume, is not one of its strong characteristics.   Besides the sermon on development, which has nothing to do with the main theme of the volume, there are sermons on Natural and Revealed Religion, on evangelical sanctity, on justice as a principle of divine governance (directed primarily at the Benthamites), on willfullness as the sin of Saul (aimed largely at the revolutionary spirit of the early 1830's), and on "Human Responsibility as Independent of Circumstances" (aimed at the fatalistic environmentalism of the age).

Readers who find the *Grammar of Assent* intolerably technical and laborious will discover, in sermons IV and X–XIV, an easy introduction to the heart of Newman's theory.   They will be protected from misunderstanding his final position regarding assent by the Preface and the footnotes which he introduced into the third edition.   They will find abundant aphorisms throughout the well-conducted argument — "It is as absurd to argue men, as to torture them, into believing," "All men have a reason, but not all men can give a reason," "Reason can but ascertain the profound difficulties of our condition, it cannot remove them." [6] And at the end of the tenth sermon the reader will find a passage which possibly suggested the image of "ignorant armies clashing by night" in Matthew Arnold's "Dover Beach":

* See Chap. III, iv, p. 64.

"Controversy, at least in this age, does not lie between the hosts of heaven, Michael and his Angels on the one side, and the powers of evil on the other; but it is *a sort of night battle*, where each fights for himself, and friend and foe stand together. When men understand each other's meaning, they see, for the most part, that controversy is either superfluous or hopeless." [7]

In the final sermon there occurs Newman's famous illustration that human nature contains within itself elements capable of expansion into infinite and eternal meanings. If God's nature is infinite, it is sometimes asked, how can a finite creature like man gain any but a hopelessly inadequate notion of Him? Newman answers by pointing to the marvels of music, with its limited number of notes:

"There are seven notes in the scale; make them fourteen, yet what a slender outfit for so vast an enterprise! What science brings so much out of so little? Out of what poor elements does some great master in it create his new world! Shall we say that all this exuberant inventiveness is a mere ingenuity or trick of art, like some game or fashion of the day, without reality, without meaning? We may do so, and then perhaps we shall also account the science of theology to be a matter of words; yet, as there is a divinity in the theology of the Church which those who feel cannot communicate, so is there also in the wonderful creation of sublimity and beauty of which I am speaking. To many men the very names which the science employs are utterly incomprehensible. To speak of an 'idea' or a 'subject' seems to be fanciful or trifling, and of the views which it opens upon us to be childish extravagance; yet is it possible that that inexhaustible evolution and disposition of notes, so rich yet so simple, so intricate and yet so regulated, so various yet so majestic, should be a mere sound which is gone and perishes? Can it be that those mysterious stirrings of heart and keen emotions and strange yearnings after we know not what and awful impressions from we know not whence, should be wrought in us by what is unsubstantial and comes and goes and begins and ends in itself? It is not so; it cannot be. No! they have escaped from some higher sphere: they are the voice of angels or the magnificat of saints, or the living laws of divine governance or the divine attributes: something are they besides themselves which we cannot compass, which we cannot utter; though mortal man, and he perhaps not otherwise distinguished above his fellows, has the gift of eliciting them." [8]

The last of Newman's Anglican sermons were published under the title of *Sermons on Subjects of the Day* (1843). Some of the twenty-six which make up the volume were preached as early as 1831, 1837, and 1838; all but five, however, were either written or preached between 1840 and Newman's final farewell, "The Parting of Friends," in September, 1843. Though their style retains some of the chaste simplicity of the earlier sermons, these adopt a rich texture of Biblical phrase, a variety of rhythm, parallelisms, and cumulative effects which later developed into the profuse and passionate eloquence of the *Discourses to Mixed Congregations*. Many of the sermons were preached when Newman was on his "Anglican deathbed," in retirement at Littlemore. They reflect an agony of indecision. To read them, says Barry, "is to overhear the soliloquy in which every possible reason is advanced against joining the Church of Rome that could yet afford ground to one whose ideals were monastic, antiquarian, but above all, unworldly." [9] A kind of pathos, says Hutton, "runs like a silver thread through the whole series of Oxford sermons." [10] Newman was now painfully uncomfortable under the conditions of the Anglican Church, not only because he wanted the Church freed from all political fetters, but also because he resented the sleek complacency, the easy worldliness, the shallow piety, to which the alliance with the state had brought the Anglican clergy. For him, there could be no true church except where the ecclesiastical motive power was in the hands of men who had renounced the comforts and joys of the world for the sake of that "other world," *i.e.* in the hands of a self-denying clergy, under the moral influence of the great monastic orders. Most of these sermons show Newman's "severity" now passing into a radical otherworldliness, a frank asceticism, which shows that he is already a convert at heart to the Church of Rome. With the same skill as on other occasions, he traces the thoughts of those who take a shallowly optimistic view of the evils of the world:

"The world promises that, if we trust it, we cannot go wrong. Why? because it is so many — there are so many men in it; they must be right. This is what it seems boldly to say, — 'God cannot punish so many.' So it is, we know, in human law. . . . They think that this world is too great an evil for God to punish; or rather that therefore it is not an evil, because it is a great one. They cannot compass the idea that God should allow so great an evil to exist, as the world would be, if it is evil; and therefore, since He does allow it, it is not an evil." [11]

No passage in Newman better illustrates his unfailing and relentless power to expose inconsistent thinking.

Throughout the volume, Newman stresses the warfare between faith and the world, and between the Church and the world; he develops his mystical interpretation of Old Testament figures — Joshua and Elisha are types of Christ, the Christian Church is a continuation of the Jewish; he also develops his sense of Christianity as a supernatural order realized both in the individual and in the corporate realm of a divine society — three sermons especially show this growing institutionalism in Newman's thought, "The Christian Church as an Imperial Power," "Sanctity the Token of the Christian Empire," and "Condition of the Members of the Christian Empire." [12] As he relentlessly pursues his thought of the Christian empire, he finally sets before his hearers an image of an institution which can be nothing else than the Roman Church —

"a universal empire without earthly arms; temporal pretensions without temporal sanctions; a claim to rule without the power to enforce; a continual tendency to acquire with a continual exposure to be dispossessed; greatness of mind with weakness of body." [13]

This empire will inevitably be persecuted (persecution is a token of the Church), yet it will claim a right to rule, direct, rebuke, exhort, denounce, condemn. No one in Newman's congregation thought he was describing the Anglican Church; all knew that he was envisaging an ideal, one which had found its historical approximation in that communion toward which he was tending. All knew, too, his meaning when he described the ideal

Christian as being "apostolical," in a sermon which must have sounded very strange to secular-minded Anglicans.

In this volume occurs the famous sermon on "Wisdom and Innocence," which so painfully impressed Charles Kingsley. Christ's followers, says Newman, were enjoined to be "wise as serpents and harmless as doves"; they were to be God's sheep, but without the witlessness of sheep; they were to be prudent and wary "in the midst of wolves," injuring no one, yet not blurting out what might merely irritate the world without succeeding in teaching it. Newman's sermon might never have been pounced on by Kingsley if he had confessed that some churchmen have mingled a good deal too much wisdom of the serpent with too little of the harmlessness of the dove. However, the sermon as a whole leaves no impression of guile or duplicity. In one of his best closing paragraphs, Newman says:

"May He, as of old, choose 'the foolish things of the world to confound the wise, and the weak things of the world to confound the things which are mighty'! May He support us all the day long, till the shades lengthen, and the evening comes, and the busy world is hushed, and the fever of life is over, and our work is done! Then in His mercy may He give us a safe lodging, and a holy rest, and peace at the last!"

But the great sermon, in some ways the very greatest of Newman's, is the final one. In preaching "The Parting of Friends," Newman speaks not merely as a preacher but as a man; he takes his farewell of his parish and of his friends; he chooses the same text he had used on preaching his first sermon nineteen years before: "Man goeth forth to his work and to his labor until the evening" (Psalm civ: 23). The sermon is a tissue of Biblical diction and imagery; hardly a sentence is without its paraphrase or quotation. One result is that Newman is able to speak personally yet without embarrassment; the borrowed imagery at once protects him and intensifies the effect of his words on his congregation, which, by the end, is in tears. With simple eloquence he parallels Christ's parting from His disciples "at a feast," with his own farewell over the communion table in his chapel at Littlemore. Carrying the thought through the Old and New Testaments, he shows how similar partings took place in the lives of Jacob, Ishmael, Naomi, David, and St. Paul. By the time he reaches his closing paragraphs, he has built up a wonderfully rich texture of allusion, quotation, association, and symbol. His congregation, whose minds are already filled with Biblical image and thought, then hears him cry: "O Jerusalem, Jerusalem, which killest the prophets!" If any of them doubt the allusion, they are quickly enlightened when Newman suddenly follows with words that are now as famous, for their pathos and eloquence, as any he ever wrote:

"O mother of saints! O school of the wise! O nurse of the heroic! of whom went forth, in whom have dwelt, memorable names of old, to spread the truth abroad, or to cherish and illustrate it at home! . . . O virgin of Israel! wherefore dost thou now sit on the ground and keep silent. . . O my mother, whence is this unto thee, that thou hast good things poured upon thee and canst not keep them, and bearest children, yet darest not own them? why has thou not the skill to use their services, nor the heart to rejoice in their love? how is it that whatever is generous in purpose, and tender or deep in devotion, thy flower and thy promise, falls from thy bosom and finds no home within thine arms? Who hath put this note upon thee, to have 'a miscarrying womb, and dry breasts,' to be strange to thine own flesh, and thine eye cruel towards thy little ones?" [14]

Only Newman could have written a sermon like this; only he, with his passionate reticence, could have so brilliantly availed himself of the shelter of scriptural phrase, so that his very rebuking of his Church could take on the mournful beauty of a religious elegy.

The *Oxford University Sermons* and the *Sermons on Subjects of the Day* may be regarded as transitional in character. Some of them are as purely Anglican as any in the *Parochial and Plain Sermons*; others are so Catholic that they might have been delivered in the Roman Church. Whoever wishes to study the growth of Newman's ideas should read chronologically the ten volumes of sermons preached during his Anglican period. There Newman will be found testing the validity and the resisting power of every new argument or theory. From year to year he moves farther and farther away from rationalistic Protestantism; his conception of religion becomes more and more intense, dogmatic, ascetic, mystical, and institutional; he lays more and more stress, as we have said, on the opposition between the world and the Church, between the natural and the supernatural, between the City of God and the city of men.

Following the two transitional volumes, Newman's third and last group of sermons appears in *Discourses to Mixed Congregations* (1849) and *Sermons Preached on Various Occasions* (1857). Newman was never very fortunate in the titles of his books; only in the titles of his sermons does he show much imagination. No one would suspect from the backstrip of the volume of 1849 that the contents were rich in eloquence and thought. These sermons were preached during the first years of Newman's Catholic ministry, when he felt the enthusiasm of the convert and the freedom of the man who has found his proper sphere of action. He is no longer the perplexed Anglican; he is now the disciple of St. Philip Neri. Released from conflicting emotions, and from the self-imposed task of reconciling the apparently irreconcilable, he has developed a mature self-confidence and a vigor of style which bring out all the more vividly his own special powers as a preacher. His sermons now have a new character; they are passionate, boldly imaginative, colorful, at times consciously rhetorical. Possibly his recent seminary studies amid Italian surroundings account for some of this sudden change in Newman's style. He permits himself greater range in effects — sharper irony, exquisite pathos, sublimity, scorn, daring imagination (as in "The Mental Sufferings of Our Lord," which we have already examined). He is also more direct, mercilessly pursuing his psychological probings into the hearts of his listeners, as in the sermon on "Neglect of Divine Calls and Warnings." He is more unsparing than ever in his delineations of worldly life, and speaks tersely in condemnation of it:

"We are not sent into this world for nothing; we are not born at random; we are not here, that we may go to bed at night, and get up in the morning, toil for our bread, eat and drink, laugh and joke, sin when we have a mind to, and reform when we are tired of sinning, rear a family and die." [15]

In such sermons as those on the "Glories of Mary," the new convert is giving free rein to what has been called the "pious impressions," with which the Catholic Fathers supplied him as interpreting and illustrating the theology of the Church. He rivals the passion of Italian and French devotion to the Virgin Mary, and even anticipates the dogma of the Immaculate Conception of the Virgin several years before it is defined. On the other hand, in such sermons as "Nature and Grace," "Faith and Private Judgment," "Faith and Doubt," and "Purity and Love," Newman employs a less colorful rhetoric, and engages in a tightly executed feat of distinction and definition. In "Faith and Private Judgment," he sharply attacks the Protestant position; with scorn he alludes to the Protestant cast of Anglicans:

"Let them stake their eternal prospects on kings and nobles and parliaments and soldiery, let them take some mere fiction of the law, or abortion of the schools, or idol of a populace, or upstart of a crisis, or oracle of lecture-rooms, as the prophet of God." [16]

This is hardly the language of the *Parochial and Plain Sermons*. It is in fact the language to appear shortly in certain parts of the *Difficulties of Anglicans*, and later, and more devastatingly, in the *Present Position of Catholics*.

In the *Sermons Preached on Various Occasions* (1857) Newman returns somewhat to his earlier Anglican reserve. His style is no longer the passionate rhetoric of the *Discourses to Mixed Congregations*, but is the style of a man who has found his place in English Roman Catholicism. The first eight of the fifteen sermons were delivered before the Catholic University of Ireland in 1856 and 1857, during the first year of the opening of its Church. The other seven sermons were preached on such occasions as the installation of Bishop Ullathorne, the funeral of James R. Hope-Scott, the anniversary of the Birmingham Oratory. The variety in these sermons is more limited than in the two preceding volumes; yet one notes the tight intellectuality of the sermons on "Dispositions for Faith" and "Omnipotence in Bonds"; the vivid contrasts drawn between St. Philip Neri and Savonarola in "The Mission of St. Philip"; the personal quality and the gentle simplicity in the sermon on Hope Scott; the searching analysis of the pharisaical "religion of mankind." But nowhere are there the flights of religious fancy which Newman permitted himself a few years earlier. Probably the most memorable single passage in the volume is that which poetically describes the conversion of England from paganism, and the rise of the Church like a solemn pageant, before which the idols of heathendom vanished like ghosts; we find it in the sermon on "Christ upon the Waters":

"In a hundred years the work was done; the idols, the sacrifices, the mummeries of paganism flitted away and were not, and the pure doctrine and heavenly worship of the Cross were found in their stead. The fair form of Christianity rose up and grew and expanded like a beautiful pageant from north to south; it was majestic, it was solemn, it was bright, it was beautiful and pleasant, it was soothing to the griefs, it was indulgent to the hopes of man; it was at once a teaching and a worship; it had a dogma, a mystery, a ritual of its own; it had an hierarchical form. A brotherhood of holy pastors, with mitre and crosier and uplifted hand, walked forth and blessed and ruled a joyful people. The crucifix headed the procession, and simple monks were there with hearts in prayer, and sweet chants resounded, and the holy Latin tongue was heard, and boys came forth in white, swinging censers, and the fragrant cloud arose, and mass was sung, and the Saints were invoked; and day after day, and in the still night, and over the woody hills and in the quiet plains, as constantly as sun and moon and stars go forth in heaven, so regular and solemn was the stately march of blessed services on earth, high festival, and gorgeous procession, and soothing dirge, and passing bell, and the familiar evening call to prayer; till he who recollected the old pagan time, would think it all unreal that he beheld and heard, and would conclude he did but see a vision, so marvelously was heaven let down upon earth, so triumphantly were chased away the fiends of darkness to their prison below." [17]

No doubt the greatest of the sermons *On Various Occasions* is that which Newman preached at the first Synod of Oscott on the occasion of the re-establishment of the Catholic hierarchy in England. He chose for his text a verse from the Song of Songs:

"Arise, make haste, my love, my dove, my beautiful one, and come.

For the winter is now past, the rain is over and gone. The flowers have appeared in our land."

This sermon, "The Second Spring," even while it celebrates the triumph of his Church, is unaggressive and meek. Its spirit in the midst of victory is that of the martyr rather than of the conqueror; it speaks of the victory that is won through suffering, persecution, and renunciation, rather than through conquest and domination.

"The opening [of this sermon]," one critic observes, "is slow and solemn and stately, like the overture to some majestic symphony. But its splendor is not heavy or barbaric. The light shines through it, as the dawn shines through a lattice." [18]

The theme of the sermon is the law of permanence behind the transiency of earthly things; the opening lines therefore run thus:

"We have familiar experience of the order, the constancy, the perpetual renovation of the material world which surrounds us. Frail and transitory as is every part of it, restless and migratory as are its elements, never-ceasing as are its changes, still it abides."

In addition to the usual phrasal felicity, and accumulating parallelisms, we note the remarkable number of "r's" and "l's" in these lines, resulting in a fragile sort of beauty, which is sharply rounded off by the concluding element, "still it abides." The theme now quietly continues, in undulating rhythms, and without imagery, which is to appear later in the rhetorical climax:

"It is bound together by a law of permanence, it is set up in unity; and, though it is ever dying, it is ever coming to life again. Dissolution does but give birth to fresh modes of organization, and one death is the parent of a thousand lives."

Then follows a series of phrases and sentences which unite rhythm with imagery, the abstract with the concrete:

"Each hour, as it comes, is but a testimony, how fleeting, yet how secure, how certain, is the great whole. It is like an image on the waters, which is ever the same, though the waters ever flow. Change upon change — yet one change cries out to another, like the alternate

Seraphim, in praise and in glory of their Maker.   The sun sinks to rise again; the day is swallowed up in the gloom of the night, to be born out of it, as fresh as if it had never been quenched.   Spring passes into summer, and through summer and autumn into winter, only the more surely, by its own ultimate return, to triumph over that grave, towards which it resolutely hastened from its first hour." [19]

Newman now approaches the specific point which he wishes to drive home to his elated listeners, namely, that man and all his works are mortal; they die, and they have no power of renovation; but through a miracle the Church of Augustine and Anselm and St. Thomas returns after three centuries to the land of St. Cuthbert and St. Chad and St. Dunstan.   The "second spring" has come.   Great sacrifices are to be demanded, perhaps even martyrdom.   Certainly few sermons of triumph were ever more humble and graceful.   It played no small part in allaying the fears of non-Catholics that the restored hierarchy would be an arrogant or aggressive force against the Anglican Establishment and the state.   Reprinted as a brochure it won admirers from all quarters, and remains today the sermon which, more than any other, keeps *Sermons on Various Occasions* a memorable volume.

iv.   *A Note on Newman's Style*

We have already touched on the sources and the general features of Newman's prose style.   We have noted its origins in Cicero and in the English eighteenth century; we have noticed its utter transparency, its sobriety, its austerity of expression which renounces the startling metaphor, its slow and cautious advance which, though sometimes falling into prolixity, never adds one link in the chain of argument without testing its strength.   Newman's fastidious and searching mind naturally delights in analysis and subtle distinctions, hence in a prose that is always supple and sinuous.   Yet Newman's style is never merely one, but several, depending on the readers he hopes to reach.   There is the "regal" style with which he closes the essay on *Development*, the elegiac style of "The Parting of Friends," the vivid drama of "The Mental Sufferings of Our Lord," the idiomatic informality of *The Tamworth Reading Room*, the casual and sometimes careless style of "Holy Scripture and the Creed" (Tract LXXXV), the affectionate style of "The Church of the Fathers," the amazingly objective and icily self-analyzing style of the Preface to the third edition of the *Via Media*, the nostalgic memorial style of much of the *Apologia*, the ironic and humorous style of parts of *The Present Position of Catholics*. What are the qualities common to all these immensely effective styles? Certainly Newman's prose is far more than what Dr. Inge has called it, "only the Oriel manner at its best." [1]

It was first of all a remarkable union of the academic style which he had learned, to some extent, from Copleston and Whately at Oxford, and the simple and informal manner which naturally resulted from his distaste for any kind of pretentiousness or pedantry. It was the style of a man delicately observant, keenly sensitive to the ridiculous, capable of sharp wit, and convinced that learning should be culture, and the scholar a gentleman. Newman thus unites the scholarly and the urbane, ease with strength, fullness of feeling with strictness of control. Though his sentences are often extremely long, they maintain their lucid and leisurely unity by various rhetorical devices: skillful repetition of key words, paralleled phrases and clauses, illuminating antitheses, adroit subordination, and well-placed climaxes. Though they often deal in abstractions, they are always concrete in diction and illustration, moving from thing to thing. Newman always prefers the homely and telling phrase or illustration, the individual and the actual, rather than the general and theoretical. Yet his imagery is never startling, but quiet and unobtrusively persuasive; his metaphors always do greater duty in his arguments than whatever logical process he may be appearing to conduct. It is the naturalness of his imagery and metaphors which, in his sermons, succeeds in making us *realize* what we are reading or hearing him say. So quiet, and sometimes so weak, is his imagery that George Moore denied him greatness as a writer.[2] But this is refusing to judge Newman's style on its own merits. Concrete and idiomatic as his style may be, it is not, one must admit, a very colorful one. Its strength lies elsewhere. Though it abounds in alliteration, assonance, and liquid consonants, it is not marked by vivid use of nouns, verbs, or adverbs.   It never becomes "poetic prose"; there are no "purple passages," such as are found in Ruskin or Pater.   Its genius lies in its rhythm.

We have already observed, frequently, how Newman's subtle music runs elusively through the mind, its cadences carried along on skillfully articulated phrases, wide-ranging and delicately shifting, adroitly modulated in accordance with the demands of each sentence.   Under the spell of Newman's sentences, rhythmical as an incantation, the mind's defences are, at least for a moment, broken down, and the reader submits to Newman's power. The source of that power is the writer's mastery of the *phrase*. He courts the mind with the simple, undulating, sometimes self-contained phrase, as in the description of the well-educated man:

"He is at home in any society, he has common ground with every class; he knows when to speak and when to be silent; he is able to converse, he is able to listen . . ." [3]

At times Newman wields this phrase in Gibbonian antithesis:

"He has a gift which serves him in public, and supports him in retirement, without which good fortune is but vulgar, and with which failure and disappointment have a charm." [4]

What Tardivel calls the "curled" (*bouclé*) — or, better still, the reverberative — phrase is often used in Newman's most closely reasoned passages, as in the following from "Theology a Branch of Knowledge":

"I say, then, that if a University be, from the nature of the case, a place of instruction, where universal knowledge is professed, and if in a certain University, so called, the subject of Religion is excluded, one of two conclusions is inevitable — either, on the one hand, that the province of Religion is very barren of real knowledge, or, on the other hand, that in such University one special and important branch of knowledge is omitted." [5]

Here the phrases "in a certain University" and "in such University," at the beginning and toward the end of the passage, illustrate the "curling" or locking of phrases with other parts of the sentence.   In addition, we have also, in the center of the passage the phrases, "the subject of Religion" and "the province of Religion," which also "curl" and reverberate each other. A third type of phrase, the cumulative and repetitive, is generally employed in parallelism, as in the last lines of the sermon on "Wisdom and Innocence":

"Then in His mercy may He give us a safe lodging, and a holy rest, and peace at the last." [6]

This kind of phrase is obviously much less organic to the subject, much more rhetorical, than the first and the second type, which in their degree lay matter before the mind. All three, however, are used by Newman with consummate skill, sometimes in the same paragraph, the writer shifting from phrase to phrase in accordance with the requirements of the subject, the reader, and the desired effect.

One of the secrets of Newman's success as an accomplished persuader was, as we have said, his stylistic skill in adapting himself to the minds he was addressing. No two collections of his sermons, for example, have the same character. His Oxford University sermons, addressed to a highly cultivated congregation, show great restraint and refinement; they are cautious, intellectual, and exploratory. Some of the Birmingham sermons, on the other hand, are of a popular, pictorial, almost scenic type suitable for the presumably less fastidious audience of a mid-Victorian commercial town. Newman paints in broader colors and introduces dramatic effects which would have seemed out of place at St. Mary's. In the Dublin lectures, he is formal, precise, academic. Realizing that he is on controversial ground, he carefully sketches his plan for his audience, then defines and redefines his terms, anticipates objections, follows up his generalizations with convincing illustrations, turning his subject round and round, keeping a perfect poise as he moves through its intricacies. In the *Essay on Development*, Newman's method is even more severe, though here his idiomatic language, his lucidity, and his illustrations give this controversial work its peculiar attraction. Another secret of Newman's rhetorical power is the sheer drudgery which went into his best prose. He never wrote easily; in fact he seems to have hated to write, and wrote only from a sense of duty. "The composition of a volume," he says, "is like gestation and childbirth." Yet he told Bellasis: "I think best when I write." [7] Newman's agony in composition is at once the mark of the craftsman and the cause of his artistic perfection. In the process of writing, Newman sacrifices all decorative impulses; he is never mannered, pretentious, or striking. Even when his prose becomes most impressive or richly imaginative, there is no effect of discontinuity; the richer passage is but a development out of his simpler and more colloquial manner.

A third and final secret of his power lies in his breadth of handling. In working out the design of the *Essay on Development*, or the *Difficulties of Anglicans*, or the *Grammar of Assent*, he might conceivably have restricted himself to technical details, analogies, examples, and to straightforward argument. Instead, he occasionally glances up from his immediate object and engages in a searching definition, or draws up one of those general observations, from a sentence in length to several pages, which makes some of the least promising of his essays a delight to explore. Who would think that in an essay on "The Theology of the Seven Epistles of St. Ignatius" would occur the brilliant and amusing portrait of a biased man who decides to write a book upon the Fathers? Newman shows the man taking notes from Gibbon, Mosheim, Lardner; then dipping into the Fathers to "confirm his anticipations"; sketching off his characters, condemning or applauding according to his preconceptions; then, finding his time running out, drawing his work to a close and publishing, without having ever really read the Fathers. Newman's comment on this procedure is acidly reserved:

"Anyhow, *he* has gained his point; he has shown that the arguments of his adversaries admit of question, has thrown the whole subject into the gulf of controversy, and given a specimen of how the age of railroads should behave towards the age of martyrs." [8]

This breadth of handling, this direction of individual details to a larger frame of reference, leads also to those epigrammatic sentences which sparkle in every volume. Present-day readers find some of Newman's sententious utterances very relevant, as the following: "Some races are like children, and require a despot to nurse, and feed, and dress them, to give them pocket money, and take them out for airings"; "Material force is the *ultima ratio* of political society everywhere; arms alone can keep the peace." [9]   Everyone knows that "Calculation never made a hero," but not many have read that "Boys are always more or less inaccurate, and too many, or rather the majority, remain boys all their lives." [10]

Newman employed this wonderfully flexible and transparent style for one of the finest audiences any writer ever had: the educated Victorian public.   On the whole, it was hostile to his teachings, but far from indifferent to the issues which they raised. It had a deep interest in theology as well as in history and science. Newman's readers welcomed with prodigious enthusiasm his own *Apologia* and Gladstone's religious pamphlets; they read *The Origin of Species* and Lecky's *Rationalism in Europe* and innumerable three-decker novels.   They were not afraid of large volumes and many of them.

"It was the existence of this public," says one writer on Newman, "which lent to the characteristic Victorian writers a perceptible consciousness, denied to many of their successors, of being heralds of large ideas on a large stage, and it was to this consciousness that they owed at least in part the quality of impressiveness, of appeal, which distinguishes them.   In this respect, if in no other, Newman is typical of the literature of his age." [11]

V. NEWMAN AND OUR WORLD

CHAPTER XIV

NEWMAN TODAY

i. *Newman's Legacy*

Newman has been dead for more than half a century; he belongs to history.   As we look back, however, we are reminded of how unmoved he was by the great practical problems of his era.   Parliamentary reform, the repeal of the Corn Laws, the Chartist agitations, educational reform, the development of local government, the passing of the Factory Acts, the triumphant advances of democracy, industrialism, and technology — all these left him unstirred.   "Progress," he said contemptuously, "is a slang term." [1]   After the excitement of the Reform Bill years, he seems to have become completely indifferent to popular agitation.   Unlike Manning, he never championed the lower classes; [2] "there was no writer of the period," says Mr. Burgum, "who wrote with a more complete unconsciousness of their existence in state or church." [3]   Newman never patronized or flattered the common man; he made no attempt to disturb or convert him; he seems to have had no faith in popular education.   In an age of expanding liberties, he was a staunch conservative of the days of the Regency, and regarded rebellion, or revolution, as a sin against "Him who forbids us to oppose constituted authority." [4] In all this Newman shows that politically he is a Tory of the early nineteenth century and shares with many of his contemporaries their limitations of outlook.

In our own time, we naturally ask, What can so Tory a mind offer a world struggling to preserve democratic values?   The answer is simple.   Though Newman was deeply conservative, his Toryism, as Christopher Dawson has pointed out, "was not that of the defenders of vested interests, the 'Conservatives' who aroused Hurrell Froude's scorn, but that of Southey and Coleridge and the young Disraeli who were among the first to denounce the injustices of the Industrial Revolution and the new Poor Law, and the evils of the factory system." [5] Though it is true, as one critic has put it, that "his sympathies were not in the least democratic, and the whole movement represented by the Revolution of '89 filled him with horror," [6] yet Newman was practical enough to recognize in certain Victorian statesmen of liberal principles a valid leadership in reform. His practical politics accepted eagerly the reforming conservatives known as the "Peelites" — men who had followed Prime Minister Robert Peel out of the hidebound Toryism of the "hungry forties" and allied themselves in varying degrees with the Whigs, or Liberals. Of these men the most famous was Gladstone. Newman placed great confidence in this statesman, whose Anglo-Catholicism he regarded as a guarantee against the adoption of any policy injurious to religion. He continued to trust the "Peelites" even after they joined the Liberal party. In his principles, however, he remained a Conservative. Like Carlyle and Ruskin, he regretted the low estate of the old Tory party, and its fatal lack of leadership. He saw with alarm that the Liberal party was deeply tinged with theological liberalism, and was hostile to institutional Christianity, especially to its most dogmatic form, Roman Catholicism. Yet he saw in the Liberal party a hope for social justice, a force for true progress, in so far as secular efforts could bring it about. Though there is nothing in his works to indicate that he lived through the seething times of Disraeli's *Sybil*, Mrs. Gaskell's *Mary Barton*, Dickens' *Hard Times*, or Hood's "Song of the Shirt," nevertheless Newman felt keenly the woes of the poor. If he did not express himself in secular and "democratic" terms, there were intelligible reasons, as we have seen.

For Newman, as for Carlyle and Ruskin, the word "democracy" still retained a great deal of its original connotation, suggesting anarchic domination by a mob. All three writers had a strong conviction that a stratified social order was somehow ordained or permitted by divine Providence. They could say with Mrs. Alexander:

"The rich man in his castle,
        The poor man at his gate,
    God made them high and lowly,
        And ordered their estate."

Yet while all three believed in social inequality, they also believed in a democracy of the spirit far more revolutionary, if practised, than any secular kind. If Newman is unsympathetic with the working man's efforts to "rise in the world," he is equally unconcerned with the rich man's acquisition, retention, or increase of his wealth; in fact he is extremely unsettling, as we have seen, to the rich man's peace of mind. Newman was concerned only with the soul of the man underneath the "social problem." In more specific terms, in sociology and politics, Newman's position becomes clear when we test it by a threefold definition of democracy offered by Jacques Maritain:

" 'Democracy' may mean (*a*) what is recommended by Popes, the desire to get for working-classes, more than ever oppressed, just conditions of life. (There has been 'a terrifying lack of attention' to the injunctions of Leo XIII.) Or, democracy may mean (*b*) political democracy as conceived by Aristotle and St. Thomas; exemplified in the old Swiss democracy. Or (*c*) the Rousseau religious myth of democracy, political pantheism, the multitude as God." [7]

It is easy to see which of these three "democracies" Newman would favor today — either (*a*) or (*b*) or both, but certainly not the Rousseauistic myth of the "General Will," and the "innate goodness of man."

Nor is it difficult to believe that were Newman alive in our own tragic times he would agree with the distinction between "the people" and "the masses" which was made in the annual Christmas message of Pius XII in 1944. He doubtless would be able to follow the Pope's explanation that "the people lives and moves of its own energy . . . The masses, on the contrary, wait for the impulse from outside, an easy plaything in the hands of anyone who exploits their instincts." [8] Newman had already noted the distinction between civilization and barbarism, in his lectures on the Turks. What he dreaded was not the spread of responsible government by the people but the triumph of what

Carlyle called *Mobocracy*, the masses led by a "rabble-rouser." One of Newman's greatest secular services to the present-day reader is to make him more constructively critical of democratic values, of leadership, and of the whole concept of liberty. His severely moral approach to human nature introduces a beneficent sophistication in one's political thinking. One realizes, with him, the possibilities of a "new Barbarism," coming not like the Goths and Vandals from northern Europe, but from our own frustrated or misguided lower classes; these, says Newman, "will rise up from the depths of the modern cities, and will be the new scourges of God" — unless, one infers, they are spiritually reconstituted and spiritually led.[9]

If Newman stood in comparative isolation from some of the most characteristic forces of his time, it was partly because he had his eyes turned steadily on certain great issues which would outlast the fever and the fret of the Victorian world and will doubtless outlast ours. Both as an Anglican and as a Roman Catholic, he took the Christian religion, as we have seen, in its original and historical sense, with primitive severity and uncompromising otherworldliness. His moral sense was constantly appalled at the world's guilt, its suffering, its horrible alienation from God. And his intellect keenly appreciated its manifold difficulties in knowledge and belief. Without abandoning any part of orthodox doctrine, he set himself to demonstrating the intelligent foundations for belief, the continuity of the great Christian doctrines which, for him, were the spiritual bedrock of western culture, and the need for free and genuine intellectual discipline. Thus, though he is unmoved by the great social problems of his day and is unencouraged by its physical achievements, he leaves us a legacy in religious and educational thought. In the first place, he has reconciled, in the *Development of Christian Doctrine*, the principle of growth with the principle of sameness or of stability, and in so doing has enhanced, in Catholic and non-Catholic religious thought, the provocative and fruitful nineteenth-century concepts of "growth" and "change" and "evolution." Secondly, Newman has left a classic definition and outline of the *Idea of a University*. And thirdly, he has contributed, in his *Grammar of Assent*, valuable suggestions on the problem of how we come to assent to truths or propositions, religious or secular. On these three books, together with the *Apologia*, Newman's fame will rest for the far future.

His legacy is not, however, confined to his books. He had his life and being in certain movements persisting to our own day. There is, first, the Anglo-Catholic movement. Though Newman deserted it to become a Roman Catholic, the movement which he helped to start still flourishes and is indeed stronger now than it ever was, both in England and in the United States. A second movement is that by which the Roman Church has grown through converts who have directly or indirectly felt Newman's influence. Without him, that Church might never have acquired some of her most valuable recruits in the last three quarters of a century. Finally, Newman's heroic effort for intellectual freedom, without license, in the field of religious thought, has certainly altered the cast of Catholicism in England for the better. Newman was a symbol of moderate and courageous Catholic thinking. His example made converts and also held many Catholics who might otherwise have seceded. It has been said that "if the extremists like Ward had prevailed, there is no telling what defections might have occurred." [10] Newman was in himself "a living apologetic" for his Church; his career was a proof of the possibility, within that Church, of a combination of dauntless intellectual inquiry with childlike claimlessness and devoted faith. To be sure, his path was thorny; Manning, W. G. Ward, Talbot, and Herbert Vaughan did everything possible to hinder his intellectual efforts, and to convict him of unsoundness, unorthodoxy, disloyalty, evil influence. But Newman's supreme distinction lies in the fact that he triumphed over the obstacles set in his path by his coreligionists. In the words of one of his Roman Catholic biographers, J. Elliot Ross:

"He is a symbol of that perpetual struggle between the reactionary and the developing, between the separatist and the progressive forces in Catholicism. . . . Newman stood bravely against the reactionary forces [and] . . . won the fight for others, in the sense that any one may now without fear preach the principles of development of doctrine, the limitation of papal infallibility, and everything else for which Newman specifically stood." [11]

Now that the tide of liberal Protestantism — the secularized "social Gospel" — has ebbed, and a new search for the transcendent has arisen; now that such radically non-immanentist religious thinkers as Kierkegaard and Karl Barth have come into their own in Europe and in America, Newman's steadfast adherence to supernatural reality is winning new followers. They recognize, as the great secularists of the nineteenth century refused to recognize, that man is a religious creature, that if he loses his heritage of genuine Christianity, he will turn to other "religions," those of nationalism, racism, communism. No longer can Newman be superficially classed either as blindly dogmatic or as subtly "modern." Since, however, there are elements in his teachings which appear unorthodox to the casual reader, or lead even a critic to say unguardedly that "it is Newman who has started Loisy," [12] the great and excommunicated French Modernist, it is important to consider him in relation to that movement of which Loisy was the most brilliant exponent.

ii. *Newman and Modernism*

As the nineteenth century drew to a close, many Catholics felt the need of meeting the attacks made on the Church and her doctrines by Biblical and historical criticism. Though this criticism had had more than half a century in which to develop, Catholics suddenly found themselves unprepared for its impact. What was more, they found within their own Church a movement, known as "Modernism," which was attempting to reconcile what seemed irrefutable in modern thought with what was permanently true and valuable in religion. At the same time Modernists were trying to free Christianity from those obsolete and accidental accretions which disfigured it, and were hoping to bring the Church "up to date." At first France seemed to be in the van of Catholic progress in this movement. Many of her Biblical scholars and critics had fallen under the spell of Newman, especially under the spell of his essay on *Development*. Thus in the French literature on Newman we find such eminent names as Loisy, Dimnet, Laberthonnière, Leroy, Houtin (all of whom, as Modernists, were condemned in the Encyclical of

1907), and Duchesne, Grandmaison, Lebreton, Brémond and Rivière.[1]

According to the encyclical, there were three aspects and elements of Modernism: evolution, symbolism, and vital immanence. The Modernists accepted the principle of variation and evolution in doctrine as opposed to the principle of immutability; they hoped to bring Darwin into theology. They also attempted a solution of the conflict of science and religion through a new method of scriptural interpretation; they simply substituted a symbolical and allegorical reading of the Bible for the literal and historical. Finally, they introduced a new philosophy of religion, a new conception of religious phenomena: they substituted the principle of "vital immanence" for the principle of "transcendency," that is, they minimized the objective, dogmatic, external side of religion and stressed the subjective and internal side.[2] Actually, the essence of their efforts was an emptying out of the supernatural, an increasing reliance on the natural, the historical and the psychological in religion, through the application of the "historical spirit" to Biblical exegesis, to the Church, and, above all, to Christology. "The non-intervention of God in history," says Inge, "is an axiom with the Modernists."[3] The real Christ is an object of faith, a power, or a force, rather than a historical fact. The test of truth for a dogma, according to Tyrrell, is its "prayer-value." In short, the Modernists saw religion as something subjective, expressed through symbols in the space-time current of history.

"Thus," summarizes Maisie Ward, "we come to the key of Modernism — that dogmas are not the statement of truths revealed by God, but expressions of the religious mind at the stage to which religious experience has brought it; and the value of dogmas is measured, not by the objective truth of what they tell us about God, but by the adequacy with which (provisionally and for the time being) they express our own religious consciousness."[4]

Modernism ran its course for several years in France, Italy, and England. Italian Modernism appeared in such figures as Murri, the social democrat; in Fogazzaro, the novelist; and Alfieri, the editor of *Rinnovamento*. In England the movement had fewer exponents, but the radical Modernism of Father George Tyrrell's audacious books, such as *Christianity at the Cross-Roads,* spread consternation among cautious British Catholics. Newman's biographer, Wilfrid Ward, and Baron von Hügel were to some extent involved in Modernism, chiefly through personal relationships, but neither writer ever took such extreme views as those of Tyrrell or Loisy.[5] It was in France that Modernism grew most virulently, and found its most startling expression in Loisy's *L'Evangile et l'Eglise* (1902), in which the Gospels were treated as a patchwork, a compound of history and legend. According to Loisy, and other extreme Modernists,

"The supernatural life of Christ in the faithful and in the Church has been clothed in an historical form, which has given birth to what we might somewhat loosely call the Christ of legend." [6]

It is not our purpose here to enter into the details of the Modernist movement. It is enough to note how incredible such views must have seemed to orthodox believers when propounded by Catholic priests, such as Hebert, Houtin, and Loisy. Suddenly the Church awoke to the fact that once the Modernist teachings were accepted, only a modern mirage would be left in place of what she regarded as objective Christian reality. The Vatican therefore decided that it could never come to terms with the new movement. It officially condemned Modernism in two documents — the decree of the Holy Inquisition, *Lamentabili sane exitu,* July 3, 1907, and the Encyclical, *Pascendi dominici gregis,* September 8, 1907.

Many readers of the encyclical, having already observed how frequently Newman's name appeared in Modernist writings, were convinced that he and many of his teachings were now condemned. Many had uncritically assumed indeed that Newman had been the father of Modernism, that, as Sarolea had uncritically suggested, Newman had been the inspirer of Loisy. However, as Guitton has pointed out, Loisy had no acquaintance with Newman's works until rather late in his career. Newman's doctrine of development merely strengthened Loisy's adherence to his own doctrine of the "relativity" of the various forms of

religious life.[7]   In fact, Vidler has well demonstrated that Newman was in no real sense a precursor of Modernism.   He was,
however, the only nineteenth-century theologian whom the Modernists found useful.   But his usefulness was limited to the prestige of his name.[8]   It was not that Newman was liberal, or progressive, or modern, but that he had been more liberal than any
other theologian whose name was held in high honor in official
circles.   The Modernists found much in Newman that was suggestive, but not until he became a cardinal under Leo XIII did
his writings win that implied authoritative approval which made
them valuable to the movement.   Had Newman died before
Pius IX, any Modernist appeal to Newman's writings would have
been utterly futile.   As for the Encyclical, though Tyrrell, and
Fawkes, and other Modernists declared Newman to be condemned in it, Cardinal Gasquet soon made it clear that the Vatican had in no sense condemned him.[9]   Wilfrid Ward explained
the *apparent* condemnation by pointing out that while the "Newman" positions formed part of the statement of the whole Modernist system, and the system could not be stated without them,
nevertheless since not all parts of an untrue system are untrue,
the encyclical did not mean to condemn such parts, only the system as a whole.[10]   Moreover, the so-called "Newman" passages
meant one thing in the highly subjective system of Modernism,
but quite another thing in Newman's context.   Newman himself
would have recoiled in horror from the destructive criticism of
Loisy, the contempt for scholastic authority of Tyrrell, the defiance hurled at the Papacy in the manifesto, the *Programma dei
modernisti* of the Italian Modernists.   He had long ago, as we
have observed, prophesied such an onslaught, in Tract LXXXV
(1838), and in the reviews of Milman's *History of Christianity*
(1841) and Seely's *Ecce Homo* (1866).   He had foreseen the
gradual abandonment, by many believers, of creeds and dogmas
and the institutional side of the Church.   In Tract LXXXV he
had predicted that for many men Christianity would be seen no
longer in documents any more than in institutions; the Bible
would be given up as well as the Church.   And Christianity
would become a vague pantheism, giving way in time to "the

religion of beauty, imagination, and philosophy, without con-
straint moral or intellectual, a religion speculative and self-
indulgent." [11]

Though Newman was in no proper sense the "father of Modernism," there are elements in his thinking which parallel or
resemble Modernist teachings.   Like the Modernists, he sub-
stitutes the religion of the heart for the religion of reason; like
them, he dreads the excesses of Catholic scholasticism and has
little interest in the theology of Thomas Aquinas, which has become the official theology of the Church.   He sees the Church
as a *growing organism,* and if he does not radically historicize
it as do the Modernists, he still likes to think of its historical
course through the world.   He sees doctrines and dogmas *developing,* and if, unlike Loisy, he insists that they become ultimately what they were originally in germ, he likes to ponder the
mystical unfolding of an idea as it passes through many minds.
This may lead to misunderstanding, and many French critics attacked him severely, notably Michaud, who declared that Newman strips dogma of divinity and leaves only "changing opinion,"
and that his theories of development and of assent amount in the
end to a sort of sentimentalism.[12]   But when examined carefully
Newman's Modernist-seeming ideas turn out to be startlingly
realistic, neither blindly reactionary nor recklessly innovative.
Brémond is undoubtedly right in holding that Newman could,
had he wished, have been one of the creators of Biblical criticism;
several remarks in Tract LXXXV, thrown out, *currente calamo,*
would, in their far-reaching import, have made the fortune of a
professional scholar.[13]

Newman was never disturbed by the Biblical critics, since his
Catholicism rested not on the Bible alone but also on tradition and
on the living ministry of the Church.   He could not have tolerated the thought of religion being bound up with the conclusions of philologists and archeologists.   Yet even had he known
the results of German criticism, he undoubtedly would have accepted such conclusions as seemed historically and rationally
warranted, and would have got over any difficulties by remembering the symbolism and allegorism of Alexandria.   He would

never, on the other hand, have resorted to the Modernist distinction between "truths of faith" and "truths of fact." As Sarolea has well said,

"One fact is certain, he would not have been content to lag behind the heels of German critics or make unwilling and inglorious concessions to the demands of science. His intellect was too clear-sighted and too manly to approve of a policy of compromise and evasion, and to see a menace to religion in every discovery of scholarship. His faith was too robust not to look dangers full in the face. He would have done what he actually did as an old man of eighty-three: he would have demanded an exhaustive inquiry into the Biblical question without reticence or afterthought, secure and certain that religion would . . . emerge from the ordeal with renewed vigor." [14]

One day in 1880 one of the Oratorian fathers drew from Newman a statement of what would be his individual policy in the improbable but not absolutely impossible event of his being called, now that he was a cardinal, to the papal throne. He replied "in a matter-of-fact manner, but with grave seriousness," that he would immediately appoint and organize commissions on various subjects, especially on Biblical criticism and the history of the early Church; and that the commissions would be obliged to make a full and candid report to be dealt with by Newman's successor as he should think fit.[15]

And yet, however "modern" some of Newman's passages or remarks may seem, a careful reading of him shows beyond all doubt that his orthodoxy was absolute, his belief literal and uncompromising. Brilliant and liberal as are some of the pages of Tract LXXXV, on the Scripture and the Catholic creed, some of its conclusions are so uncritical, as Brémond notes, that few nowadays would think of defending them.[16] The extent of his literal interpretation of the Bible may be seen in the fourth discourse of *The Idea of a University*, which deals with the bearing of various branches of study on theology. He has just declared that he considers theology to be as genuine a science as physics or mathematics. He holds, therefore, that

"Revealed Religion [based on the written and the unwritten word of God, on Scripture and Tradition] furnishes facts to the other sciences, which those sciences, left to themselves, would never reach; and it invalidates apparent facts, which, left to themselves, they would imagine. Thus, in the science of history, the preservation of our race in Noah's ark is a historical fact, which history never would arrive at without Revelation; and, in the province of physiology and moral philosophy, our race's progress and perfectibility is a dream, because Revelation contradicts it . . ." [17]

Newman's faith was so strong, his distrust of "secular reason" was so great, that he refused, as he put it, "to be eclectic in so serious a matter of fact" as Biblical texts and teachings.[18] No doubt he was unnecessarily uneclectic; certainly he suffered, as we have seen, from the limitations of his time, his temperament, his intellectual background.

Some light is thrown on Newman's position in regard to Modernism and orthodoxy when we examine his view of miracles. This is a very vexed subject. It has been perplexed by Huxley's clever attack on Newman's *Essay on the Miracles Recorded in the Ecclesiastical History of the Early Ages* (1843), by E. A. Abbott's *Philomythus: an Antidote against Credulity: a Discussion on Cardinal Newman's Essay on Ecclesiastical Miracles* (1891), and by the Abbé Brémond's witty but unsatisfactory analysis in *The Mystery of Newman* (1907). None of these works really get behind Newman's words and seek his *philosophy* of miracle. We may well begin our inquiry by admitting at the outset that Newman was, as Ward says, "ready of belief as to marvellous occurrences." He was, in a sense, superstitious: he had a curious feeling about the number seven in the scheme of things — he limited his Irish rectorship to seven years, he believed seven years to be the normal length of intimate friendships, he even toyed with the idea that the elect in the world is never more than 7,000.[19] He was always waiting for Providential "signs," and interpreted whatever happened — an unexpected act, a word, an encouragement, a meeting, a separation, a book or an article — as Providentially directed.[20] In his late thirties, as he notes in the *Apologia*, he actually conceived political movements to be the work of a race of intermediate beings, between angels and devils, the offspring of amorous intercourse between fallen angels and the daughters of men, before the Deluge; John Bull, with his genius for compromising, was such a being, "a spirit neither of heaven nor hell"! [21]   He attached a serious importance to dreams, and sometimes recorded them in his letters. This was a man always prepared to make pious sacrifices of his reason to what he regarded as supernatural reality; he was eager to humiliate "the wild living intellect, which needs to have its stiff neck bent." [22]   This was the man who in that remarkable seventh chapter in *The Present Position of Catholics*, after discussing the "reasonable probability" of miracles, concludes with breath-taking boldness and unreticence:

"I will avow distinctly, that, putting out of the question the hypothesis of unknown laws of nature (that is, of the professed miracle being not miraculous), I think it impossible to withstand the evidence which is brought for the liquefaction of the blood of St. Januarius of Naples, and for the motion of the eyes of the pictures of the Madonna in the Roman States. I see no reason to doubt the material of the Lombard crown at Monza; and I do not see why the Holy Coat at Trèves may not have been what it professes to be. I firmly believe that portions of the True Cross are at Rome and elsewhere, that the Crib of Bethlehem is at Rome, and the bodies of St. Peter and St. Paul also. I believe that at Rome too lies St. Stephen, that St. Matthew lies at Salerno, and St. Andrew at Amalfi . . . I firmly believe that saints in their life-time have before now raised the dead to life, crossed the sea without vessels, multiplied grain and bread, cured incurable diseases, and superseded the operation of the laws of the universe in a multitude of ways." [23]

In reading this, one remembers that on the day of his admission into the Roman Church, Father Dominic omitted the legend of St. Denis walking about with his head under his arm, out of deference to Newman's intellect; but he was assured that he need not have done so, for Newman's faith would have accepted it.[24]

Thus Newman was constitutionally capable of greater belief than even the orthodox of his own day. But underlying his belief was a reasoned-out theory of miracle which removes some of that "mystery of Newman" which, according to Brémond, consisted in the willingness of his acute mind to believe in fantastic mediaeval legends.   We may not agree with Newman, his theory may not convince us; but it should indicate that his oftenmentioned "credulity" is neither so simple nor so ridiculous as some of his critics have maintained.   In the first place, Newman did not make a hard-and-fast distinction between interference with the laws of nature and God's general providence.   For him, such laws were God's general rules of action, and they might be directed much as the workings of the human organism are affected by the mind and will, without any "violation" of natural law.   Newman considers that, "*philosophically*, miracle is only parallel to the interference of human volition in the blind sequence of physical cause and effect":

"Is not human volition, in its action upon mechanical processes, a miracle?   I put out my hand and stop the pendulum of a clock. The clock stops. . . .   Now, what is a miracle in theological science but the interference of such an extra-physical cause, viz. of a Being, not hypothesised for the occasion, but known already to exist as a moral governor by means of the conscience?" [25]

This line of argument satisfied Newman, as it had Dean Mansel, and he seems never to have suspected its vulnerability.   When Wilfrid Ward visited him in January, 1885, he tried to present to Newman the answer made by "the modern phenomenist school," namely, that when one stops the pendulum, both the act of will and the action are only a *part* of nature's uniformity, not an exception to it — human action can be no reliable analogy in understanding God's action.   Ward observed that Newman did not seem to get hold of this point, in fact "seemed a trifle irritated, and said: 'I only contend that what man can do God can do.' " [26]

Newman of course accepted both the scriptural and the ecclesiastical miracles.   The latter, he maintained, "are on the same level of *antecedent probability* with those of Scripture . . . Ecclesiastical miracles are *probable*, because Scripture miracles are *true*."   The basis for his acceptance of the Biblical miracles is evident in his declaration that they are "credible, i.e., proveable, on a ground peculiar to themselves on the *authority of God's*

Word." [27]　Newman defines a miracle in its strict sense as "an event in a given system which cannot be referred to any law, or accounted for by the operation of any principle, in that system." [28] It is a relative term, presupposing an assemblage of laws from which it is a deviation, but also referring to some one particular system; for the same event which is anomalous in one, may be quite regular when observed in connection with another.　For Newman, miracles are more than exceptions to physical order; they are evidences of a revelation, a criterion of a divine message, a "manifestation of the Hand of God."　However, the term miracle may be used in a wider sense:

"No evidence of a revelation is conceivable which does not partake of the character of a Miracle; since nothing but a display of power over the existing system of things can attest the immediate presence of Him by whom it was originally established; or, again, because no event which results entirely from the ordinary operations of nature can be the criterion of one that is extraordinary." [29]

Hence all evidences of revelation, such as prophecy, the rapid spread of Christianity, the teaching of the pure morality of the Gospels by illiterate fishermen, may be classified as miraculous. It is clear that, for Newman, the line between what is natural and what is miraculous is sometimes very thin, and it is easy for his mind to pass from the natural to the supernatural, where he is far more at home than most of his readers.

But willing as he is to believe what many have given up, he himself is in fact, as Brémond finally admits, "the least credulous of men."　His own faith does not rest on miracles, but on his personal experience of God.　His *Essay on Miracles* (1843) — his meticulous and hairsplitting analysis of the miracles of the thundering legion, the turning of water into oil by St. Narcissus, the sudden death of Arius, the Labarum, the discovery of the true Cross — all this is but the submissive service of the mind to the spirit; Newman is not here trying to convince, he is *worshiping.* Moreover, he knows that miracles are not the chief motive of credibility.　He knows that they add little to the force of other evidence for divine truth, that they are not even necessary, that they can easily be replaced, that a person must already be disposed to believe the doctrine to which they pretend to witness, indeed that many of those very miracles, *e.g.*, of the Old Testament, need the support of faith rather than the reverse. Newman preached a very effective sermon on "Miracles No Remedy for Unbelief," and came to the conclusion that "whatever be the reason, nothing is gained by miracles, nothing comes of miracles, as regards our religious views, principles, and habits. Hard as it is to believe, miracles certainly do not make men better; the history of Israel proves it." [30] Why, then, do miracles happen? Newman replies: because an infinitely good God gives man much when He could give him less; they are evidences of God's bounty and love as well as of His power. But of themselves, miracles are not strong enough to compel belief by a hardhearted man; they are not a metaphysical demonstration — "they do not write the Gospel on the sun" for either a good or a bad man. Like all evidences they must "presuppose the being of an Intelligent Agent to whom they may be referred," and "the admission that the doctrine they are brought to prove is, not merely not inconsistent, but actually accordant with the laws of His moral governance." [31] Thus we may see that "credulous" as Newman appears to many readers, he does not in fact rest his faith on "fantastic legends" but on a deeply mystical sense of the reality of only two beings, himself and his Creator.

Finally, we should note that Newman's whole position on the question of miracle rests on the doctrine of the divinity of Christ. On this point he challenges Protestants, who, if they are orthodox, start with this doctrine, accept various other Biblical miracles, but balk at the miracles of the Breviary or the Martyrology.

"Catholics . . . hold the mystery of the Incarnation; and the Incarnation is the most stupendous event which ever can take place on earth; and after it and henceforth, I do not see how we can scruple at any miracle on the mere ground of its being unlikely to happen. No miracle can be so great as that which took place in the Holy House of Nazareth; it is indefinitely more difficult to believe than all the miracles of the Breviary, of the Martyrology, of Saints' lives, of legends, of local traditions, put together. . . If, through divine grace, we once are able to accept the solemn truth that the Supreme Being was born of a mortal woman, what is there to be imagined which can offend us on the ground of its marvellousness." [32]

To return to Newman's relation to Modernism, we may note in conclusion that, unlike the Modernists, he denies man's ability to arrive unaided at the central doctrines of Christianity. He denies that human nature of itself could come to even the most fragmentary or embryonic knowledge of such strange and puzzling dogmas as those of the Trinity, the Incarnation of the Word, and the Sacrament of the Eucharist. The Modernists held, on the question of revelation, that the so-called supernatural is merely an outgrowth of the natural needs and aspirations of man, that "supernatural" dogma is only a natural development, or expression, of human reason and sentiment. Newman's teaching is just the reverse of this immanentism. He held that revelation of supernatural truths has been accompanied by signs which prove their divinity, by events miraculous or natural. Moreover, the whole Christian revelation is *one* and *self-existent,* yet mysterious. "God has revealed everything necessary to the fulfilment of His inscrutable designs; but He has not left us the key to the most secret recesses of His Wisdom, Goodness and Will." [33] The whole *depositum* of revelation, from the seemingly least significant fact to the profoundest principle or the loftiest dogma about the mysteries of the divine nature, has its divine economy and is offered to humanity on one and the same motive, namely, because God has revealed it. Man is to accept it as a *whole,* without laying down any conditions before accepting it, without exercising his private judgment or choosing from the doctrines those teachings which please him and rejecting or denying others. According to Newman, without this revelation man could never attain notions, either consciously or unconsciously, that would be even the faintest counterparts of the divine doctrines of Christianity. It is true, however, says Newman, that the revelation of *natural* truths has been accommodated to the needs of human nature in such a way that, properly studied, they point to the supernatural origin of revealed truth.

In view of Newman's emphasis on the abyss between human knowledge and the divine mysteries, one realizes how presumptuous and wanting in intellectual humility the Modernists would have seemed to him.

iii. *Newman's Integrity*

Few great men have suffered so much misunderstanding as Newman. Few have been so consistently labeled "insincere," "full of guile," "intellectually seductive." One critic will declare: "Never consciously insincere, Newman constantly gave the impression of insincerity." [1] Another, far more fiercely, will write of Newman's

"subtle and delicately lubricated illative rhetoric by which you are led downwards on an exquisitely elaborated inclined plane, from a truism to a probability, from a strong probability to a fair probability, and from a fair probability to a pious but most improbable belief." [2]

Still another critic will state that "Newman made mere siren style do duty for exact, penetrating and coherent thought." [3] Thomas Carlyle will opine that Newman was cursed not with insincerity but merely with "the intellect of a moderate-sized rabbit." [4] Yet other critics, like the Roman Catholic biographer, J. Elliot Ross, will write that "In Newman we have the picture of a man who was absolutely sincere"; and a brilliant non-Catholic will hold that "precisely because Newman is scrupulous and honest, he leaves upon us the impression of a restless mind." [5] Certainly few great thinkers have appeared under so many and varied aspects or seemed to pass through so many changes. As we know, early in his career, Newman appeared to many as a tortuous and subtle casuist, at heart a Roman priest, continuing for ten years to "corrupt" his fellow-Anglicans toward Rome. Later, after the publication of the *Apologia*, his position changed: the *doctor subtilis* became almost overnight a *doctor angelicus*, whose portrait, with its saintly, emaciated, ascetic face, was known in nearly every Anglican vicarage. Still later, during the Victorian "conflict between Science and Religion," a third Newman appears, "with the intellect of a skeptic and the heart of a mystic" — the Newman of Huxley and Leslie Stephen, a combination of Hamlet and Pascal, agonizing over faith and doubt, and finding in Catholicism a refuge from the terrors of modern knowledge.

Still another Newman emerges from Purcell's *Life of Manning* (1896); the martyr of ultramontane intolerance, the victim of Manning, W. G. Ward and the Jesuits, the opponent of papal infallibility, the man whom Mgr. Talbot called "the most dangerous man in England," and the recipient of the belated cardinal's hat.   Finally, at the turn of the century, Newman appears as the "liberal Catholic," the "father of Modernism," the "Darwin of theology," a man whose works misled the Abbé Brémond, who left the Society of Jesus, and Father Tyrrell and the Abbé Loisy, who were expelled from it.[6]

There are various reasons, not commonly considered, for the paradoxical character of much of Newman's work.   For one thing, as we have frequently noted, his approach to his problems was always a personal one.   This the Germans have spoken of as his "subjectivity."   Certainly his writings have little of the objective character which would give them an immediate and obvious utility as a contribution to general knowledge.   Ward reminds us that Newman never rubbed shoulders with others at a public school; that he was not quite a good member of the republic of letters — he was too individual, too solitary by nature. He did not work freely or well with other minds.[7]   The key to the difficulty is not simply that he was a Catholic.   Other Catholic writers were able, for example, in the debates of the Metaphysical Society, to isolate their philosophical arguments from their theological conclusions, to discuss free will, empiricism, intuitionism independently of religious considerations.   Newman was never able to do this;[8] in all his writings, the artist, the poet, the historian, the rhetorician, the theologian took turns, as it were, in dealing with a given subject.   He never argued objectively, philosophically, but always as an advocate.   Moreover, there are times, as Ward says, when Newman reminds one of a wilful woman, in his contempt for logic:

"In the 'Grammar of Assent,' [as we have seen] Newman dismisses a logical criticism on a certain process of thought by the remark that it leads to truth, and that therefore, if logic finds fault with it, it is 'so much the worse for logic.' "[9]

The hostile critic of Newman fastens on such passages and fails to see that it is simply the rhetorician in him which leads him to employ what one may term wilful sayings. There is no use complaining that Newman should not be so flippant on a serious subject; we must remember that as a rhetorician, his main business is to persuade and convince, not dispassionately or objectively to analyze. "This despiser of reasoning," says Brémond, "is a logician of genius"; but it is extremely rare for Newman to demonstrate anything at all.[10] Always presuming that he is addressing himself only to minds like his own, to readers who believe what he believes, he uses logic to *explore* a doctrine, to render it *alluring* to the mind which already had accepted it. Hence the abundance of "views," of probabilities, intuitions, "feelers," which he uses as the scaffolding of an argument. Brémond wittily observes that

"When intellectual principles are in question, the provisional, usually, is sufficient for him. His real and solid building is elsewhere . . . If a gust of wind overturns this hut, we will make another close by . . . 'Is not this an intelligible ground?' he asks somewhere, as if he said — 'After all, sound or not, cannot this be defended? "View" for "view," mine is at least as good as another.' " [11]

Even his theory of doctrinal development "is undoubtedly an hypothesis to account for a difficulty." This does not mean that he renounces verification, the legitimizing or defense of a hypothesis by rational and scientific proofs, with the most exact method, where proofs are available. However, this initial reservation that he is after all dealing with a "view," a theory to account for a difficulty, reminds us that if, by chance, reason or fact should destroy his edifice from top to bottom, his conviction on the subject of the divinity of the Church would not be shaken in the slightest degree. This explains the bewilderment of his friend Thomas Mozley, who had been told by Newman not to expect reasonings to propel him into the Roman Church, yet who saw Newman impose upon himself two years more of critical and historical studies before going over. "The fact was," adds Mozley, "he did not intend to work out any problem at all, but to wait for further light from his Heavenly Guide." [12]   Hence the incompleteness of the *Essay on Development*.

Everywhere in Newman's argumentative writings what strikes some readers as "immoral shiftiness" in language is really, as Wilfrid Ward has said:

"only the attempt, in view of the extraordinary delicacy of his insight into the complex problems he considered, to express more and more accurately truths which he always held to transcend words.   Truths simple to others were complex to him, because he recognized all the assumptions, prepossessions, and previous questions which they involved.   His self-criticism and the criticisms of others perpetually led him to verbal alterations." [13]

What Ward calls his "power of evasion" is unmistakably evident in all his writings, but it was used with integrity, to protect what he regarded as the true proportions of an argument as a whole. Moreover, Newman's mind revealed an unusual combination of gifts: a strong sense of fact, careful psychology, a love of truth, and intellectual subtlety.   With these, he broke down the common antithesis between the special pleader (which critics like Leslie Stephen thought him to be) who has his eye constantly on effects, and the genuine seeker after truth.   Newman was in fact both.   In the *Grammar of Assent*, he is more: he is at once the artist, the rhetorician, the theologian, and the logician; except for the opening pages, none of the *Grammar* is written in the passionless style of the typical philosopher, and none of it is merely special pleading or *mere* rhetoric.   Newman fuses his several roles in his search for concrete justification of assent. This is not the usual method in exposition or controversy, and it has always perplexed some of his critics.

The key to the problem of Newman's integrity is his complexity.   It is this which causes Sarolea and R. H. Coats to give up the "mystery of Newman" in despair.   At first we may think that Newman's is a simple mind, so candid it is, so naïve and ingenuous in some of its moods.   But we soon find ourselves wholly lost in the labyrinthine mazes of his complex personality.   Here is an ascetic who is also an artist and a literary epicure; a mystic with the corrosive intellect of a skeptic; a solitary who has troops

of friends and followers; a great religious leader and controversialist, yet a dreamer, an idealist, childlike in his simple faith;
a scorner of the world, yet shrewdly conversant with all its ways,
and deft in using it as a tool to suit his purposes; a man who is
timid and aggressive, deeply sincere and yet possessed of a subtlety which the greatest casuist might have envied, intellectually
hard, cold, glittering and analytical one moment, and meltingly
sweet, rapturously adoring, womanlike in tenderness the next
moment.[14] We shall probably never be able to resolve all the
paradoxes in Newman's character and mind. But there are no
valid grounds for questioning his sincerity and integrity.[15]

CHAPTER XV

COR AD COR LOQUITUR: *A CONCLUSION AND A BEGINNING*

And now that we have surveyed Newman in the rich variety of his mind and work — as religious thinker, poet, historian, novelist, critic, autobiographer, controversialist, preacher, educator — we come to the conclusion of our study, but not, we feel confident, to the end of our knowledge of the man. The character of Newman is as perpetually discoverable as a great book. Readers will always be fascinated by his personality, by his style, and by his insights into perennial problems in faith and in the nature of religious ideas. So complex are his personality and intellect, so fertile are the paradoxes and suggestions in his thought, that he will long continue as a potent if at times an enigmatic influence. He will exert an influence by the exploitation, by the very perversion, of his teachings. His disciples will continue to deduce from his works many conclusions which they do not contain. This has happened to many another great writer; it has happened to Plato and Aristotle, to Goethe and to Hegel; it has happened, of course, to Christianity itself. With the passing of time and the rise of new exigencies of the spirit, men will ignore those books of Newman which no longer bear a living utility, and will adapt to their needs those elements in his thought which retain their vitality. Indeed, it is quite possible, as Sarolea declared, that "the influence of Newman will be in proportion as he is more ingeniously misunderstood." [1]

We have seen how his admirers have sought to link him with evolutionism, with pragmatism, with skepticism, with Modernism. Newman has even been seen as an anticipator of Freud, in his emphasis on how childhood experiences mould and direct our egos, how they later become idealized, and how we forget the painful and the evil in them: "n'est-ce pas la thèse même du psychologue de Vienne?" asks Seillière. [2] More plausible is the

374

attempt to trace parallels between Newman and Bergson. That there was an *influence* can hardly be proved. There is, however, as Cronin shows, "a fruitful field of comparison between the illative sense and the Bergsonian intuition," [3] and Newman's insights into the problem of knowledge are again discovered to be prophetic of theories to flourish after his own day. But Newman's greatest seminal force will lie in the sphere of religious truth. His weight will increasingly be felt on the side of anti-immanentism, in the direction of greater and subtler and more enlightened supernaturalism. In a letter she wrote in 1929, Evelyn Underhill declared very succinctly that "it is really better to face up at once to what a genuinely Catholic religious philosophy teaches than to temporize with half-Christian pantheistic-immanentist books . . . [One] has got to make the transition from 'God in everything' to 'everything in God.'" [4] In the reaction from nineteenth- and early twentieth-century "socializing" and "historicizing" of Christianity, Newman's works, both as truly understood and as fruitfully and ingeniously "misunderstood," will doubtless be a major contribution. The uniqueness of Christianity, its radical otherworldliness, its uncompromising moral and spiritual demands, its explosive incommensurability with nature and history — all this appeals profoundly to a war-exhausted world. And as men awake to the shortcomings and hazards of superficial faith in secularism, many will turn, sometimes with distortion or error, to the great dogmas of Christianity. And here the silver voice of Newman will give to doctrine and dogma a fresh beauty and a new meaning without forfeiting in any degree their basic integrity. Some of his followers will see in the slogan "Communism or Catholicism" a present-day variant on Newman's "Atheism or Catholicism." [5] In any event, Newman's ideas will have a "new beginning" in the religious thought of the future.

In spite of the fact that Newman was an "occasional" writer, in spite of a lack of formal unity in his work, few great writers have been in reality more consistent. Though he never summarized his position in one or two great treatises — he left nothing like a *Treatise on Human Nature,* or an *Essay on the Human Under-*

standing — he nevertheless can be readily placed as a thinker. When he received the cardinal's hat in 1879, he chose the motto, *Cor ad cor loquitur* — "Heart speaketh unto heart." When he designed his own monument, he wrote an inscription which summed up his whole point of view: *Ex umbris et imaginibus in veritatem* — "From shadows and images unto truth." [6] It is appropriate to dwell a moment on these two mottoes. They not only tell us much about Newman's conviction that the visible world is but a shadow,[7] they also point to the distinct appeal which Newman makes as a writer. Especially is this true of the first motto. All of Newman's work was addressed to his readers' *hearts*; all his words were, after all, trying to say the unsayable, to people who, as we have elsewhere observed, had already felt what he had felt. These readers he regarded as belonging to an aristocracy of the spirit. It was they who appreciated the final quotations in the *Grammar of Assent*.* And it is such readers who will always constitute the bulk of "Newmanites." They will follow Newman in his conception of the world as *umbra et imago*; in his conviction that our direct experience is with phenomena and that our faith is in what is behind; in his teaching that "conscience is a proof of God, as a shadow is a proof of a substance"; in his regarding rites and dogmatic formulae as merely the *umbra et imago* of reality. If Newman is an enigma or a mystery to anyone, it is simply because that person is, for one reason or another, incapable of approaching him in the spirit of *cor ad cor loquitur.*

That quality in Newman which troubles and attracts us today, his lofty and sovereign spirituality, has in no way diminished since it was described in the stately words of R. H. Hutton at the time of Newman's death:

"In a century in which physical discovery and material well-being have usurped and almost absorbed the admiration of mankind, such a life as that of Cardinal Newman stands out in strange and almost majestic, though singularly graceful and unpretending, contrast to the eager and agitated turmoil of confused passions, hesitating ideals,

* See the ending of Chap. VI, of the present work.

tentative virtues, and groping philanthropies, amidst which it has been lived." [8]

Now that our material well-being has ironically grown into a liability, and our philanthropies have groped amiss, and our tentative virtues have failed to bear us up, the lonely splendor of Newman's mind, rooted in the bedrock of his religion, stands out as a warning and a comfort. His steadfast and tranquil faith that the visible is but *umbra et imago* comforts many who now know it from experience. Even in the din of these turbulent times, his silvery voice may be heard — *cor ad cor loquitur*. It is not merely his words that reach our troubled ears; "he has that in him which is beyond eloquence." For there are moments when his simplest utterances come "charged with an unearthly import, as straight from out the region where he loved to dwell." [9]

NOTES

Chapter I

i.

[1] Wilfrid Ward, "Newman and Renan," in *Problems and Persons* (London, 1903), p. 283.

[2] *Apologia pro vita sua,* ed. Wilfrid Ward (London, 1913), the edition hereafter referred to, pp. 105–06; *Letters and Correspondence of John Henry Newman,* ed. Anne Mozley (London, 1891), I, 16.

[3] Erich Przywara, *Ringen der Gegenwelt: Gesammelte Aufsätze:* 1922–1927 (Augsburg, 1929), II, 845–71, "Der Newman'sche Seelentypus in der Kontinuität katholischer Aszese und Mystik." See also L. Bouyer, "Newman et le Platonisme de l'âme Anglaise," *Revue de philosophie,* VI (1936), 286, 289, etc.

[4] *Apologia,* p. 108.

[5] *Ibid.,* p. 107.

[6] *Ibid.,* pp. 107–08.

[7] *Ibid.,* pp. 107–08. In reading Romaine, Newman was coming into contact with a thorough Calvinistic school of Evangelicalism, closely related to the Puritans of the old stock (see Y. Brilioth, *The Anglican Revival,* [London, 1925], p. 32). By "final perseverance" is meant the Calvinistic belief that the converted are given an assurance that they *will* persevere to the end and *cannot* fall away. This doctrine is eloquently treated by Romaine in *The Triumph of Faith* (1795), Chap. VI, "The Believer's Victory over the Dominion of Sin," and in Chaps. X and XI. Newman is more indebted to Romaine than is generally realized; the famous sermon on the "Neglect of Divine Calls and Warnings" (Discourse II in *Discourses to Mixed Congregations*) would seem to owe a direct debt to Romaine's sermon on "The Duty of Watchfulness Enforced" (*Works,* London, 1796, V, 359–84). Newman's early Evangelical stress on fear of eternal punishment likewise reminds one of Romaine's "Future Rewards and Punishments," (*Works,* VI, 61–109).

[8] Henry J. Jennings, *Cardinal Newman* (Birmingham, 1882),

p. 7. Jennings' admirable little volume is undeservedly neglected; it contains numerous details about Newman not elsewhere found, and benefits from having been written in Birmingham during Newman's life at the Oratory.

[9] *Apologia,* pp. 108–09. It was Scott's *Commentary* (1788–92) and his *Force of Truth* (1779) which most influenced Newman. The last pages of the latter work have an appeal to the reader remarkably like the final passage of Newman's *Development of Christian Doctrine.* "Holiness before peace" is the theme of one of Scott's *Essays on the Most Important Subjects of Religion* (1793), Essay XVI, "On the Believer's Warfare and Experience"; "Growth the only evidence of life" is the theme of Essay XXII, "On the Christian's Improvement of his Talents." Much of the terminology and a few of the general ideas in the *Grammar of Assent* seem to echo certain pages in Essay XVIII, "On the Disposition and Character Peculiar to the True Believer."

[10] It was under the influence of William Jones of Nayland (1726–1800), probably his *Catholic Doctrine of the Trinity* (1756), that Newman made his collection of Scripture texts. There is evidence, as we shall later see, that Newman was still under Jones' influence, consciously or unconsciously, when he wrote his *Arians,* his book on *Development,* and probably the *Oxford University Sermons* and the *Grammar of Assent.* — Milner's Church History came out between 1744 and 1797, and in view of Newman's later fondness for the early Fathers, was curious reading, being severely Evangelical and highly critical of Clement, Origen, Tertullian, Iraeneus, who showed an "unhappy mixture of philosophical self-righteousness and superstition" (I, 282, 286, etc.). Milner's work figures in the background of the *Arians.*

[11] *Apologia,* p. 110. Dr. Johnson referred to Newton's *Dissertations* as "Tom's great work." It is virulently anti-Roman, massive in its learning, and of course narrow in its argument.

[12] Newman's brother Francis tells us that "in none of [the games] was John Henry Newman to be seen. He did go to our bathingpond, but never *swam.* My father took care that he should learn to *ride.*" See F. W. Newman, *Contributions Chiefly to the Early History of Cardinal Newman* (London, 1891), p. 3. This book, "un méchant ouvrage," as Guitton truly says, must be consulted with caution.

[13] Geoffrey Faber, *Oxford Apostles* (New York, 1934), pp. 15, 16.

[14] On this side of Newman's nature, see Abbé Henri Brémond, *The Mystery of Newman*, transl. H. C. Corrance (London, 1907), Chap. I, "The Solitary by Choice." Brémond's work, like so many on Newman, is emotional and one-sided, and therefore of very uneven value.

[15] *Letters and Corresp.*, I, 16.

[16] F. W. Newman, *op. cit.*, p. 9.

[17] In that strangely objective "Autobiographical Memoir" which Newman wrote in the third person, he tells us that "Newman had not a grain in his composition of that temper of conviviality so natural to young men" (*Letters and Corresp.*, I, 36).

ii.

[1] See Frank Leslie Cross, "Tractarian Oxford," in *John Henry Newman: with a Set of Unpublished Letters* (London, 1933); and W. S. Knickerbocker, *Creative Oxford* (Syracuse, N. Y., 1925), pp. 30 ff. The *locus classicus* on Oxford in Newman's early years is Dean R. W. Church's account in *The Oxford Movement* (London, 1892), pp. 159 ff.

[2] See Gibbon's *Autobiography* (World's Classics ed.; London, 1907), pp. 35 ff.

[3] *Letters and Corresp.*, I, 37.

[4] E. A. Knox. *The Tractarian Movement: 1833–1845* (New York, 1933), pp. 22–26; Knickerbocker, *op. cit.*, pp. 32–34.

[5] Newman's "Autobiographical Memoir" in *Letters and Corresp.*, I, 73: Newman "never wished anything better or higher than, in the words of the epitaph, 'to live and die a Fellow of Oriel.' "

[6] Wilfrid Ward, *Life of Cardinal Newman* (London, 1912), I, 36.

[7] Faber, *op. cit.*, p. 80. Chapter III, sect. 1, "The Parties in the Church," is one of the most readable and useful summaries of the subject.

[8] Faber, *op. cit.*, p. 81. See also, for standard accounts, V. F. Storr, *The Development of English Theology in the Nineteenth Century: 1800–1860* (London, 1913), Chaps. IV–VI; Y. Brilioth, *The Anglican Revival* (New York, 1925), Chaps. II–IV; J. H. Overton, *The English Church in the Nineteenth Century* (London, 1894); and L. E. Elliott-Binns, *Religion in the Victorian Era* (London, 1936), Chap. 2.

[9] Newman's account may be read in English in Wilfrid Ward's

edition of the *Apologia*, Introduction, pp. xxii–xxviii. According to Storr, *op. cit.*, p. 78, the terms High, Low, and Broad Church were not applied to early nineteenth-century divisions; but see Ward's ed. of the *Apologia*, p. xxvii.

¹⁰ *Apologia*, p. 394.

¹¹ The Fathers of the Birmingham Oratory, who published the *Correspondence of John Henry Newman with Keble and Others: 1839–1845* (London, 1917), try to explain away as far as possible all that points to Evangelicalism in Newman (pp. 115–16); but Ward, though noting that Newman's conversion of 1816 had "none of the 'special Evangelical experiences,'" acknowledges that a certain Calvinistic austerity persisted in his nature to the end (*Life*, I, 30–31). See Brilioth, *op. cit.*, pp. 32–35, 254, n. 4.

¹² See Fernande Tardivel, *La personnalité·littéraire de Newman* (Paris, 1937), Pt. II, Chap. III.

¹³ *Letters and Corresp.*, I, 35, 39.

¹⁴ Newman, *The Idea of a University*, p. 110.

¹⁵ Jean Guitton, *La philosophie de Newman: essai sur l'idée de développement* (Paris, 1933), p. xvi: "Pour comprendre Newman il eût fallu le rattacher au XVIIIᵉ siècle anglais, dans lequel il s'enracine."

¹⁶ See *Letters and Corresp.*, I, 39, 41; *Idea of a Univ.*, p. 322; Ward, *Life*, II, 343. For an interesting discussion of Newman and Gibbon on Christianity, see S. T. McCloy, *Gibbon's Antagonism to Christianity* (London, 1933), pp. 267–75.

¹⁷ See J. Connop Thirlwall, "Cardinal Newman's Literary Preferences," *Modern Language Notes*, XLVIII (1933), 23–27; and S. T. Williams' article with the same title, in the *Sewanee Review*, XXVIII (1920), 486–97.

¹⁸ Abbé E. Dimnet, "Newman et l'intellectualisme," *Les annales de philosophie chrétienne*, CLIV (1907), 272–73.

¹⁹ Newman, *Discussions and Arguments*, p. 293.

²⁰ "Noetic," from the Greek *noesis*, means "knowing through a purely intellectual act." For an admiring but not very accurate account of the Noetics, see W. Tuckwell, *Pre-Tractarian Oxford* (London, 1909). Cf. *Letters and Corresp.*, I, 113–14; also Mark Pattison, *Memoirs* (London, 1885), pp. 78–79; Brilioth, *op. cit.*, Chap. VI.

²¹ Pattison, *op. cit.*, p. 79.

²² Brilioth, *op. cit.*, p. 82. It should be noted, too, that it was the Noetics, from the intellectual side, who drew Newman away from

his Evangelical principles, as it was Keble and Froude who drew him away on the doctrinal and ecclesiastical side.

[23] *Apologia*, pp. 119–22.

[24] *Apologia*, pp. 125–27. For another example of the importance of *personal* relations with Newman, see the *Autobiography* of Isaac Williams (London, 1892, pp. 49–50), Fellow and tutor at Trinity, and a close friend and colleague of Newman's in Tractarian days.

[25] Denys Gorce, *Newman et les Pères* (Paris, 1933), p. 34: "La lecture des Alexandrins ne fut point cependant pour Newman une révélation à proprement parler. Elle ne fit en réalité que fortifier une disposition native, une sorte de réflexe instinctif. . ." Gorce later says (p. 104): "On peut dire sans exagération aucune que Newman est tout entier dans son IVe siècle. C'est là son lieu intellectuel; c'est le paysage d'âme qu'il porte au fond de lui et qui transfigure ses journées."

[26] Newman, *Lectures on Certain Difficulties Felt by Anglicans*, II, 24.

[27] Newman, *Sermons Preached on Various Occasions*, pp. 92–93.

[28] Tardivel, *op. cit.*, p. 174.

[29] Charles Sarolea, *Cardinal Newman* (Edinburgh, 1908), p. 77; William Barry, *Newman* (London, 1905), p. 42. See also C. F. Harrold, "Newman and the Alexandrian Platonists," *Modern Philology*, XXXVII (1940), 279–91.

[30] *Apologia*, p. 127; *Letters and Corresp.*, I, 235.

[31] *Letters and Corresp.*, I, 49, 104–05.

[32] Aubrey de Vere, "Some Recollections of Cardinal Newman," *Nineteenth Century*, XL (1896), 396; J. B. Mozley, *Letters* (London, 1885), p. 35, n.

[33] W. Tuckwell, *Reminiscences of Oxford* (2nd ed., New York, 1908), p. 180; Thomas Mozley, *Reminiscences, Chiefly of Oriel College and the Oxford Movement* (London, 1882) (2 vols.), I, 205.

[34] W. Lockhart, "Cardinal Newman," *Reminiscences of Fifty Years Since* (London, 1891), p. 4.

[35] R. Blennerhassett, "Some of My Recollections of Cardinal Newman," *The Living Age*, CCXXXI (1901), 797.

[36] *Letters and Corresp.*, II, 242.

[37] *Ibid.*, I, 377.

[38] *Letters and Corresp.*, I, 373, 414, 417, etc.; Newman's re-

markable account, "My Illness in Sicily," is to be found in this work, toward the end of vol. I, pp. 413–30.

³⁹ These words were a free translation of the *Iliad*, xviii, l. 125, the words of Achilles: "And let them know that I too long have held aloof from war." Cf. the *Apologia*, pp. 135–36.

CHAPTER II

i.

¹ A. P. Stanley, *Life of Thomas Arnold, D.D.* (London, 1904), p. 278.

² S. L. Ollard, *A Short History of the Oxford Movement* (London, 1915), p. 17. Cf. R. W. Church, *The Oxford Movement*, pp. 3–12; G. Kelway, *The Story of the Catholic Revival* (2nd ed., London, 1915). Y. Brilioth (*The Anglican Revival*, pp. 6–15) attempts to correct the errors of omission and commission to be found in these conventional accounts.

³ D. C. Somervell, *English Thought in the Nineteenth Century* (New York, 1929), p. 17.

⁴ Brilioth, *op. cit.*, Chaps. II and III, especially pp. 17–20, 42, 43, etc. For a remarkably rosy picture of the 18th- and early 19th-century English Church as being in "the healthiest condition," see James Anthony Froude's "The Oxford Counter-Reformation," *Short Studies on Great Subjects* (London, 1917) (new impression), IV, 237 ff. Froude's account is strongly anti-Tractarian, partly from early disappointments over the cenobitic experiment at Littlemore.

⁵ *Letters and Correspondence,* I, 233.

⁶ *Ibid.*, I, 204–05.

⁷ Wilfrid Ward, *The Oxford Movement* (The People's Books, London, 1913), p. 13.

⁸ Richard Carlile (1790–1843) and Thomas J. Wooler (1786?–1853) were free-thinking journalists and politicians who edited such radical periodicals as *The Reasoner* and *The Republican*. Carlile (whose name Newman misspells) was a disciple and editor of Tom Paine.

⁹ See Whately's *Logic*, final paragraphs of the original preface.

[10] See A. M. Fairbairn, *Catholicism: Roman and Anglican* (London, 1899), pp. 87–88; L. E. Elliott-Binns, *Religion in the Victorian Era,* pp. 182 ff.; Storr, *Development of English Theology,* pp. 143 ff., 219–27, etc. Critics have often remarked on how little the Tractarians knew of German thought and Biblical criticism. Newman once contemplated learning German, but was apparently dissuaded by his friend Bowden (*Letters and Corresp.,* II, 56–57). Pusey had studied German theology at Göttingen in 1825–27, but never appeared to have been influenced by any German teachings. In 1828 he published the now rarely procurable *Historical Enquiry into the Probable Causes of the Rationalist Character lately Predominant in the Theology of Germany.* Possibly he was influenced, as Brilioth points out (*op. cit.,* p. 249, n. 3) by the Pietists of Halle.

[11] See Carlyle's essay on "Sir Walter Scott," *Collected Works* (Centenary Ed.), Vol. IV of *Critical and Miscellaneous Essays* (London, 1896–99), p. 49.

[12] Ollard, *op. cit.,* p. 1.

[13] See Wilfrid Ward, *W. G. Ward and the Oxford Movement* (London, 1890), pp. 53, 68, 374, and Appendix D.

[14] L. A. Willoughby, "On Some German Affinities with the Oxford Movement," *Modern Language Review,* XXIX (1934), 52 ff.; Fairbairn, *op. cit.,* pp. 94–111.

[15] See Brilioth, *op. cit.,* Chap. V, esp. p. 58; Hoxie N. Fairchild, "Romanticism and the Religious Revival in England," *Journal of the History of Ideas,* II (1941), 330–38. Typical accounts which make misleading alignments of Tractarianism and Romanticism are those by W. R. Inge, *Outspoken Essays: First Series* (London, 1924), p. 31; Fairbairn, *op. cit.,* pp. 94 ff., 294, etc.; L. E. Gates' introductory essay on Newman in his *Selections* (New York, 1895), pp. l–lviii.

[16] *The Greville Memoirs: A Journal of the Reigns of King George IV and King William IV,* by the late Charles C. F. Greville, Esq., ed. Henry Reeve (3 vols.) (London, 1874), I, 184 ff.

[17] Newman, *The Arians of the Fourth Century,* pp. 257–58.

[18] Birmingham Fathers, *Correspondence with Keble and Others,* pp. 172–73.

[19] J. A. Froude, *Short Studies,* IV, 276. Newman, says Edwin Berry Burgum, was "one of the few Englishmen of his time who actually believed the doctrines, and what is always essential to belief, the implications of the doctrines, which most Victorians supposed they

believed." ("Cardinal Newman and the Complexity of Truth," *Sewanee Review*, XXXVIII [1930], 315.)

[20] Pattison, *Memoirs*, pp. 172–73; Lord Blachford, *Letters*, ed. George E. Marindin (London, 1896), p. 15; Ward, *W. G. Ward and the Oxford Movement*, pp. 79–80. Moralism as a central element in Tractarian appeal has been given considerable attention in recent years: Brilioth, *op. cit.*, Chap. XII; Cross, *John Henry Newman*, Chap. VI; Tardivel, *La personnalité littéraire de Newman*, pp. 263 ff.; etc.

[21] See *Cardinal Newman and William Froude, F. R. S.: a Correspondence*, ed. G. H. Harper (Baltimore, 1933), p. 127; *W. G. Ward and the Oxford Movement*, p. 392.

[22] *Discussions and Arguments*, p. 284.

[23] Knox, *The Tractarian Movement*, pp. 26–27.

[24] Ward, *The Oxford Movement*, p. 21; J. A. Froude, *op. cit.*, p. 270.

[25] *Apologia*, p. 160.

[26] *Ibid.*, p. 144.

[27] The whole of Tract I is present in Church's *The Oxford Movement*, pp. 112–18; Tracts I, II, III, IV, VII, X, XV, and XVIII are summarized in Knox, *op. cit.*, pp. 157–59. (Knox's whole account of the Movement is Evangelical and severely critical.)

[28] T. Mozley, *Reminiscences*, I, 313.

[29] *Letters and Corresp.*, I, 490. One should remember, at this point, that early Tractarianism was strongly anti-Roman, seeking to avoid both the emotionalism and intellectual vacuity of popular Protestantism and the "superstitions" and "corruptions" of Roman Catholicism.

[30] T. Mozley, *op. cit.*, I, 315, 316.

[31] Church, *op. cit.*, pp. 129–30.

[32] Matthew Arnold's description of Newman, in his essay on "Emerson," in *Discourses in America* (London, 1896), pp. 139–40.

ii.

[1] See, for example, the Evangelically biased account by Knox, *op. cit.*, pp. 166–74.

[2] Newman replied to Wiseman in an article, "The Fall of De la Mennais," for the *British Critic* (1837), in which he attempted to show that the Roman Church "is after all . . . but an established

thing," like the Anglican. Newman's argument is not very effective, and it leaves untouched Wiseman's criticism of the failure of the Anglican Church to protect herself from heresy. (See Newman's *Essays Critical and Historical*, I, 138–72; and Knox's account [*op. cit.*, pp. 175–77] of the article.)

³ When Froude died, Newman chose from among his effects his copy of the Breviary, and soon began using it himself.

⁴ *Letters and Corresp.*, II, 177. From Newman's list of events, we note the predominance of personal loss, of preoccupation with theological issues, of his still vehement hostility to the Church of Rome, of his chapel at Littlemore (with which his mother and sisters had so much to do in its construction and furnishing), and of his early responsibility for the rejuvenation of the *British Critic*, which he edited from 1838 to 1841.

⁵ Published later as the first volume of the *Via Media* (2 vols., 1877).

⁶ Newman's theory of the *Via Media*, which Christopher Dawson says "still remains the best justification for the essential Anglican position" (*Spirit of the Oxford Movement* [New York, 1933], p. 102), should not be confused with the Branch Theory, put forward by another Tractarian, William Palmer, in his *Treatise on the Church of Christ* (1838).

⁷ At this time, in the Adam de Brome Chapel, Newman delivered several other lectures, some of them of considerable interest: *Lectures on Justification* (1838), usually neglected, but regarded by Brilioth (*op. cit.*, p. 140) as entitled to a more central place than the *Via Media* "in the unfortunately unwritten dogmatic history of Anglicanism"; *Lectures on the Scripture Proof of the Doctrine of the Church* (1838), later published as Tract LXXXV, and still later as part III of *Discussions and Arguments* (1872); *Advent Sermons on Anti-Christ*, published as Tract LXXXIII, and as part II, "The Patristical Idea of Anti-Christ," in *Discussions and Arguments*.

⁸ Ollard, *op. cit.*, p. 56.

⁹ *Apologia*, p. 174.

¹⁰ Church, *op. cit.*, pp. 184–85.

¹¹ J. A. Froude, *op. cit.*, pp. 282–83.

¹² T. Mozley, *op. cit.*, I, 208.

¹³ Bertram Newman (*Cardinal Newman* [London, 1925], p. 128) cites, for example, Newman's subsequent choice of Cardinal Manning "to be his right-hand man" in the Irish University enterprise. In this Brémond agrees, and quotes Newman: "I am a bad

hand at characters," and cites *My Campaign in Ireland,* pp. xxiii–xxiv. (See *The Mystery of Newman,* p. 44, n.)

[14] J. A. Froude, *op. cit.,* p. 283.

[15] *Apologia,* p. 152.

[16] *Ibid.,* p. 166.

iii.

[1] *Apologia,* p. 201.

[2] *Ibid.,* p. 208. "Home Thoughts Abroad" appeared in the March and April numbers of the *British Magazine,* 1836, and eventually as "How to Accomplish It," the first essay in *Disc. and Arg.,* an essay discussing the possibility of giving the English the benefit of Roman Catholic advantages without submitting to Rome.

[3] *Apologia,* pp. 210–11.

[4] *Ibid.,* pp. 212–13; Ollard, *op. cit.,* pp. 62–64.

[5] *Letters and Corresp.,* II, 286.

[6] *Apologia,* p. 213.

[7] *Letters and Corresp.,* II, 300.

[8] *Apologia,* p. 245.

[9] *Ibid.,* p. 235.

[10] See Ward, *W. G. Ward and the Oxford Movement,* p. 152.

[11] Cf. the *Apologia,* pp. 192–93: "I claimed, in behalf of who would in the Anglican Church, that he might hold . . . a comprecation with the Saints with Bramhall, and the Mass all but Transubstantiation with Andrewes, or with Hooker that Transubstantiation itself is not a point for Churches to part communion upon, or with Hammond that a General Council, truly such, never did, never shall err in a matter of faith, or with Bull that man had in paradise and lost inward grace by the fall, or with Thorndike that penance is a propitiation for post-baptismal sin, or with Pearson that the all-powerful name of Jesus is no otherwise given than in the Catholic Church."

[12] Church, *op. cit.,* pp. 298–99, n.

[13] J. A. Froude, *op. cit.,* pp. 305, 307.

[14] R. H. Hutton, *Cardinal Newman* (London, 1891), p. 145. Yet Brilioth (*op. cit.,* p. 155) calls Tract XC "a very melancholy document" full of "a certain double dealing," showing "how a really great man can become little in a false and ambiguous situation"; and Knox (*op. cit.,* p. 255) in a devastating, and distorting, chapter, calls the Tract the "culmination of [the] sophistries" to which the Trac-

tarians had resorted in order to "falsify history" for their own purposes.

[15] Sarolea, *Cardinal Newman,* p. 29.

[16] *Letters and Corresp.,* II, 97.

[17] Sarolea, *op. cit.,* p. 31.

[18] Ward, *W. G. Ward and the Oxford Movement,* p. 371.

[19] This retractation was really an apology for violence of language rather than a renunciation of the Anglican position. On his entry into the Roman Church, in 1845, Newman published a fresh "Recantation of Anti-Catholic Statements" (now to be found in *Via Media,* vol. II). One should note, with Brilioth (*op. cit.,* p. 166), that "the events of this year 1843 are reflected in Newman's lectures on the 'Difficulties of Anglicans,' delivered after his secession."

[20] *Apologia,* p. 318.

[21] *Ibid.,* p. 290.

[22] These words are the able summing-up by Dean Church of Newman's growing conception of the Roman Church in the Littlemore period (*Oxford Movement,* pp. 229–30).

[23] Pattison, *op. cit.,* p. 210.

[24] Ward, *Life of Newman,* I, 87. See, also, on the infinite labors of this period, *Letters and Corresp.,* II, 459–68; *Correspondence with Keble and Others,* pp. 380–83; and Harper, *op. cit.,* pp. 66–67.

[25] *Letters and Corresp.,* II, 468.

[26] For a complete account of this crucial night in Newman's life, see F. Oakeley, *Historical Notes on the Tractarian Movement,* 1833–1845 (London, 1865), pp. 98–99; otherwise, Ollard, *op. cit.,* pp. 101–02.

[27] Newman, *Essay on the Development of Christian Doctrine,* final paragraph.

iv.

[1] *Apologia,* p. 331. The "Liberal" aftermath at Oxford, after 1845, has been well described by Pattison, when "the railway mania of 1847 . . . rushed in to fill the vacuum . . . [and] 'instead of High, Low, and Broad Church, they talked of high embankments, the broad gauge, and low dividends' " (*Memoirs,* pp. 235–36). Mill's *Logic* captured Oxford, and the repeal of the Corn Laws, and the beginning of the fabulous "mid-Victorian prosperity" soon put Newman and Tractarianism out of most men's minds.

[2] Cf. Sarolea, *op. cit.,* pp. 71–78; J. N. Figgis, *The Fellowship of the Mystery* (London, 1914), pp. 249 ff.

[3] R. H. Coats, "Birmingham Mystics of the Mid-Victorian Era," *Hibbert Journal*, XVI (1917–18), 491–92.

[4] Newman, *Essays Critical and Historical*, II, 170–71.

[5] *Difficulties of Anglicans*, I, 379.

[6] *Apologia*, p. 291.

[7] *Cardinal Newman and William Froude, F.R.S.: a Correspondence*, ed. Gordon Huntington Harper (Baltimore, 1933), p. 68.

[8] J. Elliott Ross, *John Henry Newman* (New York, 1933), pp. xv–xvi.

[9] Ward, *Life*, I, 568. One might well note at this point that a carefully balanced and complete account of the Newman-Manning relationship has yet to appear. Too many readers of (and about) Newman base their knowledge of that relationship on Lytton Strachey's brilliant but highly misleading pages in his essay on "Cardinal Manning" in *Eminent Victorians*, especially section six and the famous passage about "the meeting of the eagle and the dove." Even J. Lewis May seems to fall under Strachey's spell: Newman is the "dove," Manning the "hawk" (*Cardinal Newman*, p. 190). However eagle-like or hawk-like Manning may have been, Newman does not appear, on any careful consideration of him, to be particularly dove-like — Kingsley, Pusey, Gladstone, and others who fell under his controversial blows, would never have recognized the emasculated and pathetically helpless creature so patronizingly painted by Strachey.

[10] *Ibid.*, I, 573.

[11] Ward, *Life*, II, 438.

CHAPTER III

[1] Wilfrid Ward, *Last Lectures*, p. 23. "I know," wrote Aubrey de Vere in 1850, "that [Newman] . . . anticipates an unprecedented outburst of infidelity all over the world. To withstand it he deems it his special vocation." Ward, *Aubrey de Vere: a Memoir* (London, 1904), p. 182.

[2] The Metaphysical Society met once a month to debate matters lying at the foundation of religious belief. All schools of thought were represented, from Huxley and Tyndall to Gladstone, Dean Church, and Cardinal Manning. Newman never approved of the Society and declined an invitation to membership offered by R. H. Hutton in 1869.

[3] Newman, *Oxford University Sermons*, p. 122.

i.

[1] Newman, *Lectures on Justification*, pp. 325–31, 340.

[2] Arnold, *Literature and Dogma* (London, 1891) (Popular Ed.), Chap. I, p. 16.

[3] *Apologia*, p. 150.

[4] *Oxford Univ. Sermons*, p. 297.

[5] See section III of *Discussions and Arguments* ("Holy Scripture in its Relation to the Catholic Creed"), p. 134.

[6] *Arians of the Fourth Century*, p. 221 (italics added).

[7] H. L. Stewart, *A Century of Anglo-Catholicism* (London, 1929), p. 100.

[8] *Essays Critical and Historical*, I, 42.

[9] R. W. Church, *Occasional Papers* (London, 1897), II, 457.

[10] *Essays Crit. and Hist.*, I, 45.

[11] *Ibid.*, I, 47 (italics added).

ii.

[1] So surmise the Birmingham Fathers. See *Correspondence with Keble and Others*, p. 112.

[2] Scott, *Works*, V, Essay xxii. For Newman's acknowledgment of his debt to Scott, Milner, and Jones of Nayland, see the *Apologia*, pp. 108–10.

[3] See Milner's *History of the Church of Christ* (Boston, 1809–11), I, 282, 284, etc.

[4] Brilioth, *The Anglican Revival*, p. 35.

[5] *Apologia*, p. 110.

[6] William Jones, *Theological and Miscellaneous Works* (London, 1826), III, 168. As we shall see, Newman owes an enormous debt to Bishop Butler, especially to *The Analogy*: "Christianity," says Butler, "is a particular scheme under the general plan of providence . . . : consisting itself also of various parts, and a mysterious economy . . ." (*Analogy*, London, 1857, p. 241).

[7] *Letters and Correspondence*, I, 205–06.

[8] Newman, *Parochial and Plain Sermons*, IV, 174.

iii.

[1] *Arians,* p. 146.
[2] See Ward, *Last Lectures,* pp. 39–40; *Arians,* p. 146.
[3] J. A. Froude, *Carlyle's Life in London* (London, 1884), II, 462.
[4] *Oxf. Univ. Sermons,* pp. 332–34, 336, 350. By "sacred impressions," Newman means "those living ideas of sacred things, from which alone change of heart or conduct can proceed. This awful vision is what Scripture seems to designate by the phrases 'Christ in us,' 'Christ dwelling in us by faith.'" It is a knowledge of a most intimate kind, e.g. "knowledge of Christ Jesus." But unlike the knowledge supplied by the senses, which is direct, immediate, and spontaneous, it fluctuates, is sometimes shadowy and ill-defined in the mind; hence, says Newman, "we form creeds as a chief mode of perpetuating these impressions" (pp. 332, 333).
[5] *Arians,* pp. 36–37.
[6] *Ibid.,* pp. 142 ff.
[7] *Letters and Corresp.,* II, 156. Newman was fond of distinguishing between men who *believed* in revealed religion and those (like Coleridge, Thomas Arnold, Maurice, and Carlyle) who had *opinions* or a *philosophy* of religion. The latter, he felt, being individual and subjective, are without authority and are a poor recourse for harassed mankind.
[8] *Apologia,* pp. 127–28.
[9] *Arians,* p. 84.
[10] *Apologia,* p. 128. On Newman's affinity with the Alexandrian Fathers, see C. F. Harrold, "Newman and the Alexandrian Platonists," *Modern Philology,* XXXVII (1940), 279–91.
[11] See Joseph Butler, *The Analogy of Religion Natural and Revealed to the Constitution and Course of Nature* (London, 1857), pp. 240–50, 378–79, etc.
[12] *Apologia,* p. 113. Cf. Butler, *op. cit.,* p. 246, for Butler's "sacramental" view: "The appearance of deficiencies and irregularities in nature is owing to its being a scheme, *but in part made known,* and of such a certain particular kind in other respects" (italics added). Thus Butler, like Newman, speaks frequently of the "mysterious economy" of the world, of "various dispensations" "through a succession of ages," etc. (pp. 241–43).

[13] See Milner's *History of the Church of Christ*, in his collected *Works* (Boston, 1809–11), I, 19. Milner uses the term "outpourings," rather than "effusions." The former term was probably substituted when the author's brother, Isaac, brought out a revised edition of the collected *Works*. The meaning remains the same.

[14] *Apologia*, p. 129.

[15] See Newman's severe "Postscript" to "Rationalism in Religion" (*Essays Crit. and Hist.*, I, 96–99), in which he contemns the "spurious Christianity" of Schleiermacher and his English brethren, Erskine and Abbott, who believe that religion contains nothing unintelligible to the intellect, and that its one object is "to stir the affections, and soothe the heart." This, thinks Newman, is a serious doctrinal error, a snare over the whole of Protestant Christianity.

[16] See Guitton, *La philosophie de Newman*, pp. 2, 22.

iv.

[1] Newman, *Historical Sketches*, I, 342.

[2] *Ibid.*, p. 381; Vincent of Lerins, *Commonitorium Primum*, in Migne's *Patrologia Latina*, L, 637–86, especially p. 640. It is possible that Newman got from Vincent of Lerins his habit of speaking of the "notes" of the Church.

[3] Republished in *Disc. and Arg.* as the opening section, entitled "How to Accomplish It."

[4] *Apologia*, p. 205.

[5] *Disc. and Arg.*, p. 19; *Apologia*, p. 208.

[6] *Essays Crit. and Hist.*, II, 12–13.

[7] *Ibid.*, p. 40.

[8] *Ibid.*, pp. 47, 53, 72.

[9] *Ibid.*, p. 44.

[10] *Oxf. Univ. Sermons*, p. 318.

[11] *Ibid.*, p. 318; Newman cites Butler's *Analogy*, Part II, Chap. iii. We find the following "developmental" sentence in Butler (p. 232): "If [the Biblical scheme as a whole] ever comes to be understood, before the restitution of all things, and without miraculous interventions, it must be . . . by the continuance and progress of learning and of liberty, and by particular persons attending to, comparing and pursuing, intimations scattered up and down it, which are overlooked and disregarded by the generality of the world." This is typical of the many passages in Butler which encouraged Newman in his formulation of the theory of development.

[12] *Oxf. Univ. Sermons*, p. 323.
[13] *Ibid.*, p. 334.
[14] *Ibid.*, pp. 340–41.
[15] *Ibid.*, pp. 342, 343.
[16] *Ibid.*, pp. 348–49.
[17] *Apologia*, pp. 290–92.

CHAPTER IV

i.

[1] Frank Leslie Cross, *John Henry Newman*, p. 102.
[2] *Apologia*, pp. 318–19.
[3] Frank Leslie Cross, "Newman and the Doctrine of Development," *Church Quarterly Review*, CXV (1933), pp. 245–57; *John Henry Newman*, pp. 107–09.
[4] *Ibid.*, p. 254.
[5] *Ibid.*, p. 255.
[6] Cross, *John Henry Newman*, pp. 108–09. Newman was destined to meet with disappointment when Rome came to examine his *Essay*. One of the ironies of his life was that when the Jesuits pronounced on it, "they took the part of Bull against Petavius and said Petavius went too far and retracted." They admitted the principle of development, but felt that Newman had carried it too far. (See Ward, *Life of Newman*, I, 161.)
[7] Sylvester P. Juergens, *Newman on the Psychology of Faith in the Individual* (New York, 1928), p. 265. Juergens cites, Fr. Marin-Sola, *L'Evolution homogène du Dogme catholique*. Deuxième édit., Tome II, Ch. VII, pp. 127 ff. See also E. D. Benard, *A Preface to Newman's Theology* (St. Louis, Mo., 1945), pp. 84, 96, etc.
[8] See, for example, Wilfrid Ward in *Problems and Persons*, p. 9; and Guitton, *La philosophie de Newman*, pp. 54, 137–40.
[9] Cf. Hutton, *Cardinal Newman*, pp. 165, 185; Barry, *Newman*, p. 278; Tardivel, *La personnalité littéraire de Newman*, p. 45; J. M. Flood, *Cardinal Newman* (London, 1933), p. 232; J. L. May, *Cardinal Newman* (New York, 1937), p. 55; Ross, *John Henry Newman*, pp. 30 ff; and A. Fawkes, *Studies in Modernism* (London, 1913), p. 47.
[10] Sarolea, *Cardinal Newman*, pp. 155–56; Faber, *Oxford*

Apostles, p. 111; see also Cross, *John Henry Newman*, pp. 104–05. Newman's "development," one might say, is somewhat like the *Entwicklung* of the German Romantic philosophers, such as Fichte — a logical rather than a temporal process, certainly in no sense an immanental process. Benard (*op. cit.*, pp. 96, 103, 107, 109, etc.) sees Newman's "development" simply as the Scholastics see it, i.e. *explicatio impliciti.*

[11] Barry, *op. cit.*, p. 280.

[12] J. A. Elbert, *Evolution of Newman's Conception of Faith* (Philadelphia, 1932), p. 72.

[13] Guitton, *op. cit.*: "le progrès des formules dogmatiques n'est pas pour lui [Newman] une pure 'explication,' il est une vie; le temps ne déroule pas le dépot, il le développe véritablement . . ." (p. 118). Cf. L. A. Sabatier, *Les religions d'autorité et la religion de l'esprit* (1904), pp. 126–27; George Tyrrell, *Christianity at the Cross-Roads* (1909), p. 30; and V. F. Storr, *English Theology in the Nineteenth Century* (1913), p. 302.

[14] See *Essays Crit. and Hist.*, I, 288n. (Italics added to "fixed," "enlargement," and "new.")

[15] *Difficulties of Anglicans*, II, 314.

[16] *Ibid.*, II, 327.

[17] For the English and Latin statements of Newman and Perrone, see Ward, *Life*, I, 184–85. See also "The Newman-Perrone Paper on Development," ed. T. Lynch, *Gregorianum*, XVI, fasc. iii (1935), 402–47.

[18] Guitton, *op. cit.*, p. 116.

[19] Bertram Newman, *Cardinal Newman*, pp. 92–93.

[20] R. Blennerhassett, "Some Recollections of Cardinal Newman," *Living Age*, XIII (1901), 796.

ii.

[1] Bertram Newman, *op. cit.*, p. 86.

[2] E. Przywara, *Einführung in Newmans Wesen und Werk*, p. 63.

[3] See Cross, *John Henry Newman*, p. 179. Only a few of the more important and typical alterations in the book may be noticed here. The 1878 edition of the *Essay* breaks up the text into shorter and less formidable-looking units, and each section is given an Arabic numeral and a helpful title. Many passages in the first edition are omitted entirely, but without changing the book's character. The famous discussion of the tests or notes is lifted from a sub-section of

Chapter I and in 1878 given importance as Chapter V. Section III of Chapter III becomes Section I; Section IV of this Chapter becomes Section I of Chapter IV. Section II of Chapter IV is entirely new material. These are typical shiftings and enlargements of the text. No chapter escaped alteration; in all cases more effective organization and more weighty argument resulted. Interestingly, the "Office of Saint Mary," used to illustrate the fourth test in the edition of 1845, is applied to the fifth test in 1878, as are also "Resurrection and Relics," and the "*Cultus* of Saints and Angels"; "The Merit of Virginity" becomes "The Virgin Life." The fourth test is illustrated, as we have seen, with Pardons, Penances, Satisfactions, etc. The sixth and seventh tests are virtually unchanged. — Newman's changes in the text, the addition of new footnotes, and the general effect thus produced would make an interesting study of considerable substance and value.

[4] *Development of Christian Doctrine*, p. 2.

[5] *Ibid.*, pp. 29–30.

[6] *Ibid.*, p. 40.

[7] *Ibid.*, p. 54.

[8] *Ibid.*, pp. 89–90.

[9] *Ibid.*, pp. 93–94.

[10] *Ibid.*, p. 108.

[11] *Ibid.*, p. 112.

[12] *Ibid.*, p. 129.

[13] *Ibid.*, p. 154.

[14] Guitton, *op. cit.*, p. 112.

[15] *Development*, p. 242.

[16] *Ibid.*, final paragraph of Sect. I, Chap. VI.

[17] *Ibid.*, pp. 249–72.

[18] *Ibid.*, p. 284.

[19] *Ibid.*, p. 316.

[20] *Ibid.*, pp. 321–22. Newman's second summary, that of the Church of the fourth century, is not given, for lack of space. It is readily accessible, however, not only in Newman's *Essay*, but also, and perhaps more easily, in Ward's *Life*, I, 90; and Hutton, *op. cit.*, pp. 170–71. In the 1878 ed., see pp. 271–72; in the 1845 ed., see p. 269.

[21] *Development*, pp. 364–65.

[22] *Ibid.*, p. 373.

[23] *Ibid.*, p. 402.

[24] Hutton, *op. cit.*, p. 185.

[25] *Development,* p. 442.

[26] *Ibid.,* p. 444. It is interesting to note, with Sarolea (*op. cit.,* p. 122, n.) that "in the *Theory of Development,* in which he discusses every Catholic dogma, he does not once mention the doctrine of Hell and eternal punishment." — An excellent and complete summary of Newman's *Essay,* with a brief description of the various applications, may be found in the article, "Dogme," by E. Dublanchy, in the *Dictionnaire de théologie catholique,* IV, cols. 1630 ff. A comparatively recent study of the Anglican background of the *Essay* is that by James J. Byrne, "The Notion of Doctrinal Development in the Anglican Writings of J. H. Newman," *Ephemerides theologicae Lovanienses,* XIV (1937), 230–86.

CHAPTER V

i.

[1] See Walter Pater's essay on "Style," *Appreciations* (New York, 1902), p. 14.

[2] Pattison, *Memoirs,* p. 238.

[3] Newman, *Lectures on the Present Position of Catholics in England,* p. 390.

[4] *Idea of a University,* p. 238.

[5] Ross, *John Henry Newman,* p. 83.

[6] *Idea of a Univ.,* p. 13.

[7] W. F. Stockley, *Newman, Education, and Ireland* (London, 1933), p. 39; T. Corcoran, *Newman: Selected Discourses on Liberal Knowledge, from the Text of the First Edition, Dublin,* 1852, *With an Introduction,* (Dublin: University College, 1929), pp. lxxi ff.

[8] Stockley, *op. cit.,* p. 47.

[9] Ward, *Life of Newman,* I, 351; Corcoran, *op. cit.,* p. xx.

[10] Ward, *Life,* I, 312.

[11] Corcoran, *op. cit.,* p. xvi; but see Stockley, *op. cit.,* pp. 49, 172, 173, for a view that Newman was not an "invader" seeking to impose a foreign pattern of education on Ireland. However, both May Yardley and Paul Sobry feel that Newman went beyond the needs of the Irish at the time in overstating the nature of "intellectual culture." See May Yardley, *John Henry Newman: the Idea of a University* (Cambridge University Press, 1931); pp. xxv–xxvi; and

Paul Sobry, *Newman en zijn Idea of a University* (Louvain, 1934), pp. 91–99.

[12] The second half of *The Idea of a University* is made up of lectures on Christianity and letters, on literature, on university preaching, etc., and is thus not so unified as the nine earlier Discourses.

ii.

[1] Knickerbocker, *Creative Oxford*, p. 48.

[2] *Idea of a Univ.*, p. ix.

[3] *Ibid.*, p. xiii.

[4] *Ibid.*, p. xiv.

[5] *Historical Sketches*, III, 331.

[6] Knickerbocker, *op. cit.*, pp. 33–46; *Idea of a Univ.*, p. 31.

[7] *Idea of a Univ.*, p. xx.

[8] *Ibid.*, p. xxii.

[9] *Ibid.*, p. 101.

[10] *Ibid.*, p. 147.

[11] *Ibid.*, p. 146.

[12] *Ibid.*, p. 145. Cf. Newman's contemptuous allusion to London University as "Gower Street College" in "The Tamworth Reading Room" (in *Discussions and Arguments*, p. 274), because of the new university's growing size, as well as for its Liberal support.

[13] *Hist. Sketches*, III, 74.

[14] *Idea of a Univ.*, pp. 24, 42.

[15] *Ibid.*, p. 72.

[16] *Ibid.*, p. 232.

[17] *Ibid.*, p. 471.

[18] *Ibid.*, p. 479.

[19] *Ibid.*, pp. 466–67.

[20] *Ibid.*, pp. 469–70.

iii.

[1] *Idea of a Univ.*, p. 142.

[2] *Ibid.*, pp. 143–44.

[3] *Ibid.*, p. 132; cf. the interesting anticipation of several passages in this Discourse to be found in the *Oxford University Sermons*, pp. 282 ff., 292 ff.: (i) on ways of "enlarging the mind," and (ii) the dilemma of men without "a philosophical view." Newman acknowledges in a footnote of *The Idea* (p. 130) that he is using almost *ver-*

batim some portions of the fourteenth Oxford University sermon.

[4] *Idea of a Univ.*, pp. 113–14.

[5] *Ibid.*, p. 130.

[6] *Ibid.*, pp. 151–52.

[7] *Ibid.*, pp. 107–09.

[8] *Ibid.*, p. 160.

[9] Knickerbocker, *op. cit.*, p. 47.

[10] *Idea of a Univ.*, pp. 117, 118n.

[11] *Ibid.*, pp. 120–21; cf. Newman's essay on John Davison, friend of Keble, and Fellow of Oriel shortly before Newman's time at Oxford, for quotations from Davison's "National School Sermon," in which the author holds that "education will never produce virtue, . . . that the power of reading, or the use of it, makes no man either wise or virtuous" (*Essays Critical and Historical*, II, 408). There is little doubt that Newman derived some of his ideas for his Discourses from Davison, especially the idea that secular and religious education are two quite separate disciplines.

[12] *Idea of a Univ.*, p. 101.

[13] *Ibid.*, Discourse VI, sects. 5 and 6.

[14] *Ibid.*, p. 113.

[15] *Ibid.*, pp. 122–23; Corcoran, *op. cit.*, pp. lxxi ff., "The Philosophy of Severance and its Origins." Corcoran maintains that in the Discourse of June 5, 1852, which Newman excluded from the edition of 1859, Newman "furnishes the antidote for the Oxford Philosophy of Severance between Liberal Knowledge and . . . 'Virtue or Religion,' " in declaring that Catholics view all knowledge as *one*, a system which may be said to be *in equilibrio* so long as no one branch of knowledge, such as theology, is excluded (pp. lxxi–lxxv).

[16] *Idea of a Univ.*, pp. 121–23.

[17] *Ibid.*, p. 177; however, as we shall elsewhere note, Newman was skeptical about the influence of universities on their immediate communities. (See *Historical Sketches*, III, 281.)

[18] *Idea of a Univ.*, pp. 177–78.

[19] *Ibid.*, pp. 184–86.

[20] *Ibid.*, p. 189.

[21] *Ibid.*, pp. 191–201 (Newman's italics); cf. Burke's *Reflections on the French Revolution* (London, 1790), p. 113.

[22] *Idea of a Univ.*, p. 202; *Hamlet*, III, 4, ll. 147–49.

[23] *Idea of a Univ.*, p. 192.

[24] *Ibid.*, pp. 204–08, 211.

iv.

1 *Idea of a Univ.*, pp. 208–11.
2 *Hist. Sketches*, II, 64–65.
3 H. V. Routh, *Money, Morals and Manners as Revealed in Modern Literature* (London, 1935), p. 137 (but see also the whole of Chap. IX, "The Ideals of a Gentleman"). See, too, Esmé Wingfield-Stratford's *The Making of a Gentleman* (London, 1938), especially the very amusing and informative twelfth chapter, "The Gentleman-Conscious Victorians," which ends climactically with Newman's famous definition.
4 *Kenilworth*, Chap. III (quoted in Routh, *op. cit.*, p. 133).
5 Corcoran, *op. cit.*, p. lxxviii.
6 Ward, *Life*, I, 60.

CHAPTER VI

1 Ward, *Life of Newman*, II, 262.
2 *Oxford University Sermons*, pp. 54 ff.; see Sermon IV.
3 *Ibid.*, p. 191.
4 Ward, *Life*, II, 245.
5 See the *Parochial and Plain Sermons*, VI, 249, also I, 320; *Oxf. Univ. Sermons*, p. 224.
6 *Apologia*, pp. 113–14.

i.

1 *Arians of the Fourth Century*, pp. 75–76; see an earlier passage on this subject in Newman's essay on "Cicero" (*Historical Sketches*, I, 266–73), in which he discusses The New Academy and its skeptical denial that reason and sensation can deliver ultimate truth in its purity.
2 Brilioth, *The Anglican Revival*, p. 290.
3 *Lectures on Justification*, p. 267.
4 "Tamworth Reading Room," *Discussions and Arguments*, p. 294.
5 Newman, *An Essay in Aid of a Grammar of Assent*, pp. 91–97; *Disc. and Arg.*, p. 293.
6 See *Oxf. Univ. Sermons*, No. XIII, "Implicit and Explicit Reason."

[7] *Ibid.*, pp. 203 ff.

[8] Thus Newman writes in a letter of 1840: "The human mind in its present state is unequal to its own powers of apprehension; it embraces more than it can master . . . Absolute certainty, then, cannot be attained here; we must resign ourselves to doubt as the *trial under* which it is God's will we should do our duty and prepare ourselves for His presence" (italics in text). — *Letters and Correspondence*, II, 311.

[9] F. Bacchus, "Newman's Oxford University Sermons," *The Month*, CXL (1922), 2.

[10] For an excellent analysis of Newman's teachings on faith prior to 1845, chiefly in the Oxford sermons, see J. A. Elbert, *Evolution of Newman's Conception of Faith* (Philadelphia, 1932).

[11] Ward, *Life*, I, 393–94. Newman foresaw quite early the mental attitude of many late-Victorians toward religious matters as illustrated in the 1870's by John Morley, who wrote in "Robespierre": "We will not attack you as Voltaire did; we will not exterminate you; we shall explain you . . . As History explains your dogma, so Science will dry it up; . . . the mental climate will gradually deprive your symbols of their nourishment . . ." (*Critical Miscellanies* [London, 1886], I, 81). The new attack was to be intellectually subtle, and Newman therefore resorted to the appropriate weapons.

[12] Ward, *Life*, I, 423–25.

[13] *Ibid.*, II, 242–43; Ross, *John Henry Newman*, p. 213.

[14] Thomas H. Huxley, *Science and Christian Tradition*, London, 1894, p. 333n.: "If I were called upon to compile a Primer of 'Infidelity,' I think I should save myself trouble by making a selection from these works [Tract LXXXV and the 1843 *Essay on Miracles*], and from the *Essay on Development*."

ii.

[1] Ward, *Life*, II, 243. As Dr. Benard points out, Newman had "almost no training in the theology of the Schools" and used none of their "scientific phraseology and *axiomata*." E. D. Benard, *A Preface to Newman's Theology*, pp. 16, 18–19.

[2] Letter to Aubrey de Vere, in Ward, II, 245. One might note also that Newman's intense concentration on the process of faith and assent was quietly carried on in the uproar over papal infallibility.

[3] Guitton, in his *La philosophie de Newman* (pp. 211–12), lists the titles of many of these notes — "Faculty of Abstraction," "Ele-

ments of Thought," "Objects of Conscience," "Proof of Theism," etc. Through the courtesy of the Fathers of the Birmingham Oratory, I have been able to examine their content, in a transcription made by Erich Przywara. Newman in a note of September 24, 1888, forbade their publication. Actually they are of comparatively little value in our study of the *Grammar of Assent.* Written in the late 'fifties and early 'sixties, they are highly fragmentary, and promise little of the finished arguments in the *Grammar.*

[4] Ward, *Life*, II, 278.

[5] *Ibid.*, II, 253.

[6] Letter to Henry Wilberforce, in Ward, *Life*, II, 252.

[7] Ward, *Life*, II, 257.

[8] Barry, *Newman*, p. 191. Invaluable in any close study of the *Grammar* is Gordon H. Harper's edition of Newman's correspondence with William Froude, especially the first 187 pages (letters from April 1844 to July 28, 1871).

[9] Ward, *Life*, II, 266.

[10] Jennings, *Cardinal Newman*, p. 134.

[11] Ward, *Life*, II, 267.

[12] T. Harper, "Dr. Newman's Essay in Aid of a Grammar of Assent," *The Month*, XII (1870), 599–611, 667–92.

[13] See J. H. Randall, Jr., *The Making of the Modern Mind* (New York, 1926), pp. 296–97 (Voltaire's argument from "design" and "final cause," and Huxley's similar position).

[14] Ward, *Life*, II, 269.

[15] *Ibid.*, II, 268.

iii.

[1] Dimnet, *La pensé catholique dans l'Angleterre contemporaine* (Paris, 1906), pp. xxiii–xxiv; noted in Sarolea, *Cardinal Newman*, p. 101n.

[2] *Oxf. Univ. Sermons*, p. 63: "It is as absurd to argue men, as to torture them, into believing."

[3] *Grammar*, p. 99. We should note, too, that Newman is addressing the *whole man.* In this, according to Bishop Gore (*Philosophy of the Good Life*, London, 1930, p. 289), he ranks with Tertullian, in emphasizing the "unity of the soul of man, which feels when it reasons and reasons when it feels." Moreover, his whole treatment is, to some extent, and in the best sense, "popular" — he even draws an illustration in the *Grammar* from the *Penny Cyclopaedia* (see p. 393)!

[4] Hutton, *Cardinal Newman*, p. 234.

[5] *Oxf. Univ. Sermons*, p. xii (italics added): retrospective reasoning, analyzing itself, "brings out to advantage the implicit acts on which it has proceeded." — It was this faculty, developed to a high degree in Newman, which led him to write to Hurrell Froude the often-quoted sentence, "You and Keble are the philosophers [of the Oxford Movement], and I the rhetorician" (*Letters and Corresp.*, II, 156).

[6] Sylvester P. Juergens, *Newman on the Psychology of Faith in the Individual* (New York, 1928), p. 167; see Chap. I *passim*.

[7] *Oxf. Univ. Sermons*, pp. 275–76, 332.

[8] Juergens, *op. cit.*, p. 21.

[9] "Cicero," *Historical Sketches*, I, 293–94.

[10] An anonymous writer on the *Grammar* in *The Month*, XII (1870), 366.

[11] Dimnet, "Quelques aspects du Cardinal Newman," *La revue du clergé français*, April 1 and 15, p. 459 (or see *La pensée catholique dans l'Angleterre contemporaine*, p. 99; quoted in Tardivel, *La personnalité littéraire de Newman*, p. 84, n. 2).

[12] For a good popular account of the technique of the *Grammar*, see Bertram Newman, *Cardinal Newman*, pp. 172–83.

[13] Juergens, *op. cit.*, pp. 72, 177.

[14] *Grammar*, pp. 190–94; Juergens, *op. cit.*, p. 52. Yet Newman uses "inquiry" in what seems to be the usual sense on page 425.

[15] Juergens, *op. cit.*, pp. 268, 269–70; Elbert, *op. cit.*, pp. 64–65.

[16] M. C. D'Arcy, *The Nature of Belief* (London, 1931), pp. 118, 148, 151. The *New English Dictionary* will show that Newman uses "notion" in precisely the same fashion as do Hooker, Bacon, and Boyle.

[17] See Scott's *Essays*, p. 354.

[18] Lord Blachford, *Letters*, ed. G. E. Marindin (London, 1896), p. 409 (italics added). Ward, *Life*, II, 255.

[19] See *Arians*, pp. 467–68; Newman's article on "The Development of Religious Error," *Contemporary Review*, XLVIII (1885), 458, 460, etc., in which he attempts a reply, not altogether successful, to Principal Fairbairn's charge that Newman's use of "reason" made him an "intellectual skeptic." (A. M. Fairbairn, *Catholicism, Roman and Anglican*, pp. 206 ff.)

[20] F. Bacchus, "How to Read the Grammar of Assent," *The Month*, CXLIII (1924), 107.

iv.

[1] *The Development of Christian Doctrine*, p. 330.

[2] Juergens, *op. cit.*, p. 257; cf. the *Oxf. Univ. Sermons*, Nos. XII–XIV; and Przywara, *Einführung in Newmans Wesen und Werk*, pp. 59–60; see also p. 75 (Newman seen as holding Anselm's view, *credo ut intelligam*), and Juergens, p. 259 ("Newman does not hold the principle *Credo ut intelligam*"). This is a highly debatable point, and one that will long exercise Newman's admirers, according to the emphasis they place on his mystical tendencies.

[3] See J. F. Cronin, *Cardinal Newman: His Theory of Knowledge*, pp. 4–5; Locke, *Essay Concerning Human Understanding* (London, 1753), Bk. IV, Chap. XVII, pp. 291, 299. The value of this chapter of Locke's work for the student of the *Grammar* cannot be overestimated; both its language and its ideas illuminate the thought of Newman.

[4] Locke, *op. cit.*, p. 299.

[5] J. Lebreton, "Autour de Newman," *Revue pratique d'apologétique*, III (1906–07), 493–94; L. de Grandmaison, "John Henry Newman," *Etudes*, CX (1907), 56, 61–62, 67–68, 69; E. Baudin, "La philosophie de la foi chez Newman," *La revue de philosophie*, VIII (1906), 30; Fairbairn, *op. cit.* pp. 141 ff.; and D'Arcy, *op. cit.*, pp. 148–49. On Newman's alleged anti-intellectualism, see Dimnet, "Newman et l'intellectuelisme . . , "*Annales de philosophie chrétienne*, June, 1907, pp. 261–93, 448–75 (which is a vigorous answer to Baudin's charges) and Cronin, *op. cit.*, pp. 72–94.

[6] *Grammar*, p. 277.

[7] Aristotle, *Nichomachean Ethics*, VI, viii, 9 transl. Rackham (New York, 1926), quoted in Cronin, p. 28. It is interesting that throughout the *Grammar* Newman quotes no other of Aristotle's works than the *Nich. Ethics*.

[8] *Nich. Ethics*, VI, xi, 6.

[9] *Ibid.*, VI, ii, 5; vii, 7; Cronin, *op. cit.*, p. 28.

[10] *Idea of a University*, p. 109; *Grammar*, pp. 414–15.

[11] *Apologia*, p. 121.

[12] Joseph Butler, *The Analogy of Religion* (ed. of London, 1857), p. 3.

[13] Juergens, *op. cit.*, p. 254.

[14] See *Letters and Corresp.*, II, 39n.: "During this spring (1835) I for the *first time* read parts of Coleridge's works; and I am surprised how much I thought mine, is to be found there." See *Gram-*

mar, p. 305, for Newman's quotation from Coleridge's *Aids to Reflection* (ed. 1839, p. 59) on the idea that "in all finite quantity, there is an infinite." — Many writers, such as Barry, and Gardeil (*La crédibilité et l'apologétique*, Paris, 1912, p. 283n.) erroneously inferred that Newman borrowed directly from Coleridge. For a correction of this view, see Juergens, *op. cit.*, pp. 257 ff., and Cronin, *op. cit.*, pp. 21 ff.

[15] "Prospects of the Anglican Church," *Essays Critical and Historical*, I, 269.

[16] Ward, *Life*, I, 58n.

[17] See W. R. Castle, Jr., "Newman and Coleridge," *Sewanee Review*, XVII (1909), 139–52 (the author was unaware that Newman had read Coleridge); and Cronin, *op. cit.*, pp. 22–23; Harper, *Newman and William Froude*, pp. 22–23. For Coleridge's distinction between reason and understanding, see *Aids to Reflection* (London, 1859), pp. 167–85.

[18] From "Essays on Faith," quoted in Cronin, *op. cit.*, p. 23.

[19] There is also, of course, a parallel here between Newman and Carlyle, which has been ably traced by Cronin, *op. cit.*, pp. 23–24. Needless to say, there is no influence of Carlyle on Newman.

[20] The problem of how far Newman adapted Kant's ideas to his own system, in a really un-Kantian manner, has been dealt with by Erich Przywara, who has published portions of Newman's diary in "J. H. Newmans Problemstellung," *Stimmen der Zeit*, CXII (1927), reprinted as Chap. 5 in *Ringen der Gegenwart: Gesammelte Aufsätze*, 1922–27, II (Augsburg, 1929), 815–44. The conclusion is that, in spite of superficial resemblances, Newman's theory of knowledge and faith is actually too simple and personal to be in any sense Kantian: for Newman, conscience as a personal-concrete experience gives rise to a sense of *law*, then to an awareness of a lawgiver, and thus to a concrete assent to belief in God (pp. 824, 829–30).

[21] Ward, *Life*, I, 653; *Letters and Corresp.*, II, 40–41 (italics in the text).

[22] Cronin, *op. cit.*, p. 87 and note 53. That Newman's thought has little of Berkelian "phenomenology" in it has been carefully pointed out by Przywara in his *Religionsbegründung: Max Scheler, J. H. Newman*, Freiburg im Breisgau, 1923, p. 286–87: "Newmans 'reales Denken' nicht auf logische Wesenheiten, sondern auf reale Wirklichkeiten gerichtet ist."

[23] Przywara, "J. H. Newmans Problemstellung," p. 443 (transl.

and quoted by Cronin, *op. cit.*, p. 89). The nature of Newman's ruminations on our knowledge of the external world may be further indicated by a passage from the unpublished Notes in the Birmingham Oratory. Under date of November 4, 1859, writing on "Objects of Consciousness," Newman says: "Consciousness is always an *experience*. Its objects are my impressions, sensations, judgments, affections, imaginations, etc. It does nothing more than bear testimony to facts — and must be true. At the same time its testimony is not always so immediate and prompt as to preclude all necessity of cross-examination and revision . . . I am conscious that I see what I call a tree or a house; and that consciousness is infallible. I am not conscious of the object[ive] reality, but of the subjective sensation or impression. But still, though *when* I am conscious, I am infallibly certain of that of which I am conscious, I may at times think I am conscious, when I am not. Thus St. Peter 'knew not if it was true what was spoken of the Angel, but thought he saw a vision'; that is, not that he was quite certain of the fact of the impression of the senses, and doubted only the objective reality which they represented, but he doubted, from his experience of visions, dreams, etc. whether he was awake, whether he had really the sensation, whether his sensus intimus reported that he had this impression on his retina or his sensorium." This line of reasoning is obviously much more informal and concretely psychological than anything in Kant.

[24] Przywara, "J. H. Newmans Problemstellung," p. 444 (transl. and quot. in Cronin, *op. cit.*, pp. 89–90.

[25] Guitton, *La philosophie de Newman*, p. xxxvi. Before leaving the subject of Newman and Kant, let us note a passage in Wilfrid Ward's *Witnesses to the Unseen* (pp. 21–22): Kant, says Ward, asked the three great philosophical questions: "What can I know?" "What ought I to do?" and "What may I hope?" In the Middle Ages the first question could be asked without reference to the second and third, since they were accepted as a part of Christian orthodoxy. In later times, however, skeptics like Hume separated them and wrote as though knowledge could be dealt with apart from duty and hope (or faith); ethical and religious assumptions were now under question. Kant, and Newman in his own way, attempted a new synthesis, based on the idea of "the right moral disposition" as leading to a cogent faith. Every act of faith of the intellect, says Kant, assumes the existence of moral dispositions. If we leave them aside, and suppose mind to be indifferent to moral laws, then any speculative inquiry will ultimately issue in skepticism. This was precisely New-

man's position. (Kant, *Kritik der reinen Vernunft*, ed. Harten-stein, p. 547.)

[26] See Sarolea, *op. cit.*, pp. 101–02; also Chap. VII, "Pascal and Newman," *passim.*

[27] See Newman's sermon on "Ventures of Faith," *Par. and Pl. Sermons*, IV, 295–306. Cf. Pascal *Pensées*, ed. of 1670, p. 101: "Il se joue un jeu a cette distance infinie, où il arrivera croix ou pile. . . . Oui, mais il faut *parier*; cela n'est pas volontaire; vous êtes *embarqué*" (italics added).

[28] H. F. Stewart, *The Holiness of Pascal* (Cambridge, 1915), pp. 53–59. Cf. also E. Janssens, *La philosophie et l'apologétique de Pascal* (Paris, 1906), pp. 177, 287, 291, 372, etc., for parallels between Pascal and Newman on "implicit reasoning" and other principles of the *Grammar of Assent*. Janssens actually uses Newman to explain Pascal. See also Cronin, *op. cit.*, pp. 17–20; and Ward, *Last Lectures*, pp. 29–31.

[29] *Letters and Corresp.*, II, 307.

[30] *Grammar*, pp. 307–08.

[31] Ward, *Last Lectures*, pp. 86–87; see Cronin, *op. cit.*, pp. 115–23, on which the present comparisons are largely based.

[32] F. C. S. Schiller, *Formal Logic* (London, 1912), p. 5; John Dewey, *Reconstruction in Philosophy* (New York, 1920), p. 133; Cronin, *op. cit.*, p. 120 and notes.

[33] William James, *The Will to Believe* (New York, 1905), p. 4; Cronin, *op. cit.*, p. 121.

[34] Cronin (p. xiv) has listed those writers who find "no important conflicts between the *Summa* and the *Grammar*": J. J. Toohey, "The Grammar of Assent and the Old Philosophy," *Irish Theological Quarterly*, II (1907), 482 and *passim*; "Newman on the Criterion of Certitude," *Ibid.*, V (1910), 445; M. J. Ryan, "The Philosophy of Newman," *American Catholic Quarterly Review*, XXXIII (1908), 83–84. Those who see Newman as *approximating* neo-scholasticism are T. J. Gerrard, "Newman and Conceptionalism," *New York Review*, II (1906), 433 ff.; "Dichotomy, a Study in Newman and Aquinas," *Ibid.*, III (1908), 381; "The Grammar of Assent and the Sure Future," *The Dublin Review*, ser. 4, LV (1905), 120; "Bergson, Newman, and Aquinas," *The Catholic World*, XCVI (1913), 755; A. G. Brickel, "Cardinal Newman's Theory of Knowledge," *Amer. Cath. Quar. Rev.*, XLIII (1918), 508 ff. See also Przywara, *Ringen der Gegenwart*, Tome II, Pt. VI, "Kant, Newman, Thomas," pp. 729–962.

[35] *Oxf. Univ. Sermons,* pp. 254–56; *Grammar,* p. 195.

[36] Cronin, *op. cit.,* p. 105.

[37] *Ibid.,* pp. 106–12. Cronin has further pages on the relation of Newman's thought to Fideism, Humanism, the ideas of Balfour, Ollé-Laprune, Henri Bergson, and Max Scheler and the Newman movement in Germany prior to 1939 (see pp. 83 ff., 115 ff., 123–40).

v.

[1] E. D. Benard, *A Preface to Newman's Theology,* p. 159.

va.

[1] *Disc. and Arg.,* p. 295; Cronin, *op. cit.,* pp. 33–39; see also Elbert, *op. cit.,* pp. 28–32.

[2] Cronin, *op. cit.,* p. 34.

[3] A. McRae, *Die religiöse Gewissheit bei J. H. Newman* (Jena, 1898), p. 36; cf. *Grammar,* p. 338.

[4] *Apologia,* p. 264. Cronin (*op. cit.,* p. 37) notes that in the Newman revival in Germany Theodor Haecker (*Christentum und Kultur,* München, 1927, p. 148) emphasized, Newman-like, the distinction between "person and system" in religious thinking.

[5] Ward, *Life,* II, 249.

[6] See note 25 of section iv of the present chapter.

[7] Harper, "Dr. Newman's Essay in Aid of a Grammar of Assent," *The Month,* 1870, p. 366. Contrast the impression made by Newman on Baudin, *La philosophie de la Foi chez Newman* (Montligeon, 1906), together with Grandmaison, "J. H. Newman considéré comme maître," *Etudes,* CX (1907), 39–69, both of whom *condemn* Newman for the concrete realism of his method.

[8] See Ward, *Ten Personal Studies* (London, 1908), p. 252.

vb.

[1] F. Delattre, *La pensée de J. H. Newman: extraits* . . . (Paris, 1906), p. 30; Cronin, *op. cit.,* pp. 39–40.

[2] *Grammar,* pp. 9–10, 11, 12, 20.

[3] *Ibid.,* p. 189 ff.

[4] *Ibid.,* pp. 194–96.

[5] *Ibid.,* pp. 189–91.

[6] Cf. Juergens, *op. cit.*, pp. 21–22. However, C. Bonnegent (*La théorie de la certitude dans Newman*, Paris, 1920, p. 98) denies that the difference between inference and assent is as radical as Newman holds in the *Grammar*. Most of Bonnegent's study, though well handled, seems based on numerous misconceptions of Newman's meanings.

[7] *Grammar*, pp. 40–41. At this point, if space permitted, we should consider in some detail the relation of "apprehension" to "assent." It is enough to note here that in assenting to propositions we must to some extent *apprehend* their terms, an act which, for Newman, differs from *understanding* them. Apprehension is "simply an intelligent acceptance of the idea, or of the fact which a proposition enunciates" (*Grammar*, p. 20) — "Pride will have a fall." Understanding, having the *key* to this proposition, sees the *nature* of "pride" and "fall" and also their *relation*. One may actually apprehend, in Newman's sense, without understanding. And apprehension, being either *real* (directed to things external to us) or *notional* (expressing our own thoughts) bears significantly on the nature and direction of assent: real apprehension is stronger than notional, and the more fully the mind is occupied by concrete experience the keener and fuller will be its assent. We might add that notional assent and inference are sometimes confused. However, assent is strengthened by apprehension, and apprehension is often weakened by inference. For an excellent statement of "Assent Related to Apprehension," see Juergens, *op. cit.*, pp. 26–30.

[8] *Grammar*, pp. 42–74. D'Arcy (op. cit., pp. 113–18) gives considerable critical attention to these five forms of notional assent, and comments on Newman's archaic use of such terms as "instinct," "cause," and "presumption," which he attributes to the influence of Locke.

[9] *Grammar*, p. 88.

[10] *Ibid.*, pp. 92–96; *Disc. and Arg.*, pp. 292–97.

[11] It was such a line of reasoning which led Fairbairn (*op. cit.*, p. 304) to sum up Newman's epistemology as "the struggle of English empiricism to remain empirical, and yet become imaginative and religious." For Newman on "instinct," see *Grammar*, pp. 110–11.

[12] *Grammar*, p. 104.

[13] Cf. Butler, *Analogy of Religion*, p. 181 ("The proper motives to religion are the proper proofs of it, from our moral nature, from the presages of conscience, and our natural apprehension of God under the character of a righteous governor and judge"); against

this position of Butler and Newman, cf. Bonnegent, *op. cit.*, p. 119.
[14] *Grammar*, pp. 117–18.

vc.

[1] *Grammar*, pp. 157–58, 162; Locke, *Essay Concerning Human Understanding*, Bk. IV, Chap. IX, "Of Enthusiasm," sect. 1.
[2] *Grammar*, pp. 160–61; Locke, *op. cit.*, Bk. IV, Chap. XV, "On Probability," sect. 2. See also Chap. XVI, "Degrees of Assent," sect. 6.
[3] *Grammar*, p. 175.
[4] Newman of course acknowledges his debt to Butler for his doctrine of probability. (See the *Apologia*, pp. 120–21.) Newman *quotes* and *argues with* Locke (pp. 160–64) but he has so absorbed Locke's idea of "probability" that it seems never to occur to him to acknowledge his borrowing.
[5] *Grammar*, p. 220.
[6] *Ibid.*, pp. 199–200.
[7] *Apologia*, p. 113.
[8] *Grammar*, pp. 239, 288; cf. Butler, *op. cit.*, pp. 3–8.
[9] *Grammar*, pp. 320, 321.
[10] *Ibid.*, p. 411; Leslie Stephen, "Dr. Newman's Theory of Belief," *Fortnightly Review*, N.S., XXII (1877), 801; cf. A. Bazailles, *La crise de la croyance dans la philosophie contemporaine* (Paris, 1901), pp. 167–68; Cronin, *op. cit.*, p. 51.
[11] *Apologia*, p. 121–22.
[12] *Grammar*, p. 258.
[13] *Ibid.*, pp. 259, 267, 268, 279–80.
[14] *Ibid.*, pp. 284, 330, 345.
[15] *Ibid.*, p. 403.
[16] *Ibid.*, pp. 291–92.
[17] *Ibid.*, pp. 301–02.
[18] *Ibid.*, p. 320; cf. Butler, *op. cit.*, pp. 291, 293, 296–97.
[19] *Grammar*, p. 331.

vd.

[1] The word "sense" bears here what may be called an "18th-century" meaning, and "illative sense," according to Newman, is paralleled with "good sense," "sense of beauty," "common sense," etc. (*Grammar*, p. 345). Both Locke and Whately used "illative" in Newman's fashion; "illative" is from *illatum*, passive participle of *inferre*. On Newman's term, see F. Bacchus, "How to Read the

'Grammar of Assent,'" *The Month,* CXLIII (1924), 106–15. — D'Arcy (*op. cit.*, pp. 148–49) is somewhat severe on Newman's use of the term: "The illative sense is introduced as a newcomer without antecedents and without its proper title, and is made to do duty for all manner of acts and processes of thought because in the preceding chapters thought has been deprived of some of its functions." D'Arcy is inclined to view the "illative sense" as simply the power of *interpreting* "infinitely complex and consistent data by means of indirect reference, in terms of unity" (pp. 201, 274). But see Cronin, *op. cit.*, pp. 50 ff.

² *Grammar,* pp. 343–44.

³ *Ibid.,* p. 350.

⁴ *Ibid.,* p. 351.

⁵ *Ibid.,* pp. 353–57. "The illative sense," says Cronin (*op. cit.,* p. 109, note 109), "might well be compared with Kant's 'faculty of judgment,' the faculty which subsumes particulars under the general laws of understanding. Kant gives the example of a physician who, while knowing well medical theory, gives an erroneous diagnosis. He failed in applying a universal law to particular instances." This example may be found in Kant's *Critique of Pure Reason,* Transcendental Analytic, Book II, Introduction.

⁶ E. B. Burgum ("Cardinal Newman and the Complexity of Truth," *Sewanee Review,* XXXVIII [1930], 322) makes the curiously erroneous statement that "Not every man possessed the illative sense" — not the common man, but the genius. This is one of several errors in an otherwise admirable article.

⁷ *Grammar,* p. 357.

⁸ *Ibid.,* pp. 358–59.

⁹ *Ibid.,* pp. 361–62; for a good abridgment of Newman's thought on the range of the illative sense, see Juergens, *op. cit.,* pp. 92–96.

¹⁰ Juergens, *op. cit.,* p. 95.

¹¹ *Grammar,* p. 361.

¹² *Ibid.,* pp. 344, 377.

¹³ *Oxf. Univ. Sermons,* p. 63.

¹⁴ *Ibid.,* p. 201.

¹⁵ Juergens, *op. cit.,* p. 96.

¹⁶ *Grammar,* p. 412.

¹⁷ *Essays Crit. and Hist.,* II, 353.

¹⁸ *Grammar,* p. 427; Juergens, *op. cit.,* pp. 217–19.

¹⁹ *Grammar,* p. 428.

²⁰ *Ibid.,* p. 431; Juergens, *op. cit.,* pp. 217–18. "The positive

apologetic [in Newman's last chapters]," says Benard with considerable truth, "will strike many readers as the weakest part of the *Grammar*. But this is not surprising when we consider that Newman was not professing his apologetic to be *the* proof of Christianity, but merely that evidence from the convergence of probabilities which was personally convincing to him. He does not maintain that everyone will be convinced by it, though he naturally hopes and expects that many will be." (*A Preface to Newman's Theology*, p. 168.)

²¹ *Grammar*, p. 492; Ward, *Problems and Persons*, pp. 264–65; John, x, 14, 27–28.

CHAPTER VII

¹ *Difficulties of Anglicans*, I, vi.

i.

¹ *Apologia*, p. 493; cf. also Newman's poem on "Liberalism" in *Verses on Various Occasions*, p. 140.

² Hutton, *Newman*, p. 242. However, Hutton, in this same passage, queries if "Liberalism" was a happy description of "the anti-dogmatic principle." Historically, Liberalism has been used to signify concessions to popular demands, chiefly in politics.

³ Fairbairn, *Catholicism: Roman and Anglican*, pp. 82–84.

⁴ Dawson, *Spirit of the Oxford Movement*, p. 41.

⁵ Hutton, *op. cit.*, p. 243.

⁶ Sarolea, *Cardinal Newman*, p. 150 (see Chap. VIII, "Was Newman a Liberal Catholic?").

⁷ *Essays Critical and Historical*, I, 34, 35, 38, 41–42, 68–70.

⁸ *Ibid.*, II, 190–93, 202–03, 208 ff.

⁹ *Ibid.*, II, 208–09, 213, 214–16, 219, 241–42.

¹⁰ See Albrecht Ritschl (1822–89), disciple of the great liberal theological scholar, F. C. Baur, also of Kant, Schleiermacher, and Lotze; note especially his *Die Christliche Lehre von der Rechtfertigung und Versöhnung* (1870–74).

¹¹ *Discussions and Arguments*, pp. 370–71, 398.

¹² *Essays Crit. and Hist.*, I, 96–99.

¹³ "The Fall of De La Mennais" (1837); *Essays Crit. and Hist.*, I, 154, 157, 158, etc.

¹⁴ *Disc. and Arg.*, pp. 60–61.

¹⁵ Ward, *Life of Newman*, II, 460–62.

[16] *Disc. and Arg.*, pp. 266, 300, 302, 304.
[17] *Ibid.*, p. 75.

ii.

[1] Cross, *John Henry Newman*, p. 70; Dawson, *Spirit of the Oxford Movement*, p. 102; Geoffrey Faber, *Oxford Apostles*, p. 347.
[2] "The Good Samaritan," *Verses on Var. Occ.*, pp. 149 ff.
[3] *Via Media*, I, 79.
[4] Church, *The Oxford Movement*, pp. 203–14, especially p. 211.
[5] *Via Media*, I, 137.
[6] *Ibid.*, Chapters IX–XIII: "On the Essentials of the Gospel," "On Scripture as the Record of Faith," "On Scripture as the Record of Our Lord's Teaching," "On Scripture as the Document of Proof in the Early Church," etc.
[7] *Via Media*, I, 212–13.
[8] Hutton, *op. cit.*, p. 83.
[9] Brilioth, *The Anglican Revival*, p. 282.
[10] *Lectures on Justification*, p. 30.
[11] *Ibid.*, pp. 4–5.
[12] *Ibid.*, p. 29.
[13] *Ibid.*, pp. 32–36.
[14] *Ibid.*, p. 37.
[15] Brilioth, *op. cit.*, p. 286.
[16] *Ibid.*, pp. 289–90.
[17] *Lect. on Just.*, p. 340.
[18] J. A. Froude, "The Oxford Counter-Reformation," *Short Studies on Great Subjects* (London, 1917), IV, 281.
[19] *Disc. and Arg.*, p. 234.
[20] *Ibid.*, pp. 142, 146–47.
[21] *Ibid.*, p. 148.
[22] *Ibid.*, p. 149.
[23] *Ibid.*, p. 150.
[24] *Ibid.*, p. 174.
[25] *Ibid.*, p. 178.
[26] *Ibid.*, p. 195.
[27] Hutton, *op. cit.*, p. 96.
[28] *Disc. and Arg.*, pp. 34–42.
[29] "The Theology of the Seven Epistles of St. Ignatius," *Essays Crit. and Hist.*, I, 245 (italics in the text).
[30] *Ibid.*, pp. 222–23, 237–38.

[31] "Palmer's View of Faith and Unity," *Essays Crit. and Hist.*, I, 179.

[32] *Ibid.*, p. 185.

[33] *Ibid.*, p. 195.

[34] "Prospects of the Anglican Church," *Essays Crit. and Hist.*, I, 283.

[35] "The Anglo-American Church," *Essays Crit. and Hist.*, I, 349–50.

[36] *Ibid.*, pp. 350–51.

[37] *Ibid.*, pp. 375, 376.

[38] See *Essays Crit. and Hist.*, I, 196 ff.

[39] *Ibid.*, I, 196; II, 18 ff., 47.

[40] "Reformation of the Eleventh Century," *Essays Crit. and Hist.*, II, 313.

[41] "Protestant Idea of Antichrist," *Essays Crit. and Hist.*, II, 134–40, 151–52.

[42] "Private Judgment," *Essays Crit. and Hist.*, II, 341, 367.

[43] *Ibid.*, p. 351.

[44] *Ibid.*, p. 362.

[45] *Ibid.*, p. 365.

[46] *Ibid.*, p. 374.

CHAPTER VIII

i.

[1] Hutton, *Newman*, pp. 207–08: "I shall never forget the impression which his voice and manner, which opened upon me for the first time in these lectures, made on me. Never did a voice seem better adapted to persuade without irritating. Singularly sweet, perfectly free from any dictatorial note, and yet rich in all the cadences proper to the expression of pathos, of wonder, of ridicule, there was still nothing in it that any one could properly describe as insinuating, for its simplicity, and frankness, and freedom from the half-smothered notes which express indirect purpose, was as remarkable as its sweetness, its freshness, and its gentle distinctness." However, as the Birmingham Fathers have noted, these lectures "are full of the thoughts which had been seething in Newman's mind since the autumn of 1839" and thus show a remarkable feat of self-control. See *Correspondence with Keble and Others*, ed. at Birmingham Oratory, p. 365n.

² Ross, *John Henry Newman,* p. 53.
³ *Difficulties of Anglicans,* I, 1, 9.
⁴ *Ibid.,* p. 6.
⁵ *Ibid.,* p. 107.
⁶ Hutton, *op. cit.,* p. 211.
⁷ *Diff. of Ang.,* I, 249–50; *Apologia,* p. 47.
⁸ *Diff. of Ang.,* I, 239–40.
⁹ Hutton, *op. cit.,* p. 207.

ii.

¹ Ward, *Life of Newman,* I, 264.
² Ross, *op. cit.,* p. 65.
³ Ward, *Life,* I, 264.
⁴ Ross, *op. cit.,* p. 67.
⁵ *Present Position of Catholics,* pp. 24–41.
⁶ *Ibid.,* pp. 172–73.
⁷ *Ibid.,* pp. 216–17.
⁸ *Ibid.,* p. 208.
⁹ *Ibid.,* p. 371.

iii.

¹ *Apologia,* pp. 332–33.
² *Ibid.,* pp. 333–35.
³ *Ibid.,* pp. 335, 337–40.
⁴ *Ibid.,* p. 346.
⁵ *Ibid.,* p. 353.
⁶ *Ibid.,* pp. 357–58.
⁷ *Ibid.,* p. 355.

iv.

¹ The author was Newman's Anglican friend, R. W. Church (see Ward, *Life,* II, 109).
² *Diff. of Ang.,* II, 6–7.
³ *Ibid.,* pp. 10–11; *Apologia,* p. 396.
⁴ *Diff. of Ang.,* II, 31–32.
⁵ *Ibid.,* p. 35.
⁶ *Ibid.,* pp. 46–47.
⁷ *Ibid.,* pp. 50–67.
⁸ *Ibid.,* p. 76.
⁹ *Ibid.,* pp. 79–80.

[10] *Ibid.*, pp. 80–81.
[11] *Ibid.*, p. 85.

v.

[1] Ward, *Life*, II, 399–400.
[2] Ross, *op. cit.*, pp. 196–97.
[3] See Macaulay's essay on "Gladstone on Church and State."
[4] *Diff. of Ang.*, II, 378.
[5] Ward, *Life*, II, 402.
[6] *Ibid.*, II, 403.
[7] Ross, *op. cit.*, p. 198. "It was not an accident," remarks Dr. Benard, "that [Newman] addressed his *Letter* to the Duke of Norfolk, hereditary Earl Marshal of England and head of an ancient family distinguished alike for its loyalty to the Catholic Church and for its faithful service to the English Crown" (*A Preface to Newman's Theology*, p. 58).
[8] *Diff. of Ang.*, II, 176–77.
[9] Ward, *Life*, II, 401.
[10] *Diff. of Ang.*, II, 209–11.
[11] *Ibid.*, II, 237–42.
[12] *Ibid.*, II, 248, 257.
[13] *Ibid.*, II, 243.
[14] *Ibid.*, II, 258.
[15] *Ibid.*, II, 261.
[16] *Ibid.*, II, 269–75.
[17] *Ibid.*, II, 285.
[18] *Ibid.*, II, 292–97.
[19] *Ibid.*, II, 297.

vi.

[1] *Via Media*, I, xx–xxiii.
[2] *Ibid.*, I, xxv.
[3] *Ibid.*, I, xxvii, xxviii.
[4] *Ibid.*, I, xxx–xxxi.
[5] *Ibid.*, I, xxxvii–xxxviii.
[6] *Ibid.*, I, xxxvi.
[7] *Ibid.*, I, xxxix–xli.
[8] *Ibid.*, I, xlii.
[9] *Ibid.*, I, xliii.
[10] *Ibid.*, I, lii.

[11] *Ibid.*, I, 90, 98, 104.
[12] *Ibid.*, I, 144.

Chapter IX

i.

[1] See J. J. Reilly, *Newman as a Man of Letters* (New York, 1925), Chap. V; Denys Gorce, *Newman et les pères* (Paris, 1933), pp. 106–07: "Dison le mot: c'est l'historien dans toute la plénitude du terme, pour qui l'histoire est ce qu'elle doit être en somme, sous peine de manquer son but, c'est-à-dire une résurrection."
[2] Henri Brémond, *The Mystery of Newman* (London, 1907), Chap. II, p. 111.
[3] *Historical Sketches*, I, xi.
[4] *Ibid.*, III, 272.
[5] *Ibid.*, II, xi.
[6] Brémond, *op. cit.*, pp. 107–08.
[7] Brilioth, *The Anglican Revival*, p. 117.
[8] Brémond, *op. cit.*, p. 110.

ii.

[1] "Marcus Tullius Cicero," *Hist. Sketches*, I, 249.
[2] *Ibid.*, I, 292–94; cf. p. 258 (Cicero on the doctrine of "expediency" or "reserve," suggesting that something of Newman's position on this subject goes back to Cicero, as well as to the Alexandrian Fathers).
[3] *Arians of the Fourth Century*, pp. 234–35.
[4] *Hist. Sketches*, II, 2.
[5] *Ibid.*, II, 79.
[6] *Ibid.*, II, 155.
[7] Gorce, *op. cit.*, p. 104.
[8] *Hist. Sketches*, III, 333, 334.
[9] Reilly, *op. cit.*, p. 141.

iii.

[1] *Hist. Sketches*, I, 23.
[2] *Ibid.*, I, 35, 48.

³ *Ibid.*, I, 106.
⁴ *Ibid.*, I, 139.
⁵ *Ibid.*, I, 173–74.
⁶ *Ibid.*, I, 228–29; cf. Ernest Jackh, *The Rising Crescent* (New York, 1944), for an excellent picture of present-day Turkey.

iv.

¹ *Hist. Sketches*, III, 93, 111, 112, 125.
² *Ibid.*, III, 200–01.
³ *Ibid.*, III, 20–22.
⁴ *Ibid.*, III, 81, 83, 85.
⁵ *Ibid.*, III, 263.
⁶ *Ibid.*, III, 295.
⁷ *Ibid.*, III, 281.

v.

¹ *Hist. Sketches*, II, 375.
² *Ibid.*, II, 399.
³ *Ibid.*, II, 397, 398, 400.
⁴ *Ibid.*, II, 410–11.
⁵ *Ibid.*, II, 442–43.
⁶ *Ibid.*, II, 452.

vi.

¹ Reilly, *op. cit.*, p. 156.
² *Hist. Sketches*, II, 229, 230.
³ *Ibid.*, II, 218–31.
⁴ *Ibid.*, II, 233.
⁵ *Ibid.*, II, 297–98.
⁶ *Ibid.*, II, 341.
⁷ *Ibid.*, II, 323–24.

CHAPTER X

¹ See Tardivel, *La personnalité littéraire de Newman*, Bk. III, Chap. II, pp. 202–25; Alvan S. Ryan, "Newman's Conception of

Literature," *Critical Studies in Arnold, Emerson, and Newman,* ed. J. E. Baker (University of Iowa Humanistic Studies, vol. VI, no. 1) (Iowa City, Iowa, 1942), pp. 119–75; L. G. Miller, "Newman on the Function of Literature, *Catholic World,* CLVII (1943), 510–14.

i.

[1] Stanley T. Williams, "Newman's Literary Preferences," *Studies in Victorian Literature* (New York, 1923), p. 233 (this chapter is a reprint of the paper in *Sewanee Review,* XXVIII [1920], 486–97). For other treatments of Newman as a Romantic, see Sister Mary Kiener, *John Henry Newman, the Romantic, the Friend, the Leader* (Boston, 1933); Lewis Gates, *Studies and Appreciations* (London, 1900); Calvert Alexander, *The Catholic Literary Revival* (Milwaukee, 1935); Paul Elmer More, "Newman," *The Drift of Romanticism* (Shelborne Essays, Eighth Ser.) (New York, 1913); and Brémond, *The Mystery of Newman,* also *Prière et poésie* (Paris, 1926).

[2] Sister Mary Kiener, *op. cit.,* Book I, "The Romantic."

[3] *Ibid.,* pp. 1–129, *passim;* Brémond, *op. cit.,* Introduction, Part II, Chap. 1, "The Poet," etc.

[4] "Poetry, with Reference to Aristotle's Poetics," *Essays Critical and Historical,* I, 1, 2.

[5] *Ibid.,* I, 7, 1–2, respectively.

[6] Matthew Arnold, Preface to *Poems* (London, 1853).

[7] Ryan, *op. cit.,* p. 130.

[8] *Essays Crit. and Hist.,* I, 10. Newman's interpretation of the nature of poetry was in fact so un-Aristotelian, so "Platonic," that Whately regarded it with displeasure, and Newman's brilliant friend, Blanco White, "good-humoredly called it only Platonic" (see *Apologia,* p. 114).

[9] *Essays Crit. and Hist.,* I, 16, 17. (Italics added.)

[10] *Ibid.,* I, 14. (Italics added.)

[11] Tardivel, *op. cit.,* p. 390 (italics added). (See Appendix I, notes on Newman's lecture on "The Characteristics of True Poetry," pp. 387–92.)

[12] See N. P. Stallknecht, "The Moral of the Ancient Mariner," *Publications of the Modern Language Association of America,* XLVII (1932); also Elizabeth Nitchie, "The Moral of the Ancient Mariner Reconsidered," *Ibid.,* XLVIII (1933).

[13] Ryan, *op. cit.,* p. 170 (italics added).

ii.

[1] Tardivel, *op. cit.*, p. 203, n. 2; *Letters and Correspondence*, II, 477.

[2] *Oxford University Sermons*, p. 14.

[3] *Ibid.*, p. 13 (slightly rearranged).

[4] "Truth Hidden When Not Sought After," *Parochial and Plain Sermons*, VIII, 188.

[5] *Ibid.*, II, 372, 373.

[6] *Ibid.*, VII, 25, 27; Ryan, *op. cit.*, p. 138.

[7] Przywara, *A Monument to St. Augustine* (New York, 1930), p. 286; Ryan, *op. cit.*, p. 140, n. 57.

[8] See the opening paragraphs of Matthew Arnold's essay on "The Study of Poetry," *Essays in Criticism*, 2nd Ser. (New York, 1921), pp. 2–3.

[9] *Discussions and Arguments*, pp. 274, 275.

[10] *Arians of the Fourth Century*, p. 85.

[11] Ryan, *op. cit.*, p. 142.

iii.

[1] *Essays Crit. and Hist.*, II, 421 ff.

[2] *Idea of a University*, pp. 227, 228; Ryan, *op. cit.*, pp. 148–49.

[3] *Idea of a Univ.*, pp. 227, 228.

[4] *Ibid.*, p. 229.

[5] *Ibid.*, pp. 316–17.

[6] *Ibid.*, p. 229.

[7] *Ibid.*, p. 275.

[8] *Ibid.*, pp. 276–77.

[9] *Ibid.*, pp. 279–86. Newman's context is devoted to a consideration of the "lavish richness of style" of Shakespeare, and of the "elaborateness" of many of the classics, such as Cicero. Yet in these same pages he rejects Dr. Johnson's style for its artificiality.

[10] *Idea of a Univ.*, pp. 286, 312–13.

[11] *Ibid.*, pp. 326, 291, 292–93.

[12] *Ibid.*, pp. 327–29.

iv.

[1] *Essays Crit. and Hist.*, I, 24. The quotation is from only *one* page of the essay on Aristotle's *Poetics*; yet, since nothing Newman

subsequently says in any of his writings denies it, we may let it stand
as expressing his continuing conviction.

² *Historical Sketches,* II, 386–87.   It is curious, as Ryan points
out, that Shelley, not Newman, equated poetic genius with divine
inspiration, and that Newman merely held that "the exercise of the
poetic imagination is a *natural* function, which may be linked with
personal purity or with personal profligacy" (Ryan, *op. cit.,* p. 149).
Cf. Newman's sermon on "Nature and Grace," *Discourses to Mixed
Congregations,* pp. 156–57, for his separation of the literary gift from
"divine inspiration."

³ *Idea of a Univ.,* p. 290; Ryan, *op. cit.,* p. 158.

⁴ Ryan, *op. cit.,* pp. 153–63.

⁵ *Hist. Sketches,* III, 197–98.

⁶ Tardivel, *op. cit.,* Appendix I, p. 388: "[To] cultivate the mind
of man, *that* is the province of literature, of poetry, and of criticism;
these refine the mind by making it what it was not before . . . Poetry
is the science of the beautiful. . . It is emphatically the beautiful
which refines and cultivates the mind; and by long contemplation of
beauty the mind itself, so to speak, becomes beautiful in the process."
(Italics added.)

⁷ Thirlwall, "Newman's Literary Preferences," p. 23.

⁸ See Ward's *Life of Newman,* II, 354–56; Stanley T. Williams,
loc. cit.

⁹ "Of classical poetry his special favorites were the 'Odyssey,' the
'Georgics,' the 'Prometheus' of Aeschylus; Euripides rather than
Sophocles attracted him, especially the 'Alcestis.' " (Ward, *Life,* II,
355.)

¹⁰ *Ibid.,* II, 354.   Professor Williams is thus evidently in error,
though he may have in mind a passage from the *Letters and Corresp.,*
I, 52–53, where Newman speaks of Crabbe's "monotonous gloomi-
ness," "prosaic lines," and "familiar vulgarity."   Yet Newman adds
that Crabbe is, for him, "one of the greatest poets of the present day"
and admires "Lady Barbara" as one of the "most uniformly elevated
and animated" of the *Tales of the Hall.* (Cf. S. T. Williams, *op.
cit.,* p. 497, where Newman is said to be offended by Crabbe's
realism.)

¹¹ *Idea of a Univ.,* p. 283.

¹² Ward, *Life,* II, 355.

¹³ *Ibid.,* II, 354.

¹⁴ *Ibid.,* I, 612; cf. Thirlwall, *op. cit.,* p. 24: Newman valued
Thackeray highly as re-creating Addisonian style.

[15] "But Miss Austen has no romance — none at all," cries Newman (*Letters and Corresp.*, II, 224); "what vile creatures her parsons are! she has not a dream of the high Catholic ἦθος." However, Newman is reported to have said that "he read through *Mansfield Park* every year, in order to perfect and preserve his style." (W. Tuckwell, *Reminiscences,* p. 181.)

[16] See Chapter II, and note no. 7.

[17] *Letters and Corresp.*, II, 281, 300.

[18] S. T. Williams, *op. cit.*, p. 488.

CHAPTER XI

i.

[1] See E. Baudin, *La philosophie de la foi chez Newman* (Montligeon, 1906); and L. de Grandmaison, "J. H. Newman considéré comme maître," *Etudes,* CX (1907), 62.

[2] Brilioth, *The Anglican Revival,* pp. 214–15; cf. Brémond, *op. cit.*, pp. 161–62, and Tardivel, *La personnalité littéraire de Newman,* pp. 143 ff. Whether Newman was a better writer as an Anglican or a Roman Catholic is a question much debated by some of his critics. Hutton (*Newman,* p. 190) and Bertram Newman (*Cardinal Newman,* p. 129) are certain that "in irony, in humor, in eloquence, in imaginative force, the writings of the later and, as we may call it, the emancipated portion of his career far surpass the writings of his theological apprenticeship." Geoffrey Faber, however, in *Oxford Apostles* (pp. 442–43) is of the opposite opinion, as is Dr. Inge (*Outspoken Essays,* 1st Ser., p. 173). Newman himself once declared: "What I wrote as a Protestant has had far greater power, force, meaning, success, than my Catholic works, and this troubles me a great deal." But this was written in his Journal during the years of his eclipse (the entry is dated January 8, 1860), and appears in Ward's nineteenth chapter, titled "Sad Days (1859–1864)." We are thus not obliged to accept Newman's melancholy judgment, as one of his most brilliant and telling works was to appear just four years hence — the *Apologia.* (Ward, *Life of Newman,* I, 578.) On the whole, Newman's greatest work, in the sense of distinction and quality, falls within his Catholic period.

[3] *Letters and Correspondence,* I, 242–43.

[4] *Ibid.*, I, 318.

[5] *Ibid.*, I, 287; cf. I, 306–07.

[6] *Ibid.*, I, 288.

[7] T. Mozley, *Reminiscences,* etc., I, 214.

[8] *Ibid.*, I, 215.

[9] *Letters and Corresp.*, I, 347; Mozley, *op. cit.*, I, 396.

[10] *Verses on Various Occasions,* p. 57.

[11] Tardivel, *op. cit.*, p. 124: "Cette préoccupation morale a-t-elle appauvri l'oeuvre artistique de Newman? Oui, sans aucun doute. . . . Mais l'oeuvre de Newman a connu une magnifique revanche. . . Newman moraliste a été enrichi des dépouillements de Newman artiste. . ."

ii.

[1] *Letters and Corresp.*, I, 365–66.

[2] Faber, *op. cit.*, p. 93. Even Newman's later poetry has been severely criticized, as not, at times, being poetry at all; "he was," says J. Lewis May (*Cardinal Newman,* p. 235), "a poet who did not write poetry. His real poetry is to be found . . . in his prose." Mr. May "opens at random 'The Dream of Gerontius'," and what he finds is "not poetry at all — not even the protoplasm of poetry" (p. 240). He has just quoted the Angel's speech beginning "We now have pass'd the gate . . ." (p. 350 of *Verses on Var. Occ.*). Though quite severe, Mr. May's criticism is valid for the greater portion of Newman's verses.

[3] *Letters and Corresp.*, I, 308. Newman was certainly at times too copious and facile in verse-making. During the Mediterranean tour he sometimes dashed off three poems a day. See *Verses on Var. Occ.*, pp. 164–66, 167–71, 172–76, etc.

[4] Tardivel, *op. cit.*, pp. 322, 330–31.

[5] Dawson, *Spirit of the Oxford Movement,* p. 56.

[6] Faber, *op. cit.*, p. 93.

[7] *Verses on Var. Occ.*, p. 121.

[8] *Ibid.*, p. 177.

[9] *Ibid.*, p. 206.

[10] *Ibid.*, p. 126. Reilly (*Newman as a Man of Letters,* p. 107) seems to be the first to point out the curious "angularity" of much of Newman's poetry.

[11] Hutton, *op. cit.*, p. 11; Flood, *Cardinal Newman at Oxford,* p. 114.

[12] *Verses on Var. Occ.*, pp. 184–85.

[13] *Ibid.*, pp. 188–90. Only the first of three stanzas is quoted. Cf. Hutton, *op. cit.*, p. 13.

[14] *Verses on Var. Occ.*, pp. 34–35. "Lead, Kindly Light" is so well known as to need no detailed comment here. However, Reilly (*op. cit.*, p. 112) has pointed out a confusion of metaphor in it which escapes the ordinary reader: "In the first stanza the poet prays for light amid the darkness; in the third stanza the figure is maintained and he trusts to see at last the beauty of the newborn day. But in the second stanza he has confessed as a fault his love for the day whose light he now prays Heaven to send him as a boon." Reilly adds that "it would be difficult to find another instance of so faulty a short poem winning its way so completely and holding its place so securely with persons of every type. The imagery is not novel nor is there a single striking stanza or one of those 'inevitably' adequate lines whose perfection makes it unforgettable."

[15] *Verses on Var. Occ.*, pp. 44–47.

[16] Ward, *Life*, II, 318; one more "light verse" poem may be found in *Verses on Var. Occ.*, pp. 55–56, "Seeds in the Air: for an Album."

[17] Ward, *Life*, II, 76–78; Reilly, *op. cit.*, p. 116.

[18] Ward, *Life*, II, 514–15. What may be foreshadowings of *Gerontius* are passages in certain of Newman's early sermons, "The Individuality of the Soul," "Greatness and Littleness of Human Life," "The Lapse of Time," and "Neglect of Divine Calls and Warnings" (noted by Reilly, *op. cit.*, pp. 117–18).

[19] Reilly, *op. cit.*, p. 125.

[20] *Ibid.*, p. 127.

[21] Hugh Walker, *Literature of the Victorian Era* (Cambridge, 1913, 1931), p. 340.

[22] Reilly, *op. cit.*, p. 132.

iii.

[1] *Callista*, Postscript to Advertisement of 1856.

[2] Ward, *Life*, I, 245. In Aubrey de Vere's *Reminiscences* (p. 272), we read that *Callista* "was written as he (J.H.N.) informed us, chiefly with a pencil in railway carriages, during a continental tour."

[3] See *Charles Kingsley: His Letters and Memories of His Life*, ed. by his wife (one-vol. ed., London, 1883), p. 145; Joseph E. Baker, *The Novel and the Oxford Movement* (Princeton, N.J., 1932), pp. 55–56.

[4] Baker, *op. cit.*, pp. 62, 64.

[5] *Ibid.*, p. 61.

[6] Reilly, *op. cit.*, p. 95.

[7] Newman, *Loss and Gain: the Story of a Convert* (one-vol. ed.; London, 1935), p. 37.

[8] *Ibid.*, p. 9.

[9] *Ibid.*, p. 124.

[10] *Ibid.*, p. 230.

[11] *Ibid.*, pp. 44–45.

[12] *Ibid.*, pp. 186–87. R. H. Hutton greatly admired the scene in which Reding's mother took leave of him on learning that he was going to join the Roman Catholic Church (Part III, Chap. I): "Except in *Callista*, Newman has written nothing in the form of fiction more touching than this passage" (*Cardinal Newman*, p. 196). The final scenes of the novel, however, where Reding is besieged by religious impostors Hutton dismisses as "a shade too farcical" (p. 197).

[13] *Loss and Gain*, pp. 272–73.

[14] *Ibid.*, p. 289.

[15] *Ibid.*, p. 290; *Apologia*, p. 318.

[16] Noted by Baker, *op. cit.*, p. 57.

[17] Reilly, *op. cit.*, p. 82.

[18] *Loss and Gain*, p. 91; cf. the *Apologia*, p. 186: "It was simply an impossibility," writes Newman concerning the results of Tract XC, "that I could say any thing henceforth to good effect, when I had been posted up by the marshall *on the buttery hatch* of every College of my University, after the manner of discommoned pastry-cooks" (italics added). In Appendix 3 of the Oxford ed. of the *Apologia*, on "The Anglican Church," Newman tells us that in *Loss and Gain* "all the best characters are sober Church-of-England people. No Tractarians proper are introduced. . . There *could* not be such in the Tale, without the introduction of friends, which was impossible in its very notion. . . My expedient was the introduction of what may be called Tractarians *improper*" — enthusiasts over ritual, architecture, the externals of religion, the kind of men, however, of whom Newman knew nothing. He adds that none of his friends or partisans of the Oxford Movement entered into the composition of the novel. (*Apologia*, pp. 398–99.)

[19] Newman, *Callista*, p. 57.

[20] *Ibid.*, pp. 61–63.

[21] *Ibid.*, p. 167.

[22] *Ibid.*, pp. 224–25.
[23] *Ibid.*, pp. 168–74.
[24] *Ibid.*, pp. 186–87.
[25] *Ibid.*, p. 263.
[26] *Ibid.*, pp. 380–81.
[27] *Ibid.*, p. 346.

Chapter XII

[1] W. R. Inge, *Outspoken Essays*, 1st Ser., p. 180.
[2] Ward, *Life of Newman*, II, 34. Reilly, in *Newman as a Man of Letters* (pp. 253–72), carries out an extensive and interesting comparison and contrast between the *Apologia* and the autobiographies of Augustine and Rousseau, Cellini, Marmontel, *et al.*

i.

[1] *Apologia*, pp. 5–17; Ward, *Life*, II, 1–7. The Oxford edition of the *Apologia*, ed. by Wilfrid Ward (1913), gives by typographical device the various readings of the different editions, and reprints the Newman-Kingsley correspondence, together with Kingsley's pamphlet, "What, Then, Does Dr. Newman Mean?" and the two pamphlets which Newman suppressed from the standard edition, "Mr. Kingsley's Method of Disputation" and "True Mode of Meeting Mr. Kingsley."
[2] Margaret Farrand Thorp, *Charles Kingsley: 1819–1875* (Princeton, N. J., 1937), p. 153. In fairness to Kingsley, two facts should be noted, as given by Mrs. Kingsley in her *Charles Kingsley: His Letters and Memories* (one-vol. ed.), p. 257: he was suffering from illness and depression from overwork, which was a bad preparation for dealing with so exacting an opponent as Newman; and, having heard that Newman himself was in poor health, felt a chivalrous consideration for his opponent, at least in the early stages of the controversy, and was to some extent at a disadvantage.
[3] *Apologia*, pp. 5–21.
[4] Ward, *Life*, II, 8. Ward, in his edition of the *Apologia* (pp. vi, xiv–xv) attributes to Newman a great deal of cool calculation in publishing the correspondence, knowing that Kingsley would become angry, and therefore a less able antagonist. Ward even suggests that Newman *simulated* his own feelings in the *Apologia* as part of his

controversial technique: "he evidently thought an indignant denial and angry language the appropriate retort richly deserved by Kingsley's accusation, and representing truly his own view though not any lively personal feeling" (p. xv). Other writers have made the same observations. For an opposite opinion, see Ross, *John Henry Newman* (pp. 150–52), who believes that Newman wrote at too great a speed to permit calculated effects to be developed, and that Newman really was passionately aroused, even to failing in charity, though his anger was directed less at the man Kingsley than at the Protestant bigotry which Kingsley personified. There is no doubt some truth on both sides. As a master controversialist, fighting for his Church, Newman would not be averse to simulating a passion as a part of the rhetorical method he used.

[5] Ward, *Life*, II, 5–6.

[6] *Apologia*, pp. 58–59.

[7] Thorp, *op. cit.*, p. 158 (quoting the *Quarterly Review* for October, 1864).

[8] *Apologia*, p. 83.

[9] Ward, *Life*, II, 18–19.

[10] In preparing the *Apologia* for its final appearance Newman carefully omitted all reference, so far as possible, to the occasion of the controversy, as well as all mention of Kingsley by name, and the polemical portions generally. In 1913, the Rev. J. Gamble brought out an edition as it originally appeared, in the "Scott Library."

[11] Ward, *Life*, II, 21.

[12] *Ibid.*, II, 21–25.

[13] *Ibid.*, II, 29.

[14] *Ibid.*, II, 31.

[15] *Saturday Review*, quoted in Ward, *Life*, II, 33.

[16] Bertram Newman, *Cardinal Newman*, pp. 160–61.

[17] Ward, *Life*, II, 45–46.

ii.

[1] Ward, *Life*, II, 22.

[2] Pages 97–101 of this pamphlet as it appears in the Oxford ed. of the *Apologia* are reprinted in the Preface to the standard ed. which Newman prepared (pp. xx–xxv).

[3] *Apologia*, p. 98.

[4] *Ibid.*, p. 99.

[5] *Ibid.*, p. 101.

[6] Lewis Gates, Introduction (pp. xviii-xix), *Newman: Prose Selections* (New York, 1895, 1931). Gates' essay, which still has considerable value and interest, replies to the frequent statement that the *Apologia* is "simply and sincerely autobiographic" by declaring the book, not altogether justly, to be "an enormously elaborate and ingenious piece of special pleading to prepare the way for a few syllogisms that have now become grotesquely insignificant" (p. xix).

iii.

[1] Ward, *Life*, II, 22n. (italics in text).

[2] Dom Cuthbert Butler, *The Life and Times of Bishop Ullathorne* (London, 1926), I, 332.

[3] See A. F. Hort, *Life and Letters of Fenton John Anthony Hort* (London, 1896), II, 423–25.

[4] Inge, *Outspoken Essays*, 1st Ser., p. 180.

[5] Fairbairn, *Catholicism: Roman and Anglican*, p. 241.

[6] E. A. Knox, *The Tractarian Movement*, p. vii.

[7] Cross, *John Henry Newman*, pp. 8, 132–33, 138.

[8] *Ibid.*, p. 139.

[9] See *Correspondence with Keble and Others*, p. 277.

[10] Harper, *Newman and William Froude*, pp. 60–61.

[11] Hutton, *Newman*, p. 231.

[12] *Ibid.*, pp. 231–32.

CHAPTER XIII

i.

[1] Amy Cruse, *The Victorians and Their Reading* (New York, 1935), p. 108.

[2] *Ibid.*, p. 118.

[3] *Ibid.*, p. 116.

[4] T. Mozley, *Reminiscences*, I, 315.

[5] L. E. Elliott-Binns, *Religion in the Victorian Era*, pp. 459.

[6] *Ibid.*, pp. 459–60.

[7] Cruse, *op. cit.*, pp. 35–36.

ii.

¹ See Tardivel, *La personnalité littéraire de Newman,* pp. 299–317: "Comme elles [*Discourses to Mixed Congregations*] nous semblent étrangères aux élans de Bossuet, aux exultations de Lacordaire! Il n'est qu'à rapprocher le *Panégyrique de sainte Thérèse* ou le célèbre sermon sur l'amour de quelques-uns des passages les plus chaleureux de Newman pour apprécier pleinement la réserve propre à ses moments d'effusion" (p. 316).

² Quoted in the *Letters and Correspondence,* II, 219. On Newman as a preacher, see J. J. Reilly's excellent treatment in his *Newman as a Man of Letters,* Chap. II.

³ *Idea of a University,* p. 408; cf. Ward, *Life of Newman,* II, 335.

⁴ *Idea of a Univ.,* p. 412.

⁵ *Ibid.,* pp. 412–13.

⁶ *Ibid.,* p. 418.

⁷ *Ibid.,* p. 426. Cf. Sister Mariella, "Newman's Anglican Sermons," *Catholic World,* CXLVIII (1939), 431–37 (Newman's debt to Aristotle's *Rhetoric* for eloquence, and for his habit of aiming at the *mind* of his congregation, though some emotion was permitted "because of the sorry nature of an audience," as Aristotle put it).

⁸ *Parochial and Plain Sermons,* VII, 16–18.

⁹ *Ibid.,* IV, 223, 210, respectively.

¹⁰ Hutton, *Newman,* p. 200.

¹¹ *Disc. to Mixed Cong.,* pp. 336–39.

¹² *Oxford University Sermons,* p. 122 (italics added).

¹³ Newman, *Sermons on Subjects of the Day,* p. 120, but see also p. 391; also *Par. and Pl. Sermons,* VI, 93.

¹⁴ *Serm. on Subj. of the Day,* pp. 290–91.

¹⁵ Brémond, *The Mystery of Newman,* p. 197.

¹⁶ Faber, *Oxford Apostles,* pp. 170–71. However, Faber is typical of those writers on Newman who harp uncritically on Newman's *flight* to Catholicism, as in the statement: "This sense of sin . . . drove him, like a child running from the terror of the dark to be comforted by its mother, into the consolations of religion — into, finally, the arms of his adopted Mother, the Church of Rome, and his Father, St. Philip Neri" (p. 172).

¹⁷ *Idea of a Univ.,* p. 409.

[18] Alexander Whyte, *Newman: an Appreciation* (London, 1901), pp. 94, 97, 103, 104.

[19] Brilioth, *The Anglican Revival*, p. 217n. 3.

[20] *Par. and Pl. Sermons*, I, 24, 53, 323; *Disc. to Mixed Cong.*, p. 143.

[21] *Par. and Pl. Sermons*, IV, 339; V, 66, 271; *Serm. on Subj. of the Day*, pp. 120–22. Newman has one whole sermon on "Religious Joy," *Par. and Pl. Sermons*, VIII, no. 17.

[22] J. A. Froude, *Short Studies on Great Subjects* (New York, 1883), IV, 284.

[23] F. Delattre, *La pensée de J. H. Newman* (Paris, 1914), p. 17.

[24] Whyte, *op. cit.*, p. 93.

[25] *Par. and Pl. Sermons*, I, "The Christian Mysteries," p. 211.

[26] *Ibid.*, III, 164; VI, 73, 363 ff.; *Sermons on Various Occasions*, pp. 77–81. It was no doubt the second of these three sermons, "The Incarnate Son, a Sufferer and Sacrifice," to which J. A. Froude alluded in a well-known passage in his *Short Studies* (IV, 286). Newman had described in detail some of the incidents of Christ's Passion: "He then paused. For a few moments there was a breathless silence. Then, in a low, clear voice, of which the faintest vibration was audible in the farthest corner of St. Mary's, he said, 'Now, I bid you recollect that He to whom these things were done was Almighty God.' It was as if an electric stroke had gone through the church, as if every person present understood for the first time the meaning of what he had all his life been saying." (See *Par. and Pl. Sermons*, VI, 74.) Other "definitions" of God may be found in the *Idea of a Univ.*, pp. 61–66; *Grammar of Assent*, p. 101; *Disc. to Mixed Cong.*, pp. 318–20; *Par. and Pl. Sersons*, III, 117–25.

[27] *Par. and Pl. Sermons*, IV, no. 1; II, no. 2; *Serm. on Var. Occ.*, no. 1; *Serm. on Subj. of the Day*, nos. 5 and 7. See also *Disc. to Mixed Cong.*, pp. 113–14 (the lecherous man of the world).

[28] *Par. and Pl. Sermons*, I, no. 24.

[29] *Ibid.*, IV, no. 10; II, no. 20, and *Serm. on Var. Occ.*, no. 9; *Serm. on Subj. of the Day*, nos. 6 and 7; *Disc. to Mixed Cong.*, no. 5, and *Serm. on Var. Occ.*, nos. 7, 5, and 12, respectively.

[30] *Par. and Pl. Sermons*, I, 20.

[31] *Ibid.*, I, 36, 42, 50; II, 361; III, 144.

[32] *Ibid.*, I, 111 (italics in text).

[33] *Ibid.*, VI, 369–70.

[34] *Serm. on Subj. of the Day*, p. 409.

iii.

¹ This latter date is for the next-to-the-last sermon; that for the final sermon is not known.   See the valuable chronological lists of Newman's parochial and plain sermons and those published as *Sermons on Subjects of the Day* in this latter volume, edited by W. J. Copeland.   The term "parochial" in Newman's title alludes to the fact that the sermons so designated were preached before his parochial congregation of St. Mary's (1828–43).

² See Brémond, *op. cit.*, pp. 145–52.

³ *Par. and Pl. Sermons*, III, 123–25.

⁴ *Ibid.*, V, 325–26; cf. *Loss and Gain*, last paragraph of Chap. XII of Part I, p. 81.

⁵ *Par. and Pl. Sermons*, II, 362.

⁶ *Oxf. Univ. Sermons*, pp. 63, 259, 351.

⁷ *Ibid.*, p. 201 (italics added).   Cf. the final lines of "Dover Beach":

> "And we are here as on a darkling plain
>   Swept with confused alarms of struggle **and flight,**
>   Where ignorant armies clash by night."

⁸ *Oxf. Univ. Sermons*, pp. 346–47.

⁹ Barry, *Newman*, p. 81.

¹⁰ Hutton, *op. cit.*, p. 115.

¹¹ *Serm. on Subj. of the. Day*, pp. 91–92.

¹² "No one," says Christopher Dawson (*Spirit of the Oxford Movement*, pp. 124–25), "can understand the Oxford Movement who has not read and meditated these great [last Anglican] sermons, especially the series of Nov.–Dec., 1841, on the inward notes of the Church and that of Nov.–Dec., 1842, on "The Christian Empire," for they express the spirit of the Movement in its purest form, disentangled from the ecclesiastical polemics and the controversial special pleading that disfigured its external history."

¹³ *Serm. on Subj. of the Day*, pp. 260–61.

¹⁴ *Ibid.*, pp. 406–07.   This apostrophe to the Anglican Church is followed, in the sermon, with the paragraph of farewell quoted in sect. ii of the present chapter.

¹⁵ *Disc. to Mixed Cong.*, p. 111.

¹⁶ *Ibid.*, p. 211.

¹⁷ *Serm. on Var. Occ.*, pp. 127–28.

¹⁸ J. Lewis May, *Newman*, p. 108.
¹⁹ *Serm. on Var. Occ.*, pp. 163–64.

iv.

¹ Inge, *Outspoken Essays*, 1st Ser., p. 173.
² Tardivel, *op. cit.*, p. 370, n. 3; George Moore, *Hail and Farewell* (London, 1911–12), I, 54.
³ *Idea of a Univ.*, p. 178.
⁴ *Ibid.*, pp. 178–79.
⁵ *Ibid.*, p. 21; Tardivel, *op. cit.*, p. 357.
⁶ *Serm. on Subj. of the Day*, p. 307.
⁷ E. Bellasis, *Memorials of Mr. Serjeant Bellasis* (London, 1895), p. 177n.
⁸ *Essays Critical and Historical*, I, 231–32.
⁹ *Discussions and Arguments*, pp. 336, 355. The two aphorisms are from a seldom-read article, "Who's to Blame," which Newman published in the *Catholic Standard* in March, 1855. The occasion was the Crimean War. Newman shows how the British Constitution is excellent in time of peace, slow and lumbering in time of war. The blame for the "untoward events in the Crimea" should rest on "the ignorant, intemperate public" which clamored for an unwise war and now abuse their public servants for not doing the impossible. As in "The Tamworth Reading Room," Newman shows his skill at informal, journalistic discussion; his article contains a number of shrewd political observations.
¹⁰ *Idea of a Univ.*, p. 332. Besides being studded with aphoristic expressions, Newman's style is now and then quickened by unexpected slang, or highly colloquial phrases. When he gave up the theory of the *via media*, he regarded it as "standing on one leg" (*Apologia*, p. 247); in the *Difficulties of Anglicans* (II, 92) he says that Protestants charge that "our devotions to our Lady must necessarily throw our Lord in the shade"! His use of slang is of course much more marked in his letters, which, however, are usually as formal and correct as his other prose. To his sister, after Tract XC was condemned, he wrote: "I fear I am clean dished" (*Letters and Corresp.*, II, 326). To Henry Wilberforce, in 1859, during his "years of eclipse," he wrote: "All through my life I have been plucked" (Ward, *Life*, I, 573).
¹¹ Bertram Newman, *Cardinal Newman*, p. 201.

CHAPTER XIV

i.

[1] Ward, *Life of Newman*, II, 81. The modern reader, says H. L. Stewart, is puzzled at the absence in the *Tracts for the Times* and in Newman's *Sermons on Subjects of the Day* of any reference to social problems. "The famine in Ireland, the vast selfishness of the Corn Laws, Chartism, the opium war in China — how a Hebrew prophet would have dealt with them! But one would gather from Newman's sermons that the social passion of an Isaiah or a Jeremiah had no place in Christianity." (H. L. Stewart, *A Century of Anglo-Catholicism* [London, 1929], p. 122.) That Newman was not entirely blind to the economic and political progress of the day is evidenced by a passage in the *Rise and Progress of Universities* (*Historical Sketches*, III, 59): "What largeness of view, what intrepidity, vigor, and resolution are implied in the Reform Bill, in the Emancipation of the Blacks, in the finance changes, in the Useful Knowledge movement, in the organization of the Free Kirk, in the introduction of the penny postage, and in the railroads! This is an age, if not of great men, at least of great works." (It should be added that Newman is not justifying or exalting "mercantile undertakings" or political measures, but is urging the Church to show as much vigor and enterprise as was the political and commercial world in the 1850's.)

[2] Unlike Newman, Cardinal Manning "would stand on a van or a cart as occasion served" while mediating in a strike, or cooperating with Protestants in their war against intemperance. Newman's brother, F. W. Newman, tells a story which, in spite of the brother's bias, is at least credible as showing Newman's disdain for histrionic effects or for overemphasizing venial sins. In October, 1867, F. W. Newman attended a meeting in Manchester at which Manning spoke eloquently on the evils of drink. Writing at once to his brother, hoping "at length to find some interest in common," F. W. Newman described the occasion, only to receive in reply a note which included the following sentence: "As to what you tell me of Archbishop Manning, I have heard that some also of our Irish bishops think that too many drink-shops are licensed. As for me, I do not know whether we have too many or too few" (F. W. Newman, *Contributions Chiefly to the Early History of the Late Cardinal Newman*

[London, 1891], pp. 109–10). See also L. E. Elliott-Binns, *Religion in the Victorian Era*, pp. 422–25.

[3] E. B. Burgum, "Cardinal Newman and the Complexity of Truth," *Sewanee Review*, XXXVIII (1930), 320.

[4] *Oxford University Sermons*, p. 150; *Difficulties of Anglicans*, II, 262 ff., 268–69.

[5] Dawson, *Spirit of the Oxford Movement*, p. xi; cf. Southey's *Sir Thomas More: or Colloquies on the Progress and Prospects of Society* (1829), which shows the general anti-Liberal traditionalist attitude toward social questions of the period. Southey's book was brilliantly attacked by Macaulay in a review in the *Edinburgh Review* for January, 1830. That the traditionalist view was not simple or merely reactionary becomes clear on reading P. E. T. Widdrington, "The Social Mission of the Catholic Revival," *Christendom* (June, 1932); or Harold J. Laski, *Studies in the Problem of Sovereignty* (New Haven, Conn., 1927), Chaps. III, IV, and V. See also Ruth Kenyon, "The Social Aspect of the Catholic Revival," *Northern Catholicism: Centenary Studies in the Oxford and Parallel Movements*, ed. N. P. Williams and Charles Harris (London, 1933), pp. 367–400; and W. G. Peck, *The Social Implications of the Oxford Movement* (New York, 1933).

[6] Maisie Ward, *The Wilfrid Wards and the Transition*, II, 377.

[7] Jacques Maritain, *The Things That Are Not Caesar's*, transl. J. F. Scanlan (New York, 1930), p. 131; quoted by W. F. Stockley, *Newman, Education and Ireland* (London, 1933), p. 92n.

[8] *Time*, January 8, 1945, p. 26.

[9] Ward, *Life*, II, 344.

[10] Ross, *John Henry Newman*, p. 244.

[11] *Ibid.*, p. 246.

[12] Sarolea, *Cardinal Newman*, p. 157.

ii.

[1] Maisie Ward, "What Was Modernism?" *The Wilfrid Wards and the Transition*, II, *Insurrection Versus Resurrection*, p. 182; Nédoncelle, "The Modernist Crisis," *Baron Friedrich von Hügel*, transl. Marjorie Vernon (New York, 1937), pp. 12–13; H. L. Stewart, *Modernism, Past and Present* (London, 1932), p. 355.

[2] See Sarolea, *op. cit.*, "Newman and Modernism," pp. 154–73. One of the best books on Modernism is that by J. Rivière, *Le modernisme dans l'Eglise* (Paris, 1929); on Newman's relation to the

Movement, see especially L. Gougaud, "Le prétendu modernisme de Newman," *La revue du clergé français*, LVII (1909), 560–65.

[3] Inge, "Roman Catholic Modernism," *Outspoken Essays*, 1st Ser., p. 153.

[4] Maisie Ward, *op. cit.*, II, 195.

[5] Von Hügel has sometimes been thought of as a Modernist, at least as a liaison officer between the Modernists and the Orthodox, but Nédoncelle has successfully shown this to be false (*op. cit.*, pp. 35–36).

[6] Quoted from the very radical Italian *Programma dei modernisti* in Inge, *op. cit.*, p. 152.

[7] Guitton, "Newman et le modernisme," *La philosophie de Newman*, p. 172.

[8] A. R. Vidler, *The Modernist Movement in the Catholic Church* (Cambridge, 1934), pp. 51–52, 59.

[9] Stewart, *Modernism, Past and Present*, p. 326; Maisie Ward, *op. cit.*, II, 265; A. Fawkes, *Studies in Modernism*, pp. 380–81; Gougaud, *op. cit.*, pp. 560–61; Guibert, *Le réveil du catholicism en Angleterre* (Paris, 1907); Benard, *Preface to Newman's Theology*, pp. 155–56 (giving portions of Pope Pius X's letter to Bishop O'Dwyer, clearing Newman of any charge of Modernism).

[10] Maisie Ward, *op. cit.*, II, 275–76.

[11] See *Discussions and Arguments*, pp. 232–33. Cf. S. G. Dimond, "The Philosophy and Theology of the Oxford Movement and Anglo-Catholicism," *London Quarterly and Holborn Review*, CLVIII (1933), 445: "[Newman] saw clearly enough the forces which led Renan, two days after he himself was received into the Roman Church in the village of Littlemore, to walk down the steps of the College of Saint Sulpice, and leave the Church forever. He foresaw the tendencies which resulted in Tyrrell being deprived of the Sacraments in 1907, and Loisy being excommunicated in 1908." Newman would no doubt have been shocked even by High Anglican advanced thought as seen in *Lux Mundi*: "It is our likeliest guess," says H. L. Stewart, "that he would have seen in *Lux Mundi* a development, not of what the Tractarians had taught, but of what they had so inadequately resisted" (*A Century of Anglo-Catholicism*, p. 199).

[12] E. Michaud, "Le Newmanisme," *Revue internationale de théologie*, XIII (1905), 641, 646. In France, Brémond (*The Mystery of Newman*) has been the best known of the liberal theologians who claimed Newman as a Modernist; but they include also

Tyrrell and Loisy. Defending his orthodoxy are Dimnet, Guibert, Gougaud, Sarolea, Barry, Hutton, *et al.* The most recent, and one of the most successful, attempts to define Newman's position in relation to Modernism is that of E. D. Benard (*Preface to Newman's Theology*, Pt. II), especially in regard to the *Essay on Development* and the *Grammar of Assent.*

[13] Brémond, *op. cit.*, p. 94.

[14] Sarolea, *op. cit.*, pp. 159–60.

[15] Ward, *Life*, II, 476–77.

[16] Brémond, *op. cit.*, p. 97.

[17] *Idea of a University*, p. 73.

[18] *Disc. and Arg.*, p. 397.

[19] Ward, *Life*, II, 342–44.

[20] T. Mozley, *Reminiscences*, etc., I, 208; II, 48–49.

[21] *Apologia*, pp. 129–31. "I am aware," says Newman of his idea, "that what I have been saying will, with many men, be doing credit to my imagination at the expense of my judgment — 'Hippoclides doesn't care'."

[22] Ward, *Life*, II, 506.

[23] *Present Position of Catholics*, pp. 312–13.

[24] E. A. Knox, *The Tractarian Movement*, p. 193. In 1847, while in Italy Newman visited the Holy House at Loreto, and had "no antecedent difficulty in the matter," but believed completely. Ward (*Life*, I, p. 198) reminds us, however, that in 1847 "recent criticism as to the history of the Holy House was unknown, and the tradition was far more widely received among Catholics than it is at present." Yet how far criticism would have affected Newman at that date is difficult to surmise.

[25] From long-unpublished memoranda quoted in Wilfrid Ward, *Witnesses to the Unseen* (London, 1893), p. 150.

[26] Ward, *Life*, II, 494–95.

[27] *Pres. Position of Cath.*, pp. 412–13 (italics added).

[28] Newman, *Two Essays on Biblical and Ecclesiastical Miracles* (1918), p. 4; cf. Juergens, *Newman on the Psychology of Faith in the Individual*, p. 201.

[29] *Essay on Miracles*, pp. 6–7; Juergens, *op. cit.*, pp. 201–02.

[30] *Parochial and Plain Sermons*, VIII, 77; Juergens, *op. cit.*, p. 200.

[31] *Oxf. Univ. Sermons*, p. 196; Juergens, *op. cit.*, p. 204.

[32] *Pres. Position of Cath.*, p. 305.

[33] Juergens, *op. cit.*, p. 191.

iii.

[1] Fawkes, "Newmañ," *Studies in Modernism,* p. 27. Cf. *Letters of Lord Acton to Mary Gladstone,* ed. Herbert Paul (New York, 1904), p. 70. Actòn regarded Newman as a "sophist, the manipulator, and not the servant, of truth."

[2] E. Abbott, *Philomythus, an Antidote against Credulity: a Discussion of Cardinal Newman's "Essay on Ecclesiastical Miracles"* (London, 1891), p. 32.

[3] John Morley, *Miscellanies,* ser. IV (London, 1908), p. 161.

[4] J. A. Froude, *Carlyle's Life in London* (London, 1884), II, 247.

[5] Ross, *op. cit.,* p. 239; Sarolea, *op. cit.,* p. 69.

[6] See Sarolea, *op. cit.,* pp. 4–6.

[7] Ward, *Last Lectures,* pp. 14–15.

[8] Ward, *Life,* II, 333n.: "Newman never quite approved of the Metaphysical Society. He writes thus to Dean Church in 1876: 'I hear that you and the Archbp. of York (to say nothing of Cardinal Manning, etc.) are going to let Professor Huxley read in your presence an argument in refutation of our Lord's Resurrection. How can this possibly come under the scope of a Metaphysical Society? I thank my stars that, when asked to accept the honor of belonging to it, I declined. Aren't you in a false position? Perhaps it is a ruse of the Cardinal to bring the Professor into the clutches of the Inquisition.' "

[9] Ward, *Last Lectures,* p. 17; *Grammar of Assent,* p. 403. This passage has been quoted, of course, in Chap. VI, sect. vc.

[10] Brémond, *op. cit.,* pp. 66, 69.

[11] *Ibid.,* pp. 71–72.

[12] T. Mozley, *op. cit.,* II, 398; Brémond, *op. cit.,* p. 74.

[13] Ward, *Witnesses to the Unseen,* p. 129.

[14] See Sarolea, *op. cit.,* pp. 58–59; R. H. Coats, "Birmingham Mystics of the Mid-Victorian Era," *Hibbert Journal,* XVI (1917–18), 490–92. Cf. Brilioth, *The Anglican Revival,* p. 140. Tract LXXXV, says Brilioth, "makes us forecast the inner discord between modernism and mediaevalism, which alone can explain the riddle of [Newman's] personality."

[15] No doubt a great deal of one's misunderstanding of Newman could be avoided if one observed the four "principles of interpretation" recently drawn up by Dr. Benard (*Preface to Newman's Theology,* pp. 55, 63, 70, 74): any particular work of Cardinal

Newman should be judged and interpreted in the light of (i) "the particular phase of religious and intellectual development during which it was written, (his later and more mature views on a question must be preferred to the earlier)"; (ii) "the precise purpose for which the work was written and . . . the persons for whom it was intended"; (iii) "the two doctrines which form the foundation of his idea of religion, the principle of dogma and the principle of the existence of a visible Church, with sacraments and rites that are the channels of invisible grace"; and (iv) the absence of Newman's intention of producing works of systematic theology, or of employing scholastic terminology or conventional logical method.

Chapter XV

[1] Sarolea, *op. cit.*, p. 174. No study has been attempted in the present work of Newman's *Meditations and Devotions,* because we have been primarily concerned with Newman's thought and literary method.

[2] See E. Seillière, *La religion romantique et ses conquêtes:* 1830–1930 (Paris, 1930), p. 58. See Livre I, Chap. x, "Les précautions de la mystique chrétienne contre l'orgueil de la surhumaine alliance. L'enseignement de Newman" (pp. 56–63).

The effort to understand Newman in our own time has, as one would expect, included an effort to interpret him in the light of Freudian psychology. Since this inevitably attracts the attention of Newman's readers, it is desirable to examine the extent to which the psychoanalysts can be of service in furthering one's understanding of him. They can, of course, point out Newman's dreamy, sensitive, introspective childhood, his early tendency to "escape" from the buffetings of the world by retreating to the world of spirit where he and God alone were real. They can remind us of Newman's highstrung nature, and of some deep inner conflict, partly evidenced in his "near escape from being a stammerer." They can "account" for Newman's decision at fifteen to "lead a single life" by emphasizing the training he received from his mother, which may have exaggerated his sense of "separation from the visible world," and which may have wounded or frustrated his animal instincts on their first appearance. They can "account" for Newman's decision on celibacy also by stressing a physiological fact about him, namely, his "feminine" character and charm, which has been attested to by so many who knew him. Finally, they can point to the important part played by passionate friendships in the Tractarian Movement, and to the exalted place which the "high severe idea of virginity" occupied in the minds of both Newman and Hurrell Froude. However, when they have done all this, they have failed to individualize Newman's "case." The same facts which are brought out here concerning a man of great religious genius may be brought out concerning a person of no religious distinction whatever. The successful application of Freudian exegesis to Newman is unfortunately — or fortunately — impossible, because of the lack of adequate documentary evidence. Newman's letters are really a disappointment if we seek in them much of the writer's personality; they reveal no important secrets, no hidden "springs of action," very little of Newman's daily life. And Newman left no Rousseauistic autobiography, no secret-disclosing diaries. The "Autobiographical Memoir" in the *Letters and Correspondence,* written with remarkable aloofness, in the third person, is a very barren quarry for the psychoanalyst.

The result of one attempt to see Newman through Freudian spectacles, Mr. Geoffrey Faber's *Oxford Apostles,* is to reduce the severe moralism of the Tractarian ethos to nothing more or less than morbid emotionalism. Christopher Dawson (*op. cit.,* pp. v–ix) has observed that in Mr. Faber's hands, the history of the Oxford Movement becomes an essay in sexual psychopathy. This is largely because the author bases his account of the Movement on his interpretation of the characters of its leaders, which is in turn based not on their theological and moral conceptions but on various teachings of Freudian psychology, as interpreted by Mr. Faber. Hence Newman appears throughout the book not as a great religious thinker but as an unhappy example of infantile repression; and his religious principles are seen as nothing more than "unconscious instruments of a maimed personality struggling to attain equilibrium without abandoning 'the citadel where his infantile self lay entrenched' " (p. vi). Similarly Hurrell Froude and Pusey are depicted as different types of the same psychic perversion, while some of the lesser Tractarians are referred to as Newman's "escort of hermaphrodites" (Faber, *op. cit.,* p. 346). Here we see the typical errors of the literary psychologist: the confusion of moral and medical values, and the tendency to regard every spiritual or self-transcending act as a disguised form of sexual impulse. In its own domain the Freudian method is indifferent to moral considerations; but once applied by the historian or man of letters, it ceases to be objective and becomes marked with the moral convictions — or lack of them — in the lay critic. Thus the Freudian concept of homosexuality, which involves no moral judgment, becomes charged, in Mr. Faber's application, with an ethical significance, and finally becomes equivalent to a lack of "manliness" in the moral sense. This, as Dawson notes, is simply the old prejudices of Kingsley and Abbott in a new Freudian dress. Brilliant as is the *Oxford Apostles*, remarkable as is its humanization of the Tractarians, it suffers from the weaknesses of most literary applications of Freudian doctrine: an explanation of personality by reducing human behavior to its physical and non-rational elements. In view of the paucity of materials with which to psychoanalyze Newman, it is natural that, at one important point in his discussion, Mr. Faber admits, "Certainly this is pure hypothesis" (p. 31). This admission really covers the whole question of understanding Newman through the Freudians. It suggests also that the safest and most profitable way is to read Newman's works, and to keep our minds on what he says, not on hypothetical moods and motives behind his pages.

[3] Cronin, *Cardinal Newman*, pp. 130–36. Cronin also has some interesting pages on "Max Scheler and the Newman Movement in Germany" (pp. 136–40) involving Laros, Haecker, Przywara, Husserl. It would be possible, of course, to examine also the parallels between Newman's theory of thought as proceeding "from wholes to wholes" and certain elements in present-day *Gestalt* psychology.

[4] Evelyn Underhill, *Letters* (London, 1943), p. 183.

[5] See the *Apologia*, p. 291: "I came to the conclusion that there was no medium, in true philosophy, between Atheism and Catholicity." Guitton (*op. cit.*, pp. xxviii–xxix, n. 3) reminds us that a similar alternative was put to John Stuart Mill by Auguste Comte in a letter of May 15, 1845, "entre le catholicisme et le positivisme." The letter is given in Ward, *W. G. Ward and the Oxford Movement*, p. 304.

[6] See Ward, "Two Mottoes of Cardinal Newman," *Problems and Persons* (London, 1903), pp. 262–67.

[7] See L. Bouyer, "Newman et le platonisme de l'âme Anglaise," *Revue de philosophie*, VI, nouv. sér. (1936), 285–305; and C. F. Harrold, "Newman and the Alexandrian Platonists," *Modern Philology*, XXXVII (1940), 279–91.

[8] Hutton, *Newman*, p. 251.

[9] B. Newman, *Cardinal Newman*, p. 212.

A SELECT BIBLIOGRAPHY

I. Principal Works *

The Arians of the Fourth Century. London, 1833.

Tracts for the Times. Oxford, 1833–1841. (Of the tracts, Newman wrote nos. 1, 2, 3, 6, 7, 8, 10, 11, 15, 19, 20, 21, 33, 34, 38, 40, 41, 45, 47, 71, 73, 75, 76, 79, 82, 83, 85, 88, and 90.)

Lyra Apostolica. Oxford, 1836. (Of the poems in this volume, Newman wrote those signed δ. Most of these poems were subsequently republished in the volume entitled *Verses on Various Occasions*, 1868.)

Lectures on the Prophetical Office of the Church, Viewed Relatively to Romanism and Popular Protestantism. London, 1837. (Republished as part of the *Via Media*, 2 vols., 1877, 1883.)

Parochial and Plain Sermons, 8 vols. 1834–1843.

Lectures on Justification. London, 1838.

Sermons on Subjects of the Day. London, 1843.

Oxford University Sermons. London, 1843.

Two Essays on Biblical and Ecclesiastical Miracles. London, 1825, 1843.

Essay on the Development of Christian Doctrine. London, 1845.

Loss and Gain: the Story of a Convert. London, 1848.

Discourses to Mixed Congregations. London, 1849.

Lectures on Certain Difficulties Felt by Anglicans. 2 vols. London, 1850, 1872.

Lectures on the Present Position of Catholics in England. London, 1851.

The Idea of a University. London, 1852.

Callista. London, 1855.

Sermons Preached on Various Occasions. London, 1857.

Apologia pro vita sua. London, 1864. (Rev. ed. 1865.)

The Dream of Gerontius. London, 1865.

Letter to the Rev. E. B. Pusey on his Recent "Eirenicon." London, 1866.

Verses on Various Occasions. London, 1868.

An Essay in Aid of a Grammar of Assent. London, 1870.

---

* The standard edition of Newman's collected works is that published by Longmans, Green, and Co., 40 volumes, 1874–1921 (Index by J. Rickaby). All references in the present study are to this edition, except those references to the *Apologia*, which is used in the edition of Wilfrid Ward, Oxford University Press, 1913, and *Callista*, for which references are to the one-volume edition of London, 1935. For a more complete bibliography of Newman, see the *Cambridge Bibliography of English Literature*, Vol. III, pp. 686–91.

Essays Critical and Historical. 2 vols. London, 1872.
Discussions and Arguments. London, 1872.
Historical Sketches. 3 vols. London, 1872.
Tracts Theological and Ecclesiastical. London, 1874.
Letter to the Duke of Norfolk. London, 1875.
Meditations and Devotions. London, 1893.
Addresses to Cardinal Newman, with His Replies, 1879–81. Ed. W. P. Neville. London, 1905.
Sermon Notes of John Henry Cardinal Newman, 1849–78. Ed. Fathers of the Birmingham Oratory. London, 1913.

II. Letters

Letters and Correspondence of John Henry Newman During His Life in the English Church, with a Brief Autobiography. Edited, at Cardinal Newman's request, by Anne Mozley. 2 vols. London, 1891.
Correspondence of John Henry Newman with Keble and Others: 1839–1845. Edited at the Birmingham Oratory. London, 1917.
Cardinal Newman and William Froude, F. R. S.: a Correspondence. Ed. Gordon H. Harper. Baltimore, 1933.

III. Biography

Atkins, Gaius Glenn. *Life of Cardinal Newman.* New York, 1931.
Barry, William. *Newman.* New York, 1905.
Bucaille, V. *Newman: histoire d'une âme.* Paris, 1912.
Cross, Frank L. *John Henry Newman: with a Set of Unpublished Letters.* London, 1933.
Dark, Sidney. *Newman* (Great Lives Series). London, 1934.
Donahue, G. J. *Newman.* Boston, 1927.
Flood, J. M. *Cardinal Newman and Oxford.* London, 1933.
Goyau, L. F. F. *Newman: sa vie et ses oeuvres.* Paris, 1901.
Hutton, R. H. *Cardinal Newman* (Leaders of Religion Series). London, 1891.
Jennings, Henry J. *Cardinal Newman.* Birmingham, 1882.
May, J. Lewis. *Cardinal Newman.* New York, 1930.
Meynell, Wilfrid. *Cardinal Newman.* London, 1890.
Newman, B. *Cardinal Newman: a Biographical and Literary Study.* New York, 1925.
Ross, J. E. *John Henry Newman.* New York, 1933.
Waller, A. R., and Barrow, G. H. S. *John Henry, Cardinal Newman.* Boston, 1901.
Ward, Wilfrid. *Life of Cardinal Newman.* 2 vols. London, 1912.

IV. Critical and Expository Works

Abbott, E. A. *The Anglican Career of Cardinal Newman.* 2 vols. London, 1892.

Benard, E. D. *A Preface to Newman's Theology.* St. Louis, Mo., 1945.

Blennerhassett, C. J., Lady. *John Henry Kardinal Newman.* Berlin, 1904.

Bonnegent, C. *La théorie de la certitude dans Newman.* Paris, 1920.

Brémond, Henri. *L'inquiétude religieuse.* Première Serie: Aubes et lendemains de conversion . . . Paris, 1919.

———— *Essai de biographie psychologique.* Paris, 1906. Translated as *The Mystery of Newman,* by H. C. Corrance. London, 1907.

Bucaille, V. *Newman: histoire d'une âme.* Paris, 1912.

Corcoran, T. *Newman: Selected Discourses on Liberal Knowledge, with an Introduction.* Dublin, 1929.

———— *Newman's Theory of a Liberal Education.* Dublin, 1929.

Croly, D. *Index to "Tracts for the Times."* Oxford, 1842.

Cronin, J. F. *Cardinal Newman: His Theory of Knowledge.* Washington, D.C., 1935.

D'Arcy, M. C. *The Nature of Belief.* London, 1931. (See Chaps. IV, V and VI.)

D'Cruz, F. A. *Cardinal Newman, His Place in Religion and Literature.* Madras, India. N.D.

Delattre, F. *La pensée de J. H. Newman: extraits* . . . Paris, 1914.

Elbert, J. A. *The Evolution of Newman's Concept of Faith Prior to 1845: a Genetic Presentation and Synthesis.* Cincinnati, 1933.

Fairbairn, A. M. *Catholicism: Roman and Anglican.* London, 1889.

Folghera, J. D. *Newman's Apologetic.* Trans. Philip Hereford. Int. Bede Jarrett. London, 1930.

Friedel, F. J. *The Mariology of Cardinal Newman.* New York, 1928.

Goyau, L. F. F. *Newman: sa vie et ses oeuvres.* Paris, 1901.

Grappe, G. J. H. *Newman: essai de psychologie religieuse.* Pref. Paul Bourget. Paris, 3rd ed., 1902.

Guitton, Jean. *La philosophie de Newman: essai sur l'idée de développement.* Paris, 1933.

Harper, G. H. *Cardinal Newman and William Froude, F.R.S.: a Correspondence.* Baltimore, 1933. (See Int., pp. 1–30.)

Houghton, W. *The Art of Newman's "Apologia."* New York, 1945.

Juergens, S. P. *Newman on the Psychology of Faith in the Individual.* New York, 1928.

Kassner, R. *Newman.* Munich, 1920.

Kattenbusch, F. "Newman." *Realencyklopädie für protestantische Theologie und Kirche,* XIV.

Kiener, Sister Mary Aloysi. *John Henry Newman, the Romantic, the Friend, the Leader.* Boston, 1933.

Lamm, W. R. *The Spiritual Legacy of Newman* (Religion and Culture Series. Joseph Husslein, S.J., Ph.D., general editor). Milwaukee, 1934.

Laros, M. *Kardinal Newman.* Wiesbaden, 1921.

MacRae, A. *Die religiöse Gewissheit bei J. H. Newman.* Jena, 1898.

Mozley, J. B. *The Theory of Development.* London, 1878.

Newman, F. W. *Contributions Chiefly to the Early History of Cardinal Newman.* London, 1891.

O'Dwyer, E. T. *Cardinal Newman and the Encyclical Pascendi dominici gregis.* London, 1908.

Olivero, Frederico. *La teoria poetica di Newman.* Milan, 1930.

Palmer, W. *Narrative of Events Connected with "Tracts for the Times."* London, 1883.

Przywara, E. *Einführung in Newmans Wesen und Werk.* Vol. IV of *Christentum.* Freiburg im Breisgau, 1922. (Transl. as *Introduction to the Principles and Works of Newman.* Freiburg, 1923.)

Reilly, J. J. *Newman as a Man of Letters.* New York, 1925.

Rickaby, Joseph. *Index to the Works of J. H. Newman.* London, 1914.

Sarolea, Charles. *Cardinal Newman and His Influence on Religious Life and Thought.* Edinburgh, 1908.

Sobry, D. P. *Newman en zijn "Idea of a University."* Louvain, 1935.

Stockley, W. F. P. *Newman, Education, and Ireland.* London, 1933.

Stoel, H. *Kardinal Newman.* Groningen, 1915.

Tardivel, Fernande. *La personnalité littéraire de Newman.* Paris, 1937.

—————— *John Henry Newman, Éducateur.* Paris, 1937.

Toohey, J. J. *An Indexed Synopsis of the Grammar of Assent.* New York, 1906.

Tristram, H. *Newman and His Friends.* London, 1933.

Whyte, Alexander. *Newman: an Appreciation.* Edinburgh, 1901.

Yardley, May. *John Henry Newman: the Idea of a University.* Cambridge University Press, 1931. (See Introduction.)

V. Short Critical Works: Articles, Chapters, Essays, Monographs

Bacchus, F. "How to Read the 'Grammar of Assent,' " *The Month,* February 1924, pp. 106–115.

—————— "Newman's Oxford University Sermons," *The Month,* July 1922, pp. 1–12.

Baker, A. E. *Prophets for an Age of Doubt: Job, Socrates, Pascal, Newman.* London, 1934.

Baker, J. E. "Newman as Novelist," *The Novel and the Oxford Movement.* Princeton, N. J., 1932.

Barry, William. "Catholicism and Reason," *Contemporary Review*, XLVIII (1885), 656–75.

Baudin, E. "La philosophie de la foi chez Newman," *La revue de philosophie*, VIII (1906), 571–598; IX (1906), 20–55, 253–285, 373–390.

Baynes, Bishop Hamilton. "From Newman to Gore," *Hibbert Journal*, XXXII (1933), 1–8.

Birrell, A. "Cardinal Newman," *Scribner's Magazine*, III (1888), 735–743. (See *Res Judicatae*, London, 1892.)

Blennerhassett, R. "Some of My Recollections of Cardinal Newman," *Living Age*, CCXXXI (1901), 793–804.

Boardman, G. N. "John Henry Newman: a Study," *Bibliotheca Sacra* (Oberlin), LXIX (1912), 618–41.

Bouyer, L. "Newman et le platonisme de l'âme anglaise," *Revue de philosophie*, XXXVI (1936), 285–305.

Brémond, Henri. "Apologie pour les newmanistes français," *Revue pratique d'apologétique*, III (1906–1907), 655–666.

Brickel, A. G. "Cardinal Newman and Edmund Burke," *Catholic World*, CIX (1919), 637–645.

——— "Cardinal Newman and Gilbert K. Chesterton," *Catholic World*, CIX (1919), 744–752.

——— "Newman's Criteria of Historical Evolution," *American Catholic Quarterly Review*, XLIV (1919), 588–594.

——— "Newman's Theory of Knowledge," *American Catholic Quarterly Review*, XLIII (1918), 507–518.

——— "The Newman Revival in Germany," *Catholic World*, CXVII (1923).

Brinton, Crane. *English Political Thought in the 19th Century*. London, 1933. (See chapter on Newman.)

Burgum, E. B. "Cardinal Newman and the Complexity of Truth," *Sewanee Review*, XXXVIII (1930), 310–327.

Byrne, J. J. "The Notion of Doctrinal Development in the Anglican Writings of J. H. Newman," *Ephemerides theologicae Lovanienses*, XIV (1937), 230–86.

Castle, W. R., Jr. "Newman and Coleridge," *Sewanee Review*, XVII (1909), 139–152.

Cecil, A. "John Henry Newman," *Six Oxford Thinkers*. London, 1909.

Chesterton, C. "Art of Controversy: Macaulay, Huxley, and Newman," *Catholic World*, CV (1917), 446–456.

Chevalier, Jacques. *Trois conférences d'Oxford: Aristotle, Pascal, Newman*. Paris, 1933.

Church, R. W. *Occasional Papers*. 2 vols. London, 1897. (See II, 379–482.)

Coats, R. H. "Birmingham Mystics of the Mid-Victorian Era," *Hibbert Journal*, XVI, (1918), 485–494.

Collin, W. E. "Cardinal Newman and Recent French Thought," *Royal*

Society of Canada Transactions (Ottawa). Ser. 3, vol. XXXI (1937), 33–43.

Conacher, W. A. "Personal Influence of Cardinal Newman," *Catholic World*, CX (1920), 773–780.

Cross, F. L. "Newman and the Doctrine of Development," *Church Quarterly Review*, CXV (1933), 245–257.

Delattre, F. "J. H. Newman, éducateur," *Etudes anglaises*, II (1938), 144–150.

De Vere, A. "Some Recollections of Cardinal Newman." *Nineteenth Century*, XL (1896), 395–411.

Dimnet, l'Abbé E. "Newman et l'intellectualisme," *Les annales de philosophie chrétienne*, CLIV (1907), 260–293, 448–475.

———— "Quelques aspects du Cardinal Newman," *La revue du clergé français*, April 1 and 15, 1903.

———— *La pensée catholique dans l'Angleterre contemporaine.* Paris, 1905.

Dimond, S. G. "The Philosophy and Theology of the Oxford Movement and Anglo-Catholicism," *London Quarterly and Holborn Review*, CLVIII (1933), 433–446.

Donaldson, A. B. *Five Great Oxford Leaders.* London, 1900.

The English Way: Studies in English Sanctity from St. Bede to Newman. By various authors. London, 1933.

Evans, A. W. "Historical Commentary," *Tract Ninety.* Rptd. from ed. 1841. London, 1933. (See pp. vii–lv.)

Faber, Geoffrey. *Oxford Apostles.* London and New York, 1933.

Falconer, R. A. "Newman's Life and Work," *Constructive Quarterly*, IX (1921), 510–536.

Farges, A. *La crise de la certitude: étude des bases de la connaissance et de la croyance, avec la critique du Neo-Kantisme, du Pragmatisme, du Newmanisme. . .* Paris, 1907.

Fawkes, A. "Newman," *Studies in Modernism.* London, 1913.

Firmin, A. (l'Abbé Loisy). "Le développement chrétien d'après le Cardinal Newman," *La revue du clergé français*, XVII (1898), 5–20.

Fletcher, Jefferson B. "Newman and Carlyle: an Unrecognized Affinity," *Atlantic Monthly*, XCV (1905), 669–79.

Froude, J. A. "The Oxford Counter-Reformation," *Short Studies on Great Subjects: Fourth Series.* New York, 1883.

Gates, L. E. *Selections from the Prose Writings of . . . Newman.* New York, 1895. (See Introduction.)

Gorce, D. *Newman et les Pères: le secret de sa conversion.* Paris, 1933.

Gougaud, L. "Le prétendu modernisme de Newman," *La revue du clergé français*, LVII (1909), 560–565.

Gout, R. *Du protestantisme au catholicisme.* Montauban, Auduse, 1904. (Thèse.)

Grandmaison, L. de. "J. H. Newman considéré comme maître," *Etudes*, CX (1907), 39–69.

———— "Le développement du dogme chrétien," *Revue pratique d'apologétique*, V (1907–1908), 521–542; VI (1908–1909), 5–33; 81–104; 401–436; 881–905.

Guibert, J. "Newman et l'encyclique 'Pascendi,'" *Revue pratique d'apologétique*, V (1907–1908), 277–278.

Hardt, J. H. *J. H. Kardinal Newman als Prediger.* Vienna, 1928.

Harper, T. "Dr. Newman's Essay in Aid of a Grammar of Assent," *The Month*, XII (1870), 599–611, 667–692.

Harrold, C. F., "Newman and the Alexandrian Platonists," *Modern Philology*, XXXVII (1940), 279–291.

Healy, Martinus. "The Logical Cogency of Faith in the Writings of John Henry Newman," Louvain, 1939. (Diss. outline.)

Hermans, F. "Portrait de Newman," *Revue générale*. Bruxelles, 1938. *Année* 71, pp. 453–71.

Holloway, O. E. "The Tractarian Movement in Oxford," *Bodleian Quarterly Record*, VII (1933), 213–232.

Hutton, R. H. "The Two Great Oxford Thinkers, Cardinal Newman and Matthew Arnold," *Essays on Some of the Modern Guides of English Thought in Matters of Faith*, London, 1887.

Inge, W. R. "Cardinal Newman," *Outspoken Essays: First Series*. London, 1919.

———— *Faith and Its Psychology.* London, 1909. (See pp. 99–103, 179, 234, etc.)

Johnson, L. "Cardinal Newman," *Post Liminium*. London, 1911.

Jörimann, A. Pl. *Exposé critique de la doctrine de Newman.* (Thesis: Univ. of Geneva.) Geneva, 1904.

Joye, D. *La théorie du Cardinal Newman sur le développement du dogme chrétien.* Paris, 1896. (Thèse.)

Juergens, S. P. "What is Newman's Deepest Message?" *Ecclesiastical Review*, LXXVIII (1928), 142–51.

Lebreton, J. "Autour de Newman," *Revue pratique d'apologétique*, III (1906–1907), 488–504. (See also pp. 542–557; 666–675; etc.)

Leibell, J. F. "Newman's Philosophy of Education," *Catholic Educational Review*, XXII (1924), 193–200.

Leslie, S. "Cardinal Newman." In *Great Catholics*, ed. C. C. H. Williamson. London and New York, 1938.

———— *Studies in Sublime Failure.* London, 1932.

Lilly, W. A. "Cardinal Newman and the New Generation," *Fortnightly Review*, LXXXII (1904), 211–224.

———— "Last Words on Cardinal Newman," *Fortnightly Review*, CIX (1918), 899–913.

Lockhart, W. "Cardinal Newman: or 'tis Fifty Years Since," *Dublin Review*, CVII (1890), 408–423.

Lucas, H. "The Life's Work of J. H. Newman," *Catholic World*, CXII (1920–1921), 171–179, 303–315, 473–485, 660–673.

Lynch, J., (Ed.) "The Newman-Perrone Paper on Development," *Gregorianum*, XVI, fasc. iii (1935), 402–47.

MacRae, A. *Die religiöse Gewissheit bei J. H. Newman.* Jena, 1898.

Mariella, O. S. B., Sister. "Newman's Anglican Sermons," *Catholic World*, CXLVIII (1939), 431–37.

Meynell, W. "Cardinal Newman and His Contemporaries," *Contemporary Review*, LVIII (1890), 313–332.

Michaud, E. "Le Newmanisme," *Revue internationale de théologie*, XIII (1905), 633–660.

Miller, L. G. "Newman on the Function of Literature," *Catholic World*, CLVII (1943), 510–14.

More, P. E. "Cardinal Newman," *The Drift of Romanticism.* (Shelburne Essays, Eighth Series.) Boston, 1913.

Mozley, J. F. "Newman's Opportunity." *Quarterly Review*, CCXLVI (1926), 75–92.

———"Newman in Fetters," *Quart. Rev.*, CCXLVI (1926), 272–293.

———"Newman and Manning," *Quart. Rev.*, CCVI (1907), 354–383. (See also CCXVI [1912], 458–479.)

Mozley, T. *Reminiscences Chiefly of Oriel College and the Oxford Movement.* 2 vols. London, 1882.

Overmans, J. "Harnack und Newman," *Stimmen der Zeit*, LXVII (1936–1937), 20–31.

Przywara, E. "The Newmanian Type of Soul in the Tradition of Catholic Mysticism and Askesis," *Yearbook* (1923) *of the Union of Catholic Academies.* Augsburg, 1923.

——— "Zur Geschichte des 'Modernistischen' Newman," *Stimmen der Zeit*, CII (1922), 443–451.

——— *Ringen der Gegenwart* [Kant, Newman, Thomas]. Augsburg, 1929. (See Tome II, Part VI, pp. 729–962.)

——— *Religionsbegründung: Max Scheler; J. H. Newman.* Freiburg im Breisgau, 1923.

Reilly, J. J. "Saints and Charlatans," *Catholic World*, CXVI (1922), 19–32.

——— "Some Critics of Cardinal Newman," *Catholic World*, CXXIV (1927), 587–595.

Rivière, J. "Newman, apologiste," *Revue des sciences religieuses*, July 1926, pp. 394–410.

Routh, H. V. *Towards the 20th Century.* Cambridge, 1937. See Chapters IV and V.

Ryan, Alvan S. "Newman's Conception of Literature," *Critical Studies in Arnold, Emerson, and Newman.* Ed. J. E. Baker. University of Iowa Humanistic Studies, VI, no. 1. Iowa City, 1942.

——— "The Development of Newman's Political Thought," *The Review of Politics*, VII (1945), 210–240.

Ryan, M. J. "The Philosophy of Newman," *American Catholic Quarterly Review*, XXXIII (1908), 77–86.

Sanday, W. *England's Debt to Newman.* Oxford, 1892.

Scott-Holland, H. *Personal Studies.* London, 1905.

Shafer, R. *Christianity and Naturalism.* New Haven, 1926.

Shairp, J. C. "Prose Poets: Cardinal Newman," *Aspects of Poetry.* Boston, 1891.

Shuster, G. N. *The Catholic Spirit in Modern Literature.* New York, 1922.

Slanton, R. M. "Some Reminiscences of the Early Days of Cardinal Newman's Catholic Life," *Dublin Review,* CVII (1890), 402–408.

Stapfer, Paul. "L'évolution religieuse d'un penseur catholique — Newman," *Bibliothèque Universelle* (Lausanne), LXXII (1913), 225–57.

Stephen, L. "Newman's Theory of Belief," *An Agnostic's Apology.* London, 1893.

Stockley, W. F. P. "Education According to Newman," *The Month,* CXL (1922), 303–11.

Strong, L. A. G. "Was Newman a Failure?" *Nineteenth Century,* CXIII (1933), 620–28.

Tardivel, F. *J. H. Newman: éducateur.* Paris, 1937.

Thirlwall, J. C. "Cardinal Newman's Literary Preferences," *Modern Language Notes,* XLVIII (1933), 23–27.

Toohey, J. J. "The Grammar of Assent and the Old Philosophy," *Irish Theological Quarterly,* October, 1907, pp. 466–484.

Tristram, H. "Newman and the Novelists," *Cornhill Magazine,* LXII (1927), 495–509.

——— "Newman and Matthew Arnold," *Cornhill Mag.,* LX (1926), 309–319.

——— "School-days of Cardinal Newman," *Cornhill Mag.,* LVIII (1925), 666–677.

——— "Two Leaders: Newman and Carlyle," *Cornhill Mag.,* LXV (1928), 367–382.

——— "Two Suppressed Passages from Newman's Autobiographical Memoir . . . ," *Revue anglo-américaine,* Paris, 1934, année 11, pp. 481–94.

Tristram, H., and Bacchus, F. "John Henry Newman." In J. Vacant, E. Mangenot, and E. Amann, *Dictionnaire de Théologie catholique,* vol. XI. Paris, 1931.

Tucker, W. J. "Newman as Philosopher and Littérateur," *Catholic World,* CXXV (1927), 155–163.

Tynan, Michael. "The Approach to Newman," *Irish Ecclesiastical Record* (Dublin), LV (1940), 260–73.

Underhill, Evelyn. "The Spiritual Significance of the Oxford Movement," *Hibbert Journal,* XXXI (1932–33), 401–12.

Walter, Luke. "Newman's Approach to the Church," *Blackfriar's* (Oxford), XIV (1933), 545–50.

Ward, Wilfrid. "Cardinal Newman's Sensitiveness," "Cardinal Newman on Constructive Thought," *Men and Matters.* London, 1914.

—— "Witnesses to the Unseen," "Some Aspects of Newman's Influence," "Philalethes: Some Words on a Misconception of Cardinal Newman." *Witnesses to the Unseen*, London, 1893.

—— "Two Mottoes of Cardinal Newman," "Newman and Renan," *Problems and Persons*, London, 1903.

—— "John Henry Newman: an Address," "Newman and Manning," *Ten Personal Studies*. London, 1908.

—— "Newman and Sabatier," *Fortnightly Review*, LXXV (1901), 802–822.

—— "The Genius of Cardinal Newman" [Lowell Lectures, 1914]: Newman and the Critics; The Unity of Newman's Work; The Sources of Newman's Style; Newman's Philosophy; Personality in Apologetic; Newman's Psychological Insight. *Last Lectures*, London, 1918.

Williams, S. T. "Newman's Literary Preferences," *Sewanee Review*, XXVIII (1920), 486–497. (Rptd. in *Studies in Victorian Literature*, New York, 1923.)

Williams, W. J. *Newman, Pascal, Loisy, and the Catholic Church.* London, 1906. (Cf. review by Wilfrid Ward, *Dublin Review*, CXLI [1907].)

Windle, B. C. A. *Who's Who in the Oxford Movement.* New York, 1926.

Woodruff, D. "On Newman, Chesterton and Exorbitance," *For Hilaire Belloc, Essays in Honor of His Seventy-first Birthday.* Ed. D. Woodruff. New York, 1942.

Wright, C. "Newman and Kingsley," *Harvard Graduates' Magazine*, XL (1931), 127–134.

VI. Some Works in Which Newman Material or Allusion May Be Found

Letters of Lord Acton to Mary Gladstone. Ed. Herbert Paul. New York, 1904.

Selections from the Correspondence of the First Lord Acton. Ed. J. N. Figgis and R. V. Laurence. London, 1917.

Baldensperger, F. *Le mouvement des idées dans l'émigration française: 1789–1815.* 2 vols. Paris, 1924.

Bazailles, A. *La crise de la croyance dans la philosophie contemporaine.* Paris, 1901.

Bellasis, E. *Memorials of Mr. Serjeant Bellasis.* London, 1895.

Bowden, J. E. *Life and Letters of Frederick William Faber, D.D.* London, 1869.

Butler, Cuthbert. *The Life and Times of Bishop Ullathorne.* London, 1926.

Chapman, E. M. *English Literature and Religion: 1800–1900.* London and New York, 1910.

Cruse, Amy. *The Victorians and Their Reading.* New York, 1935.

de Vere, Aubrey. *Recollections.* New York and London, 1897.

Eastwood, Dorothy M. *The Revival of Pascal: A Study of His Relation to Modern French Thought.* Oxford, 1936.

Figgis, J. N. *The Fellowship of the Mystery.* London, 1914.

Gasquet, Abbot. *Lord Acton and His Circle.* London, 1906.

Gore, Charles. *The Holy Spirit and the Church.* London, 1924.

Guibert, J. *Le réveil du catholicisme en Angleterre.* Paris, 1907.

Hort, A. F. *Life and Letters of Fenton John Anthony Hort.* 2 vols. London, 1896.

Huxley, T. H. "Agnosticism and Christianity," *Science and Christian Tradition.* New York, 1896.

Janssens, A. *Anglicaansche bekeerlingen.* Antwerp, 1928. (See Chap. I.)

——— *La philosophie et l'apologétique de Pascal.* Paris, 1906.

Charles Kingsley: His Letters and Memories of His Life. Ed. by his wife. One-vol. ed. London, 1883.

Knickerbocker, W. S. *Creative Oxford.* Syracuse, N. Y., 1925.

Laski, H. J. *Studies in the Problem of Sovereignty.* Yale University Press, 1927.

Leslie, Shane. *Henry Edward Manning, His Life and Labors.* 2nd ed. London, 1921.

Liddon, H. P. *Life of E. B. Pusey.* 4 vols. London, 1893–97.

Lock, Walter. *John Keble.* London, 1892.

Lunn, Arnold. *Roman Converts.* London, 1924.

Marin-Sola, F. *L'évolution homogène du dogme catholique.* 2nd ed. Paris, 1924.

May, J. Lewis. *Fénelon.* London, 1938.

McCloy, S. T. *Gibbon's Antagonism to Christianity.* London, 1933.

Meyrick, Frederick. *Memories of Life at Oxford . . .* London, 1905.

Mozley, J. B. *Letters.* London, 1885.

Nédoncelle, Maurice. *Baron Friedrich von Hügel.* Transl. Marjorie Vernon. New York, 1937.

Pattison, Mark. *Memoirs.* London, 1885.

Przywara, E. *A Monument to St. Augustine.* London, 1930.

Purcell, E. S. *Life of Cardinal Manning.* 2 vols. London, 1896.

Rivière, J. *Le Modernisme dans l'Eglise.* Paris, 1929.

Rogers, Frederick. *Letters of Lord Blachford.* Ed. G. E. Marindin. London, 1896.

Ruggiero, Guido de. "English Liberalism: Religious Development," *History of European Liberalism.* Transl. R. G. Collingwood. London, 1927.

Sabatier, Paul. *Les Modernistes.* Paris, 1909.

Seillière, E. "Les précautions de la mystique chrétienne contre l'orgueil de la surhumaine alliance. L'enseignement de Newman." *La religion romantique et ses conquêtes: 1830–1930.* Paris, 1930.

Somervell, D. C. *English Thought in the Nineteenth Century.* New York, 1929.

Stewart, H. F. *The Holiness of Pascal.* Cambridge, 1915.

Stewart, H. L. *A Century of Anglo-Catholicism.* London, 1929.

—— *Modernism, Past and Present.* London, 1932.

Strachey, Lytton. *Eminent Victorians.* London, 1918.

Thorp, Margaret F. *Charles Kingsley.* Princeton University Press, 1937.

Tuckwell, W. *Reminiscences of Oxford.* 2nd ed. New York, 1908.

—— *Pre-Tractarian Oxford: a Reminiscence of the Oriel "Noetics."* London, 1909.

Tyrrell, G. *Through Scylla and Charybdis, or the Old Theology and the New.* London, 1907.

—— *Christianity at the Cross-Roads.* London, 1909.

Vidler, A. R. *The Modernist Movement in the Catholic Church.* Cambridge, 1934.

Ward, Bernard. *Dawn of Catholic Revival in England.* 2 vols. London, 1909.

Ward, Maisie. *The Wilfrid Wards and the Transition: I. The 19th Century; II. Insurrection vs. Resurrection.* 2 vols. New York, 1934, 1937.

Ward, W. *Aubrey de Vere: A Memoir.* London, 1904.

—— *Life and Times of Cardinal Wiseman.* 2 vols. London, 1897. (2nd. ed.)

Memoirs of Richard Whately, Archbishop of Dublin: With a Glance at His Contemporaries and Times. By W. J. Fitzpatrick, J. P. 2 vols. London, 1864.

Life of the Rev. Joseph Blanco White. Written by himself with portions of his correspondence. Ed. J. H. Thom. 3 vols. London, 1845.

Williams, Isaac. *Autobiography.* Ed. Sir G. Prevost. London, 1892.

Wilson, J. A. *Life of Bishop Hedley.* London, 1930.

VII. WORKS ON THE OXFORD MOVEMENT

Brilioth, Yngve. *The Anglican Revival.* London, 1925, 1933.

Broicher, C. "Anglikanische Kirche und deutsche Philosophie," *Preussiche Jahrbücher,* CXLII (1910), 205–33, 457–98.

Church, R. W. *The Oxford Movement.* London, 1894.

Croly, D. *Index to Tracts for the Times.* Oxford, 1842.

Dawson, Christopher. *The Spirit of the Oxford Movement.* New York, 1933.

Elliott-Binns, L. E. "The Oxford Movement to 1845," "The Roman Church in England," "The Oxford Movement: the Second Phase," *Religion in the Victorian Era.* London, 1936.

Harper, Gordon H. *The Froude Family in the Oxford Movement.* Baltimore, 1933.

Hutton, W. H. "The Oxford Movement," *Cambridge History of English Literature.* Vol. XII, 1916, pp. 280–308.

Knox, E. A. *The Tractarian Movement: 1833–1845* . . . London, 1933.

Leslie, Shane. *The Oxford Movement.* Milwaukee, 1933.

May, J. Lewis. *The Oxford Movement.* London, 1933.

Northern Catholicism: Centenary Studies in the Oxford and Parallel Movements. Ed. N. P. Williams and Charles Harris. London, 1933.

Oakeley, F. *Historical Notes on the Tractarion Movement: 1833–45.* London, 1865.

Ollard, S. L. *A Short History of the Oxford Movement.* London, 1915.

Overton, J. H. *The English Church in the Nineteenth Century.* London, 1894.

The Oxford Movement: Being a Selection from the Tracts for the Times. Ed. W. G. Hutchison. London, 1913.

Peck, W. G. *The Social Implications of the Oxford Movement.* New York, 1933.

Simpson, W. J. S. *The History of the Anglo-Catholic Revival from 1845.* London, 1932.

Storr, Vernon F. "The Oxford Movement," "The Philosophy of the Oxford Movement," *The Development of English Theology in the Nineteenth Century: 1800–1860.* London, 1913.

Thureau-Dangin, P. *The English Catholic Revival in the Nineteenth Century.* 2 vols. Transl. W. Wilberforce. London, 1914.

Tulloch, John. *Movements of Religious Thought in Britain.* New York, 1885. (See Chap. III.)

Ward, Wilfrid. *W. G. Ward and the Oxford Movement.* London, 1889.

——— *W. G. Ward and the Catholic Revival.* London, 1912.

——— *The Oxford Movement.* New York, 1912.

Webb, C. C. J. *Religious Thought in the Oxford Movement.* New York, 1928.

Widdrington, P. E. T. "Social Mission of the Catholic Revival," *Christendom,* June 1932.

Willoughby, L. A. "On Some German Affinities with the Oxford Movement," *Modern Language Review,* XXIX (1934), 52 ff.

INDEX